Manual for the Strong-Campbell Interest Inventory

Form T325 of the Strong Vocational Interest Blank

David P. Campbell & Jo-Ida C. Hansen

MANUAL FOR THE
SVIB-SCII

Strong-Campbell Interest Inventory

Form T325 of the Strong Vocational Interest Blank

THIRD EDITION   1981

For use with the Revised and Expanded (1981) Profile

Published by
STANFORD UNIVERSITY PRESS
Stanford, California 94305

Distributed by
CONSULTING PSYCHOLOGISTS PRESS, INC.
577 College Avenue
Palo Alto, California 94306

STANFORD UNIVERSITY PRESS, STANFORD, CALIFORNIA

ISBN 0-8047-1104-6   LC 80-54735

Last figure below indicates year of this printing:
89 88 87 86 85 84 83

Publisher's Note

The Strong-Campbell Interest Inventory (Form T325) is the current edition of the Strong Vocational Interest Blank (SVIB), an interest inventory that has the longest history of any psychological test in widespread use today. It is used chiefly as an aid in making curricular or occupational choices and in planning career options. It measures *interests*, not aptitude or intelligence. Although its materials are essentially self-explanatory, no one should be administered the SCII without benefit of professional counseling; and the profile should be used to encourage wide-ranging vocational exploration, whatever the respondent's sex, social class, or ethnic background.

Although this edition of the *Manual for the SVIB-SCII* has been extensively revised, the instrument itself and the answer sheet are unchanged. The one fundamental change is in the profile: as the Preface to the Third Edition makes clear, the profile now reports 162 Occupational Scales, 99 of them developed since 1977 —a monumental achievement in scale construction.

The new samples collected for this revision are undoubtedly the best that have ever been used for the development of Strong scales. Every occupation is represented by a national sample, and the characteristics of the criterion samples were studied carefully to ensure that they were representative of their respective occupations. Factors such as occupational specialty and primary job task were examined to reduce the possibility of unwarranted bias, and younger and older age groups within an occupation were compared to ensure that the interests of recent entrants into the world of work were not different from those of older workers. We take particular satisfaction in the fact that these efforts have also produced such a remarkable balance between male-normed scales and female-normed scales: only four male and four female scales are not yet capable of being matched by scales for the opposite sex.

Of course, the SCII continues to score six General Occupational Themes, 23 Basic Interest Scales, an Academic Comfort and an Introversion-Extroversion Scale, and several Administrative Indexes. All play important roles, and only the SCII offers the checks and balances inherent in the use of both empirical and homogeneous scales.

The SCII was published in April 1974, and the first edition of this *Manual* was also published at that time. Since that time, the SCII has been in widespread use, and the collective experience of counselors and research psychologists has led to refinements in interpretation and valuable guidelines for continued development.

The publication of the SCII was marked by a number of important innovations. Chief among these were the merging of the men's and women's forms into a single booklet (the answer sheets and profiles, too, were merged into single forms); and the introduction of a theoretical framework (the General Occupational Themes) to guide the layout of the profile and the interpretation of the scores. The virtues of the second of these innovations are illustrated in the chapter on interpretation (Chapter 10).

The virtues of the first are more evident but more complex, for the goal of eliminating sex bias in psychological instruments is an ethical, moral, and legal issue as well as a psychometric issue. As the data in this *Manual* demonstrate, the route to *equal* treatment is not necessarily through *identical* treatment: men and women, on the average, respond differently to the items in the SCII inventory. To have ignored the various sex-linked differences in the norming of the scales would have been to introduce substantial error. Chapter 7 explains how this issue was resolved with the SCII, and an appendix (Appendix A) shows the ways in which the SCII met the most reasonable views of this dilemma. More recent research, also reported in Chapter 7, confirms—at least for the foreseeable future—the wisdom of employing separate scales for the two sexes.

As in the past, research for this latest edition of the SCII has drawn upon the priceless stores of longitudinal data that are one of the great traditional strengths of the Strong. As before, that research has been carried out for the publisher, under contract, by the Center for Interest Measurement Research at the University of Minnesota, under the direction of Dr. Jo-Ida C. Hansen, Director. A number of agencies, geographically dispersed in the United States and Canada, are now licensed to score the SCII; the names of these agencies are available upon request.

Preface to the Third Edition

The publication of this edition of the *Manual for the SVIB-SCII* marks another important milestone in the instrument's empirical evolution. Although there have been no theoretical or conceptual changes, and no change in the instrument itself, the expansion of coverage of the occupational samples—both in numbers and in breadth—has been extensive: the project turned out to be the largest testing program of employed adults in history. For this version of the profile, 162 occupational samples, containing a total of 40,197 people, were assembled. In general, each occupational sample consisted of people who:

1. were between the ages of 25 and 55;
2. had been in their occupation for at least three years;
3. reported that they enjoyed their work;
4. met at least some minimal standard of occupational performance, such as certification, licensure, or an advanced degree; or were otherwise performing at the average level or above in their occupation; and
5. pursued their occupation with the typical tasks and duties, not in some unusual way.

Thus each sample represents the experienced, satisfied, capably functioning, and typically engaged workers of that occupation. Of course, satisfying these criteria meant rejecting a great many candidates; for the first three criteria were pretty rigorously adhered to, and the fourth and fifth were observed where the necessary data were available. The 162 samples and the 40,197 sample members were in fact drawn from a total of 107,807 people actually tested in the course of research.

These standardization samples were not college students, not military recruits, not job applicants, not prison inmates, not hospital patients. Nor were they random samples of people-in-the-street. Each respondent was a happily employed adult—a point worth emphasizing—sought out and tested as a typical representative of a specific occupation.

Only 57 of the samples were collected prior to 1972, and none before 1966. The bulk of the testing was done in the late 1970's and more than half of the samples were surveyed in 1978 and 1979.

Of the 162 samples, half contained men, half women. The number making up each sample ranged from 100 male licensed practical nurses and 92 female restaurant managers to 498 male ministers and 400 female college professors. The average sample contained 248 people.

The samples ranged in average age from the relatively youthful, male flight attendants (mean age 28.4 years) and female foresters (mean age 26.6 years), to the middle-aged, male bankers (mean age 49.0 years) and female interior decorators (mean age 52.0 years). The overall mean age (the mean of the sample means) was 39.2 years.

Each person surveyed was asked to report his or her level of education and number of years of experience in the occupation being studied. In educational level, the samples ranged from male skilled craftsmen (11.6 years of education) and female licensed practical nurses (11.7 years of education) up to male biologists (21.7 years of education) and female sociologists (21.4 years of education). The average level of education over all samples (the mean of the sample means) was 16.6 years.

In terms of experience, the samples ranged from the relatively junior, male flight attendants (4.0 years of experience) and female foresters (3.4 years of experience), to the well established, male farmers (24.4 years of experience) and female bankers (23.0 years of experience). The average length of experience over all samples was 12.2 years.

In terms of experience, the samples ranged from the relatively junior, male flight attendants (4.0 years of experience) and female foresters (3.4 years of experience) to the well established male farmers (24.4 years of experience) and female bankers (23.0 years of experience). The average length of experience over all samples was 12.2 years.

Forty-four employees, all part-time, were involved in this revision of the occupational samples. Although each performed a variety of tasks, the one common denominator was a stringent demand for accuracy. Every Holland type was represented in the group; but in the end, they were all required to manifest the "attention-to-detail" behavior of the Conventional type. Those who persisted to the end of the revision demonstrated a sense of commitment, as well as a pride in performance that allowed them to work diligently in areas other than those reflecting their primary interests.

Jean Forsberg, who had also been at the Center during the 1974 revision, was responsible for the smooth day-to-day operation of the office, and the timely preparation of manuscript copy under time pressure.

Four students worked on this project for over five years, an unusual duration of work concentration for undergraduate or graduate students. Rosangélica Aburto trained and coordinated the office assistants, research assistants, and secretaries. She was the one person accountable for every detail of sample collection; without her, there would have been chaos. Carol Grams, imaginative and persistent, solved many of the problems associated with testing hard-to-obtain samples: she wrote over 500 letters, made over 400 telephone calls, wrote press releases, maneuvered through complicated government systems, and outlasted the executive secretaries of several organizations. Kevin Larkin supervised the computer operations over a six-year period while pursuing his own student responsibilities; his long evening and weekend hours not only made exacting deadlines possible, but kept down costs (computer time is less expensive after midnight). Valerie Steffenson joined the staff as a sophomore, and will leave as an alumna of the University of Minnesota; she was personally responsible for over 20 occupational samples (not too many years ago, people completed Ph.D. dissertations by collecting a single sample).

Jane Swanson worked on the tabulation of demographic data and the compilation of Appendix C for the past year. Her predecessor was Jeffrey Stocco, who received his master's degree in counseling psychology in 1979. Jane's calculator-battery bills attest to the hours she has worked. Tamara Nelson worked with Jane during the summer of 1980 to provide summary reports on the new occupations.

Also particularly involved were Sandra Cerda, Dana Benassi (who handled some especially touchy samples), John Barnier, and Betsy McInerny.

The theme throughout these acknowledgments is accuracy and a willingness to work very hard when the project demanded. As often happens under such circumstances, a camaraderie developed among very diverse people. We celebrated births and birthdays, the opening of the baseball season, and all the major holidays. We had parties for graduations, passed preliminary exams, and gave our farewells and welcome backs. We had a collaboration that allowed a ten-year project to be completed in five. The result is, we think, the best interest inventory ever available for public use.

DAVID P. CAMPBELL
JO-IDA C. HANSEN

October 1980

Preface to the Second Edition

E. K. Strong, Jr., the original author of this inventory, was one of the most intense, dedicated, effective psychologists produced by America in the first half of the twentieth century. Over a 40-year span he developed—without benefit of modern funding or data-processing machinery—one of the country's most widely used psychological inventories. His research instincts were remarkable, his persistence astonishing, and his insistence on producing a practical product of high quality all too rare among academic psychologists.

He has been my scientific model. I am an ardent and unabashed admirer, and his impact on my life and professional career has been enormous. Further evidence of that can be found in the final chapter of the *Hand-book for the Strong Vocational Interest Blank* (Campbell, 1971), which is a history of the Strong blank.

These comments are a necessary prelude to this *Manual,* for in what follows I am reporting several changes in his test that would have made Strong quite uncomfortable. Two of these merit special comment: the first is the introduction of a theoretical framework to guide the layout of the profile and the interpretation of the scores; the second is the merging of the men's and women's forms into a single booklet.

I am not certain what Strong would think about the theoretical structure introduced here. He was an empiricist, and his major contribution was a determined empiricism at a time—the 1920's and 1930's—when the systematic collection of large amounts of test data was uncommon. He doggedly tested sample after sample to build a repository of data showing that people in different occupations can be distinguished from each other by the simple procedure of asking them to check their likes and dislikes on a long checklist. Much of his career was devoted to expanding his data bank and to developing statistical techniques for working with the inventory.

Yet he was also concerned with the sensible organization of his data in a theoretical sense. He went beyond the blind empirical approach in at least two ways: the first was the development of his occupational globe, which was essentially a three-dimensional representation of the relationship between occupations; the second was the grouping of occupations on the profile on the basis of the scale intercorrelations. These beginnings of an occupational taxonomy were expanded by John Holland after Strong's death, and the result, Holland's theory drawing heavily on Strong's data, is being used here for the first time to guide the layout of the Strong profile.

Holland was himself trained in the empirical tradition. He took his degree at the University of Minnesota in 1952 under J. G. Darley, the earliest of the Strong experts spawned at Minnesota. Darley's 1941 monograph, *Clinical Aspects and Interpretation of the Strong Vocational Interest Blank*, was the first major published work on the use of the Strong, and was an attempt to organize Strong's data for the benefit of the counselor. It had little direct impact because it was overwhelmed two years later, in 1943, by the publication of Strong's massive work *Vocational Interests of Men and Women*. Still, Darley's clinical approach (which was expanded in 1955 in Darley and Hagenah's influential *Vocational Interest Measurement*) was one of the early major factors leading to the success of the SVIB.

Now, 30 years later, all of these themes—Strong's empiricism, Darley's clinical stance, and Holland's theory —have converged in the publication of this revision.

The other major change that might have made Strong uncomfortable is the merger of the men's and women's forms. Since the 1930's, men and women have been analyzed separately, mostly because they give substantially different responses to many of the items in the inventory. Strong and I never specifically discussed this aspect of his system, for at the time of his death ten years ago we both accepted the general, if unexamined, view that this was the way the world sorted itself out, that is, with vocational distinctions between the sexes. Strong would have been offended by the current charge of sex discrimination. He probably felt, as I have, that the provision of a separate system for women was a rational reflection of statistical and social realities; to have thrown men and women into the same norming tables would have reduced the usefulness of the inventory for both sexes.

But what has been acceptable in the past does not offer adequate answers now, for either practice or theory. Accordingly, the rationale for having separate forms for men and women has been reexamined and rejected, and I have sought in the data some means of merging the forms to more accurately reflect current occupational trends. As part of this process, the views of women in various settings have been actively sought out. Acting on their suggestions—sometimes contradictory, usually stimulating, always interesting—has been challenging. A solution was sought that would do justice to all viewpoints—to statistical truth, to redressing genuine injustice, and to the practical constraints imposed by history.

Here are the major changes that have been made to "neutralize" the inventory:

1. The men's and women's test booklets have been combined into a single form.

2. Items that appear to have sexual bias have been eliminated.

3. References to gender have been eliminated from the inventory by changing *policeman* to *police officer*, and so forth.

4. New scales have been developed to allow individuals of both sexes to be scored on all scales, and the scores are reported on a single profile form, used for both sexes (norms are still separated by sex; the necessity for this is discussed at length in Chapter 7).

5. To reflect changes in the pattern of traditional male-female vocational separations, several new empirical scales have been added — for example, *female* college professors, pharmacists, credit managers, veterinarians, physicists, optometrists, and advertising executives; *male* nurses, elementary teachers, speech pathologists, and dietitians.

6. New theoretical scales have been added to the profile, and the profile layout stresses them over the empirical scales, which of course must still respond to the existing subject-pool and accordingly to historical job patterns.

7. The Masculinity-Femininity scale included on the earlier profiles has been dropped.

With the publication of this *Manual*, there are now two basic reference sources for this latest, merged form of the SVIB, the Strong-Campbell Interest Inventory (SCII, Form T325): the first is this *Manual*; the second is the *Handbook for the SVIB* (Campbell, 1971). The two overlap in coverage, and some guidance about what is, and is not, in each may be helpful to the user. The *Handbook*, which was published three years before this *Manual*, continues to be useful in several functions: as a test manual, as a statistical handbook, as a summary of relevant research information, and as a historical account of the Strong inventory. This *Manual* has a more specific focus: it reports the developmental work and statistical data for the SCII. Although the earlier SVIB and its *Manual* (1966; *Supplement*, 1969) are still available (and although some scoring agencies will continue to score the earlier SVIB), for the purposes of the SCII the 1966/1969 *Manual* is completely superseded.

When the *Handbook* was published, in 1971, it was the latest and most complete treatment of the SVIB, and as such it contained lengthy sections on topics such as scale development, validity, reliability, and usage. Almost immediately following the publication of the *Handbook*, intense work on the SCII began, and this has resulted in advances in some areas beyond what is in the *Handbook*. These advances are treated in this *Manual*. For the other, unaffected areas, the *Handbook* is still the best source, and those areas have merely been summarized here. This *Manual*, then, reports advances in three important areas:

1. *Item technology*. More information on the rationale underlying the choice of the items for the booklet, and on the way the individual items behave, appears here than has been published heretofore.

2. *The General Occupational Themes*. These themes, which are based on John Holland's theory, are being used here for the first time to guide the layout of the Strong profile.

3. *Male-female differences and similarities*. Because this is the first form of the SVIB to be used with both sexes, this is the first time that direct comparisons have been possible.

Following are the topics, summarized in this *Manual*, for which the *Handbook* remains the primary source:

1. Detailed information on predictive validity.
2. Construction of the Basic Interest Scales.
3. Test-retest reliability and change over time.
4. Stability of interests within occupations.
5. Stable and changing interests within our society.
6. The interests of outstanding people.
7. The history of the SVIB.
8. Discussion of the various past forms of the SVIB.

For most users, the *Manual* will be a sufficient source of information on the SCII. For those who want more detail, such as researchers and those responsible for training other professionals, the *Handbook* will continue to be an important reference work.

I would like to emphasize one final point: in psychology in general, and in psychological testing specifically, there has been little emphasis on building on the work of previous investigators. Most psychologists seem to feel they must have their own system, their own theory, their own technique. Most test developers start from scratch, authoring their own tests instead of improving on what is already available. I have of course done just the opposite; I have tried to take one of the best inventories in existence and make it better. In so doing, I have built on the immense contributions of E. K. Strong, Jr., and I have tried also to integrate the work of other researchers. Thus, the development of the SCII has drawn not only on Strong's work but also on that of K. E. Clark (1961) in the construction of the Basic Interest Scales, John Holland (1973) in incorporating the General Occupational Themes, and, through Holland's work, J. P. Guilford (Guilford et al., 1954) in identifying the major themes of vocational interests. If there is any single accomplishment that I am proudest of in this inventory, it is this integration of the work of earlier researchers.

In producing this revision, I have had considerable help. Phyllis Campbell has played the difficult, conflicting roles of sounding board, consultant, security blanket, and women's advocate. She has been intimately involved and her contributions were many. My colleagues in the Student Counseling Bureau and Department of Psychology, too numerous to mention individually, were never reticent in helping me find a path acceptable to both hard-headed empiricists and highly aware feminists. The University of Minnesota student body continued to provide me with productive research assistants. That the complex of elements that make up this *Manual* was completed in reasonable time is due largely to the expertise and energy level of Leslie Crichton and Patricia Webber, who were responsible for the statistical analyses and computer processing. Jean Forsberg prepared and organized a manuscript that at first had almost no sequential coherence. Mark Taylor and Joyce Schomberg suffered graciously while working through the innumerable daily clerical tasks assigned to undergraduates. Jo-Ida Hansen became our resident "Holland expert" and helped solve the tricky procedural problems of applying Holland's theory to Strong's data. Nothing has been more satisfying in my career than working with the many competent people who have found their way to the top floor of Eddy Hall at the University of Minnesota to work on the Strong inventory.

DAVID P. CAMPBELL

Minneapolis, Minnesota
January 1974

Contents

Figures and Tables

Manual for the
Strong-Campbell Interest Inventory

Form T325 of the Strong Vocational Interest Blank

CHAPTER ONE

Making Use of the SCII

Vocational-interest inventories are carefully constructed questionnaires that ask the respondent to indicate a degree of preference for a wide range of occupations, occupational activities, hobbies, amusements, school subjects, and types of people. With the Strong-Campbell Interest Inventory (SCII), the current edition of the Strong Vocational Interest Blank (SVIB), the person is given a list of 325 items and asked to respond either "Like," "Indifferent," or "Dislike" to each of them. The answers are then analyzed, by computer (the SCII cannot be scored by hand), and the results are reported on a sheet called a profile, which presents scores on a number of "scales" in an organized format and offers interpretive information. Although the profile is largely self-explanatory, it is essential that a counselor guide the respondent to an understanding of the scales and an interpretation of the scores.

Briefly, the SCII gives the respondent three main types of information: first, scores on six General Occupational Themes, which reflect the respondent's overall occupational orientation; second, scores on 23 Basic Interest Scales, which report consistency of interests or aversions in 23 specific areas, such as art, science, or public speaking; and third, scores on 162 Occupational Scales, which indicate degree of similarity between the respondent's interests and the characteristic interests of men and women in a wide range of occupations.

Scores are arranged on the profile to encourage the respondent to note overall trends, and then to see how these trends are related to the world of work. The emphasis is on organizing the information to help the respondent develop a general strategy toward approaching career decisions.

Interest inventories can be used effectively for a variety of purposes. This chapter reviews the more common applications.

Counseling the Individual Student or Employee

Interest inventories should perform one or both of two principal functions. First, they should provide people with information about themselves and their relationship to the working world, information that will lead them to greater self-understanding and to better decisions about the course of their lives. Second, interest inventories should provide people who must make decisions about others—counselors, teachers, administrators, personnel managers, supervisors—with comparable information, as well as strategies for interpreting it, so that their decisions can consider the unique qualities of each individual.

Interest inventories can be used in many ways to serve these functions. The following does not exhaust the possibilities; it does list the applications that have been found to be the most effective.

As an aid in making educational and occupational choices. This is by far the most common use. People must make decisions about the course of their lives, and because their choices of educational major and eventual occupation may have more impact on their lives than any other decisions they make, those choices should be well informed.

When students make these decisions, they should have access to good occupational information, to professional advice, and to the best possible data about themselves. The SCII was designed specifically for these situations, and the information it provides about a person's pattern of interests is directly applicable to making educational and occupational choices. Of course, other information, such as experiences and abilities, should also be considered in making these choices; the SCII profile offers only a measure of interests.

Some counselors use interest inventories only with students who are uncertain about what they want to do, but many students who have already made firm decisions are reassured in seeing their choices confirmed. One common reaction to the profile is, "Yes, my scores look reasonable: that's about what I figured. I'm glad the computer and I agree; it's reassuring."

As a vehicle in discussions between student and counselor. Many students who are seeking vocational guidance feel more comfortable in counseling sessions if the initial discussion is structured, and they are grateful for an organized assessment of their interest patterns. Test scores provide a focus that moves conversation quickly to areas of concern to the student. Many counselors, especially inexperienced ones, also appreciate the focusing qualities of the profile scores. Tests, of course, should not be used as a crutch, but that is seldom a problem once the counselor has accumulated some experience.

As a catalyst in discussions between student and parent. Although experienced teachers and counselors can guide discussions with students quite adroitly without the aid of tests, many parents do not have the same facility. Again, interest-test scores can stimulate discussion of topics such as career choice and personal development. These scores present the parent with specific information about the student's interests—information that may not have surfaced in earlier discussions—and they afford the student an opportunity to explain personal feelings in ways not usually possible. In such settings, useful decisions can often be reached.

Several years ago, a university student reported, with considerable relief, that his results on the inventory had helped him convince his parents that he had good reason for not wanting to go to medical school. He was from a family with a long history of physicians—a parent, two siblings, a grandparent, and two other relatives had all gone to medical school—but he had never wanted to be a doctor. Whenever he said this to his family, they always responded, "Sure, we all felt that way when we were your age. After you get into it, you'll like it." Years of protest on his part had not availed, but the evidence provided by the interest profile—that his interests were quite different from those of physicians—finally convinced them that he was not destined to follow in the family tradition. With no further protest on their part, he took his degree in architecture and today is contentedly designing schools and industrial facilities.

In a similar situation, a student whose parents were advising her to enter nursing training had set her sights higher—she wanted to go to medical school—and she used her profile (and tests of ability) to demonstrate to them that her interests (and aptitudes) were similar to those of physicians and other biological scientists. Shown this evidence, the parents supported her plans.

As a selection device for those who must make employment decisions. Precisely how test scores should be used in employee selection will vary with the situation and with the training of the individual who is doing the hiring. Employment decisions are important for all concerned, and they should be made by people with professional training. Using the inventory simply as a "go/no-go" employee-selection device, and making each decision on the basis of a fixed cutoff score, is not recommended, though such a strategy is better than basing the decision on whether or not the applicant is friendly and has a good handshake.

For employee-selection purposes, the inventory is most effective when it is part of a general screening process developed by someone with professional training. Similarly, using an inventory to make placement decisions about people already on the payroll is handled best by a trained personnel worker who can study the respondent's scores, then discuss them with her/him along with other considerations dictated by the practical setting.

As a tool in helping people understand their job dissatisfaction. Some people are dissatisfied with their jobs because they are in positions that fail to allow them outlets for their dominant interests, or because they are in settings in which they have little in common with their colleagues. Many times an interest profile can identify the problem by showing the individual how he/she is different. When an accountant is shown that her interests tend much more toward the artistic than those of most executives, she has information that can help her contend with the boredom of her job. Even if she cannot change careers, she can take steps to improve her situation, perhaps by becoming active in the local art institute during her off-hours or by seeking employment as an accountant in some art-related firm, such as an advertising agency. What plan she develops depends on her imagination and energy, but the inventory can give her some direction.

Conducting Research on Groups

Most of the practical, day-to-day applications of the SCII have been discussed. But the instrument need not be confined to the individual; researchers studying groups should consider the following possibilities: This list, like the first, is incomplete, for imaginative scientists can find many novel uses for good measuring instruments.

Studying characteristic interests of particular occupations. Data such as item-response percentages, scale means, and intercorrelations of a new scale with existing scales provide information about the dominant interests of people in a given occupation. For example, the interest-inventory data from the sample of women geologists showed that their likes were concentrated in academic areas such as science and mathematics, as well as in nature and outdoor activities and mechanical activities. Their aversions focused on social service and religious activities, and on the traditional home and family activities. They also showed an aversion to enterprising endeavors such as merchandising and sales.

Detailed information about an occupation is useful for many purposes, such as helping people decide if they would like employment in the occupation, planning recruiting efforts to attract to the occupation those people who would be most likely to remain, or identifying people already in the occupation who might be more happily and more effectively assigned elsewhere.

Studying change in groups. Interest inventories have been used to test groups at one point in time and then to retest them at some later time to see how they have changed. In a study by the American Association of Medical Colleges, 2,800 medical school students were tested as entering freshmen and retested four years later upon graduation (Hutchins, 1964). The results, discussed in more detail in Chapter 5 and in the *Handbook for the SVIB* (Campbell, 1971), indicated that these students showed a decline in both scientific and social-service interests, on which they had scored very high as freshmen, and a mild increase in adventuresome interests. These findings run counter to expectations, and afford an interesting basis for psychometric research and speculation.

Interest inventories are not precise enough to detect small, subtle, short-term changes in groups. Because the items for the inventory were selected for long-term stability and validity, small day-to-day shifts are not reflected in the scores. For example, teachers who test students before and after a specific course to determine the impact of the course will usually find that the SCII shows little, if any, change. Most people's interests, as measured by the SCII, are quite stable over the short range.

Over a longer period, such as two or three years, substantial changes do occur in some people—especially young people—and the inventory scores should reflect those changes.

Studying change in institutions. Interest inventories can be used to compare different classes, different pools of applicants, or different recruit or volunteer groups at various times. One study examined the characteristics of freshmen classes at Dartmouth College over a 20-year period (Campbell, 1969). These results, which were available only because the answer sheets had been meticulously filed over the years by Clark Horton, an educational researcher at Dartmouth, showed that the more recent classes were much more academically oriented—with stronger interests in science and the arts—than their predecessors, who were more attracted to business endeavors.

Studying general societal trends. When samples tested in the 1930's are compared with analogous samples tested in the 1960's or 1970's, estimates of general change within our society can be drawn. The results of such studies (Campbell, 1966b) show that vocational-interest patterns are much more stable over long time spans than the average person (or psychologist, for that matter) might think. One general shift—a mild increase in extroverted interests—did occur: people today report more attraction for working with others in a variety of settings than did men and women in analogous occupations who were tested in the 1930's. More details on this topic are given in the *Handbook*.

Studying change within an individual. Interest inventories can be used in case studies of change over time, or lack of it, with a single person representing some generalized societal phenomenon. Several examples of this application are given in the *Handbook*.

Studying cross-cultural influences. Several projects have used the inventory to study occupations in other countries. For some of these, the form has been translated into another language; for others—studies in Ireland and Pakistan, for example—the English-language version was used. Examples include Lonner's work with German-speaking psychologists and accountants (Lonner, 1968, 1969); Shah's work with Pakistani physicians and engineers (Shah, 1970); Hanlon's study of Irish students (Hanlon, 1971); and Stauffer's work with the German and French translations of the Strong (Stauffer, 1973). The results of these studies show considerable similarity of interests, across several countries, among people in the same occupation; generally, American norms are usable in other countries as representations of the interests of specific occupations there.

One problem in using the earlier editions of the Strong cross-culturally was that a few items—such as *Be a cheerleader* or *Work with Democrats*—were peculiarly American. These items bemused or irritated foreign respondents. Though the number of items was too small to have an appreciable effect on scoring, the loss of goodwill was substantial. This problem was addressed in the development of the SCII, and many troublesome items were eliminated. In consequence, when the SCII is translated into other languages, problems are minimal; most items (for example, *Operating machinery, Writing reports, Watching an open-heart operation*) translate easily into most languages, eliciting the same responses as they do in English.

Some Potential Research Uses

The foregoing covers the usual research applications of interest inventories. Because of the improvements being made in the SCII, other applications may become common. Here are some likely possibilities.

Identifying homogeneous types on which to do further research. Dimensions of interests can be used in the same way that we have learned to use measures of general intelligence or socioeconomic status. The Holland, or General Occupational Theme, scales (discussed in later chapters) may be especially useful. People can be grouped into realistic types, artistic types, social types, and so forth as a prelude to other investigations. Almost certainly, people of these types will behave differently in various environments, and researchers could use this typology as a classifying variable. For example, investigators studying the reactions of people to crowding might first separate their subjects into predominantly social and predominantly artistic groups, since these groups are likely to have different reactions to crowds.

Helping to understand influences on career development. Strange as it may seem, almost no knowledge exists about the ways in which various patterns of interest develop. Virtually all of the previous research has concentrated on the technology of measuring interests, describing group characteristics, determining the degree of predictability of vocational behavior by inventoried interests, or studying other correlates of interests. Little has been done to learn how different patterns of interest form in the first place. To a large extent, this neglect has persisted because the measuring instruments have not lent themselves to this type of research. The bulky empiricism of traditional approaches—dealing with dozens of scales—has restricted the range of applicability of the inventories, leaving no easy way to study early determinants of various patterns of scores. Now that the profile has a more definite theoretical framework, research of a more theoretical nature can be organized.

Carrying out a census of interest patterns. How many people in a given society have scientific interests?

How many have artistic interests? Are cultures with many enterprising individuals more progressive than cultures with few? Interest inventories can help research such questions.

Studying interpersonal relationships. Marriages between people of similar interests might be more successful than others. Parents and children with different patterns of interest might need more help in communicating with each other than do those with similar interests.

Studying the behavioral-type composition of groups. Groups exhibiting heterogeneous interest patterns may be more or less efficient than homogeneous groups. The characteristics of the individuals within any group have an impact on overall group behavior, and interest inventories can help in studying such issues.

Helping to design jobs around the interests of people. Interest inventories are a systematic means of asking people what they like and dislike. Such information should be useful—indeed, crucial—in designing work environments that people will find appealing. Given the current level of knowledge, this may be, at the moment, a grandiose goal. Still, if we know, for example, that psychologists have strong artistic interests, perhaps departments of psychology and psychological clinics would do well to allocate some portion of their supply budgets to making their environments more artistically exciting. If we know that people in sales have high levels of adventuresome interests, perhaps we should design sales incentives that capitalize on that knowledge. And perhaps we should design clerical work out of the technician's job, since we know that these people abhor those activities.

Similar, but more subtle, modifications of working environments have been made by the workers themselves, often through decades of gradual change, but we should learn to shape environments more systematically, to create a greater impact sooner. Such an approach could lead to greater diversity in work environments. In the absence of forces to the contrary, conformity, not diversity, is the rule in most contemporary work settings. The better we can document that different people, or different subgroups of people, like different things, the more successfully we can adapt their work environments.

This chapter has discussed the major ways in which interest inventories are being used, and has suggested several applications for future research. The chapters that follow examine the development of the SCII in detail and report data on its statistical characteristics.

CHAPTER TWO

Testing and Scoring Materials

The materials for the SVIB-SCII include the inventory booklet (Form T325), an answer sheet, and a profile form. Some scoring agencies also offer an interpretive profile, an option yielding several sheets of tailored interpretation in addition to the scores and generalized interpretation of the basic profile. All of these materials are discussed in this chapter.

The SCII is also available in Spanish translation (Form T325S).

The Inventory Booklet

The core of the SVIB-SCII system is the inventory booklet (Fig. 2-1; in Spanish, Fig. 2-2). This form lists 325 items, to most of which the person responds by filling in either "Like," "Indifferent," or "Dislike" on the answer sheet.

Types of items in the inventory. The test booklet has seven sections:

Section I. Occupation (131 items). These items are all names of occupations, and this is the best section in terms of measurement power; that is, these items elicit more variability in response from one occupation to the next than any other section. People respond to the stereotypic nature of occupational titles, and their responses signal their own occupational orientation.

Section II. School Subjects (36 items). The school subjects cover a wide range of educational situations, including academic and other areas. Most people, even students as young as 13 or 14, have little trouble in deciding how they feel about a given subject, even though they may never have studied it.

Section III. Activities (51 items). This section contains a diverse collection of activities, such as *Repairing electrical wiring, Making statistical charts,* and *Interviewing clients.* This is another powerful section; occupations differ widely in the percentage of people answering "Like" or "Dislike" to these items.

Section IV. Amusements (39 items). These items cover spare-time activities, hobbies, games, and a variety of entertainments. Some examples are *Poker, Symphony concerts,* and *Preparing dinner for guests.*

Section V. Types of People (24 items). This section asks whether the respondent would enjoy working day-to-day with various types of people, such as *Highway construction workers, High school students,* and *Babies.*

Section VI. Preference Between Two Activities (30 items). This section asks the respondent to contrast two activities or circumstances, such as *Taking a chance* versus *Playing safe,* or *Having a few close friends* versus *Having many acquaintances,* and to decide which is the more appealing, or whether the two should be marked as equally attractive or unattractive.

Section VII. Your Characteristics (14 items). The respondent is asked to read a statement such as *Usually start activities of my group,* and to respond either "Yes," "?," or "No" to indicate if the statement is an apt self-description. Almost everyone appears to answer this section honestly, if with a general tendency toward self-flattery, and these answers furnish another type of information about the respondent's occupational orientation. (See the case studies in Chapter 10.)

The value of a varied item format. Variation in item content and format from section to section is helpful in two ways; first, the variety provides some redundancy and subtlety in the scales (a person's interests can thus be tapped from several approaches and at several levels); second, it presents a more interesting task to the person filling in the inventory (to respond to several hundred items of the same format can be boring).

Selecting items for the booklet. There are two paramount concerns in selecting items for interest inventories: first, the items must collectively produce valid, reliable scales; and second, the items should not irritate, offend, strain, or embarrass the respondent in any way, if the inventory is to be effective in a variety of situations.

The items for the SCII were, with two exceptions, taken from the earlier Strong booklets, either the men's form, published in 1966, or the women's, published in 1968. Excellent item statistics are available on these items, and the best of them were selected for inclusion in the SCII booklet. The following guidelines or criteria were used in selecting items from the two booklets:

1. Each item should elicit a wide range of response among occupations. Specifically, the range of "Like" or "Dislike" percentages across occupations should be large; if people in most occupational samples give the same response to an item, the item cannot add much to the scales. Examples of items eliminated because of restricted range of response were *Funeral director,* to which virtually everyone answers "Dislike," and *Geography*, to which most people in every occupation answer "Like." Examples of items eliciting a wide range of response are *College professor*, where the range of "Like" responses runs from 5 percent among farmers, people in the skilled crafts, and some lower-level business occupations to 99 percent among psychologists, political scientists, and anthropologists; and *Operating machinery*, where the range is from 5 percent among artists and writers to 97 percent among farmers and machinists.

This empirical criterion of response range—essentially a measure of item validity—was the single most important factor in deciding whether an item was to be retained: if the distribution over several hundred occupational samples was narrow, the item was discarded; if the distribution was broad, the item then faced the other criteria below. A more extensive discussion of this criterion appears in Chapter 3.

2. Items should cover a wide range of occupational content. Evaluating items on this criterion calls for some judgment in defining the universe of vocational interests across all occupations: How do we know what breadth of content that universe contains, and whether or not the items selected address all of its more important components? We cannot be sure, but the general goal was to seek diversity in items. Combining the men's and women's booklets helped considerably: The items in the merged booklet cover far more area than did the items in either of the original booklets.

3. Items should be free of sex-role bias. Because one of the primary motivations for merging the two forms was the elimination of sex-role bias, considerable attention was given to this factor in the selection and wording of items. Wherever possible, existing items were modified to eliminate gender: for example, *Policeman* became *Police officer*, *Salesman* became *Salesperson*. And where gender was an integral part of an item, versions for both sexes were included: for example, *Actor/Actress*, *Dressmaker/Tailor*, *YMCA/YWCA staff member*.

The words "man, men, woman, women" were eradicated. Thus, *Prominent businessmen* became *Prominent business leaders*, *Athletic women* became *Athletic people*, and *Advertising man* became *Advertising executive*.

One item, *Draftsman*, was not modified in 1974. At that time, a committee of women who helped to judge the sex fairness of the items agreed that the term "draftsman" had a unisex occupational connotation. At that time also, the U.S. Department of Labor used that term, as did the *Dictionary of Occupational Titles*. However, since 1974, opinion has changed, and the item has now been modified to *Drafting technician* to avoid any possibility of suggesting that the occupation is appropriate only for men.

No item was eliminated simply because of a large male-female difference in response. Although discarding such items might solve a few technical problems—

such an expedient was followed in the early days of intelligence testing—its effect would be misleading. About half of the items in the inventory show large differences in the responses of men and women; our task is to learn how to work with differences in ways that do not disadvantage either sex, not to ignore them. Chapter 7 discusses these issues further.

4. Items should not be culture-bound. Two chief reasons require that items be judged against this criterion. First, psychologists and educators in other countries are interested in adapting well-proven American techniques to their own needs; if items can be translated easily, the adaptation will be more successful. Second, and perhaps more important, items that are easily adapted for a variety of foreign cultures are more appropriate for the wide range of subcultures in the United States.

5. Items should be up to date. Even one or two dated items out of several hundred is sufficient to create a loss of confidence in an inventory. Because the Strong inventories, which were originally published in the 1920's and 1930's, were revised in the 1960's, most of the obviously dated items—*Floorwalker* or *Tearoom proprietress*, for example—had already been removed. A few borderline items remained, however, because they offered good validity statistics. Because more items were available than were needed for the merged form, the pruning this time was more severe, and the remaining dated items were discarded.

One obviously dated item, *Pursuing bandits in a sheriff's posse*, was retained: no one ever complains about it; the validity statistics are good, with "Like" responses ranging from 5 percent among ministers, school superintendents, and physicians to 80 percent among police officers and highway patrol officers; it usually evokes a smile or a chuckle; and, falling as it does about midway through the inventory, it offers a welcome departure in tone.

6. Items should be unambiguous; everyone who reads them should interpret them the same way. This is seldom a problem with items that are occupational titles or activities, but problems do occur occasionally. For example, the item *City or state employee* is not as precise as some respondents would like, but it was retained because the validity statistics are good.

Another example is the item *Interviewing men for a job*. This item was occasionally interpreted as taking the role of interviewee rather than interviewer. The problem was solved by rewording the item to *Interviewing job applicants*, which also eliminated its male orientation.

A third case, *Have good judgment in appraising values*, clearly demonstrates the problem of ambiguity. The highest percentage of "Yes" responses was, in men, among accountants (98 percent) and psychologists (92 percent); and, in women, among buyers (86 percent) and physicians (77 percent). Obviously, not everyone was interpreting the word "value" in the same way. This item was discarded.

Strong-Campbell Interest Inventory

Merged Form of the

Strong Vocational Interest Blank

EDWARD K. STRONG, JR. 1884-1963   DAVID P. CAMPBELL

This inventory is used to help you understand your work interests in a general way, and to show you some kinds of work in which you might be comfortable. The following pages list many jobs, activities, school subjects, and so forth, and you are asked to show your liking or disliking for each. Your answers will be compared with the answers given by people already working in a wide range of jobs, and your scores will show how similar your interests are to the interests of these people. But this is not a test of your *abilities*; it is an inventory of your *interests*.

Directions:

1. With this booklet, you should have a **special answer sheet** on which to mark your answers.
2. **Please make no marks on this booklet**; it will be used again by other people.
3. Use any soft, black, lead pencil (such as a No. 2) to make your marks on the answer sheet.
4. Fill in your name and other information on the answer sheet. Follow carefully the instructions for filling in your name.
5. **Instructions for marking your answers** are given on the next page of this booklet and also on the answer sheet.
6. **Make a heavy, dark mark for each answer**—not a cross or a check mark.
7. If you make a mistake or change your mind, **erase carefully and thoroughly**.
8. Your answer sheet will be processed by computer. **Please keep it neat and free from stray marks,** so that it will be scored correctly.
9. Try to answer each question. **Work quickly;** first impressions usually give the best results with this inventory. Turn the page and begin.

Fig. 2-1. SVIB-SCII inventory booklet (see also following three pages)

Part I. Occupations

Many occupations are listed below. For each of them, show how you would feel about doing that kind of work.

> Mark on the answer sheet in the space labeled "L" if you think you would **like** that kind of work.
>
> Mark in the space labeled "I" if you are **indifferent** (that is, if you think you wouldn't care one way or another).
>
> Mark in the space labeled "D" if you think you would **dislike** that kind of work.

Don't worry about whether you would be good at the job or about not being trained for it. Forget about how much money you could make or whether you could get ahead. Think only about whether you would like to do the work done in that job. **Work fast. Answer every one.**

1 Actor/Actress
2 Advertising executive
3 Architect
4 Art museum director
5 Art teacher
6 Artist
7 Artist's model
8 Astronomer
9 Athletic director
10 Auctioneer
11 Author of children's books
12 Author of novels
13 Author of technical books
14 Auto mechanic
15 Auto racer
16 Auto sales
17 Bank teller
18 Beauty and haircare consultant
19 Biologist
20 Bookkeeper
21 Building contractor
22 Business teacher
23 Buyer of merchandise
24 Carpenter
25 Cartoonist
26 Cashier in bank
27 Chemist
28 Children's clothes designer
29 Church worker
30 City or state employee
31 City planner
32 Civil engineer
33 College professor
34 Computer operator
35 Corporation lawyer
36 Costume designer
37 Courtroom stenographer
38 Criminal lawyer
39 Dancing teacher
40 Dental assistant
41 Dentist
42 Designer, electronic equipment
43 Dietitian
44 Drafting technician
45 Dressmaker/Tailor

46 Editor
47 Electrical engineer
48 Electronics technician
49 Elementary school teacher
50 Employment manager
51 Factory manager
52 Farmer
53 Fashion model
54 Florist
55 Foreign correspondent
56 Foreign service officer
57 Free-lance writer
58 Governor of a state
59 High school teacher
60 Home economics teacher
61 Hospital records clerk
62 Housekeeper
63 Hotel manager
64 Illustrator
65 Income tax accountant
66 Interior decorator
67 Inventor
68 Jet pilot
69 Judge
70 Labor arbitrator
71 Laboratory technician
72 Landscape gardener
73 Librarian
74 Life insurance agent
75 Machine shop supervisor
76 Machinist
77 Manager, Chamber of Commerce
78 Manager, child care center
79 Manager, women's style shop
80 Manufacturer
81 Mechanical engineer
82 Military officer
83 Minister, priest, or rabbi
84 Musician
85 Newspaper reporter
86 Nurse
87 Nurse's aide/Orderly
88 Office clerk
89 Office manager
90 Opera singer

91 Orchestra conductor
92 Pharmacist
93 Photographer
94 Physician
95 Playground director
96 Poet
97 Police officer
98 Politician
99 Private secretary
100 Professional athlete
101 Professional dancer
102 Professional gambler
103 Psychologist
104 Public relations director
105 Rancher
106 Realtor
107 Receptionist
108 Retailer
109 Sales manager
110 School principal
111 Scientific illustrator
112 Scientific research worker
113 Sculptor
114 Secret service agent
115 Social worker
116 Specialty salesperson
117 Sports reporter
118 Statistician
119 Flight attendant
120 Stockbroker
121 Surgeon
122 Toolmaker
123 Traveling salesperson
124 Travel bureau manager
125 Typist
126 TV announcer
127 Vocational counselor
128 Waiter/Waitress
129 Wholesaler
130 X-Ray technician
131 YMCA/YWCA staff member

Fig. 2-1 (cont.). SVIB-SCII inventory booklet (page 2)

Part II. School Subjects

Show in the same way whether you are interested in these school subjects, even though you may not have studied them.

Mark "L" for **Like**.
Mark "I" for **Indifferent** (when you don't care one way or the other).
Mark "D" for **Dislike**.

132 Agriculture
133 Algebra
134 Arithmetic
135 Ancient languages (Latin, Sanskrit, etc.)
136 Art
137 Bible history
138 Bookkeeping
139 Botany
140 Calculus
141 Chemistry
142 Civics (government)
143 Dramatics
144 Economics
145 English composition
146 Geometry
147 Home economics
148 Industrial arts
149 Journalism
150 Literature
151 Mathematics
152 Mechanical drawing
153 Military drill
154 Modern languages (French, German, etc.)
155 Nature study
156 Penmanship
157 Philosophy
158 Physical education
159 Physics
160 Physiology
161 Political science
162 Psychology
163 Public speaking
164 Sociology
165 Statistics
166 Typewriting
167 Zoology

Part III. Activities

Show your interests in the same way as before. Give the first answer that comes to mind.

168 Making a speech
169 Doing research work
170 Repairing a clock
171 Cooking
172 Operating machinery
173 Writing reports
174 Discussing politics
175 Taping a sprained ankle
176 Adjusting a carburetor
177 Going to church
178 Heading a civic improvement program
179 Raising flowers and vegetables
180 Interviewing job applicants
181 Teaching children
182 Teaching adults
183 Meeting and directing people
184 Taking responsibility
185 Sewing
186 Making statistical charts
187 Operating office machines
188 Giving first aid assistance
189 Decorating a room with flowers
190 Interviewing prospects in selling
191 Drilling soldiers
192 Pursuing bandits in a sheriff's posse
193 Watching an open-heart operation
194 Checking typewritten material for errors
195 Repairing electrical wiring
196 Organizing cabinets and closets
197 Adjusting difficulties of others
198 Starting a conversation with a stranger
199 Cabinetmaking
200 Being a forest ranger
201 Bargaining ("swapping")
202 Looking at things in a clothing store
203 Buying merchandise for a store
204 Displaying merchandise in a store
205 Competitive activities
206 Regular hours for work
207 Continually changing activities
208 Interviewing clients
209 Arguments
210 Developing business systems
211 Doing your own laundry work
212 Saving money
213 Contributing to charities
214 Raising money for charity
215 Expressing judgments publicly, regardless of what others say
216 Climbing along the edge of a steep cliff
217 Living in the city
218 Discussing the purpose of life

Part IV. Amusements

Show in the same way how you feel about these ways of having fun. Work rapidly. Do not think over various possibilities. Give the first answer that comes to mind.

219 Golf
220 Fishing
221 Jazz or rock concerts
222 Looking at things in a hardware store
223 Boxing
224 Poker
225 Bridge
226 Solving mechanical puzzles
227 Planning a large party
228 Religious music
229 Drilling in a military company
230 Amusement parks
231 Conventions
232 Formal dress affairs
233 Electioneering for office
234 Art galleries
235 Leading a scout troop
236 Writing a one-act play
237 Symphony concerts
238 Night clubs
239 Church young people's group
240 Sports pages in the newspaper
241 Poetry
242 Skiing
243 Business magazines
244 Popular mechanics magazines
245 Reading the Bible
246 Magazines about art and music
247 Building a radio or stereo set
248 Attending lectures
249 Family pages in newspapers
250 Performing scientific experiments
251 Camping
252 Playing chess
253 Preparing dinner for guests
254 Entertaining others
255 Trying new cooking recipes
256 Being the first to wear the latest fashions
257 Organizing a play

Fig. 2-1 (cont.). SVIB-SCII inventory booklet (page 3)

Part V.
Types of People

Most of us choose jobs where we can work with people we enjoy. Show in the same way as before how you would feel about having day-to-day contact with the following types of people. Work fast. Don't think of specific examples. Just give the first answer that comes to mind.

258 Highway construction workers
259 High school students
260 Military officers
261 Artistic people
262 Foreigners
263 Ballet dancers
264 Nonconformists
265 People who assume leadership
266 Religious people
267 Aggressive people
268 Physically sick people
269 Babies
270 Very old people

271 Emotional people
272 People who have made fortunes in business
273 Thrifty people
274 Musical geniuses
275 Outspoken people with new ideas
276 Fashionably dressed people
277 Prominent business leaders
278 Athletic people
279 People who daydream a lot
280 Outstanding scientists
281 People who live dangerously

Part VI.
Preference Between Two Activities

Here are several pairs of activities or occupations. Show which one of each pair you like better: if you prefer the one on the **left**, mark in the space labeled "**L**" on the answer sheet; if you prefer the one on the **right**, mark in the space labeled "**R**"; if you like or dislike **both the same**, or if you **can't decide**, mark in the space labeled "=." Work rapidly. Make one mark for each pair.

Airline pilot	282	Airline ticket agent
Taxicab driver	283	Police officer
Headwaiter/Hostess	284	Lighthouse keeper
Selling things house to house	285	Gardening
Developing plans	286	Carrying out plans
Doing a job yourself	287	Telling somebody else to do the job
Dealing with things	288	Dealing with people
Taking a chance	289	Playing safe
Drawing a definite salary	290	Receiving a commission on what is done
Outside work	291	Inside work
Work for yourself	292	Carrying out the program of a superior whom you respect
Superintendent of a hospital	293	Warden of a prison
Vocational counselor	294	Public health officer
Physical activity	295	Mental activity
Dog trainer	296	Juvenile parole officer
Thrilling, dangerous activities	297	Quieter, safer activities
Physical education director	298	Free-lance writer
Statistician	299	Social worker
Technical responsibility (in charge of 25 people doing scientific work)	300	Supervisory responsibility (in charge of 300 people doing business-office work)
Going to a play	301	Going to a dance
Teacher	302	Salesperson
Experimenting with new grooming preparations	303	Experimenting with new office equipment
Being married to a research scientist	304	Being married to a sales executive
Working in a large corporation with little chance of being president before age 55	305	Working for yourself in a small business
Working in an import-export business	306	Working in a research laboratory
Music and art events	307	Athletic events
Reading a book	308	Watching TV or going to a movie
Appraising real estate	309	Repairing and restoring antiques
Having a few close friends	310	Having many acquaintances
Work in which you move from place to place	311	Work where you live in one place

Part VII.
Your Characteristics

Show here what kind of person you are: if the statement describes you, mark in the space labeled "**Y**" (for "Yes"); if the statement does **not** describe you, mark in the space labeled "**N**" (for "No"); if you cannot decide, mark in the space labeled "**?**." (Be frank in pointing out your weak points, because these are as important as your strong points in choosing a career.)

312 Usually start activities of my group
313 Have more than my share of novel ideas
314 Win friends easily
315 Make decisions immediately, not after considerable thought
316 Prefer working alone rather than on committees
317 Have mechanical ingenuity (inventiveness)
318 Am concerned about philosophical problems such as religion, meaning of life, etc.

319 Can prepare successful advertisements
320 Stimulate the ambitions of my associates
321 Can write a concise, well-organized report
322 Enjoy tinkering with small hand tools
323 Can smooth out tangles and disagreements between people
324 Put drive into an organization
325 Have patience when teaching others

Fig. 2-1 (cont.). SVIB-SCII inventory booklet (page 4)

Parte I. Ocupaciones

A continuación se enumeran varias ocupaciones. Indique cómo se sentiría usted desempeñando el trabajo relacionado con cada una de ellas. En la hoja de respuestas:

Marque el espacio designado "**G**" si usted cree que le **gustaría** ese tipo de trabajo.

Marque el espacio designado "**I**" si le es **indiferente** (es decir, si ni le gusta ni le disgusta).

Marque el espacio designado "**D**" si usted cree que le **disgustaría** ese tipo de trabajo.

No se preocupe acerca de sus habilidades para desempeñar el trabajo o de si tiene la preparación necesaria para hacerlo. No piense tampoco en el sueldo que podría ganar ni en los posibles ascensos. Concéntrese solamente en si le gustaría desempeñar ese tipo de trabajo. **Trabaje con rapidez y conteste cada una de las preguntas.**

1 Actor/actriz
2 Director(a) de publicidad
3 Arquitecto
4 Director(a) de museo de arte
5 Maestro(a) de bellas artes
6 Artista
7 Modelo para artistas
8 Astrónomo
9 Director(a) de deportes
10 Rematador(a)
11 Autor(a) de libros para niños
12 Novelista
13 Autor(a) de libros técnicos
14 Mecánico(a) de automóviles
15 Automovilista de carrera
16 Vendedor(a) de automóviles
17 Dependiente bancario
18 Asesor(a) de salones de belleza
19 Biólogo(a)
20 Contador(a) mercantil
21 Contratista de construcción
22 Maestro(a) de comercio
23 Comprador(a) de mercancías
24 Carpintero
25 Caricaturista
26 Cajero(a) bancario(a)
27 Químico(a)
28 Diseñador(a) de ropa para niños
29 Asistente voluntario de iglesias
30 Empleado(a) municipal o estatal
31 Urbanista
32 Ingeniero(a) civil
33 Profesor(a) universitario(a)
34 Experto(a) en manejo de computadoras
35 Abogado(a) de sociedad mercantil
36 Diseñador(a) de trajes
37 Estenógrafo(a) de corte de justicia
38 Abogado(a) penal
39 Maestro(a) de baile
40 Ayudante de dentista
41 Dentista
42 Diseñador(a) de equipo electrónico
43 Especialista en dietética
44 Dibujante
45 Modista/sastre
46 Redactor(a)
47 Ingeniero(a) electricista

48 Técnico(a) en electrónica
49 Maestro(a) de enseñanza primaria
50 Gerente de personal
51 Gerente de fábrica
52 Agricultor(a)
53 Modelo de alta costura
54 Florista
55 Corresponsal extranjero(a)
56 Oficial del servicio diplomático y consular
57 Escritor(a) independiente
58 Gobernador(a) de estado, provincia o departamento
59 Maestro(a) de enseñanza secundaria
60 Maestro(a) de economía doméstica
61 Escribiente de expedientes médicos
62 Mayordomo(ama) de llaves
63 Gerente de hoteles
64 Ilustrador(a)
65 Contador(a) de impuestos sobre la renta
66 Decorador(a)
67 Inventor(a)
68 Piloto de avión a reacción
69 Juez
70 Árbitro(a) de disputas laborales
71 Técnico(a) en laboratorios
72 Diseñador(a) de jardines
73 Bibliotecario(a)
74 Agente de seguros de vida
75 Supervisor(a) de taller de maquinaria
76 Maquinista
77 Administrador(a), Cámara de Comercio
78 Administrador(a) de guarderías
79 Gerente de modistería
80 Fabricante
81 Ingeniero(a) mecánico(a)
82 Oficial militar
83 Sacerdote, pastor, o rabí
84 Músico(a)
85 Periodista
86 Enfermero(a)
87 Ayudante de enfermero(a) o de hospital
88 Oficinista

89 Gerente de oficina
90 Cantante de ópera
91 Director(a) de orquesta
92 Farmacéutico(a)
93 Fotógrafo
94 Médico(a)
95 Director(a) de campo de recreo
96 Poeta
97 Policía
98 Político(a)
99 Secretario(a) particular
100 Deportista profesional
101 Bailarín(a) profesional
102 Apostador(a) profesional
103 Psicólogo(a)
104 Director(a) de relaciones públicas
105 Ranchero(a)
106 Corredor(a) de bienes raíces
107 Recepcionista
108 Comerciante al por menor
109 Gerente de ventas
110 Director(a) de escuela primaria/secundaria
111 Ilustrador(a) de material científico
112 Investigador(a) científico(a)
113 Escultor(a)
114 Agente de la policía secreta
115 Asistente social
116 Vendedor(a) de novedades
117 Reportero(a) deportivo(a)
118 Perito(a) en estadística
119 Aeromoza
120 Corredor(a) de bolsa
121 Cirujano(a)
122 Fabricante de herramientas
123 Viajante
124 Gerente de agencia de viajes
125 Mecanógrafo(a)
126 Anunciador(a) de televisión
127 Consejero(a) de orientación profesional
128 Mozo(a) de café o restaurante
129 Comerciante al por mayor
130 Tecnico(a) en rayos X
131 Oficial de una sociedad para jóvenes tal como la YMCA/YWCA

Fig. 2-2. SVIB-SCII inventory booklet, Spanish edition, Form T325S (second page)

7. Items should be in good taste. People should not be asked to respond to items that offend them; questionnaires with offensive items continually create problems for users.

The items in the SCII booklet were screened closely on the criterion of good taste, and few of them will offend anyone. No doubt a few individuals will still wince occasionally. For example, some people think that all references to religious activities should be eliminated; others believe that all military occupations should be expunged; and a few are uncomfortable with the item *Professional gambler,* because they consider gambling illegal. In general, however, the items accord well with most people's criteria of good taste.

8. Items should have predictive as well as concurrent validity. Concurrent validity is the power to discriminate between individuals who are, at the same point in time, in different occupations; predictive validity is the power to discriminate between those who will, at some future time, enter different occupations. Because interest inventories are generally used to help people make long-range plans, the emphasis should be on predictive validity.

Some items, however, offer only concurrent validity. An extreme example, to make the point, would be the item *I am an engineer,* which would have perfect concurrent validity but little usefulness in a predictive sense, especially when used with students. No such extreme items have ever appeared in the Strong booklets, but other, more subtle items of the same nature have. The vast array of statistics available on each SVIB item made it possible to ferret out such items and eliminate them. Some examples of eliminated items are: *Do my best work late at night,* answered "Yes" most often by nightclub entertainers and highway patrol officers; *My advice is asked for often,* answered "Yes" most often by psychiatrists, lawyers, and high-level executives; and *Worry a good deal about mistakes,* answered "Yes" most often by surgeons and musicians. Though one could argue that these items have potential predictive power, the pattern of responses in the SVIB archives suggests strongly that people learn to give these answers *after entering their occupations* and being exposed to particular job activities, and that similar responses among young people would therefore not necessarily be predictive of a tendency to enter these occupations.

Cleaning out the more manifest of these items improved the psychometric quality of the inventory, but the effect was not substantial, since only a dozen or so items were affected. Predictive validity, however, is an important element in test construction; one could, by stacking up items deficient in that respect, build an interest inventory with excellent concurrent-validity statistics but one that would be useless in any predictive sense. Thus, longitudinal research is crucial in test development; without long-range studies, predictive or nonpredictive items could not be identified.

9. Items should be easy to read. The reading level of the items, the instructions, and the profile should be kept as low as possible. For the SCII, the reading level is at about the junior high level; 90 percent of the students in a typical eighth-grade class can handle the inventory, although they will occasionally inquire about the precise meaning of some items, especially some of the advanced school subjects like *Botany, Calculus,* or *Physiology.*

10. Responding to the items should be interesting, perhaps even entertaining. No empirical data are available concerning what makes tests fun to take; but if people are to enjoy the experience of answering a psychological test or inventory, the booklet and answer sheet must be free of various irritants, such as fuzzy instructions, illogical layouts, glib assertions, coarse typography or printing, or inadequate space for writing one's name.

Moreover, the item content of the inventory must make sense to the respondent; if vocational interests are being surveyed, then the items should be perceived as having direct relevance to that issue, and should not inquire into such topics as sex, family relationships, or personal finances.

Answer Sheets

The SVIB-SCII test booklet is designed to be used with a separate answer sheet. The publisher's answer sheet is shown in Fig. 2-3. (Some scoring services use a format combining the booklet and answer sheet into one form.) Computers read the answers from the answer sheets, calculate scores on scales and administrative indexes, and print out the results on preprinted profile forms. Since each scoring agency uses its own scoring machine, and each machine works from its own adaptation of the SCII answer sheet, the sheet used depends on which agency is scoring the inventory. Thus, each agency provides its own answer sheets, under license from the publisher.

It is important that answer sheets ask for sex of respondent. Although everyone is scored on all scales, regardless of sex, men and women—even those in the same occupation—often respond differently to the same item or scale. Thus, the interpretive comments—which compare the respondent's scores to the scores of a sample of his or her own sex, rather than to a combined-sex scale—supply much valuable information, but only when sex of respondent is known.

Profile Forms

The respondent's SCII scores are reported on a specially designed form called a "profile" (Fig. 2-4). The profile is a preprinted form upon which scores are entered by computer.

The layout of the profile has been guided by the occupational taxonomy devised by John Holland, a scheme that organizes the world of work into six basic patterns of occupational interest—realistic, investigative, artistic, social, enterprising, and conventional. These patterns, or General Occupational Themes, are

Strong-Campbell Interest Inventory

Merged Form of the
STRONG VOCATIONAL INTEREST BLANK

Answer Sheet for use with Form T325

Directions:
1. Fill in your name as explained below.
2. Indicate your sex in one of the circles at the right.
3. Fill in the other information at the right.
4. Read the directions at the right and begin.

Print your name in the boxes below, one letter to a box. Print your last name first, skip a box, then print your first name. Put your middle initial (if any) in the last box. Then, in each column of the circles below the name boxes, blacken the lettered circle that matches the letter you have printed in the box above it. Wherever there is no letter in a box, blacken the unlettered circle in the top row below that box, as shown below next-to-last box.

| SEX |
| F M |

Date

Address (number & street)

City   State   Zip

Age

School (if you are now a student)

Location (city & state)

Degree and major

Occupation, if you are now employed (be specific)

Employer

Number of years experience

Use a soft, black (No. 2) lead pencil. The answer spaces below are numbered the same as the items in the booklet. Fill in one circle for each item. Make no stray pencil marks.

If you **like** the item, mark the "L"
If you are **indifferent**, mark the "I"
If you **dislike** the item, mark the "D"
Erase completely any answer you wish to change.

OCCUPATIONS

SCHOOL SUBJECTS

Fig. 2-3. Publisher's answer sheet for the SVIB-SCII (see also following page)

PLEASE DO NOT WRITE IN SHADED AREA

SVIB-SCII

Strong-Campbell Interest Inventory
Merged Form of the
STRONG VOCATIONAL INTEREST BLANK

ANSWER SHEET FOR USE WITH FORM T325

Stanford University Press
Stanford, California 94305

ITEMS 312–325:

If the item describes you, mark "Y" (for "Yes")

If you are not sure, mark the "?"

If the item does **not** describe you, mark "N" (for "No")

ITEMS 282–311:

If you prefer the item on the **left**, mark the "L"

If you like **both** items or **can't decide**, mark the "="

If you prefer the item on the right, mark the "R"

ITEMS 168–281:

Continue as before. Work quickly.

ACTIVITIES

AMUSEMENTS

TYPES OF PEOPLE

PREFERENCE BETWEEN TWO ACTIVITIES

YOUR CHARACTERISTICS

Fig. 2-3 (cont.). Publisher's answer sheet for the SVIB-SCII (reverse side)

quite similar to the scale groupings that appeared on earlier editions of the profile, but they have the advantage of being more precisely defined, more inclusive, and exhaustive. Further, because Holland has developed and explicitly stated the theoretical structure underlying these categories, many useful inferences can be drawn from both the theory and the test results. Chapter 4 takes up Holland's General Themes in detail, and the reverse side of both copies of the profile (see the discussion immediately following) gives useful general information on the themes and on other aspects of the profile.

Profile layout. The publisher's form for the SCII profile is shown in Fig. 2-4; each scoring agency produces its own adaptation of the profile form under license from the publisher. Details of computer programming and profile format may differ from one scoring agency to another, but the results printed out on the various agencies' adaptations of the publisher's profile are invariant in substantive detail.

Two copies of the profile form normally are returned to the customer (that is, to the institution administering the inventory) by the scoring agency—one for the person who completed the inventory, the other for the institution's counseling service, to use in counseling the person and perhaps to retain on file. The two copies are identical on the front (scoring) side; and both carry the entire printout of scores. The reverse sides, however, carry different explanatory material: the notes on the respondent's copy are written in nontechnical language; the notes on the counselor's copy are more technical. The reverse sides, as well as the front of the profile, are reproduced in Fig. 2-4.

The first line of the profile form carries, on both copies, the name of the person who has completed the inventory, printed by the computer. The name is usually picked up from the name grid on the answer sheet. The date the form was scored (not the date the inventory was completed) is also printed at the top of the form. Sex of respondent is not indicated on the profile, but if it has not been indicated on the answer sheet, the computer (in most cases) will print on the profile a statement of the form "Because sex indication was omitted, some interpretive comments cannot be included on this profile."

Although the profile-form adaptations used by the different scoring agencies differ slightly, the following comments apply, in all important particulars, to all versions.

General Occupational Themes. The scales for the six General Occupational Themes appear in the upper left-hand corner of the profile. The respondent's standard scores are printed next to the scale names by the computer, and interpretive comments, based on the level of score with respect to that of a norm group of the person's own sex, are printed in the column to the right of the standard scores. Each score is also plotted visually, in the form of an asterisk or similar mark printed at the appropriate point along the scale range.

On each scale, the average score and scoring range for the Men- and Women-in-General samples (see p. 48) are given in the form of preprinted bars. See the reverse sides of the respondent's and counselor's copies of the profile (second and third sheets of Fig. 2-4) for a good general discussion of these themes; and see Chapter 4 for more detailed information.

Basic Interest Scales. Below the scales for the General Occupational Themes are the 23 Basic Interest Scales, grouped into six categories corresponding to the General Occupational Themes. Scores are reported in the same format as are scores on the General Occupational Themes (see above). See the reverse sides of both copies of the profile for an explanation of the scoring ranges; and see Chapter 5 for more detailed information.

Occupational Scales. The 162 Occupational Scales, listed in the three columns at the right, occupy most of the profile. Like the Basic Interest Scales, they are assembled into groups corresponding to the six General Occupational Themes. In addition, each scale is code-typed with initials representing from one to three of the General Occupational Themes, depending on that occupation's mean scores on the theme scales; the method used to code the scales is described in Chapter 6.

Scores for the Occupational Scales are printed to the left of the scale names. The standard score is printed in the column headed "Std. Score," and an asterisk is plotted on the scale range at the point corresponding to that score, graphically representing the degree of similarity with the scores of people in that occupation. Scores of 7 and below are plotted on the lowest point on the scale range; scores of 60 and above are plotted on the highest point.

As with earlier SVIB-SCII profiles, the highest scores are plotted as "Very Similar," the lowest as "Very Dissimilar," with respect to scores of people working in those occupations, and intermediate scores are plotted accordingly. But the central portion of the scale range is now termed "Mid-Range," instead of "Average" (labeling scores "Average" was found to be misleading); and it has been expanded to provide easier interpretation of scores in that range (on the 1974 SCII profile, the central portion was truncated, and all scores falling in that range were plotted in a narrow, shaded column).

Although all scales are scored, regardless of the respondent's sex or the sex norms of the scales, only those scores on scales normed on the same sex as the respondent are plotted graphically (that is, with an asterisk, on the scale range). This approach resolves the dilemma of providing the maximum number of scores to each individual while at the same time emphasizing those scores that are normed in the most technically accurate manner. Scores on other-sex scales are given only in the "Std. Score" column. Chapter 7 discusses these points at length.

Administrative Indexes and Special Scales. The

Fig. 2-4 (*following three pages*). Publisher's profile form for the SVIB-SCII: front; reverse side of respondent's copy; reverse side of counselor's copy

SVIB-SCII Profile for

Date scored

General Occupational Themes

Theme	Std. Score	Comment	Theme Score
R-THEME			
I-THEME			
A-THEME			
S-THEME			
E-THEME			
C-THEME			

Basic Interest Scales

Th.	Scale	Std. Score	Comment	Scale Score
R-THEME	AGRICULTURE			
	NATURE			
	ADVENTURE			
	MILITARY ACTIVITIES			
	MECHANICAL ACTIVITIES			
I-THEME	SCIENCE			
	MATHEMATICS			
	MEDICAL SCIENCE			
	MEDICAL SERVICE			
A-THEME	MUSIC/ DRAMATICS			
	ART			
	WRITING			
S-THEME	TEACHING			
	SOCIAL SERVICE			
	ATHLETICS			
	DOMESTIC ARTS			
	RELIGIOUS ACTIVITIES			
E-THEME	PUBLIC SPEAKING			
	LAW/ POLITICS			
	MERCHANDISING			
	SALES			
	BUSINESS MANAGEMENT			
C-Th	OFFICE PRACTICES			

Occupational Scales

Code	Scale	Sex Norm	Std. Score						
hC	AIR FORCE OFF'R	f							
RC	AIR FORCE OFF'R	m							
RC	ARMY OFFICER	f							
RC	ARMY OFFICER	m							
R	NAVY OFFICER	f							
R	NAVY OFFICER	m							
RE	POLICE OFFICER	f							
RE	POLICE OFFICER	m							
RCE	VOC. AGRIC. TCHR.	m							
RC	FARMER	f							
R	FARMER	m							
R	FORESTER	m							
R	SKILLED CRAFTS	m							
RI	RAD. TECH.(X-RAY)	f							
RI	RAD. TECH.(X-RAY)	m							
RI	FORESTER	f							
RI	ENGINEER	f							
RI	ENGINEER	m							
RI	VETERINARIAN	f							
RIC	LIC. PRACT. NURSE	f							
RAS	OCCUP. THERAPIST	f							
RAS	OCCUP. THERAPIST	m							
IR	VETERINARIAN	m							
IR	CHEMIST	f							
IR	PHYSICIST	m							
IR	GEOLOGIST	f							
IR	GEOLOGIST	m							
IR	MED. TECHNOL.	f							
IR	MED. TECHNOL.	m							
IR	DENTAL HYGIENIST	f							
IR	DENTIST	f							
IR	DENTIST	m							
IR	OPTOMETRIST	f							
IR	OPTOMETRIST	m							
IR	PHYS. THERAPIST	f							
IR	PHYS. THERAPIST	m							
IR	PHYSICIAN	f							
IR	PHYSICIAN	m							
IRS	REGIST. NURSE	f							
IRC	MATH-SCI. TCHR.	f							
IRC	MATH-SCI. TCHR.	m							
IRC	SYSTEMS ANALYST	m							
IRC	SYSTEMS ANALYST	f							
IRC	COMPUTER PROGR.	f							
IRC	COMPUTER PROGR.	m							
IRE	CHIROPRACTOR	m							
IRE	CHIROPRACTOR	f							
I	PHARMACIST	m							
I	PHARMACIST	f							
I	BIOLOGIST	f							
I	BIOLOGIST	m							
I	GEOGRAPHER	f							
I	GEOGRAPHER	m							
I	MATHEMATICIAN	m							
I	MATHEMATICIAN	f							
IA	COLLEGE PROF.	f							
IA	COLLEGE PROF.	m							
IA	SOCIOLOGIST	f							
IA	SOCIOLOGIST	m							
IAS	PSYCHOLOGIST	m							
IAS	PSYCHOLOGIST	f							
AIR	ARCHITECT	f							
AIR	ARCHITECT	m							
AI	LAWYER	f							
AI	LAWYER	m							
AE	PUBLIC REL. DIR.	f							
AE	ADVERTISING EXEC.	f							
AE	ADVERTISING EXEC.	m							
AE	INT. DECORATOR	f							
AE	INT. DECORATOR	m							
A	MUSICIAN	m							
A	COMM'L ARTIST	f							
A	COMM'L ARTIST	m							
A	FINE ARTIST	f							
A	FINE ARTIST	m							
A	ART TEACHER	f							
A	ART TEACHER	m							
A	PHOTOGRAPHER	f							
A	PHOTOGRAPHER	m							
A	LIBRARIAN	f							
A	LIBRARIAN	m							
A	FOR. LANG. TCHR.	f							
A	FOR. LANG. TCHR.	m							
A	REPORTER	f							
A	REPORTER	m							
AS	ENGLISH TEACHER	f							
AS	ENGLISH TEACHER	m							
SA	SPEECH PATHOL.	f							
SA	SPEECH PATHOL.	m							
SA	SOCIAL WORKER	f							
SA	SOCIAL WORKER	m							
SA	MINISTER	m							
SIE	MINISTER	f							
SI	REGIST. NURSE	m							
S	LIC. PRACT. NURSE	m							
S	SPECIAL ED. TCHR.	f							
S	SPECIAL ED. TCHR.	m							
S	ELEM. TEACHER	f							
S	ELEM. TEACHER	m							
SR	PHYS. ED. TCHR.	f							
SR	PHYS. ED. TCHR.	m							
SRE	RECREAT. LEADER	f							
SRE	RECREAT. LEADER	m							
SE	YWCA DIRECTOR	f							
SE	YMCA DIRECTOR	m							
SE	SCHOOL ADMINST.	f							
SE	SCHOOL ADMINST.	m							
SCE	GUID. COUNSELOR	m							
SEC	GUID. COUNSELOR	f							
SEC	SOCIAL SCI. TCHR.	f							
SEC	SOCIAL SCI. TCHR.	m							
EA	FLIGHT ATTEND'T.	f							
EA	FLIGHT ATTEND'T.	m							
EA	BEAUTICIAN	f							
E	BEAUTICIAN	f							
E	DEPT. STORE MGR.	f							
E	DEPT. STORE MGR.	m							
E	REALTOR	m							
E	LIFE INS. AGENT	f							
E	LIFE INS. AGENT	m							
E	ELECT. PUBL. OFF.	f							
E	PUBLIC ADMINST.	m							
EI	INVEST. FUND MGR.	m							
EI	MARKETING EXEC.	f							
EI	MARKETING EXEC.	m							
E	PERSONNEL DIR.	f							
E	CH. OF COMM. EX.	m							
EC	RESTAURANT MGR.	f							
EC	CH. OF COMM. EX.	f							
EC	BUYER	m							
EC	PURCH'G AGENT	f							
EC	PURCH'G AGENT	m							
ERC	AGRIBUS. MGR.	m							
ECS	HOME ECON. TCHR.	f							
EC	NURS. HOME ADM.	f							
ECR	DIETITIAN	f							
CER	EXEC. HOUSEK'P'R	f							
CER	EXEC. HOUSEK'P'R	m							
CES	BUS. ED. TEACHER	m							
CES	BUS. ED. TEACHER	f							
CE	BANKER	f							
CE	BANKER	m							
CE	CREDIT MANAGER	f							
CE	CREDIT MANAGER	m							
CE	IRS AGENT	f							
CA	PUBLIC ADMINST.	m							
C	ACCOUNTANT	m							
C	ACCOUNTANT	f							
C	SECRETARY	f							
C	DENTAL ASSISTANT	f							

Administrative Indexes

	Response %		
	LP	IP	DP
TOTAL RESPONSE			
INFREQUENT RESPONSE			

	Response %		
	LP	IP	DP
Occupations			
School Subjects			

	Response %		
	LP	IP	DP
Activities			
Amusements			

	Response %		
	LP	IP	DP
Types of People Preferences			

	Response %		
	LP	IP	DP
Characteristics			
All Parts			

Special Scales

ACADEMIC COMFORT

INTROVERSION-EXTROVERSION

Strong-Campbell Interest Inventory of the Strong Vocational Interest Blank

Revised and expanded (1981) profile for use with test booklet T325

Stanford University Press, Stanford, California

Understanding Your Results on the SCII

First, a caution. There is no magic here. Your answers to the test booklet were used to determine your scores; your results are based on what you said you liked or disliked. The results can give you some useful systematic information about yourself, but you should not expect miracles.

More important, *this test does not measure your abilities;* it can tell you something about the patterns in your interests, and how these compare with those of successful people in many occupations, but the results are based on your *interests,* not your abilities. The results may tell you, for example, that you like the way engineers spend their day; they do *not* tell you whether you have an aptitude for the mathematics involved.

Although most of us know something of our own interests, we're not sure how we compare with people actively engaged in various occupations. We don't know "what it would be like" to be a writer, or receptionist, or scientist, or whatever. People using these results are frequently guided to considering occupations to which they had never given a thought before. In particular, this inventory may suggest occupations that you might find interesting but have not considered simply because you have not been exposed to them. Or the inventory may suggest occupations that you ignored because you thought they were open only to members of the opposite sex. Sexual barriers are now falling, and virtually all occupations are open to qualified people of either sex—so don't let imagined barriers rule out your consideration of any occupation.

Men and women, even those in the same occupation, tend to answer some items on the test differently. Research has shown that these differences should not be ignored—that separate scales for men and women provide more meaningful results. Generally, the scales for your sex—those marked with the "Sex Norm" corresponding to your sex ("m" or "f")—are more likely to be good predictors for you than scales for the other sex would be. Still, you have been scored on *all* the scales, female and male, so that you can make use of the maximum possible information. In a few cases, such as Agribusiness Manager and Home Economics Teacher, Occupational Scales have not been established yet for both sexes.

Studies of employed people who completed this form as students have shown that about one-half are happily employed in occupations compatible with their profile scores. Among those in occupations not compatible with their results, many say they don't like their work, or are doing the job in some unusual manner.

Your answers have been analyzed in three main ways: first, under "General Occupational Themes," for similarity to six important overall patterns; second, under "Basic Interest Scales," for similarity to clusters of specific activities; third, under "Occupational Scales," for similarity to the interests of men and women in 85 occupations. The other two groups of data on the profile—labeled "Administrative Indexes" and "Special Scales"—are of interest mainly to your counselor. The first are checks to make certain that you made your marks on the answer sheet clearly and that your answers were processed correctly. The second are scales that have been developed for use in particular settings and require special interpretation; your counselor will discuss them with you.

The Six General Occupational Themes

Psychological research has shown that vocational interests can be described in a general way by six overall occupational-interest themes. Your scores for these six themes were calculated from the answers you gave to the test booklet. The range of these scores is roughly from 30 to 70, with the average person scoring 50. If your score on one of these themes is considerably above average, say 60, you share many of the characteristics of that theme; if your score is low, say below 40, you share very few; and if your score is close to the average, you share some characteristics but not many.

Men and women score somewhat differently on some of these themes, and this is taken into account by the printed statement for each score; this statement, which might be, for example, "Very high," is based on a comparison between your score and the average score for your sex. Thus, you can compare your score either with the scores of a combined male-female sample, by noting your numerical score, or with the scores of only the members of your own sex, by noting the phrasing of the printed comment.

The differences between the sexes in these themes are also shown on the profile: the open bars indicate the middle 50 percent of female scores, the shaded bars the middle 50 percent of male scores. The extending, thinner lines cover the middle 80 percent of the scores; and the mark in the middle is the average.

Following are descriptions of the "pure," or extreme, types for the six General Occupational Themes. These descriptions are only generalizations; none will fit any one person exactly. In fact, most people's interests combine all six themes to some degree or other.

R-Theme: People scoring high here are usually rugged, robust, practical, physically strong; they usually have good physical skills, but sometimes have trouble expressing themselves or in communicating their feelings to others. They like to work outdoors and to work with tools, especially large, powerful machines. They prefer to deal with things rather than with ideas or people. They generally have conventional political and economic opinions, and are usually cool to radical new ideas. They enjoy creating things with their hands and prefer occupations such as mechanic, construction work, fish and wildlife management, laboratory technician, some engineering specialties, some military jobs, agriculture, or the skilled trades. Although no single word can capture the broad meaning of the entire theme, the word Realistic has been used here, thus the term R-Theme.

I-Theme: This theme centers around science and scientific activities. Extremes of this type are task-oriented; they are not particularly interested in working around other people. They enjoy solving abstract problems, and they have a great need to understand the physical world. They prefer to think through problems rather than act them out. Such people enjoy ambiguous challenges and do not like highly structured situations with many rules. They frequently have unconventional values and attitudes and tend to be original and creative, especially in scientific areas. They prefer occupations such as design engineer, biologist, social scientist, research laboratory worker, physicist, technical writer, or meteorologist. The word Investigative characterizes this theme, thus I-Theme.

A-Theme: The extreme type here is artistically oriented, and likes to work in artistic settings that offer many opportunities for self-expression. Such people have little interest in problems that are highly structured or require gross physical strength, preferring those that can be solved through self-expression in artistic media. They resemble I-Theme types in preferring to work alone, but have a greater need for individualistic expression, are usually less assertive about their own opinions and capabilities, and are more sensitive and emotional. They score higher on measures of originality than any of the other types do. They describe themselves as independent, original, unconventional, expressive, and tense. Vocational choices include artist, author, cartoonist, composer, singer, dramatic coach, poet, actor or actress, and symphony conductor. This is the Artistic theme, or A-Theme.

S-Theme: The pure type here is sociable, responsible, humanistic, and concerned with the welfare of others. These people usually express themselves well and get along well with others; they like attention and seek situations that allow them to be near the center of the group. They prefer to solve problems by discussions with others, or by arranging or rearranging relationships between others; they have little interest in situations requiring physical exertion or working with machinery. Such people describe themselves as cheerful, popular, and achieving, and as good leaders. They prefer occupations such as school superintendent, clinical psychologist, high school teacher, marriage counselor, playground director, speech therapist, or vocational counselor. This is the Social theme, or S-Theme.

E-Theme: The extreme type of this theme has a great facility with words, especially in selling, dominating, and leading; frequently these people are in sales work. They see themselves as energetic, enthusiastic, adventurous, self-confident, and dominant, and they prefer social tasks where they can assume leadership. They enjoy persuading others to their viewpoints. They are impatient with precise work or work involving long periods of intellectual effort. They like power, status, and material wealth, and enjoy working in expensive settings. Vocational preferences include business executive, buyer, hotel manager, industrial relations consultant, political campaigner, realtor, sales work, sports promoter, and television producer. The word Enterprising summarizes this pattern, thus E-Theme.

C-Theme: Extremes of this type prefer the highly ordered activities, both verbal and numerical, that characterize office work. People scoring high fit well into large organizations but do not seek leadership; they respond to power and are comfortable working in a well-established chain of command. They dislike ambiguous situations, preferring to know precisely what is expected of them. Such people describe themselves as conventional, stable, well-controlled, and dependable. They have little interest in problems requiring physical skills or intense relationships with others, and are most effective at well-defined tasks. Like the E-Theme type, they value material possessions and status. Vocational preferences are mostly within the business world, and include bank examiner, bank teller, bookkeeper, some accounting jobs, financial analyst, computer operator, inventory controller, tax expert, statistician, and traffic manager. The word Conventional more or less summarizes the pattern, hence C-Theme.

These six themes can be arranged in a hexagon with the themes most similar to each other falling *next* to each other, and those most dissimilar falling directly *across* the hexagon from each other.

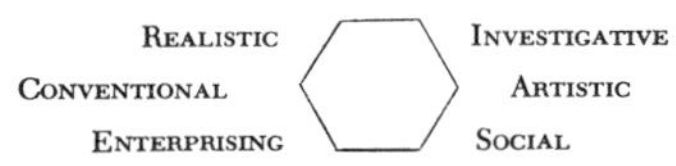

Few people are "pure" types, scoring high on one and only one theme. Most score high on two, three, or even four, which means they share some characteristics with each of these; for their career planning, such people should look for an occupational setting that combines these patterns.

A few people score low on all six themes: this probably means they have no consistent occupational orientation and would probably be equally comfortable in any of several working environments. Some young people score this way because they haven't had the opportunity to become familiar with a variety of occupational activities.

The Basic Interest Scales

These scales are intermediate between the General Occupational Themes and the Occupational Scales. Each is concerned with one specific area of activity. The 23 scales are arranged in groups corresponding to the strength of their relationships to the six General Themes.

For each scale, the level of your score shows how consistently you answered "Like" to the activities in that area. If, for example, you consistently answered "Like" to such items as *Making a speech, Expressing judgments publicly,* and *Be a TV announcer,* you will have a high score on the Public Speaking scale, and you will probably have a higher than average score on the E-Theme.

On these scales, the average adult scores about 50, with most people scoring between 30 and 70. If your score is substantially higher than 50, say about 60, then you have shown more consistent preferences for these activities than the average adult does, and you should look upon that area of activity as an important focus of your interests. The opposite is true for low scores.

As with the other scales, your scores are given both numerically and graphically, and an interpretive comment, based on a comparison between your scores and the average score for your sex, is also provided.

Your scores on some of the Basic Interest Scales might appear to be inconsistent with scores on the corresponding Occupational Scales. You might, for example, score high on the Mathematics scale and low on the Mathematician scale. These scores are not errors; they are in fact a useful finding. What they usually mean is that although you have an interest in the subject matter of an occupation (mathematics), you share with people in that occupation (mathematicians) very few of their other likes or dislikes, and you probably would not enjoy the day-to-day life of their working world.

The Occupational Scales

Your score on an Occupational Scale shows how similar your interests are to the interests of people in that occupation. If you reported the same likes and dislikes as they do, your score will be high and you would probably enjoy working in that occupation or a closely related one. If your likes and dislikes are different from those of the people in the occupation, your score will be low and you would probably not be happy in that kind of work. Remember that the scales for your sex—those marked in the "Sex Norm" column with the sex corresponding to yours—are more likely to be good predictors for you than scales for the other sex would be.

Your score for each scale is printed in numerals—for those scales normed for your sex—and also plotted graphically. Members of an occupation score about 50 on their own scale—that is, female dentists score about 50 on the Dentist "f" scale, male artists score about 50 on the Artist "m" scale, and so forth. If you score high on a particular scale—say 45 or 50—you have many interests in common with the workers in that occupation. The higher your score, the more common interests you have. *But note that on these scales your scores are being compared with those of people working in those occupations;* in the scoring of the General Themes and the Basic Interest Scales you were being compared with "people-in-general." If your score on any of the Occupational Scales is in the "Mid-Range"—between 28 and 39—you have responded *in the way people-in-general do.*

The Occupational Scales differ from the other scales also in considering your dislikes as well as your likes. If you share the same *dislikes* with the workers in an occupation, you will score moderately high on their scale, even if you don't agree with their *likes.* For example, farmers, artists, and physicists generally dislike working with large groups of people; if you don't like working with large groups, you share this attitude with the people in these occupations, and may score fairly high—40, for example—on these scales even if you don't like agriculture, art, or science. But a higher score—50—reflects an agreement on likes *and* dislikes.

Occupational Groupings

The Occupational Scales have been arranged on the profile in six clusters corresponding to the six General Occupational Themes. Within each cluster, occupations expressing similar interests are listed together.

To the left of each Occupational Scale name are one to three letters indicating the General Themes characteristic of that occupation. These will help you to understand the interest patterns found among the workers in that occupation, and to focus on occupations that might be interesting to you. If you score high on two themes, for example, you should scan the list of Occupational Scales and find any that have the same two theme letters, in any order. If your scores there are also high—as they are likely to be—you should find out more about those occupations, and about related occupations not given on the profile. Your counselor can help you.

Using Your Scores

Your scores can be used in two main ways: first, to help you understand how your likes and dislikes fit into the work; and second, to help you identify possible problems by pointing out areas where your interests differ substantially from those of people working in occupations that you might be considering. Suppose, for example, that you have selected some field of science, but the results show that you have only a moderate interest in the daily practice of the mathematical skills necessary to that setting. Although this is discouraging to learn, you are at least prepared for the choice between (1) abandoning that field of science as a career objective, (2) trying to increase your enthusiasm for mathematics, and (3) finding some branch of the field that requires less use of mathematics.

In the world of work there are many hundreds of specialties and professions. Using these results and your scores on other tests as guides, you should search out as much information as you can *about those occupational areas where your interests and aptitudes are focused.* Ask your librarian for information on these jobs and talk to people working in these fields. Talk with your counselor, who is trained to help you, about your results on this test and other tests, and about your future plans. Keep in mind that choosing an occupation is not a single decision, but a series of decisions that will go on for many years; whenever a new decision must be made, you should seek the best possible information about yourself and about the work areas you are considering. Your scores on this inventory should help.

Comments for the Counselor

The SVIB-SCII can be used with anyone who understands the vocabulary of the test items, that is, most people over 16. The inventory can be used for special projects as early as the eighth grade (age 14), but although profiles for students of 14 or 15 do reflect their current interests, they may not accurately predict future interests or careers. At this age, the inventory should be used mainly to discuss the world of work. By age 17, definite patterns emerge that remain fairly stable, and by age 25, most people's interests are well established.

The profile reflects the patterns of answers made to the inventory. The best help a counselor can give is to help students realize the importance of these patterns. Most students tend to overemphasize the importance of one or two high (or low) scores, to see in them the basis for immediate decisions; but these scores may, for various reasons, be misleading, and the emphasis should be on long-term development, on studying the patterns in *all* of the scores. Students need help, too, in finding more information about the areas where they scored high, and they usually need to be reminded that this is a test of interests, not aptitudes.

An individual's scores are determined by the responses that he or she made to the inventory, and these responses are in turn determined by that person's perception of what he or she likes and dislikes, perceptions that are developed from a variety of experiences and attitudes. Counselors should therefore be alert to situations in which a person is ignoring an occupation that looks appropriate from the profile pattern simply because he or she has had no exposure to that occupation. When a young woman scores high in the medical science/medical service area, and is considering nursing as a career, she should also be encouraged to consider other possibilities, such as medical or dental school. In general, the inventory should be used to help people focus on such special areas of interest and, within these areas, to look at the broadest possible range of occupations. In the past, some people have restricted their career options because of real or imagined barriers to their entry into certain occupations, especially racial, sexual, or age barriers. Such barriers are now falling, and virtually all occupations are legally open to all qualified persons; thus, students and others completing this inventory should give serious consideration to *all* occupations falling within their indicated sphere of interest.

Men and women, however, even those in the same occupation, give somewhat different responses to the inventory. These differences are most prominent in the artistic and domestic areas, which tend to be favored by women, and in the mechanical area, favored by men. To have ignored the various sex-linked differences in the norming of the Occupational Scales would have introduced significant error. Until men's interests no longer differ notably from women's, separate scales will provide more meaningful results. And because some occupations continue to be dominated by one sex—Agribusiness Manager, for example, or Home Economics Teacher—Occupational Scales have not been developed for both sexes in a few cases.

On the reverse side of the student's copy of the profile is an explanation of the three principal classes of scales; with the help of these comments, most students can understand their own scores. The counselor can help, first, by leading the student through an initial look at the profile (see the *Manual*, Chapter 10); second, by explaining the finer technical details; third, by explaining any apparent inconsistencies between scores of different types; and fourth, by helping the student integrate this information with data on his or her aptitudes and experiences.

The General Occupational Themes

These six themes, described briefly on the student's copy of the profile, are based on J. L. Holland's work, *Making Vocational Choices: A Theory of Careers* (Prentice-Hall, 1973). His book is an excellent source for further information about these themes and the world of work.

Holland's chief premise is that each of us can be described in terms of relative similarity to one or more of six idealized occupational-interest personality types, and that each type seeks out a different kind of occupational environment. Thus, personality types do as much as job requirements to establish the working tenor of a given occupation. This formulation offers a useful structure for analyzing the differences between people and between the occupations they choose.

The six themes or scales each contain 20 items, scored positively for "Like" responses and negatively for "Dislike" responses. Norms have been established by scoring a general sample of 600 people (300 men and 300 women), then assigning this sample a mean of 50 and a standard deviation of 10, as a basis for converting future raw scores to standard scores. The numerical score, printed out under "Std. Score," is based on this combined norm sample. Because males and females score somewhat differently on these scales, printed interpretive comments—"Very High," "Average," and so forth—are also supplied; these comments are based on comparisons with people of the same sex as the person being tested (and for this reason the correct sex must be indicated on the answer sheet). In some cases, therefore, men and women with the same numerical score will be furnished different printed comments. Within each sex, the interpretive comments correspond to the following percentile ranges:

Very high	94th and above
High	85th-93rd
Moderately high	70th-84th
Average	31st-69th
Moderately low	16th-30th
Low	7th-15th
Very low	6th and below

The distribution of scores for the two sexes is indicated by the bars printed on the scales: the shaded bar refers to men, the open bar to women. The thick portion of the bar defines the middle half of the sample, from the 25th to the 75th percentile; the thin, extending lines run from the 10th to the 90th percentile; and the vertical line indicates the mean.

The six themes can be arranged in the form of a hexagon, as shown on the student's copy of the profile, in such a way that themes falling next to each other are the most similar to each other, and those directly across the hexagon from each other are the most dissimilar.

The General Themes should be used to help the student identify a general section of the occupational world for more intensive study. The two or three themes on which the student has scored highest should be noted, and then (in conjunction with results on the Basic Interest Scales) compared with the occupations listed in the Occupational Scales section that relate strongly to the same themes. Matchings of high scores on particular Occupational Scales *and* their related General Theme and Basic Interest Scales are particularly worth noting.

The Basic Interest Scales

The Basic Interest Scales are homogeneous scales; they were constructed by clustering together items with high intercorrelations. Because the item content for each scale is closely focused on the single topic indicated by the scale name, the scales are relatively easy to understand. "Like" responses to these items are scored positively, "Dislike" responses negatively. Thus the level of scores is somewhat related to the percentage of "Like" and "Dislike" responses given; people who give many "Like" responses, say 50 percent or more, will have many more high scores here than those who give only a few, say 15 percent or fewer. For this reason, the LP and DP indexes, described below under "Administrative Indexes," will be useful in interpreting these scales. (In these respects—as in scoring and score reporting, discussed above—the Basic Interest Scales are handled like the General Occupational Themes.)

The Basic Interest Scales have been arranged in clusters corresponding to their relationships to the General Occupational Themes. Usually, the patterns of scores on the two scale types are consistent. For example, a person who scores high on the Realistic theme will usually have at least some high scores in the corresponding cluster of Basic Interest Scales.

Workers in occupations directly related to a given scale score 8-10 points higher on that scale than the general sample does; that is, salespeople average about 60 on the Sales scale, scientists about 60 on the Science scale, artists about 60 on the Art scale, and so forth. Thus, scores over 60 should be considered high; on those few scales showing substantial sex differences, scores 10 points above the relevant sex mean are high.

Scores on the Basic Interest Scales do not change much with age, though there is a tendency for scores to creep upward slightly, perhaps 3 or 4 points on the average, between the teenage years and adulthood. One major exception is the Adventure scale, on which teenage boys score about 8-10 points *higher* than adults. Scores on Athletics and Military Activities also tend to decrease slightly with age.

The Occupational Scales

Each Occupational Scale was developed by testing 200-300 happily employed men or women in that occupation, then isolating the items that they and the general sample answered differently; these items then became the scoring scale. The scales were normed by setting the mean of the occupational sample equal to 50, the standard deviation to 10. Thus, a student scoring 50 on a given scale has responded to these characteristic items in the same way the average member of that occupation does. A student scoring in the "Mid-Range"—between 28 and 39—has responded to these items in the same way that people-in-general do.

Each of the occupations has been given a code type corresponding to its high General Theme scores; the code types have been used to order the scales on the profile. Students should be encouraged to note that the Occupational Scales on which they score high usually have code types corresponding to their high scores on the General Occupational Themes and Basic Interest Scales.

The Occupational Scales are more complex than either of the other two types of scales; they include more items; they include items with a wider variety of content; and they score some "Dislike" responses positively. Thus a person can score high on an Occupational Scale by sharing patterns of aversions with the members of that occupation, as well as by sharing their "Likes."

The Occupational Scales should not be viewed as precise predictors of occupations in which the student will be happy, but only as suggestions. High scores should also be used as leads to related occupations that are not on the profile. And the student should be cautioned especially to infer not that "I scored high on the Farmer scale, therefore I'd be a good farmer," but rather that "I have answered the inventory in much the way farmers do."

Following each Occupational Scale is an "f" or "m" indicating the sex of the sample used to establish the scale. Although same-sex scales are more valid for the individual than other-sex scales, everyone is scored on all scales to ensure that maximum information is made available to everyone.

The Administrative Indexes

These indexes are checks to make certain that the answer sheet was completed and processed correctly. The first one, Total Responses, shows how many answer marks the computer has read from the answer sheet; since there are 325 items, the score on this index should be 325 or close to it. Up to 20 items can be omitted without significantly affecting the results.

The second index, Infrequent Responses, shows the number of rare responses given. It is weighted so that almost everyone scores zero or higher; if the score is below zero, the person has marked an uncommonly high number of rare responses (this weighting technique permits the counselor simply to ignore this index unless it is negative). Usually a negative score indicates some confusion, such as skipping a number on the answer sheet, or random marking.

The remaining indexes show the percentages of "Like" (LP), "Indifferent" (IP), and "Dislike" (DP) responses made to the various sections of the inventory. These percentages can be useful in detecting problems—for example, if a section was left blank on the answer sheet, the percentages for it will be 0-0-0. Although these percentages are useful in understanding the student's response style and in identifying unusual response patterns, they should not be overinterpreted; some people produce extreme percentages, yet still have a "normal" pattern on the profile. The tolerance of the scoring system for extreme test-taking strategies is considerable.

The Special Scales

The AC (Academic Comfort) scale contains items that discriminate between students who do well in academic settings and those who do not. Students graduating with a B.A. from a liberal arts college average about 50, M.A.s about 55, Ph.D.s about 60. Most students gain about 10 points on this scale over their four years of college; thus, the scores of freshmen should be judged with that in mind. The item content is heavily oriented toward science and the arts (weighted positively) and business and blue-collar activities (weighted negatively).

On the IE (Introversion-Extroversion) scale, high scores (60 and above) indicate introversion, and low scores (40 and below), extroversion. The item content is concerned almost entirely with working with people in social services, educational, entertainment, or sales settings.

Males and females score about the same, on both scales.

Inconsistencies Between Scales

There are three main types of scores on the profile, and one of the tasks of the counselor is to straighten out misunderstandings about the differences.

The three types of scores can be better understood by using an analogy to descriptions of physical build. The General Occupational Themes are concerned with global categories, and are similar to such overall descriptions as "She is tall and slender" or "He is small and wiry." The Basic Interest Scales are concerned with specific attributes and are similar to statements such as "She weighs 118 pounds" or "He has a reach of 38 inches." The Occupational Scales are concerned with how the person resembles other types of people, and are analogous to statements such as "She has the build of a swimmer" or "He looks like a jockey." Thus, although the three types of scales report three types of scores, a thread of consistency runs through all of them.

One kind of confusion arises when the score on a Basic Interest Scale—such as Art or Agriculture—is high and the score on the related Occupational Scale—Artist or Farmer—is low. This happens because the Occupational Scales are more complex in content than the Basic Interest Scales; they contain *all* of the substantial differences between people in those occupations and people-in-general. The Farmer scale, for example, contains items involving mechanical activities as well as agriculture, and also items involving rejection of social service, artistic, and leadership pursuits. To score high, one must resemble farmers in many of these areas, and not simply share their agricultural interests.

Apparent inconsistencies can be useful in counseling. The student who questions this one is likely to be receptive to a discussion of the "environment" of the occupation—and to be receptive to the idea that satisfaction with farming as a career involves more than simply liking agriculture. Farming involves a way of life, working with machines and animals and not so much with people; it is physically demanding; and for many "intellectual types" it has little appeal. Other inconsistencies—between, for example, Art and Artist, Mathematics and Mathematician, or Military Activities and Army Officer—can lead to equally fruitful discussions.

Further Information

The SVIB-SCII *Manual* contains more detailed information, and should be studied before the inventory is administered. Considerably more background information on the history and technical issues of interest measurement is reported in the *Handbook for the SVIB* (D. P. Campbell, Stanford University Press, 1971).

STRONG VOCATIONAL INTEREST BLANK
STRONG-CAMPBELL INTEREST INVENTORY RESULTS FOR

** CHARLOTTE HANSEN **

THE FOLLOWING STATISTICAL RESULTS HAVE BEEN COMPILED FROM YOUR ANSWERS
TO THIS INVENTORY.

THREE TYPES OF INFORMATION ARE PRESENTED-

      1) YOUR SCORES ON 6 GENERAL OCCUPATIONAL THEMES. THESE GIVE
         SOME IDEA OF YOUR OVERALL OCCUPATIONAL OUTLOOK.

      2) YOUR SCORES IN 23 BASIC INTEREST AREAS. THESE SHOW THE
         CONSISTENCY, OR LACK OF IT, OF YOUR INTERESTS IN EACH OF
         THESE SPECIFIC AREAS.

      3) YOUR SCORES ON 162 OCCUPATIONAL SCALES. THESE TELL YOU
         HOW SIMILAR YOUR INTERESTS ARE TO THOSE OF EXPERIENCED
         WORKERS IN THE DESIGNATED OCCUPATIONS.

    FIRST, A CAUTION. THERE IS NO MAGIC HERE. THIS REPORT WILL GIVE YOU
SOME SYSTEMATIC INFORMATION ABOUT YOURSELF BUT YOU SHOULD NOT EXPECT MIRACLES.
YOUR SCORES ARE BASED SIMPLY ON WHAT YOU SAID YOU LIKED OR DISLIKED.

    MOST IMPORTANTLY---THIS TEST DOES NOT MEASURE YOUR ABILITIES-IT IS CONCERNED
ONLY WITH YOUR INTERESTS.

THE GENERAL OCCUPATIONAL THEMES

    PSYCHOLOGICAL RESEARCH HAS SHOWN THAT OCCUPATIONS CAN BE GROUPED
INTO SIX GENERAL THEMES. ALTHOUGH THESE ARE CRUDE, THEY DO PROVIDE
USEFUL GUIDELINES. HERE IS AN ANALYSIS OF HOW YOUR INTERESTS
COMPARE WITH EACH OF THESE THEMES-

R-THEME- THIS TYPE IS RUGGED, ROBUST, PRACTICAL, STRONG, AND
        FREQUENTLY AGGRESSIVE IN OUTLOOK. THEY HAVE GOOD PHYSICAL SKILLS
        BUT SOMETIMES HAVE TROUBLE COMMUNICATING THEIR FEELINGS TO OTHERS.
        THEY LIKE TO WORK OUTDOORS AND WITH TOOLS, ESPECIALLY WITH LARGE
        POWERFUL MACHINES. THEY PREFER TO DEAL WITH THINGS RATHER THAN
        WITH IDEAS OR PEOPLE. THEY USUALLY HAVE CONVENTIONAL POLITICAL AND
        ECONOMIC OPINIONS, LIKE TO CREATE THINGS WITH THEIR HANDS, AND
        PREFER OCCUPATIONS SUCH AS MECHANIC, LABORATORY TECHNICIAN, SOME
        ENGINEERING SPECIALTIES, FARMER, OR POLICE OFFICER. THE TERM
        "REALISTIC" IS USED TO SUMMARIZE THIS PATTERN, THUS, R-THEME.

        YOUR ANSWERS SHOW THAT FOR YOUR SEX YOU ARE HIGH IN THESE
        CHARACTERISTICS AS YOUR STANDARD SCORE WAS 57.

Fig. 2-5. SVIB-SCII interpretive profile, sample generated and printed by computer (first sheet only)

boxes below the Occupational Scales contain scores for the Administrative Indexes and Special Scales. The Special Scales are discussed in detail in Chapter 8, the Administrative Indexes in Chapter 9; both are discussed briefly on the reverse side of the counselor's copy of the profile (see Fig. 2-4).

Interpretive Profiles

Some of the scoring agencies offer, as an option, a second type of profile, one that is produced completely by computer (a portion of a sample is shown in Fig. 2-5). No preprinted form is used, and a great wealth of information, including scores and interpretations of scores, is printed by the computer. Such profiles are produced expressly for the individual respondent, and the printed comments vary according to the responses made by that person to the inventory. Computer-produced interpretive profiles are more convenient in many contexts; they are also, of course, more expensive. Costs and other information are available from the scoring agencies.

Administering the Inventory

The SVIB-SCII is simple to administer; and it can be given individually or in groups, in person or by mail. The respondent needs only a place to write, a test booklet, an answer sheet, and a dark lead pencil.

Time required. Fast readers can complete the inventory in about 20 minutes; slow readers may require an hour. The average adult takes about 30 minutes.

Reading level. The SCII booklet reads at about the sixth-grade level, though a few items (for example, *Physiology, Botany, Calculus*) are unfamiliar to some students at that level. Some people who read at the sixth-grade level do not have a sufficiently long attention span to complete the inventory in one sitting, and counselors have reported cases in which they have allowed these clients to complete the inventory during several shorter sessions.

Appropriate age level for use. About 90 percent of an average eighth-grade class—students aged 13-15—can read and complete the inventory; above this age, virtually everyone can complete it successfully.

Whether eighth-grade students *should* complete the inventory, even though they *can,* is another question, and the answer depends on why the test is given, what the results are used for, and the type of professional counseling available to the students. Under the proper

circumstances, 14-, 15-, and 16-year-old students can benefit from the inventory, though they must be cautioned that their results are likely to be somewhat transitory. Counselors who wish to stimulate career planning can use the inventory with students of this age as a vehicle for discussion, showing the students something about choices and about structure in the world of work.

Historically, the major use of the Strong has been with 17- and 18-year-olds, or with older students. At 17 or 18, interests begin to solidify for most students, and the results begin to be useful for long-range career-planning purposes. By age 21, interests have become even more established, and by 25, interest patterns have stabilized for nearly everyone. Because most of the history and research on this inventory has been based on subjects 17 years old or older, this is the most appropriate age range for routine use.

Faking. The *Handbook for the SVIB* (Campbell, 1971) includes a general review of the issues of faking on the Strong; what follows is a summary.

When instructed to do so, respondents can bias their scores substantially. For example, students who are told to "Answer like the average engineer" raise their scores on the ENGINEER scale by 10 points or more, usually scoring higher than the average engineer. But when people respond to the items in customary fashion, in situations where they might be expected to bias their scores—such as when applying for a job or for admission to medical school—they usually answer truthfully. In studies of these situations, the detectable bias is seldom more than a few points. Although we should not naively suppose everyone always to be truthful, most people appear to answer this inventory honestly, even in highly competitive selection environments.

Scoring the Inventory

Completed answer sheets are normally sent to one of the commercial scoring agencies for scoring. Usually the answer sheets are scored, and the printed profiles returned, within a day or two of receipt. Details of computer programming and profile format may differ from one scoring agency to another, but the results printed out on the various agencies' adaptations of the publisher's profile are invariant in substantive detail. A listing of commercial agencies scoring the SCII, or distributing SCII test materials, under license to the publisher can be obtained by writing directly to the publisher.

CHAPTER THREE

Item Technology

Interest inventories are effective because different people give different responses to the individual inventory items, and because people who have found satisfying work in a particular occupation tend to respond to particular inventory items in a characteristic way. These two facts, illustrated and documented in the following pages, are the foundation for the entire enterprise of interest measurement.

Item-Response Distributions

As examples of the different responses that people in different occupations give to particular items, item-response distributions for the SVIB-SCII items *Artist, Farmer,* and *Night clubs* are given in Figs. 3-1 to 3-3 (for another example, see Fig. 7-1). These three items were chosen to illustrate the variance in sample response distribution from one item to the next. Each increment of cross-hatching in the distributions represents one sample (male and female samples are cross-hatched distinctively); and each sample is plotted at the point corresponding to the percentage of its members answering "Like" to the item in question. The samples are the occupational samples stored in the archives of the Center for Interest Measurement Research at the University of Minnesota. Except for unusual groups like astronauts and famous football coaches, the samples range in size from 72 to 1,199. For the *Artist* and *Farmer* items, data from 438 samples are presented; for the *Night clubs* item, which did not appear in some previous editions of the inventory, data are presented for 300 samples. For each item, the five highest- and lowest-ranking samples of each sex are identified above the distributions; these lists convey the essence of the distribution extremes and illustrate the occupational differences in responses to interest-inventory items.

Most of the samples included in these distributions are the adult criterion samples that have been tested over the years—from 1927 to 1979—to develop the Occupational Scales; the others are miscellaneous samples that have been tested for various research projects. Collectively, these samples represent an extremely diverse array of employed adults, male and female.

Fig. 3-1 shows the distribution of item-response percentages for the *Artist* item. Psychometrically, this is an excellent item, because it produces a broad distribution of responses: in some occupations, almost everyone re-

sponded "Like" to this occupation; in others, almost no one did. In contrast are those items to which nearly everyone responds in the same manner; such items, which elicit minimal discrimination among people or among groups, contribute nothing to the purposes of the inventory, and in successive editions of the SVIB-SCII they have gradually been dropped. Most SCII items produce roughly the same spread that the *Artist* item does—over 90 percentage points from lowest- to highest-response sample—though the shapes of the distributions vary considerably, as comparison of Figs. 3-1 to 3-3 indicates (another item distribution is given in Fig. 7-1).

The *Farmer* item (Fig. 3-2) is an example of an item with only a moderate variability of response; most of the samples, both male and female, fell within a 20 percent range. This item is useful chiefly because it separates agricultural occupations from the others; unlike the *Artist* item, it does not spread the other occupations across a broad response range.

The third item, *Night clubs* (Fig. 3-3), is included here to demonstrate the power of the items to elicit subtle differences between occupations. The ranking of the occupational responses to this item, too, is reasonable, but the high and low clusters are less obvious than those for the other two items illustrated. This ability to uncover characteristic, but less readily inferable, differences between occupations is one of the inventory's major strengths.

Item-response distributions such as those in Figs. 3-1 to 3-3 are available for all of the SCII items, in computer-accessible storage; collectively, they illustrate several important points:

1. The popularity of the individual item varies greatly from occupation to occupation. The distributions in Figs. 3-1 to 3-3 are typical, showing as they do a range of "Like" responses extending over 90 percent—from lows of 4 or 5 percent to highs of over 95 percent. Most of the SCII items show similar ranges. The power of the individual items to discriminate between occupations directly establishes the usefulness of the inventory. Valid scales can be constructed only from individually effective items.

2. The content of each item is related to the occupations endorsing or rejecting it. Occupational samples respond to the SCII items as one would expect: artists

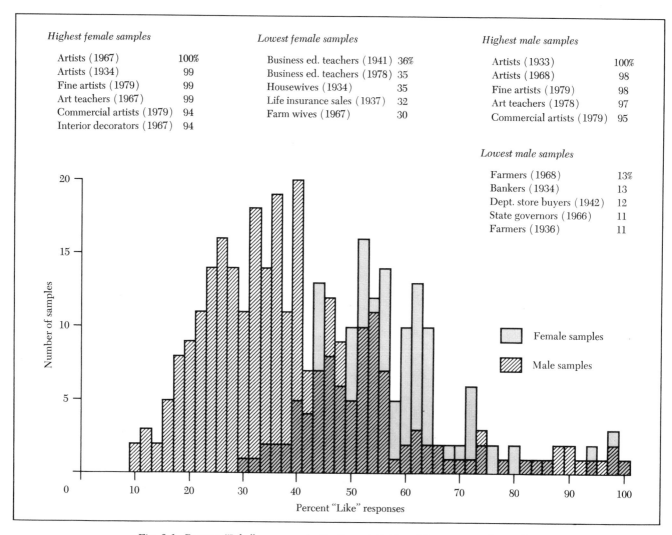

Fig. 3-1. Percent "Like" responses to the item *Artist* for 438 occupational samples

endorse artistic items; scientists, scientific items; and mechanics, mechanical items. The rank ordering of the five highest- and five lowest-scoring male and female samples in Figs. 3-1 and 3-2 emphasizes the general reasonableness of the item responses. The point is worth stressing, for in some quarters psychological tests are viewed as highly adroit probers into a mysterious, otherwise inaccessible portion of the psyche. They are not. Although systematic arrangement of obvious data can lead us to subtle insights about individuals that we might otherwise overlook (as demonstrated by the distribution of percentages for the *Night clubs* item), psychological tests—or interest inventories at least—generally operate in a straightforward manner, having as their basis the systematic arrangement of empirically detectable differences between occupations.

This is not to imply that the measurement of interests is simple-minded. Quite the contrary. The systematic use of empirical data, which incidentally happen to be reasonable, is probably the most effective way to proceed in measuring important psychological charac-

teristics. But because the information is generally so reasonable, it is sometimes seen as trivial; people often ask, "Why did you go to all that trouble to prove the obvious? Don't you already know that farmers will say they like to be farmers, and artists that they like to be artists?" The answer to this charge is that much of what seems so obvious becomes apparent *only after* the data have been organized.

Of course, the chief benefit of the systematic, empirical approach is that concepts can be quantified, then compared quantitatively *and* qualitatively.

3. Many items identify strong but subtle or unexpected differences in interests between occupations. The *Night clubs* item (see the item-response percentages in Fig. 3) is not occupationally obvious, yet like the *Artist* and *Farmer* items it spreads occupations over a wide response range, almost 80 percentage points. Again, when the percentages are rank-ordered, the data appear reasonable, with flight attendants, astronauts, sales managers, beauticians, and entertainers at the high end, and artists, scientists, ministers, and directors

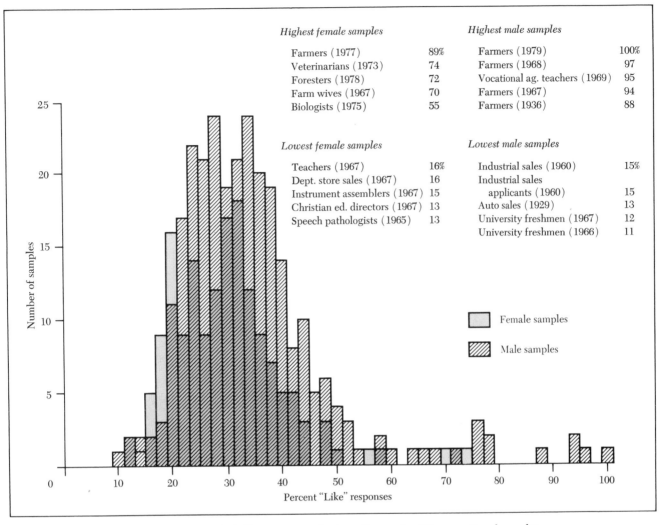

Fig. 3-2. Percent "Like" responses to the item *Farmer* for 438 occupational samples

of Christian education at the low end. Even the low percentage among retired Army officers seems right; at an average age of 69 years, it is understandable that they might reject night life. But again, the reasonableness of the data becomes apparent only *after* the high- and low-percentage occupations are identified; few people, shown an unlabeled distribution, can list correctly any of the occupations at the high and low ends of the response range.

The inventory items do, then, capture subtle differences between occupations, and even identify a few surprising characteristics of some, all of which leads to a precision of measurement not possible with cruder assessments of interests.

4. The items vary in their characteristics, especially in average popularity and in the range of spread they create among the occupational samples. The graphic presentation of the *Artist, Farmer,* and *Night clubs* item distributions illustrates the two most important characteristics of individual items: first, their overall popularity, represented by the mean of the distribution; and

second, their popularity spread, represented by the standard deviation of the distribution. These two characteristics vary considerably, and independently, across the items in the inventory, and most of the scale-construction and scoring techniques that have been developed, such as the General Reference Sample (men- or women-in-general) and the establishment of base-rate norms, are intended to control for these item differences. If all of the items operated identically—that is, if all of them were equally popular and if all were equally effective in separating occupations—reference samples and norms would not be necessary.

5. For the most part, the items are stable over time. A sample tested in one decade gives about the same responses as does another sample, from the same occupation, tested three or four decades later. Table 3-1 presents data on the stability of items over time. In 27 instances, three different samples of the same sex in the same occupation were tested, each in a different decade: one in the 1930's, generally by Strong; a second in the 1960's, by Campbell; and a third in the 1970's,

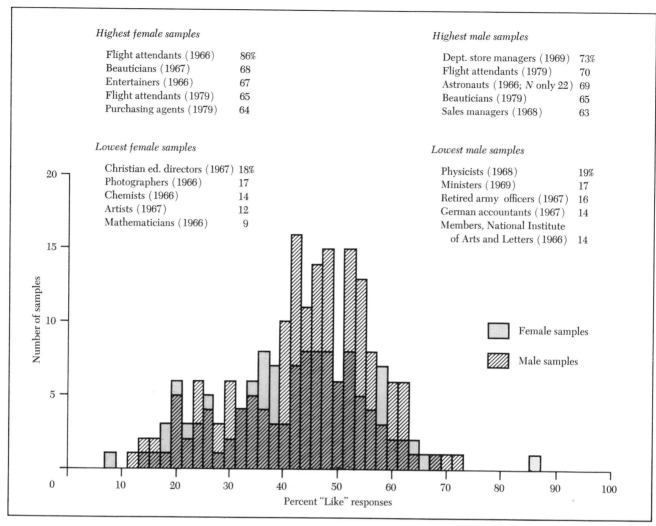

Highest female samples

Flight attendants (1966)   86%
Beauticians (1967)   68
Entertainers (1966)   67
Flight attendants (1979)   65
Purchasing agents (1979)   64

Highest male samples

Dept. store managers (1969)   73%
Flight attendants (1979)   70
Astronauts (1966; N only 22)   69
Beauticians (1979)   65
Sales managers (1968)   63

Lowest female samples

Christian ed. directors (1967) 18%
Photographers (1966)   17
Chemists (1966)   14
Artists (1967)   12
Mathematicians (1966)   9

Lowest male samples

Physicists (1968)   19%
Ministers (1969)   17
Retired army officers (1967)   16
German accountants (1967)   14
Members, National Institute
 of Arts and Letters (1966)   14

Fig. 3-3. Percent "Like" responses to the item *Night clubs* for 300 occupational samples

by Hansen. The percentages responding "Like" to the *Farmer* and *Artist* items are given in Table 3-1; the table also gives the response differences, over three time intervals, between successive samples of the same occupation.

Some of the differences over time are undoubtedly due to sampling differences, not time differences; the samples were seldom selected or tested in exactly the same way by the three investigators. Still, the differences over time are impressively small. As the summary statistics at the bottom of the table show, the average difference over time was modest, ranging from 0 to 10 percent. The data also indicate that the number of individual comparisons showing "substantial" differences is in no case more than 8 out of 27, and is usually smaller. (In the discussion of item-response percentage, below, a "substantial" difference is defined essentially as one 16 percent or larger.) These data demonstrate that the item-response percentages from a given occupational sample can be used safely over many years to represent that occupation.

Of course, the finding that in some comparisons, over

25 percent of the occupation shifted "substantially" on an item over a 30-year period argues that the occupational norms should be checked periodically. And, as data in the *Handbook* indicate, the items, too, can shift in popularity, some more than others. Criterion samples and items alike need periodic monitoring.

Still, in these comparisons, as in most others in the area of vocational interest measurement, stability over time is the rule, not the exception.

6. Male and female samples, even in the same occupation, give different responses to many items. The distributions of the male and female samples in Figs. 3-1, 3-2, 3-3, and 7-1 demonstrate that the two sexes do not respond identically to SCII items. On the *Farmer* and *Night clubs* items, the two sex distributions are fairly similar, with the male samples slightly more positive in their response; on the *Artist* item, the two distributions are quite dissimilar, with the women's mean considerably higher. Clearly, sex of respondent is an important factor in analyzing the responses to some items. This is a major concern in the development of the SCII scoring system; Chapter 7 is devoted entirely to this issue.

TABLE 3-1

Comparisons of Percent "Like" Responses to the Items *Farmer*
and *Artist* Between 1930's, 1960's, and 1970's for 27 Occupational Samples

Occupational sample	Sex	Farmer item						Artist item					
		Percent "Like" responses			Difference			Percent "Like" responses			Difference		
		1930's	1960's	1970's	30's vs. 60's	30's vs. 70's	60's vs. 70's	1930's	1960's	1970's	30's vs. 60's	30's vs. 70's	60's vs. 70's
Accountants	m	25	25	39	0	+14	+14	20	26	32	+6	+12	+6
Architects	m	27	28	42	+1	+15	+14	87	88	82	+1	−5	−6
Artists	f	31	22	25	−9	−6	+3	99	100	99	+1	0	−1
Artists	m	29	28	34	−1	+5	+6	100	98	98	−2	−2	0
Business education teachers	f	22	17	26	−5	+4	+9	36	39	35	+3	−1	−4
Chemists	m	36	27	37	−9	+1	+10	25	46	39	+21	+14	−7
Dietitians	f	33	31	38	−2	+5	+7	39	57	42	−18	+3	−15
Engineers	m	26	30	51	+4	+25	+29	28	42	35	−14	+7	−7
Farmers	m	88	97	100	+9	+12	+3	11	13	18	+2	+7	+5
Foresters	m	47	64	73	+17	+26	+9	21	37	34	+16	+13	−3
Home economics teachers	f	24	31	36	+7	+12	+5	50	67	42	+17	−8	−25
Lawyers	f	31	22	32	−9	+1	+10	47	50	52	+13	+5	+2
Lawyers	m	26	35	45	+9	+19	+10	19	37	44	+18	+25	−7
Librarians	f	31	26	35	−5	+4	+9	57	64	60	+7	+3	−4
Life insurance agents	f	21	19	28	−2	+7	+9	32	53	57	+21	+25	+4
Life insurance agents	m	29	28	38	−1	+9	+10	21	22	28	+1	+7	+6
Nurses	f	33	29	41	−4	+8	+12	53	54	55	+1	+2	+1
Personnel directors	m	27	32	36	+5	+9	+4	32	40	33	+8	+1	−7
Physical education teachers	f	21	32	51	+11	+30	+19	41	53	45	+12	+4	−8
Physicists	m	25	23	47	−2	+22	+24	37	53	43	+16	+6	−10
Police officers	m	27	32	44	+5	+17	+12	16	30	29	+14	+13	−1
Public administrators	m	45	28	38	−17	−7	+10	28	40	44	+12	+16	+4
Purchasing agents	m	26	35	34	+9	+8	−1	15	36	39	+21	+15	−6
School administrators	m	37	39	46	+2	+9	+7	16	26	30	+10	+14	+4
Reporters	f	35	24	35	−11	0	+11	72	73	62	+1	−10	−11
Reporters	m	28	23	40	−5	+12	+17	54	55	56	+1	+2	+1
YWCA directors	f	31	23	33	−8	+2	+10	49	62	51	+13	+2	−11
Average difference					0	9.7	10				7.5	6.2	−3.7
Differences larger than 15 percent					2	6	4				8	3	1

7. The shape of the item-response distributions varies from one item to the next, but which distribution shape is best is not clear. Obviously, items having narrow, peaked distributions are of little value; just as obviously, items with broad distributions are useful. What other attributes of the item distributions are desirable is impossible to say within present knowledge of psychometrics. The various functions of the instrument are probably served best by drawing upon a variety of distributions, and variety was a criterion in the selection of items for the SCII booklet.

The item-response archives. The foregoing has drawn upon the extensive archives of item-response distributions in the files at the University of Minnesota. These distributions, which are extraordinarily useful in understanding how individual items perform, have been available only since about 1970, and the SCII edition of the Strong is the first that has had the benefit of such data in item selection and scale construction. Although E. K. Strong's methodical care in preserving and stor-

ing his data made it possible for these distributions to be available today, Strong himself never saw them, for he conducted his research before the days of the electronic computer. Strong's data, along with those collected during the last 17 years at Minnesota, have been organized into a computer-accessible archive of vast utility.

The Use of Statistics and the Construction of Scales

Some of the earlier research on vocational interests has been ineffective because of the misuse of statistics, and future investigators will want to avoid the mistakes of the past. By far the most common misuse of statistics in vocational-interest research, indeed in most psychological research, has centered around the concept of statistical significance; a statistic is tested to see if it could have occurred by chance. But we know with absolute certainty that people do not give random (that is, chance) responses to psychological inventories, and testing their responses, or any combination of them, against chance is an almost useless pursuit. An investigator who tests two samples, compares their means and calculates T-tests, finds more differences than one would expect by chance, and then reports that the inventory has successfully differentiated the interests of the two samples, has made virtually no contribution to our understanding of either the two samples or the general nature of interests. If we are to look seriously into these questions, we need more substantial information about the *magnitude* and *content* of the differences.

In the discussion that follows—of guidelines for the interpretation of data collected with the SCII, including the construction of scales—all of the minimum standards suggested are far beyond the levels of chance. These guidelines have come to be respected because statistical theory has given them sanction, and because they produce valid and reliable scales. They are of course applicable only to three-choice items, that is, to items with response choices similar to the "Like," "Indifferent," "Dislike" categories; true-false items or items with five or more choices have different characteristics, and require different statistical guidelines.

Item-response percentages. One of the most frequent uses made of interest-inventory data is the comparison of item-response percentages between two or more samples. Each of the Occupational Scales, for example, is nothing more than a collection of items that have shown large differences in response percentages between a sample of people in that occupation and a general sample. To identify items that are suitable for that Occupational Scale, some decision must be made concerning what is meant by "large."

Item-percentage differences are calculated by systematically comparing the "Like" and "Dislike" response percentages of the two samples (the occupational and general samples), one item at a time. (The difference on the "Indifferent" response, which is rarely if ever the largest difference of the three, is ignored at this step; as discussed in Chapter 6, it is sometimes used, if large enough, to refine the item weights.) This comparison yields, for each item, two percentage differences, one between the two "Like" percentages, one between the two "Dislike" percentages. The larger of the two differences then becomes the ranking of that item, with respect to other items, toward its possible selection for an Occupational Scale based on the responses of the criterion sample; that is, an item is called a "12-percent item," or a "30-percent item," or whatever, depending on the size of the larger difference.

Substantial experience has shown that 10 percent and smaller differences should be ignored completely. Samples tested and retested over short periods typically yield at least two or three item-response differences of 10 percent or larger between test and retest. Consequently, ignoring differences of this size or smaller eliminates the risk of selecting items that reflect only the normal fluctuations within a sample. In general, 12-percent items are barely important, 16-percent items moderately so; every extra point above that becomes

more important, and 20-percent and larger items are extremely important. "Important" means that the items reflect a real difference between the samples, one that will replicate on repeated sampling, and one that will manifest itself in differential behavior of most of the individuals making up the two samples—they will, for example, choose different activities, not only on paper but in their actual behavior.

Just as important as the *size* of the item-response differences, in the construction of an Occupational Scale, is the *number* of items, across the full range of the inventory, that exhibit large response differences. The average occupational sample provides about 60 items that have a 16-percent or larger difference vis-à-vis the general (reference) sample. That number of items (60) with that large a difference (16-percent) will produce a scale that will separate the occupational sample from the general sample by about two standard deviations. Scales with more items or larger differences will discriminate even better. Tables 6-1 and 6-2, which report for each Occupational Scale the number of items used, the minimum percent differences scored, and the resultant overlap between score distributions for the criterion and reference samples, provide many illustrations of this point.

These guidelines for the use of item-response differences are based on the assumption that both samples contain at least 200 people. If the samples are smaller than that, the item-percentage differences should be increased, to at least 18-20 percent for samples as small as 50. But for samples containing more than 200 people, the minimum-percentage guidelines should *not* be lowered; though much smaller differences are *statistically significant* with larger samples, they are *in a practical sense insignificant*.

Differences between means. Once the selection of items for an Occupational Scale has been completed, the next step is to determine whether or not the scale clearly distinguishes the new sample from other samples—reference samples or otherwise.

When the mean scores of two samples on a given Occupational Scale are compared, differences of 4 points or less should be ignored; 5-point differences, which represent half a standard deviation, are the minimum worth noting, and then only when the samples are large enough (at least 30 people) to ensure that the differences are stable. Obviously, although 5-point differences are worth commenting on, greater differences—of 10 or 20 points—are much more impressive. Similarly, 100-person samples are much more impressive than 30-person samples. Mean differences between occupational samples on the Occupational Scales range as high as 45 points, but such enormous differences are found only between occupations with patently different outlooks, such as psychologists and military officers, or scientists and salespeople.

The range of response differences on the Basic Interest Scales and the General Occupational Themes is smaller than that for the Occupational Scales because of their different purposes and psychometric characteristics. The next four chapters discuss these differences in detail. Briefly, an Occupational Scale contains all of the items discriminating between an occupational sample and a reference sample, some weighted positively and some negatively, depending on the direction of the difference; its purpose is to produce maximum discrimination between the occupational and reference samples (preferably also between its sample and other occupational samples). In contrast, the Basic Interest Scales are designed for maximum ease in interpretation, and the General Occupational Theme scales are designed specifically to represent the Holland occupational categories; because their content is more homogeneous, that is, more focused on a single content area, these scales are shorter than the Occupational Scales. Consequently, the range of individual and mean scores is smaller, and thus smaller differences are worth noting. For the Basic Interest Scales and General Occupational Themes, 3-point differences are indicative of "real" differences between groups, that is, differences that will replicate and that will be reflected in the behavior of most members of the groups. Greater differences, of course, are more impressive.

Scores for individuals. When the scores for a particular person are considered, the minimum differences worth studying are much larger, but there is no good empirical method for specifying how different two scale scores have to be on the same profile before the difference is worth noting: in general, acceptable minimums appear to be 5-8 points on the Holland scales or the Basic Interest Scales and at least 10-15 points on the Occupational Scales. The same levels apply to comparisons across profiles; that is, person X should differ from person Y by at least 10 points on an Occupational Scale before one concludes that the two people differ with respect to that scale.

Item intercorrelations. A different type of statistical guideline for analyzing the SCII items grew out of the original research on the Basic Interest Scales. That project clustered together items with high intercorrelations to produce homogeneous scales; consequently, some definition of "high" was needed. To arrive at a practical definition for these purposes, all of the possible item intercorrelations between the 400 items of

TABLE 3-2

Median Test-Retest Correlations for the Men's SVIB Occupational Scales for Varying Ages and Test-Retest Intervals

Age at first testing	Test-retest interval					
	2 weeks	1 year	2–5 years	6–10 years	11–20 years	20+ years
17–18	—	.80	.70	.65	.64	—
19–21	.91	.80	.73	.67	.67	.64
22–25	—	—	.78	.69	.75	.72
26+	—	—	.77	.81	.80	—

the SVIB—80,000 correlations for the men's booklet and 80,000 more for the women's booklet—were calculated. Frequency distributions of these correlations were made for both booklets (they are presented on p. 90 of the *Handbook for the SVIB*), and they showed that item intercorrelations above .30 are rare, occurring less than 5 percent of the time. Consequently, the items were clustered together with that figure as a guide; most of the items finally included on each Basic Interest Scale are intercorrelated .25 or above with the other items on that scale. Because these scales have proved valid and reliable, that figure of .30 can be adjudged a useful guideline, one that can be adopted by other investigators working with three-choice (that is, L-I-D) items.

Test-retest statistics. The most common measure of stability over time is test-retest reliability, which is usually represented by a Pearson product-moment correlation between the test and retest scores. However, though this statistic can be made available, there is no good test of its importance. A test-retest correlation of .97 over three days obviously is good; how much lower the figure goes before we conclude that it is "poor"— .90, .85, .80, .60, .30—is difficult to say. No easy answer exists, but again we can use some typical findings as guidelines. Table 3-2, taken from Johansson and Campbell (1971), gives median correlations for various ages and various test-retest time intervals, for earlier editions of the Strong. These figures can be used for comparisons with other samples. See also p. 53 and Table 6-5, which report 3-year SCII test-retest data; stability over even longer periods remains high.

CHAPTER FOUR

The General Occupational Themes

In the development of the SCII, one type of analysis was the search for general occupational themes in people's responses to the test booklet, specifically those six themes represented by the occupational types hypothesized and identified by John Holland (1966, 1973). This chapter discusses these themes and their role in the construction and scoring of the SCII General Occupational Theme scales.

The SVIB and Occupational Theory

From its inception in 1927, the Strong Vocational Interest Blank was an empirical, atheoretical instrument. Employing hard work and boundless energy, and without benefit of automatic data-processing equipment, E. K. Strong, Jr., learned to develop empirical scales that had impressive validity and reliability statistics and great utility. But his profile presented a person's scores with only the laconic statement that "This score represents the degree of similarity between your interests and [those of] workers in this occupation." The person was left to decide, with the aid of a counselor, what those interests were for each occupation.

The empirical success of the Strong Blank obscured the lack of an organizing theory. As Darley and Hagenah (1955) said, "We may have attempted to isolate the individual's occupational life from his total life and life style. We may have given inadequate operational definitions to our terms and concepts, . . . we have been too concerned with the empirical aspects of our problem." John Holland, a student of Darley's, later elaborated the point (1966, p. 7).

Because of our repeated failure to define *interests* conceptually, they have come to mean no more than the scales of the Kuder Preference Record and the Strong Vocational Interest Blank. That is, we have accepted methods of assessment in place of definitions. Our reliance on empirical definitions has cost us much. . . . It has led to a vocational interest literature that has only tentative and ambiguous relationships with the mainstream of social psychology and the psychology of personality. . . . And because interest scales have lacked "surplus" meaning, these studies fail to indicate that "interests" are an expression of personality and personal development. The accumulation of many such studies has led to a relatively independent literature known as "interest measurement."

Profile groupings. Strong realized early, in the late 1930's, that systematic clustering of the scales was

necessary. He was testing more and more occupations, and he wanted to arrange their scales in groupings that would make interpretations more fruitful. His first tentative step toward a theory was to gather the scales into groups on the profile; he formed the groups by using scale intercorrelations, and he was guided to some extent by factor analyses carried out by L. L. Thurstone.

Because these groupings of related occupations were a great aid in scale interpretation, they soon were used widely in both applied and research applications of the inventory. Several classification schemes were developed on the basis of these profile groupings, but the scheme that had the greatest impact was Darley and Hagenah's tabulation of Primary, Secondary, and Tertiary interest patterns on the basis of the incidence of high scores within these groupings (Darley and Hagenah, 1955).

The most serious of several problems with these profile groupings was the lack of a general theoretical structure—which led to a proliferation of irritating idiosyncrasies and aberrations. For example, several scales—those for PRODUCTION MANAGER, CPA OWNER, and PRESIDENT, MANUFACTURING CORPORATION—defied grouping with any others. They were an embarrassment to the system, and counselors usually skipped over them quickly. Researchers working with the profile groups also ignored these scales.

What was needed was an organizing structure that would be at once global and parsimonious, one that would embrace all of Strong's scales and all scales to come.

Strong's Group Scales. Strong's next attempt in this direction was his development of Group Scales, each of which was based on a combination of the occupations in a single profile group. He was not satisfied with these scales, partly because of their questionable psychometric qualities. Strong tried to evaluate the Group Scales in the same way that he evaluated the Occupational Scales—by calculating percent overlap with men-in-general. The results were not impressive, and rather than consider whether these scales might be evaluated in a different way, he dropped them.

The Basic Interest Scales. The next attempt to find a guiding theoretical structure was the development of the SVIB Basic Interest Scales (Campbell, Borgen, Eastes, Johansson, and Peterson, 1968). The objective of constructing these scales was to identify homogeneous clusters of items that would be easy to interpret. The result was a set of scales (about 20) that was too large and unwieldy to serve as a theoretical structure, especially since most experts agree that a much smaller number of basic dimensions, probably not more than five to seven, underlies the structure of interests. Although the Basic Interest Scales are useful for other purposes, they do not provide a parsimonious organization for the domain of interests.

Holland's six categories. In an attempt to develop an occupational-classification system closely tied to psychometric research, John Holland (1959) proposed six basic categories of occupational interests, categories closely resembling the dimensions usually seen in research on vocational interests with the Strong Blank. In succeeding years, Holland refined and expanded his classifications into a theory encompassing the broad area of educational and vocational behavior, retaining as its foundation the original six categories (Holland, 1965, 1973). As reported elsewhere in more detail (Campbell and Holland, 1972; Hansen and Johansson, 1972), scales using SCII items were developed for these six categories and then applied to Strong's data; the results provide a structure that is helpful in understanding both the Basic Interest Scales and the Occupational Scales; and on the strength of this research, Holland's system was used to organize the profile scores for the SCII. Some background on Holland's theoretical structure is necessary for an understanding of this approach.

Holland's Theory and Categories

Holland's theory, which he presented in an excellent book, *Making Vocational Choices: A Theory of Careers* (1973), is based on four main assumptions:

First, in our culture, most people can be categorized in terms of six types—realistic, investigative, artistic, social, enterprising, or conventional—and each person may be characterized by one, or some combination, of these types. The six types, which are described in detail below, correspond closely to the groupings on the earlier SVIB men's profile—one indication of the utility of the theory in working with the SCII.

Second, occupational environments can be divided into the same six types, and each environment will be found to be dominated by a particular type of person. Thus, the personality types of co-workers, as much as job requirements, establish the working tenor of a given occupation.

Third, people search for environments that will let them exercise their skills and abilities, express their attitudes and values, take on problems and roles they find stimulating and satisfying, and avoid chores or responsibilities they find distasteful or formidable.

Fourth, behavior is determined by an interaction between a person's personality and the characteristics of his or her working environment. Factors such as job performance, satisfaction, and stability are influenced by this interaction.

Obviously, a classification system of only six types is insufficient for the wide diversity of either human personalities or working environments, and Holland expanded his classification to incorporate combinations of the six types, using terms such as realistic-investigative, artistic-social, or enterprising-social-conventional, depending on the relative strength of each theme in a given individual or a given working situation. In theory, using all possible combinations of the six themes, 720 classifications can be established. In practice, the use of the most strongly manifested one, two or three themes seems sufficient for most purposes.

The core of Holland's system is his six basic occupational categories. He has described their genesis (1966, pp. 15, 10):

The formulation for the types grew out of my experience as a vocational counselor and a clinician, and out of my construction of a personality inventory from interest material. After reviewing the vocational literature—especially factor-analytic studies of personality and vocational interests—I concluded that it might be useful to categorize people into six types.

The present types are analogous in some ways to those proposed earlier by Adler, Fromm, Jung, Sheldon, and others. They differ from these earlier typologies in their origin—which is largely our vocational literature—and in their definitions. The six major factors identified in Guilford's comprehensive factor analysis of human interest—mechanical, scientific, social welfare, clerical, business, and aesthetic—approximate the present types. To the best of my knowledge, Guilford's factor analysis is the most explicit forerunner of the present typology.

The archetypal models of Holland's six types can be described as follows:

REALISTIC: Persons of this type are robust, rugged, practical, physically strong, and often athletic; have good motor coordination and skills but lack verbal and interpersonal skills, and are therefore somewhat uncomfortable in social settings; usually perceive themselves as mechanically inclined; are direct, stable, natural, and persistent; prefer concrete to abstract problems; see themselves as aggressive; have conventional political and economic goals; and rarely perform creatively in the arts or sciences, but do like to build things with tools. Realistic types prefer such occupations as mechanic, engineer, electrician, fish and wildlife specialist, crane operator, and tool designer.

INVESTIGATIVE: This category includes those with a strong scientific orientation; they are usually task-oriented, introspective, and asocial; prefer to think through rather than act out problems; have a great need to understand the physical world; enjoy ambiguous tasks; prefer to work independently; have unconventional values and attitudes; usually perceive themselves as lacking in leadership or persuasive abilities, but are confident of their scholarly and intellectual abilities; describe themselves as analytical, curious, independent, and reserved; and especially dislike repetitive activities. Vocational preferences include astronomer, biologist, chemist, technical writer, zoologist, and psychologist.

ARTISTIC: Persons of the artistic type prefer free, unstructured situations with maximum opportunity for self-expression; resemble investigative types in being introspective and asocial but differ in having less ego strength, greater need for individual expression, and greater tendency to impulsive behavior; they are creative, especially in artistic and musical media; avoid problems that are highly structured or require gross physical skills; prefer dealing with problems through self-expression in artistic media; perform well on standard measures of creativity, and value aesthetic qualities; see themselves as expressive, original, intuitive, creative, nonconforming, introspective, and independent. Vocational preferences include artist, author, composer, writer, musician, stage director, and symphony conductor.

SOCIAL: Persons of this type are sociable, responsible, humanistic, and often religious; like to work in groups, and enjoy being central in the group; have good verbal and interpersonal skills; avoid intellectual problem-solving, physical exertion, and highly ordered activities; prefer to solve problems through feelings and interpersonal manipulation of others; enjoy activities that involve informing, training, developing, curing, or enlightening others; perceive themselves as understanding, responsible, idealistic, and helpful. Vocational preferences include social worker, missionary, high school teacher, marriage counselor, and speech therapist.

ENTERPRISING: Persons of this type have verbal skills suited to selling, dominating, and leading; are strong leaders; have a strong drive to attain organizational goals or economic aims; tend to avoid work situations requiring long periods of intellectual effort; differ from conventional types in having a greater preference for ambiguous social tasks and an even greater concern for power, status, and leadership; see themselves as aggressive, popular, self-confident, cheerful, and sociable; generally have a high energy level; and show an aversion to scientific activities. Vocational preferences include business executive, political campaign manager, real estate sales, stock and bond sales, television producer, and retail merchandising.

CONVENTIONAL: Conventional people prefer well-ordered environments and like systematic verbal and numerical activities; are usually conforming and prefer subordinate roles; are effective at well-structured tasks, but avoid ambiguous situations and problems involving interpersonal relationships or physical skills; describe themselves as conscientious, efficient, obedient, calm, orderly, and practical; identify with power; and value material possessions and status. Vocational preferences include bank examiner, bookkeeper, clerical worker, financial analyst, quality control expert, statistician, and traffic manager.

Holland's classification system is an extension of the trait and factor theory that dominated occupational theory from the 1920's to the 1950's. That approach, at its worst and simplest, implied that the main goal of vocational counseling is to match people and jobs—in other words, to see that round pegs find their way into round holes.

Holland's theory, which considers such broad concepts as the individual's total life style and the global occupational environment, is a more sophisticated version of this earlier approach. Although the concept of matching the individual to a setting is still salient, Holland addresses other concerns, especially developmental issues. He describes the effects of different environments on various types: for example, he points out that investigative, artistic, social, and conventional types usually do well in school because they have attitudes and values compatible with those of their teachers and thus find the atmosphere supportive; in contrast, the realistic and enterprising types tend to do poorly because the match between their dominant characteristics and the dominant characteristics of academic environments is poor.

Holland's extension of earlier work on vocational development, especially his theoretical expansion of the meaning of individual scores, is a major contribution to the area of interest measurement. With scales for his occupational types now available on the SCII, further research can concentrate on both empirical and theoretical aspects of vocational interests.

Development of the General Occupational Theme Scales

A detailed account of the construction of the Holland SVIB scales for men is given in Campbell and Holland (1972); a similar project for women was reported by Hansen and Johansson (1972). Essentially, what was done in both projects was to select 20 SVIB items to represent each type, on the basis of the descriptions given by Holland (1966). A variety of statistical evidence was used in the selection of specific items: item intercorrelations, popularity of the items among occupations of designated Holland types, and item-scale correlations.

Item selection. The same procedure was followed in constructing the General Occupational Themes for the SCII. In most instances, the SVIB and SCII Holland scales are nearly identical, though a few new items had to be substituted for those dropped in developing the SCII booklet. The items making up each SCII Holland scale are all "reasonable," in the sense that they correspond either obviously or intuitively to the descriptions of the six occupational-personality types. The same items are used for both men and women, and the items are weighted +1, 0, and −1, respectively, for the "Like," "Indifferent," and "Dislike" responses. This pattern of item weights was used because "Likes" of each of these patterns are more precisely defined by Holland's theory than are the "Dislikes." In addition, as experience with the Basic Interest Scales has shown (Campbell et al., 1968), "Likes" tend to cluster statistically, whereas "Dislikes" do not.

TABLE 4-1

Means, Standard Deviations, and Standard-Score Interpretive Boundaries of the General Occupational Theme Scales
for the Men- and Women-in-General Samples (Each $N = 300$)

(Numbers in parentheses are percentiles)

Scale	Sex	Mean	S. D.	Interpretive boundaries						
				Very low (0–6)	Low (7–15)	Mod. low (16–30)	Average (31–69)	Mod. high (70–84)	High (85–93)	Very high (94–100)
REALISTIC	f	45.5	9.9	27–31	32–35	36–39	40–50	51–56	57–61	62–75
	m	54.5	10.1	27–38	39–44	45–49	50–61	62–64	65–67	68–75
INVESTIGATIVE	f	48.5	10.1	20–32	33–37	38–42	43–55	56–59	60–63	64–69
	m	51.5	9.9	20–35	36–41	42–46	47–57	58–61	62–64	65–69
ARTISTIC	f	53.2	8.9	24–38	39–43	44–49	50–59	60–62	63–64	65–67
	m	46.8	11.0	24–30	31–35	36–39	40–53	54–59	60–63	64–67
SOCIAL	f	51.3	9.0	19–37	38–43	44–47	48–54	55–61	62–64	65–73
	m	48.7	10.9	19–32	33–38	39–43	44–53	54–60	61–65	66–73
ENTERPRISING	f	48.1	8.8	30–36	37–38	39–43	44–51	52–56	57–61	62–77
	m	51.9	11.1	30–35	36–40	41–45	46–57	58–63	64–69	70–77
CONVENTIONAL	f	50.1	10.2	23–36	37–40	41–45	46–53	54–60	61–67	68–79
	m	49.9	9.8	23–36	37–40	41–44	45–54	55–58	59–65	66–79

Norming. The raw-score-to-standard-score conversion of the General Occupational Themes is based on a distribution of 600 people, half males, half females. The mean age for the sample is 34.3 years and the mean level of education is two years beyond high school. Their raw-score means and standard deviations on the six scales are used in a standardization formula to convert all scores into distributions with standard-score means of 50 and standard deviations of 10. By this formula,

$$\text{standard score} = \left(\frac{X - Mc}{SDc}\right)10 + 50$$

where X is an individual's raw score, and Mc and SDc are the General Reference Sample raw-score mean and raw-score standard deviation. Thus, a respondent's scores can be compared quickly on common numerical measures; a standard score of 60, for example, falls one standard deviation (50 plus 10) above the combined mean, no matter which scale is used.

Because men and women have different distributions on these scales, interpretation should usually be pursued separately for the two sexes. Consequently, the interpretive comment printed by the computer on the profile for each of the General Occupational Themes is based on the distribution for the respondent's sex. For each theme, the computer prints one of the comments in the left-hand column below; the comment selected corresponds to the particular percentile band in the right-hand column that includes, for the general sample of the appropriate sex, the respondent's score on that scale.

Comment printed	Percentile in general sample
Very high	94th and above
High	85th to 93rd
Moderately high	70th to 84th
Average	31st to 69th
Moderately low	16th to 30th
Low	7th to 15th
Very low	6th and below

Again, an individual's score may be compared to the combined male and female distribution by using the printed standard scores, or to the distribution of scores for the respondent's sex by using the interpretive comments and bars.

Table 4-1 lists the standard-score means and standard deviations of the Men- and Women-in-General samples (p. 48) and the ranges used to define each interpretive category. The lower and upper bounds for each scale are the minimum and maximum possible scores; these are the scores that will be earned by anyone answering all items "Dislike" or "Like," respectively.

The distributions of the Men- and Women-in-General samples are illustrated on the profile form by two bars for each scale. The shaded bar represents the men's distribution, the open bar the women's. For each distribution for every scale, the vertical line in the middle indicates the mean; the thick portion of the bar represents the middle 50 percent of the sample (from the 25th to the 75th percentiles); and the thin-line extensions represent the middle 80 percent (from the 10th to the 90th percentiles).

General Theme intercorrelations. Scale intercorrelations for the General Occupational Themes are presented in Table 4-2. On the strength of such correlations, Holland suggested that his types be arranged in a hexagon, as shown in Fig. 4-1. Although the sides of the hexagon may not be as regular as Holland's theory states, the patterns of intercorrelations support the overall structure; especially for men, the strongest correlations occur between adjacent scales, the weakest usually between scales directly opposite each other. (These relationships are shown with great clarity in Table 4-4.) Probably because women were excluded from many occupations until recent years, the hexagon arrangement is not as obvious for them at this time as it is for men. But as women move into occupations previously restricted to men, the world-of-work map will undoubtedly be rearranged, and a clearer configuration should emerge.

Reliability. Three samples have been tested and then retested over various time intervals to determine the stability of the SCII scales. Test-retest statistics for the three samples on the General Occupational Themes are presented in Table 4-3; analogous statistics for the Basic Interest and Occupational Scales are reported in Tables 5-5 and 6-4 and 6-5, respectively.

The two-week sample was collected by Mary Whitton of North Carolina State University. She tested and retested 180 people—106 females and 74 males—who were mostly high school seniors or college students who had volunteered for this project. Their average age was 18.7 years. The test-retest interval ranged from 11 to 22 days, with a mean of 14 days. As shown in Table 4-3, the median test-retest correlation over this short time period was .91, indicating substantial stability.

The thirty-day sample, which included 35 women and 67 men, came from three sources: an Army Reserve unit under the direction of Colonel James Crawford; students at the University of Minnesota; and women in a career development course at the Resource Center for Women in Palo Alto, California, under the direction of Martha Hargadon. It was a diverse sample, mainly in the 25-40 age range. The median test-retest correlation in this sample was .86, somewhat lower than that for the two-week sample, but still comfortably high.

The three-year test-retest sample, collected by the

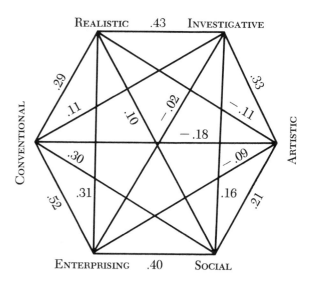

Fig. 4-1. Intercorrelations between the General Occupational Themes, arranged in hexagonal order (correlations based on sample of 300 females and 300 males)

Center for Interest Measurement Research at the University of Minnesota, included 65 females and 75 males; all were employed full-time, both when tested and when retested, in occupations ranging from semiskilled to professional—again, a diverse sample. The median test-retest correlation over the three-year period was .81, a figure high enough to indicate that the theme scores are generally stable, but low enough to indicate that some shifting around did occur.

In all three of the test-retest samples, the means were roughly 50, indicating that they were indeed general samples. The means were also quite stable between testing and retesting, never changing more than 2 points, usually less; again, these scales are quite reliable.

Interpreting the scores. The six General Theme scores provide a global view of the respondent's occupational orientation. High scores suggest the general activities the person will enjoy, the type of occupa-

TABLE 4-2

Intercorrelations Between the General Occupational Themes
(Correlations above the diagonal based on 300 women; those below the diagonal based on 300 men)

Scale	REAL-ISTIC	INVESTI-GATIVE	ARTIS-TIC	SOCIAL	ENTER-PRISING	CONVEN-TIONAL
REALISTIC	—	.55	.17	.21	.16	.27
INVESTIGATIVE	.26	—	.36	.23	.03	.12
ARTISTIC	−.09	.43	—	.15	.07	−.20
SOCIAL	.13	.15	.22	—	.43	.32
ENTERPRISING	.35	−.11	−.10	.42	—	.47
CONVENTIONAL	.38	.11	−.18	.29	.59	—

TABLE 4-3

Test-Retest Reliability Statistics for the General Occupational Themes

Theme	Two-week statistics (N = 106 women, 74 men)					Thirty-day statistics (N = 35 women, 67 men)					Three-year statistics (N = 65 women, 75 men)				
	Test-retest corre-lation[a]	Test		Retest		Test-retest corre-lation[b]	Test		Retest		Test-retest corre-lation[c]	Test		Retest	
		Mean	S.D.	Mean	S.D.		Mean	S.D.	Mean	S.D.		Mean	S.D.	Mean	S.D.
REALISTIC	.91	47	10.6	49	11.7	.87	50	8.7	51	9.2	.82	51	10.8	51	11.0
INVESTIGATIVE	.90	47	10.1	48	11.5	.84	52	8.4	52	8.7	.78	52	8.9	52	9.6
ARTISTIC	.93	49	10.5	50	11.2	.91	51	10.0	53	10.0	.87	51	10.4	51	10.9
SOCIAL	.89	49	11.2	49	12.1	.86	51	9.7	51	10.5	.82	48	10.7	47	10.2
ENTERPRISING	.85	47	8.4	49	9.8	.85	53	9.6	54	10.5	.80	50	9.1	50	9.3
CONVENTIONAL	.91	47	10.8	48	11.5	.84	49	9.8	50	10.2	.79	49	9.8	49	10.7

[a] Median correlation = .91.   [b] Median correlation = .86.   [c] Median correlation = .81.

TABLE 4-4
Occupations Scoring High and Low on Each General Occupational Theme

REALISTIC	INVESTIGATIVE	ARTISTIC	SOCIAL	ENTERPRISING	CONVENTIONAL
			High Scores		
Agribusiness managers	Astronomers	Actors	Flight attendants	Agribusiness managers	Accountants
Carpenters	Biologists	Advertising executives	Guidance counselors	Auto sales dealers	Auto sales dealers
Cartographers	Chemists	Architects	Mental health workers	Business education teachers	Bankers
Engineers	College professors	Art teachers	Ministers	Buyers	Business education teachers
Farmers	Geologists	Artists	Physical education teachers	Chamber of Commerce executives	Credit managers
Foresters	Mathematicians	Broadcasters	Recreation leaders	Computer sales	Department store managers
Highway patrol officers	Medical technologists	Interior decorators	Rehabilitation counselors	Department store managers	Executive housekeepers
Industrial arts teachers	Physicians	Ministers	School administrators	Food service managers	Farmers
Military officers	Physicists	Musicians	Social science teachers	Life insurance agents	IRS agents
Police officers	Psychologists	Music teachers	Social workers	Realtors	Nursing home administrators
Veterinarians		Photographers	Special education teachers	Retail clerks	Office workers
Vocational agriculture teachers		Public relations directors	YMCA/YWCA directors	Sales managers	Purchasing agents
		Reporters		Stockbrokers	
			Low Scores		
Advertising executives	Bankers	Agribusiness managers	Architects	Actors	Actors
Artists	Beauticians	Bankers	Artists	Anthropologists	Anthropologists
Broadcasters	Business education teachers	Correctional officers	Carpenters	Artists	Art teachers
Florists	Buyers	Farmers	Engineers	Astronomers	Artists
Foreign language teachers	Carpenters	Foresters	Farmers	Biologists	Broadcasters
Interior decorators	Chamber of Commerce executives	Industrial arts teachers	Florists	Economists	Florists
Life insurance agents	Correctional officers	Military officers	Geologists	Geologists	Interior decorators
Poets	Farmers	Physical education teachers	Geographers	Mathematicians	Musicians
Political scientists	Florists	Sales personnel	Marketing executives	Physicists	Occupational therapists
Psychologists	Interior decorators	Skilled trades	Mathematicians	Psychologists	Reporters
Public relations directors	Realtors	Veterinarians	Musicians	Writers	
Writers	Writers	Vocational agriculture teachers	Photographers		
			Physicists		

tional environment he/she will find most comfortable, the problems he/she will be most willing to tackle, and the kind of people who will be most appealing as co-workers. The scores offer a useful, immediate overview of an individual's interests.

To understand each type or combination of types better, the counselor should study the descriptions given above and the occupations scoring high and low on each scale (see Table 4-4 and Appendix B). Most people do not score high on just one theme; some have several high scores, some have few, and some have none; many have two high scores, usually on adjacent themes (see Chapter 10).

Assigning occupations to code types. One of the most important contributions of the General Occupational Themes is the structure accorded the profile by assigning the Basic Interest Scales and Occupational Scales to code types. Table 6-5 (in Chapter 6) demonstrates how this was done. Essentially, each Occupational Scale was assigned to a code type corresponding to the highest General Theme scores of the

people in that occupation. With scales then arranged on the profile in the order of the Holland hexagon, interpretation of the scores and patterns of scores is greatly enhanced; similarities and dissimilarities between occupations become more obvious, and the clustering of occupations along lines of common interests becomes more apparent. (The interpretive value of the code types is discussed at length in Chapter 10.)

The code types for several hundred occupations are given in Appendix B; students often find it useful to identify occupations with codes similar to their own.

Consistency among scales. Normally, there is considerable consistency among an individual's scores on the General Occupational Themes, the Basic Interest Scales (see Chapter 5), and the Occupational Scales (see Chapter 6). One of the counselor's main tasks is to help the respondent perceive that pattern in his/her scores or, if the consistency is in fact low, to help the person understand what causes the inconsistency. More is said on this subject in Chapter 5.

CHAPTER FIVE

The Basic Interest Scales

The SVIB-SCII Basic Interest Scales were constructed by gathering together clusters of statistically related items. This technique generates homogeneous scales, that is, scales with items highly consistent in content. For example, the ART Basic Interest Scale includes, among others, the following items: *Artist, Cartoonist,* and *Interior Decorator.* These items, and other similar items, were clustered together because most people tend to react to them in one of two ways, by responding either "Like" to all (or nearly all) of them or "Indifferent" or "Dislike" to all (or nearly all) of them.

The strength of this tendency to respond in a similar way to two items can be measured by assigning weights of +1, 0, and −1, respectively, to the three possible responses for each item and then calculating the product-moment correlations between the two items. In the case of the items mentioned above, among 500 women (in a general sample) the correlation between *Artist* and *Cartoonist* was .47, between *Artist* and *Interior decorator* .52, and between *Cartoonist* and *Interior decorator* .27; the analogous figures among 500 men were .49, .45, and .37. As discussed in Chapter 3, item intercorrelations of this size indicate a substantial relationship between the items.

A scale formed by using clusters of statistically related items has three important characteristics: first, it represents, by virtue of its internal consistency, an important focus around which people group their own interests; second, because the items are all drawn from one area, the content of the scale is easy to understand; and third, the concentration of related items in a single scale provides a more reliable measure than the same number of unrelated items would.

Purpose and Origin of the Basic Interest Scales

The main purpose in developing the Basic Interest Scales was to improve the understanding of the Occupational Scales. The latter, which historically preceded the former, are constructed by gathering together into a scale all items that discriminate between an occupational sample and a general reference sample, no matter what the item content. The resulting scale, though powerful statistically, may be difficult to interpret because the items are quite varied. The Psychologist Occupational Scale, for example, incorpo-

rates a wide range of items, including subgroups that reflect interests in science, social service, and the arts, weighted positively, and other subgroups encompassing religion, business, and military activities, weighted negatively. A person can score high (or low) on this scale in countless ways, and only those counselors with extensive clinical experience can search out the factors underlying a particular profile.

Kenneth Clark, in his work with the Minnesota Vocational Interest Inventory (Clark, 1961), proposed the use of two types of scales to overcome this problem: empirically developed Occupational Scales, such as those that had always been part of the SVIB, and statistically developed homogeneous scales. Clark's rationale was that the combination of these two types of scales would provide more information than either type used separately would. For example, if a person scored high on an Occupational Scale, such as the Psychologist scale, her/his scores on the homogeneous scales could be scanned to see precisely what combination of interests was present—science, social service, art, or whatever. The homogeneous scales could be used to describe the general patterns reflected in the scores of empirical scales. For this reason, the profile for the Minnesota Vocational Interest Inventory contained both types of scales; at the time it was published, it was the only inventory to do so (Clark and Campbell, 1965). Shortly thereafter, the SVIB profile was also expanded to include both types of scales (Campbell, 1969).

Clark, in his award-winning book *Vocational Interests of Non-Professional Men* (1961), discussed at length the differences between the two types of scales: empirical scales are heterogeneous in content and constitute an "open" system to which new occupations can continually be added as they are tested. Homogeneous scales, by contrast, each focus on only one area of item content and constitute a "closed" system, since the number of scales in the system will never be increased unless the inventory itself is expanded.

The two types of scales serve different purposes, and to understand their complementary nature one must understand the differences in their development and in their operating characteristics.

Scale Construction

To some extent, the SCII Basic Interest Scales formed themselves; for the most part, the clusters of correlated items making up the scales fell out of the item-intercorrelation matrix. A few arbitrary decisions were made in borderline cases, especially in those instances where an item correlated highly with some items in a cluster but not with others. And in a few instances an item was not used because it did not "feel" right for a given scale. For example, the item *Sculptor* correlated moderately with the science items but was not added to that scale because it seemed out of place. Such actions were rare; the bulk of the scale-construction decisions were based on hard data.

The details of the construction of the Basic Interest Scales are given in the *Handbook for the SVIB*. Briefly, the procedure was as follows:

First, item-intercorrelation matrices containing correlation coefficients between all possible pairs of items were generated for both male and female samples.

Second, frequency distributions of these correlations were made for each sex. The two distributions, presented in the *Handbook,* were virtually identical, with means of about .03 and standard deviations of about .12. Because most of the correlations were less than .30, that figure was considered "high," and pairs of items with correlations of .30 or greater were considered closely related.

Third, scales were constructed by gathering together those items with intercorrelations of .30 or higher. In many cases, the selection criterion had to be dropped to .20, especially in those instances where, for example, item A correlated .30 with B and .30 with C, but B correlated only .20 with C.

The item-intercorrelation matrices for all of the earlier SVIB Basic Interest Scales are presented in the *Handbook;* scanning them affords a good impression of the level of correlation one can expect when working with individual items.

The original SVIB Basic Interest Scales were constructed separately for the men's and women's booklets. In constructing the SCII Basic Interest Scales, the male and female SVIB sets were merged into a single set, in most cases by combining the parallel men's and women's scales. Where there was only one form of the scale, that form was usually retained. Dropping or rewording of items in the SCII booklet also led to minor changes in a few of the scales. (Scale-by-scale changes are given in the 1974 *Manual for the SVIB-SCII.*)

This work resulted in the construction of 23 Basic Interest Scales ranging in length from five to 24 items, with a median length of 11 items.

Norming the Scales

The Basic Interest Scales were normed against the General Reference Sample, 300 men and 300 women. For each scale, the mean and standard deviation of this sample were set equal to 50 and 10, respectively, and all future scores are converted to this distribution for ready comparison.

As is the case with the General Occupational Themes, the Basic Interest Scale standard-score column on the profile is followed by a column of interpretive comments. These comments are based on the distribution for the respondent's own sex, and the comments for the Basic Interest Scales correspond to the percentile bands used for the General Occupational Themes (p. 31). Table 5-1 lists the standard-score means and standard deviation of the Men- and Women-in-General samples and the ranges used to define each interpretive category. The extremes of the lower and upper bands for each scale are the minimum and maximum possible scores; these are the scores that will be earned by anyone answering all items "Dislike" or "Like," respectively—and they are thus the same for both sexes, on all scales.

The distributions of the Men- and Women-in-General samples are illustrated on the profile by two bars for each scale. The shaded bar represents the men's distribution, the open bar the women's. For each distribution for every scale, the vertical line in the middle indicates the mean; the thick portion of the bar represents the middle 50 percent of the sample (from the 25th to the 75th percentiles); and the thin-line extensions represent the middle 80 percent (from the 10th to the 90th percentiles). With the use of the standard scores, the bars, and the interpretive comments, an individual's score may be compared with either the male or female distribution or the combined male and female distribution.

Relationships to the General Occupational Themes

The SCII Basic Interest Scales are clustered on the profile into the six General Occupational Theme (Holland) categories, as indicated in the left-hand column of Table 5-1. This clustering was based on the scale intercorrelations, which appear in Tables 5-2 and 5-3. In most cases, the Basic Interest Scales in one Holland category correlate at least moderately with each other, and in some cases correlate so highly that the decision to create two scales instead of one was arbitrary. For example, the SALES and MERCHANDISING scales, both of which fit easily into Holland's ENTERPRISING category, might well have been combined; they were kept separate, even though their intercorrelation is .74, because they have different item content. Other pairs—SCIENCE and MATHEMATICS, MUSIC and ART, TEACHING and SOCIAL SERVICE—are similarly related. One must opt either for parsimony and a small number of scales, or for purity of item content and a larger number. The two types of scales—the General Occupational Themes and the Basic Interest Scales—provide the best of both approaches; and their high correlations suggest that the two types rest on the same underlying structure.

TABLE 5-1

Means, Standard Deviations, and Standard-Score Interpretive Boundaries of the Basic Interest
Scales for the Men- and Women-in-General Samples
(Each $N = 300$; numbers in parentheses are percentiles)

General Theme[a]	Scale	Sex	Mean	S.D.	Interpretive boundaries						
					Very low (0–6)	Low (7–15)	Mod. low (16–30)	Average (31–69)	Mod. high (70–84)	High (85–93)	Very high (94–100)
R	AGRICULTURE	f	48.6	10.0	30–32	33–35	36–42	43–54	55–58	59–64	65–68
		m	51.4	10.0	30–35	36–39	40–45	46–57	58–61	62–66	67–68
R	NATURE	f	51.6	9.3	17–34	35–41	42–46	47–57	58–60	61–64	65–67
		m	48.4	10.6	17–30	31–34	35–41	42–53	54–60	61–62	63–67
R	ADVENTURE	f	46.1	10.2	30–31	32–35	36–39	40–52	53–56	57–62	63–71
		m	53.9	9.8	30–37	38–43	44–47	48–58	59–64	65–68	69–71
R	MECHANICAL ACTIVITIES	f	45.5	10.2	30–32	33–34	35–38	39–49	50–56	57–63	64–72
		m	54.5	9.8	30–39	40–43	44–49	50–60	61–65	66–68	69–72
R	MILITARY ACTIVITIES	f	47.3	8.1	41–42	43–44	45–46	47–48	49–54	55–61	62–76
		m	52.7	11.6	41–42	43–44	45–46	47–58	59–65	66–74	75–76
I	SCIENCE	f	48.4	10.3	28–32	33–36	37–41	42–54	55–58	59–63	64–69
		m	51.6	9.7	28–36	37–39	40–45	46–57	58–61	62–64	65–69
I	MATHEMATICS	f	48.3	10.1	31–32	33–34	35–42	43–54	55–58	59–64	65–67
		m	51.7	9.8	31–34	35–40	41–46	47–58	59–62	63–65	66–67
I	MEDICAL SCIENCE	f	49.9	10.4	29–31	32–38	39–43	44–55	56–60	61–65	66–68
		m	50.1	9.6	29–33	34–38	39–43	44–55	56–60	61–65	66–68
I	MEDICAL SERVICE	f	52.6	11.4	33–34	35–39	40–44	45–58	59–65	66–70	71–76
		m	47.4	8.3	33–34	35–37	38–42	43–51	52–53	54–61	62–76
A	MUSIC/ DRAMATICS	f	54.0	9.7	26–36	37–43	44–50	51–58	59–63	64–67	68–73
		m	46.0	10.3	26–31	32–35	36–38	39–50	51–57	58–62	63–73
A	ART	f	54.6	9.3	26–37	38–43	44–49	50–60	61–64	65–66	67–68
		m	45.4	10.6	26–30	31–33	34–37	38–52	53–57	58–61	62–68
A	WRITING	f	52.5	9.4	26–37	38–41	42–47	48–59	60–62	63–64	65–66
		m	47.5	10.6	26–30	31–35	36–41	42–54	55–59	60–61	62–66
S	TEACHING	f	51.9	9.0	23–34	35–42	43–47	48–56	57–61	62–63	64–67
		m	48.1	10.8	23–30	31–34	35–42	43–54	55–59	60–63	64–67
S	SOCIAL SERVICE	f	52.5	9.3	24–38	39–42	43–46	47–56	57–62	63–66	67–69
		m	47.5	10.7	24–32	33–34	35–40	41–52	53–58	59–64	65–69
S	ATHLETICS	f	47.1	9.6	27–33	34–37	38–40	41–53	54–56	57–62	63–70
		m	52.9	10.4	27–37	38–40	41–46	47–60	61–63	64–65	66–70
S	DOMESTIC ARTS	f	57.3	10.4	27–40	41–45	46–50	51–65	66–67	68–70	71–75
		m	42.7	9.6	27–28	29–33	34–35	36–45	46–53	54–57	58–75
S	RELIGIOUS ACTIVITIES	f	51.5	9.7	31–34	35–39	40–47	48–57	58–61	62–65	66–68
		m	48.5	10.3	31–32	33–34	35–43	44–55	56–59	60–63	64–68
E	PUBLIC SPEAKING	f	48.0	10.0	31–34	35–36	37–42	43–54	55–60	61–64	65–71
		m	52.0	10.0	31–36	37–40	41–46	47–58	59–64	65–66	67–71
E	LAW/ POLITICS	f	47.5	10.3	30–32	33–36	37–39	40–52	53–58	59–65	66–69
		m	52.5	9.7	30–36	37–40	41–47	48–57	58–63	64–66	67–69
E	MERCHANDISING	f	49.7	9.4	31–33	34–38	39–44	45–54	55–60	61–63	64–72
		m	50.3	10.6	31–33	34–38	39–43	44–55	56–61	62–66	67–72
E	SALES	f	47.3	8.4	37–38	39–40	41–42	43–49	50–56	57–60	61–81
		m	52.7	11.4	37–38	39–40	41–43	44–58	59–65	66–73	74–81
E	BUSINESS MANAGEMENT	f	48.0	9.4	29–34	35–37	38–42	43–53	54–57	58–62	63–72
		m	52.0	10.5	29–34	35–40	41–45	46–57	58–63	64–68	69–72
C	OFFICE PRACTICES	f	52.9	10.8	36–37	38–40	41–46	47–57	58–63	64–71	72–79
		m	47.1	9.1	36–37	38–39	40–41	42–48	49–57	58–63	64–79

[a]R = Realistic; I = Investigative; A = Artistic; S = Social; E = Enterprising; C = Conventional.

TABLE 5-2

Intercorrelations Between the Basic Interest Scales for Women and Men

(Correlations above the diagonal based on 300 women; those below, on 300 men. Decimal points have been omitted.)

Basic Interest Scale	AGR	NAT	ADV	MIL	MEC	SCI	MAT	MSC	MSE	MUS	ART	WRI	TEA	SOC	ATH	DOM	REL	PUB	LAW	MER	SAL	BUS	OFF
AGRICULTURE		68	15	17	32	19	06	25	25	-16	-03	-11	-01	01	37	29	19	-19	-16	-01	01	-06	12
NATURE	55		10	10	36	40	11	46	31	11	25	10	08	13	22	32	21	-06	-06	05	-02	-02	-04
ADVENTURE	15	06		38	33	17	17	26	19	21	09	17	10	16	39	-06	03	38	39	14	14	19	-17
MILITARY ACTIVITIES	22	02	28		18	09	09	16	25	02	-09	-05	03	09	32	14	20	14	13	11	10	17	19
MECHANICAL ACTIVITIES	34	27	16	29		62	49	38	19	04	08	12	05	-12	16	-07	08	06	16	-01	-07	12	-03
SCIENCE	-03	29	09	-04	48		61	60	25	14	08	17	17	-04	01	-15	04	06	14	-21	-25	-06	-15
MATHEMATICS	-01	-01	09	10	46	66		26	12	-06	-14	-06	05	-12	09	-05	01	10	-08	-12	06	18	
MEDICAL SCIENCE	14	49	24	01	21	48	22		71	19	16	13	14	27	24	10	15	19	20	04	-03	07	-06
MEDICAL SERVICE	19	43	12	14	32	37	13	63		02	-03	-11	04	35	40	38	31	02	-03	03	04	06	23
MUSIC/DRAMATICS	-14	25	15	-05	-06	18	-04	35	28		66	53	23	25	-08	-01	11	40	30	12	-04	08	-26
ART	-14	32	19	-10	03	18	-12	32	27	78		58	17	15	-14	09	-04	23	15	16	-01	01	-26
WRITING	-23	14	20	-13	-17	19	-07	29	13	64	62		33	23	-22	-08	-01	46	47	21	03	17	-30
TEACHING	-19	17	03	02	00	23	-04	34	32	39	41	38		45	02	14	22	33	33	17	-03	21	-08
SOCIAL SERVICE	-03	22	10	05	-08	-05	-22	29	40	33	31	32	59		30	40	40	40	36	38	24	35	13
ATHLETICS	33	14	32	25	08	-12	-02	16	18	-07	-10	-11	12	31		27	24	13	08	23	23	21	25
DOMESTIC ARTS	12	37	13	09	21	05	-05	29	45	41	43	25	35	42	14		37	02	-09	35	25	21	42
RELIGIOUS ACTIVITIES	23	21	-17	16	13	-07	00	05	27	18	10	00	13	44	22	26		14	02	14	14	11	30
PUBLIC SPEAKING	-11	-04	25	20	-04	-02	19	15	33	21	44	36	51	27	23	35			81	49	39	54	-07
LAW/POLITICS	-11	-06	34	15	-17	02	02	25	12	25	14	45	32	45	23	13	15	83		40	27	50	-10
MERCHANDISING	16	03	19	30	12	-23	-01	08	18	08	04	02	00	26	32	23	31	44	30		74	81	37
SALES	21	-04	10	26	07	-29	02	-03	12	-08	-18	-16	-22	15	25	13	28	31	20	81		66	42
BUSINESS MANAGEMENT	14	02	13	36	12	-17	02	12	24	-02	-06	-04	11	36	33	20	29	49	36	84	73		44
OFFICE PRACTICES	15	06	-21	25	18	-05	17	01	33	-04	-12	-17	04	14	12	24	34	11	-01	49	51	55	

Only one Basic Interest Scale, OFFICE PRACTICES, fits into Holland's CONVENTIONAL category. Whether this is because that Holland category (and that part of the real world it represents) has a smaller bandwidth than the others, or because other Basic Interest Scales appropriate for that category have not been isolated is not clear. This is a problem for future research.

Validity of the Basic Interest Scales

There is no single index of validity for the Basic Interest Scales; instead, a variety of information has been drawn together to show that scores on these scales are reasonable and are related to the respondent's behavior.

Content validity. The emphasis in constructing these scales was to pull together related items; hence, each scale is focused on one content area, and the items reflect this focus. For example, the SCIENCE scale contains items like *Astronomer, Biologist, Chemist,* and *Working in a research laboratory.* Obviously, these items have content validity; responses to them provide direct information about the person's feelings toward scientific activities. The same is true of the other scales.

Concurrent validity. *Concurrent* validity is the power of a psychological measure to discriminate between two groups whose behavior at the same point in time differs; *predictive* validity is the power to discriminate between two groups who will behave differently sometime in the future.

The concurrent validity of the SCII Basic Interest Scales can be checked by comparing scores of people who are currently in different occupations; if the scales are working as they should, people should score high on scales relevant to their own occupations: artists should score high on the ART scale, scientists high on the SCIENCE scale, teachers high on the TEACHING scale; further, people in unrelated occupations should score at only average levels or lower on scales *not* related to their occupations.

A substantial body of such data has been collected for the SCII during the last eight years. In addition, data are available for the earlier SVIB Basic Interest Scales; and because the SCII scales are based directly on these earlier scales, these data also are relevant. The SCII and SVIB data include scores for over 450 occupational samples ranging in size from seven to over 1,000 people, with a median sample size of about 250. These samples, stored in the Center for Interest Measurement Research at the University of Minnesota, include a majority of the adults ever tested for research purposes with the SVIB and SCII.

Each sample has been scored with the Basic Interest Scales. Generally, the occupations' scores on each scale are spread over 2 to 2½ standard deviations, or a range of 20 to 25 points, demonstrating that the scales spread occupations apart in a reasonable fashion. Table 5-4 lists the highest- and lowest-scoring samples on each scale. The patterns of high- and low-scoring occupations demonstrate that scores on these scales are substantially related to the occupations that people pursue. Accordingly, counselors should study these lists of occupations carefully, for

TABLE 5-3

Correlations Between the General Occupational Themes and the Basic Interest Scales for Women and Men

(Female correlations based on 300 women; male, on 300 men. Decimal points have been omitted.)

Basic Interest Scale	General Occupational Theme and sex											
	REALISTIC		INVESTIGATIVE		ARTISTIC		SOCIAL		ENTERPRISING		CONVENTIONAL	
	F	M	F	M	F	M	F	M	F	M	F	M
AGRICULTURE	55	60	16	−05	−07	−18	14	08	01	24	14	09
NATURE	50	40	42	33	22	25	21	27	08	07	05	−01
ADVENTURE	48	32	27	25	21	25	25	09	23	18	05	−08
MILITARY ACTIVITIES	33	45	10	−03	−04	−10	21	19	16	34	20	28
MECHANICAL ACTIVITIES	90	88	61	38	17	−06	07	06	06	15	26	36
SCIENCE	53	31	92	90	23	22	09	01	−09	−20	13	15
MATHEMATICS	40	36	59	61	−06	−07	04	−09	−00	05	50	46
MEDICAL SCIENCE	41	22	68	64	23	38	34	33	13	08	11	09
MEDICAL SERVICE	27	34	28	40	−01	23	41	46	11	21	24	30
MUSIC/DRAMATICS	05	−08	27	37	83	88	19	26	10	−00	−16	−08
ART	08	−01	21	35	86	89	09	24	07	−08	−19	−15
WRITING	13	−18	30	39	76	81	19	19	15	−06	−16	−16
TEACHING	10	−05	29	36	22	41	62	66	11	−04	01	05
SOCIAL SERVICE	02	−03	11	12	20	32	83	86	35	29	17	11
ATHLETICS	30	24	05	−04	−08	−06	43	45	25	36	30	17
DOMESTIC ARTS	08	22	−09	18	−01	37	42	44	28	20	30	17
RELIGIOUS ACTIVITIES	15	19	05	−06	02	06	57	59	17	35	29	33
PUBLIC SPEAKING	09	−06	24	16	37	32	48	56	55	46	12	23
LAW/POLITICS	19	−06	31	22	29	28	39	42	48	32	14	13
MERCHANDISING	09	28	−06	−11	12	01	43	39	86	91	44	55
SALES	02	24	−16	−22	−05	−19	29	24	87	91	38	51
BUSINESS MANAGEMENT	19	29	06	−07	04	−09	49	51	81	84	57	64
OFFICE PRACTICES	01	26	−21	−11	−34	−18	22	27	39	54	81	81

they are useful in helping students think about their high and low scores.

Predictive validity. The predictive validity of the Basic Interest Scales—that is, their ability to discriminate between two groups who will at some future time behave differently—is not as good as their concurrent validity, since a long-range discrimination is harder to make than a concurrent one. Nevertheless, there is considerable agreement between the scores earned by students and their eventual occupations. Because the nature of the scales does not permit detailed predictions, there is no way of tallying "hits" or "misses"; all one can say is that students with high scores on, for example, the SCIENCE scale tend to end up in occupations of a generally scientific character. Studies documenting that conclusion are summarized in the *Handbook*.

Some of the scales are less predictive than others. Scores on the ADVENTURE scale, in particular, decrease with age and do not seem particularly related to eventual occupation. People who are in "adventuresome" occupations, such as astronauts, police officers, and military officers, have high scores, but so do many young people who will not be entering such occupations.

A study by Douce (1977) investigated the relationship between scores on the ADVENTURE scale and various aspects of the career development of women. She found that scores on ADVENTURE were related to

both current and future status. High-adventure women reported extroverted interests: they were more autonomous and independent, more willing to take physical and social risks; they expected to marry later than the low-adventure women did; and they tended to have higher salaries and to hold more full-time positions.

Douce also found that ADVENTURE scores were not significantly related to the sex-role traditionalism of occupations actually entered; nor were they related to educational aspirations or to parental variables such as education level, number of years mothers worked outside the home, or the sex-role traditionalism of parents' occupations.

Among young women, scores on the RELIGIOUS ACTIVITIES, DOMESTIC ARTS, and OFFICE PRACTICES scales are frequently high; scores on these scales decrease somewhat with age, and are less predictive than scores on other scales.

In general, the less a student's pattern resembles the typical teenage pattern, the more predictive it is. Any student with high scores on such scales as SCIENCE, ART, or BUSINESS MANAGEMENT, which are fairly uncommon high scores among young people, is likely to be more predictable in career selection than are students with high scores on the more "adolescent" scales.

Also, the more consistent the pattern is across the entire profile, the more predictive. Johnson and

TABLE 5-4

Occupations Scoring High and Low on Each SCII Basic Interest Scale

Scale	Some occupations scoring high	Some occupations scoring low	Scale	Some occupations scoring high	Some occupations scoring low
ADVENTURE	Astronauts Military officers Police officers Recreation leaders Sales personnel	Bankers Business education teachers Home economics teachers Judges Language teachers Mathematicians	LAW/POLITICS	Chamber of Commerce executives Elected public officials Judges Lawyers Political scientists Public administrators Sales personnel	Artists Beauticians Farmers Geologists Musicians Physicists Sewing machine operators
AGRICULTURE	Agribusiness managers Agriculture extension agents Animal husbandry professors Farmers Foresters Veterinarians Vocational agriculture teachers	Foreign language teachers Librarians Political scientists Psychologists Public relations directors Sociologists Writers	MATHEMATICS	Accountants Astronauts Astronomers Chemists Computer programmers Engineers Mathematicians Physicists Systems analysts	Art instructors Artists Fashion models Interior decorators Public relations directors Reporters Social workers
ART	Actors Actresses Architects Artists Interior decorators Musicians Occupational therapists Photographers Public relations directors	Accountants Bankers Business education teachers Farmers Physical education teachers Sewing machine operators Veterinarians	MECHANICAL ACTIVITIES	Carpenters Chemists Engineers Machinists Medical technologists Physicists Skilled trades	English teachers Language teachers Lawyers Political scientists Public relations directors Sales personnel Writers
ATHLETICS	Football coaches Physical education teachers Physical therapists Police officers Recreation leaders YMCA directors	Artists Biologists Interior decorators Librarians Mathematicians Musicians Physicists Social scientists	MEDICAL SCIENCE	Dentists Medical technologists Pharmacists Physical therapists Physicians Veterinarians	Artists Business education teachers Public relations directors Sales personnel Writers
BUSINESS MANAGEMENT	Business education teachers Chamber of Commerce executives Credit managers Department store managers Personnel directors Purchasing agents	Anthropologists Artists Biologists Geologists Musicians Physicists Writers	MEDICAL SERVICE	Dental assistants Dentists Licensed practical nurses Nurses Physical therapists Physicians Radiologic technicians	Architects Artists Farmers Public relations directors Sales personnel Writers
DOMESTIC ARTS	Dietitians Executive housekeepers Flight attendants Home economics teachers Special education teachers	Artists Military officers Sales personnel Scientists Writers	MERCHANDISING	Business education teachers Buyers Department store managers Food service managers Purchasing agents Sales personnel	Artists Biologists Chemists Geologists Physicists Sociologists

(Continued)

TABLE 5-4 (*continued*)

Scale	Some occupations scoring high	Some occupations scoring low	Scale	Some occupations scoring high	Some occupations scoring low
MILITARY ACTIVITIES	Airplane pilots Executive house-keepers Military officers Police officers	Actors Anthropologists Artists Musicians Psychologists Sociologists	SALES	Business education teachers Buyers Department store buyers Funeral directors Sales managers Sales personnel	Anthropologists Artists Biologists Geologists Physicists Sociologists
MUSIC/DRAMATICS	Actors Actresses Artists Flight attendants Librarians Music performers Music teachers Nightclub entertainers	Beauticians Factory workers Farmers Military personnel Physical education teachers	SCIENCE	Astronomers Biologists Chemists College professors Geologists Physicians Physicists	Artists Beauticians Business executives Interior decorators Public relations directors Sales personnel Writers
NATURE	Animal husbandry professors Biologists Farmers Foresters Veterinarians Vocational agriculture teachers	Accountants Business executives Fashion models Nightclub entertainers Sales personnel	SOCIAL SERVICE	Guidance counselors Ministers Priests Social science teachers Social workers Special education teachers YMCA/YWCA directors	Architects Chemists Engineers Geographers Geologists Interior decorators Military officers Physicists
OFFICE PRACTICES	Bankers Business education teachers Credit managers IRS agents Office workers Telephone operators	Anthropologists Architects Artists Geologists Photographers Writers	TEACHING	Elementary teachers Foreign language teachers Guidance counselors Home economics teachers Music teachers School administrators Special education teachers	Advertising executives Farmers Laboratory technicians Sales personnel Skilled trades
PUBLIC SPEAKING	Elected public officials Lawyers Ministers Public relations directors Sales personnel Speech pathologists	Artists Beauticians Carpenters Farmers Laboratory technicians Physicists Sewing machine operators	WRITING	Advertising executives English teachers Librarians Ministers Public relations directors Reporters Writers	Carpenters Factory workers Farmers Physical education teachers Vocational agriculture teachers
RELIGIOUS ACTIVITIES	Directors, Christian education Ministers Nuns Priests YMCA/YWCA directors	Artists Chemists Geographers Geologists Physicians Psychologists			

Johansson (1972) have shown that consistency between scores on the Basic Interest Scales and the Occupational Scales leads to greater predictive accuracy. A student with a high score on one of the sales-area Occupational Scales—such as REALTOR or LIFE INSURANCE AGENT—and a high score on the SALES Basic Interest Scale is more likely to enter sales work than is a student with an equally high score on these same Occupational Scales but a low or mod-erate score on the SALES Basic Interest Scale. Students with the latter pattern of scores are more likely to enter a people-oriented but non-sales occupation, such as public relations.

Inconsistency with Respect to the Occupational Scales

From his research on the relationships between the Basic Interest Scales and the Occupational Scales,

Johnson (1972) reported that approximately 20 percent of SVIB profiles exhibit one or more apparent inconsistencies between the Basic Interest and Occupational scales. Because these profiles will often crop up, counselors must understand the implications of the inconsistencies and how to explain them to the respondents.

The inconsistencies appear as highly contrasted scores on pairs of scales that are obviously related, such as ART and FINE ARTIST, MATHEMATICS and MATHEMATICIAN, MILITARY ACTIVITIES and ARMY OFFICER. Such situations provide excellent examples of the effects of the different strategies used to construct the Basic Interest and Occupational Scales; properly interpreted, they can give the student (and the counselor) considerable insight into what the scores mean for each type of scale. That is, the inconsistency can be turned to positive advantage.

An example: Mathematics/Mathematician. The Basic Interest Scales reflect the respondent's answers to items directly concerned with certain well-defined areas of activity; the score on the MATHEMATICS Basic Scale, for example, is based on responses to only nine items, all heavily mathematical in nature. The "Like" responses for these items are all weighted positively, the "Dislikes" negatively; thus, the only way an individual can score high on the MATHEMATICS scale is by indicating "Like" to most of the specifically mathematical items, and the only way to score low is by indicating "Dislike" to most of these items.

In contrast, the Occupational Scales are much more heterogeneous in content. The male MATHEMATICIAN Occupational Scale includes 69 items covering a wide range of subjects and activities. Each item was included because mathematicians responded differently to it than men-in-general did. (The female MATHEMATICIAN scale was analogously constructed.)

The heterogeneity of item content of the Occupational Scales is illustrated in the following sample of items from the MATHEMATICIAN Occupational Scale:

Items weighted positively

Astronomer	*Geometry*
Author of technical books	*Physics*
Designer, electronic equipment	*Symphony concerts*
Scientific research worker	*Teaching adults*
Statistician	

Items weighted negatively

Auctioneer	*Machine shop supervisor*
Advertising executive	*Fishing*
Employment manager	*Boxing*
Sports reporter	*Drilling in a military company*
Office manager	*Going to church*
Life insurance agent	*Leading a scout troop*
Manager, Chamber of	*Night clubs*
Commerce	*Planning a large party*
Playground director	*Giving first aid assistance*
Secret Service agent	

Again, these items were included in the MATHEMATICIAN scale because (and only because) of the large difference in response frequencies between mathematicians and men-in-general; there was no attempt

to screen them intuitively for any special type of content.

Both the number and the diversity of the items emphasize the many ways male mathematicians differ from other men in their interests. Mathematicians are particularly interesting in having many more of their items weighted negatively than most occupations do; they are, in a sense, "Dislikers." Consequently, one way of scoring high on the MATHEMATICIAN scale, or "looking like a mathematician," is to answer "Dislike" to all the negatively weighted items in the list, and thus to share the aversions of mathematicians—a different way of expressing commonality of interests than is generally the case. This is a valuable illustration of the psychometric differences between the Basic Interest and Occupational Scales, for one cannot score high on a Basic Interest Scale by reporting a particular pattern of aversions.

An analogous explanation holds for other pairs of scales where apparent inconsistencies can occur—ART and FINE ARTIST, SOCIAL SERVICE and SOCIAL WORKER, MILITARY ACTIVITIES and ARMY OFFICER. The explanation is always the same: the Basic Interest Scales are homogeneous, and high scores can be earned only by indicating preferences for those activities; the Occupational Scales are heterogeneous, and high scores can be earned in many different ways, including reporting the same pattern of dislikes that people in the indicated occupation do.

If a conflict occurs between related scales of the two types, the Basic Interest Scale score will usually be high and the related Occupational Scale score low; seldom will the inverse occur.

Interpreting the inconsistencies. Conflicting scores on the profile provide an opportunity to discuss the all-encompassing nature of occupations; they emphasize vividly that interest in one particular activity is not sufficient for a person to enjoy the occupational environment surrounding that activity. An intense interest in mathematics is only one element in the interests of professional mathematicians; artists are unique in ways other than their intense interest in artistic activities; people in social-service settings stand apart on factors other than "service-to-humanity" concerns.

Patterns of scores that appear to be inconsistencies are an asset to the system, because they literally force the counselor and the client to understand the meaning of the scales. Integrating the two types of scales in the discussion of the profile leads to the realization that they are reflecting interests in two different, but related, ways—a realization that in turn leads to more accurate interpretation.

Basic Interest Scales and Leisure Interests

The Basic Interest Scales may be used to help a client explore not only vocational interests but also avocational interests, and counselors should encourage their clients to consider both work and leisure interests as they examine their SCII results.

TABLE 5-5

Test-Retest Reliability Statistics for the SCII Basic Interest Scales

Scale	Two-week statistics (N = 106 women, 74 men)					Thirty-day statistics (N = 35 women, 67 men)					Three-year statistics (N = 65 women, 75 men)				
	Test-retest correlation[a]	Test		Retest		Test-retest correlation[b]	Test		Retest		Test-retest correlation[c]	Test		Retest	
		Mean	S.D.	Mean	S.D.		Mean	S.D.	Mean	S.D.		Mean	S.D.	Mean	S.D.
AGRICULTURE	.87	50	9.9	51	9.6	.84	50	9.1	49	8.8	.81	51	9.3	51	9.5
NATURE	.92	49	11.2	49	11.4	.87	49	9.2	49	9.6	.81	51	10.5	51	10.1
ADVENTURE	.90	52	10.9	54	11.4	.89	52	9.7	53	9.5	.81	49	10.3	49	9.9
MILITARY ACTIVITIES	.83	48	9.1	49	9.9	.90	50	11.0	51	11.8	.82	51	10.2	51	9.8
MECHANICAL ACTIVITIES	.92	47	10.6	48	11.4	.90	50	8.9	50	9.2	.87	50	11.2	51	11.4
SCIENCE	.91	48	9.8	49	10.7	.85	50	9.0	51	9.2	.84	52	9.6	51	10.1
MATHEMATICS	.91	47	9.6	48	10.2	.89	49	10.7	49	10.3	.92	51	11.3	51	11.5
MEDICAL SCIENCE	.86	49	10.8	50	11.2	.82	51	9.2	52	9.5	.74	51	8.9	51	9.9
MEDICAL SERVICE	.82	51	10.1	52	10.8	.86	49	10.5	50	10.9	.75	49	9.3	48	9.9
MUSIC/DRAMA	.91	50	11.8	51	12.0	.93	51	10.5	52	10.9	.84	51	11.3	51	11.8
ART	.91	50	10.6	50	11.2	.91	51	10.6	53	10.6	.87	50	11.1	51	11.6
WRITING	.93	46	10.8	47	11.3	.87	51	9.2	53	9.3	.83	51	9.5	51	10.2
TEACHING	.89	47	11.0	48	11.8	.83	51	9.7	51	10.0	.78	50	10.0	48	10.2
SOCIAL SERVICE	.90	50	10.5	50	11.2	.79	51	8.9	50	9.4	.80	47	10.1	46	9.6
ATHLETICS	.92	51	9.7	53	10.5	.89	49	9.1	50	9.1	.91	49	10.7	48	10.7
DOMESTIC ARTS	.93	49	13.7	50	13.9	.86	50	10.0	50	10.6	.82	49	12.5	50	12.0
RELIGIOUS ACTIVITIES	.92	49	10.6	49	10.9	.91	47	9.5	47	9.5	.86	49	10.4	49	10.4
PUBLIC SPEAKING	.88	47	8.9	48	9.9	.89	53	9.1	53	9.3	.83	50	10.3	50	10.6
LAW/POLITICS	.91	47	9.5	48	10.4	.89	53	9.5	54	10.0	.82	49	10.3	49	10.3
MERCHANDISING	.87	47	9.1	48	10.2	.89	53	10.8	54	11.0	.76	50	9.4	50	9.7
SALES	.83	48	7.7	49	8.6	.85	51	9.3	52	9.7	.82	49	9.9	49	10.0
BUSINESS MANAGEMENT	.87	45	10.0	47	11.0	.83	54	10.1	54	10.4	.81	50	9.5	50	10.1
OFFICE PRACTICES	.92	49	10.4	49	10.7	.84	47	7.8	49	9.1	.84	48	10.1	49	10.4

[a] Median correlation = .91.   [b] Median correlation = .88.   [c] Median correlation = .82.

Cairo (1979), in a study designed to determine the validity of the Basic Interest Scales, found that the scales identify leisure interests as well as they identify occupational interests. Although the scales used to measure leisure activities were in most cases different from the scales used to measure occupations, 79 percent of the subjects had Basic Interest Scale scores that were congruent with occupational or avocational activities; and about half of the subjects who had congruent measured interests and occupations also had congruent measured interests and leisure activities.

Cairo's findings suggest that the Basic Interest Scales of the SCII may be used to explore the entire interest pattern of an individual rather than vocational interests alone.

Test-Retest Reliability

The median test-retest correlations for the Basic Interest Scales, over two-week, thirty-day, and three-year periods, are .91, .88, and .82, respectively, as reported in Table 5-5. Correlations of this magnitude indicate substantial short-term stability. Analogous statistics for the General Occupational Themes and Occupational Scales are reported in Table 4-3 and Tables 6-4 and 6-5, respectively.

Test-retest reliability of the earlier SVIB Basic Interest Scales was thoroughly studied. Generally the correlations range from the .50's, for 16-year-olds re-

tested 36 years later, to the .90's, for samples tested and retested over a few weeks. The correlations vary mainly with the age of the person at the time of the first testing and the length of the retest interval, with the first factor being more important. A recent study of high school and college students (Hansen and Stocco, in press) once again demonstrates the effect of age on test-retest reliabilities. Although Basic Interest Scale median three-year test-retest correlations were lower for the high school students (r = .56) and college students (r = .68) than for adults (r = .82), the correlations were nonetheless sufficiently high to warrant the use of the Basic Interest Scales with young adults. But especially with high school students, some score changes are likely over a three-year period.

Changes with Age

Most of the SCII Basic Interest Scales are quite similar to the older SVIB scales; consequently, research findings based on earlier SVIB scales can be generalized to SCII scales. The following discussion does that, using the results from several samples tested two, three, or even four times over periods of two weeks to 36 years.

Stability over time. The most important finding is that mean scores on these scales are usually quite stable, even over long time spans, seldom shifting more than 2 or 3 points except in certain situations discussed below. Of course, these are averages; some individuals show much greater changes. In working with individual scores on these scales, the counselor must be aware of the possibility of such changes; still, on the average, stability, not change, is the norm.

Scores increasing over time. The level of scores on most of the Basic Interest Scales tends to increase slightly from age 15 into adulthood. Teenagers tend to mark "Like" to a smaller number of items than adults do; why this is so is not clear. Probably because students have not been exposed yet to a wide range of occupational activities, they tend to say "Indifferent" more often. As their experience expands, so does the number of their likes. One could suppose that an increasing self-confidence and sense of personal identity are also involved.

The general increase in number of likes is most apparent in areas where students accumulate the greatest experience. The most obvious example is the TEACHING scale, which shows the largest gain across many different samples; the gains are most evident in those samples continuing further in school, especially those continuing on to advanced professional degrees. Other scales showing substantial gains among samples continuing in school are the ART, MUSIC/DRAMATICS, and WRITING scales, those generally reflecting a liberal-arts orientation.

Another scale that shows a mild increase in mean score into the adult years is the NATURE scale, which contains items such as *Gardening, Raising flowers and vegetables,* and other outdoor activities. Many people in all occupations show an increased interest in such activities as they grow older.

Scores decreasing with age. The only scale showing a consistent, sizable decrease with age is the ADVENTURE scale. On the average, people score about 10 points lower—a full standard deviation—on this scale as adults than they did as teenagers. This decrease, along with increasing scores on the NATURE scale, reflects the general mellowing of people's interests with age, particularly a decreasing interest in physically risky activities. Related scales showing smaller decreases are the ATHLETICS and MILITARY ACTIVITIES scales—again, scales covering physically demanding and adventuresome activities.

These changes reflect the aging process; one of its components is an increased reluctance to participate in rough, boisterous, physically dangerous pursuits.

Change across time in specific samples. Occasionally, some interesting changes appear in particular samples, changes that evidently occur only within those samples. The best documented example concerns medical school students. Several samples were tested on entrance to medical school and retested at exit four years later. The results, which were quite consistent over several schools, showed a sizable decrease on the SOCIAL SERVICE, MEDICAL SERVICE, SCIENCE, and RELIGIOUS ACTIVITIES scales and a modest increase on the ADVENTURE scale. The increase on ADVENTURE is

quite significant, for these medical students are the only samples ever tested that showed an *increase* with age on this scale; usually this scale shows a substantial drop.

One explanation might be that these students, who were first tested upon entering medical school, were trying either consciously or unconsciously to appear as intense, dedicated young scientists, and as humanists with strong social-service drives. Consequently, they scored high on these scales, perhaps—to some extent—artificially high. They also may have repressed some of their youthful energy and recklessness, thus scoring artificially low on the ADVENTURE scale. Four years later, as graduating seniors, they were perhaps more realistic about their interests in both science and social service—which were still quite high but no longer so overwhelming. The increase on the ADVENTURE scale, unique to these samples, reflects the same reaction in the contrasting direction; generally, medical school students were more open, daring, and less conscientious as seniors than as freshmen.

Almost certainly, these trends do *not* represent simple regression toward the mean, which has not shown up in any other samples tested and retested with these scales. Most likely, these decreases in mean scores were reflecting some human process.

More information on these students and their scores can be found in the *Handbook;* they provide a model of how the Basic Interest Scales can be used to study changes within a population.

Interpreting the Basic Interest Scales

The Basic Interest Scales are easily interpreted, since their item content is straightforward: the items on the ART scale are concerned exclusively with artistic activities; the items on the MECHANICAL ACTIVITIES scale, with mechanical activities; those on the SALES scale, with sales. High scores can be achieved only by answering "Like" to the items on a scale, low scores only by answering "Dislike." (For more on interpretation, see Chapter 10.)

Profile plotting. The plotting arrangement on the profile is designed to make the scores easy to interpret, in a normative sense. Plotted asterisks in the extreme ranges indicate the most noteworthy Basic Interest scores on each profile. For each scale, the distributions of scores for the Men-in-General and Women-in-General samples are indicated by the horizontal bars, as discussed above, under "Norming the Scales."

High and low scores. Experienced workers usually average 58 or above on the Basic Interest Scale that most closely corresponds to their particular occupation: artists and interior decorators average 58 or above on the ART scale; ministers, 58 or above on the RELIGIOUS ACTIVITIES scale; and lawyers, elected public officials, and public administrators, 58 or above on the LAW/POLITICS scale. Thus, scores that high and above can be considered high.

Conversely, scores of 42 and below can be considered low. Scores at this level indicate that the respondent reported substantially more dislikes than average for the activities represented by the scale.

Relationships to the LP, IP, and DP percentages. The level of scores on the Basic Interest Scales is influenced by the percentages of "Like," "Indifferent," and "Dislike" responses given. Because the items on these scales are weighted +1 for the "Like" response and −1 for "Dislike," people who give many more "Like" than "Dislike" responses will usually have higher scores on these scales. Those who give an unusually high number of "Like" responses—60 to 70 percent or higher—will have several scores in the High or Very High ranges. But although these high scores indicate a positive response to a large number of activities in each of the designated areas, they probably are not as important indicators of strong interests as are scores of the same level that are the *only* high scores among the Basic Interest Scales.

This artifact means that allowances should be made in profile interpretation when a person has responded with a high percentage of "Likes" or "Dislikes." In such cases, the *ranking* of scores must be considered, as well as the absolute *level* of scores. The three or four highest—and the three or four lowest—scores are worth noting, no matter the level, since these are the areas where the individual has most consistently responded "Like" or "Dislike."

Sensitivity to overall level of "Like" and "Dislike" responses is a minor disadvantage of the SCII item format, but only minor, since not many individuals give extreme numbers of either "Like" or "Dislike" responses. (For some data on this point, see Chapter 9.) The problem could be eliminated entirely, of course, by the use of a forced-choice item format that requires the respondent to give a fixed number of likes and dislikes. However, forced-choice formats have serious drawbacks: they irritate respondents; the decisiveness they force upon the respondent is artificial; they therefore tend to produce scales with lower reliabilities; and they have no demonstrated advantage in validity.

Further, people do differ dramatically both in the numbers of activities they like and in how they go about taking pencil-and-paper tests, and this in itself is useful information. We must learn to use it, not ignore it.

Underlying themes. The Basic Interest Scales were developed to help users in the difficult task of interpreting the profile scores. The pre-1969 versions of the profile had no Basic Interest Scales, only Occupational Scales, and interpretation proceeded by inferring the underlying themes of the respondent's interests from the pattern of scores on the Occupational Scales. Because those scales are complex in content, interpretation was difficult, especially for inexperienced counselors. And even experienced counselors often could not be sure which factors had led to the observed patterns of scores.

The Basic Interest Scales are particularly useful in providing a direct reflection of the clustering in the person's responses. Used in conjunction with the Occupational Scales, they provide direct information about major themes in the individual's interests, which can then be mapped into the occupational world via scores on the Occupational Scales.

But again, the rationale for selecting items for the Basic Interest Scales is fundamentally different from that used in making up the Occupational Scales: the former use only "direct" items (*Artist*, for example, for the ART scale); the latter use both "direct" and "indirect" items (including, for example, the minister's aversion to *Poker*). The discussion above, "Inconsistency with Respect to the Occupational Scales," shows how this distinction can be turned to advantage in interpreting the profile.

An example: social-service interests. The Basic Interest Scales can be used to sharpen profile interpretation beyond Occupational Scales. For example, one presumably established finding in interest measurement is that as people grow older, their level of social-service interests increases. This "truth" was first established in Strong's longitudinal study of Stanford students over 18 years; his data showed that their scores increased on the old Group V scales, the Social Service cluster. This finding appealed particularly to social-service types such as psychologists, possibly because it implied, "As people get older and wiser, they come around more to an appreciation of what we [social service types] do." Perhaps for this reason, this finding was commented on frequently in counseling sessions and in training programs for new counselors.

That comforting thought was shaken, however, by the development of the Basic Interest Scales, including the SOCIAL SERVICE scale, which contains items such as *Social worker, Sociology, Work in a YMCA*, and *Contributing to charities*. When this scale was used to score the SVIB test-retest samples, not one of them showed any noteworthy increase of scores on this scale with age. Because that was an unexpected finding, the figures were studied carefully. The changes that did occur in these samples, which are reported in detail in Chapter 5 of the *Handbook*, were increases on the TEACHING, MEDICAL SERVICE, ART, MUSIC, and WRITING scales. Because these areas are popular among people in social-service occupations, items from them appear on their Occupational Scales; consequently, when interests in these areas increase, the Occupational Scale scores are raised. Although these areas do have a social-service flavor to them, especially the TEACHING and MEDICAL SERVICE scales, the dominant theme here is *not* social service *but rather a more generalized cultural interest*. By using the specific Basic Interest Scales to help explain the changes observed in the more global Occupational Scales, we can better understand the change that occurred. The two scale types, then, are complementary; they are more effective used jointly than either is used separately.

CHAPTER SIX

The Occupational Scales

The Occupational Scales have been the bulwark of the Strong inventory since its inception in 1927. Strong constructed them by comparing the item responses of an occupational sample with those of a general reference sample, identifying items yielding large response differences between the two samples, and then drawing these items together into a scale. The scale was normed on the occupational sample, and raw scores were converted to standard scores on the basis of the occupational sample's distribution.

Essentially the same methods are used today. Strong's original techniques·have been refined, and the important ingredients in scale construction are more systematized, but the empirical brilliance of the approach can be traced to E. K. Strong.

The 1981 Revision

Between 1927 and 1969, the SVIB was revised infrequently—only twice for the male form (1938 and 1966) and twice for the female form (1946 and 1969). Thus, the 1974 SCII and the 1981 SCII have emerged from the most active period of research in the inventory's history. One of the major goals of the 1981 revision was to match all extant male-normed Occupational Scales with the corresponding female-normed scales, and vice versa; another goal was to update the 1974 scales that had been developed with criterion samples collected prior to 1966; a final objective was to add new occupations.

Equalizing male- and female-normed Occupational Scales. The 1981 SVIB-SCII profile carries 162 Occupational Scales representing 85 occupations. All but eight of the 162 scales are in matched pairs: for each of 77 occupations there is a scale based on a male-normed criterion sample and a scale based on a female-normed sample; this more than doubles the analogous number of matched pairs (37 occupations) on the 1974 SCII. Of the new scales on the profile, 17 are female scales developed to match existing male scales:

AIR FORCE OFFICER	MINISTER
ARCHITECT	NAVY OFFICER
BIOLOGIST	PERSONNEL DIRECTOR
CHAMBER OF COMMERCE	PHOTOGRAPHER
EXECUTIVE	POLICE OFFICER
CHIROPRACTOR	PUBLIC ADMINISTRATOR
DEPARTMENT STORE	PURCHASING AGENT
MANAGER	REALTOR
FARMER	SCHOOL ADMINISTRATOR
FORESTER	

Eleven new male scales have been developed to match existing female scales:

ART TEACHER	OCCUPATIONAL THERAPIST
BEAUTICIAN	PHYSICAL EDUCATION
CHEMIST	TEACHER
EXECUTIVE HOUSEKEEPER	PHYSICIST
FLIGHT ATTENDANT	RADIOLOGIC TECHNOLOGIST
FOREIGN LANGUAGE	YMCA DIRECTOR
TEACHER	

Every effort was made to obtain criterion samples for the development of matching scales for every occupation, generally with success; but that was not always possible. For example, the American Dental Assistants Association was very willing to assist our attempts to sample male dental assistants, and offered the names and addresses of the *two* men who belonged to the ADAA. Thinking that the military might provide a source, we undertook a pilot study of a dozen male dental assistants stationed around the country. Universally, they reported that they disliked being dental assistants, had not chosen to be trained in dental assisting but rather had been assigned arbitrarily to that specialty by the military, and would not pursue careers as dental assistants once they left the service.

Four occupations are represented only by female-normed scales, compared to 20 on the 1974 SCII profile; four are represented only by male-normed scales, compared to 30 in 1974. These eight scales have proved useful for occupational exploration in the past, and they have been retained on the profile to augment the SCII occupations representing the world of work.

Occupational Scales normed only for females are

DENTAL ASSISTANT	HOME ECONOMICS TEACHER
DENTAL HYGIENIST	SECRETARY

Scales normed only for males are

AGRIBUSINESS MANAGER	SKILLED CRAFTS
INVESTMENT FUND	VOCATIONAL AGRICULTURE
MANAGER	TEACHER

Updating criterion samples. Any scale that had been developed before 1971 used samples collected on the T399 and TW398 forms. This meant that the SCII item-response data for these scales were incomplete, since samples collected on T399 responded to only 254 of the SCII's 325 items, and those collected on TW398 responded to only 249 items. Although the scales developed with these reduced item pools are reliable—testimony to the excellence of the empirical technique of scale development—scales drawing upon response data to all of the items tend to be longer and therefore even more stable.

Occupations do not change much, across time, in their item-endorsement frequency. Nonetheless, criterion samples should be updated periodically to detect such fluctuations as occasionally occur. Thus, all scales based on criterion samples collected prior to 1966 have been revised.

All of the new scales are based on criterion groups tested with the T325 booklet. Whereas in 1974, when the SCII was introduced, all but 15 of the 124 Occupational Scales were based on criterion samples tested on the old single-sex inventories, for the 1981 edition all but 35 of the 162 scales are based on samples tested on the merged-form T325. (Data on all criterion groups are given in Appendix C.)

Adding occupations. Twelve new occupations (24 scales) have been added to the profile. In selecting these occupations, special attention was paid to predictions of future growth and opportunities. For example, faster-than-average growth is predicted for geographers, geologists, marketing executives, nursing home administrators, public relations directors, restaurant managers, special education teachers, and systems analysts; all of these have been added to the profile, for both sexes.

Other Occupational Scales have been added for other reasons: sociologists were collected to develop a scale to replace the more general SOCIAL SCIENTIST scale, IRS agents to add to the limited number of occupations coded Conventional on the profile, elected public officials in response to burgeoning interest in our political system, and commercial artists to provide a more applied alternative to the FINE ARTIST scale.

Characteristics of the Occupational Samples

The first step in the construction of an Occupational Scale is testing a sample from that occupation; and because the characteristics of the sample greatly influence the characteristics of the resulting scale, the sample should be selected with care. Through years of research with the SVIB, the following sample characteristics have emerged as important.

Job satisfaction. Because the inventory is so often used in career planning, the eventual scale should reflect the interests of *satisfied* workers. The most practical way to ascertain job satisfaction for the purposes of scale construction is to use the item *Do you like your work?* (I couldn't be more satisfied; I like it; I am indifferent to it; I dislike it), and then eliminate from the sample any respondent choosing either of the last two options.

Success. Whenever possible, some measure of success or achievement should be used to screen the sample; the measure might be sales-production figures, or ratings by superiors, or an index of formal achievement, such as earning an advanced degree or being licensed or certified. The purpose is not to restrict the sample to outstanding people, but to exclude the bottom 10 or 15 percent of the working population—the inadequate practitioners—from the sample.

Age. Samples are restricted to people between the ages of 25 and 55, where possible. These limits exclude the very young members of the occupation, whose interests may not have stabilized, and the older members, who entered the occupation several decades earlier.

A study by Hansen (1978) examined possible effects of age differences on measured occupational interests. She studied three age groups (26-35; 36-45; 46-55) for each of six occupational samples that represented a mixture of traditional and untraditional occupations for one sex or the other. Her findings indicated that people of different ages who are in the same occupation do not have different interests. Nor was any evidence found to suggest a female/male role reversal in the home: younger men are not beginning to say "Like" to more domestic activities than older men do, and no large differences existed between age groups on the Academic Orientation (now Academic Comfort) scale. Thus, the current practice of combining people from across a wide age range into one occupational criterion group is both suitable and valid.

Experience. Almost all of the SCII samples are restricted to workers who have been on the job at least three years. Experience is a crude but effective index of many pertinent qualities, and screening for it helps purify the final sample. After three years, workers know enough about their occupation to answer validly the question whether they like their jobs. Thus, persistence in an occupation for three years represents, at the minimum, a modest level of both achievement and satisfaction.

"Performing in the typical manner." The samples are also screened to reject people who are not performing the occupation in the typical way. A physician who is now a writer would not be included with the physician sample; a lawyer who is now an actor would likewise be rejected. Although this circumstance usually affects less than 1 or 2 percent of an occupational base, some address lists carry numerous "nontypical" individuals.

An unintended criterion. Since most of the data collection is done by mail, a criterion that inevitably imposes itself is willingness to cooperate with the research project. Self-selection—the automatic implication of cooperation—raises the question of sample bias, which is worth discussing at length.

Bias in the Occupational Samples

Random influences. When questionnaires are collected by mail, as is usually the case, a few members of the intended sample can be expected not to respond because of some current, usually transient, disruption in their lives. Years of interest-measurement research, requiring large-scale sample collection, indicate that this particular influence is harmless. The reasons people fail to respond are legion: most of them are completely irrelevant to the research. On any address list, for example, a few people will be deceased, and their failure to respond scarcely constitutes harmful bias. Others do not respond because they are in the hospital, or their spouse is, or they are in the middle of an exhausting divorce, or they have just won a trip to the Caribbean, or their house was flooded, or their dog chewed up the test booklet—all of these are circumstances reported in past SVIB research projects, and all are apparently random events unrelated to any sample bias. Another 2 or 3 percent will not respond because they are opposed to psychological tests, questionnaires, surveys, opinion polls, and other "nefarious devices of manipulative social scientists." For these and similar reasons, about 15 percent of most samples will be inaccessible for research; thus the maximum return possible is about 85 percent.

Self-selection. That some recipients fail to respond may actually be an advantage. A few do not answer simply because they think they do not belong in the criterion sample: if the covering letter states that we are attempting to develop a job-interest profile of physical therapists, and one of the recipients is trying to leave this field for another, he/she may conclude, correctly, that we would not want his/her response. Another source of probable positive bias is general identification with the occupation: although there are no hard data on this point, the people most committed to their occupation tend to cooperate more earnestly with research studying the occupation than do those who feel more indifferent about it; to whatever extent this bias exists, it is desirable.

The initial SVIB samples, collected by E. K. Strong in the 1920's, 1930's, and 1940's, capitalized on these sources of respondent bias. Though he never reported, or perhaps even calculated, his percent returns, informal comments by Strong suggest that the effective rate of return in his research was about 25 percent. In a letter to a student who had asked about using the SVIB with an occupational sample, Strong commented that about four inventories had to be mailed out to get one usable one in return. That estimate agrees with more recent research: there is no evidence in Strong's research files to suggest that he ever used follow-up letters, and our experience at Minnesota has been that a one-time mailing, with no special care, will result in about a 25- to 30-percent return. Because Strong's samples have proved useful, one can conclude that the sampling bias was not too debilitating. Indeed, some self-selection may be an advantage.

From a well-executed mailing, one can expect about a 35- to 40-percent return, assuming an up-to-date address list, a good covering letter, and one follow-up postcard. To push the return rate higher requires an inordinate amount of time, energy, and money, with

no guarantee that the quality of the final sample will be improved—and the uneasy suspicion that the quality could in fact be lowered (the survey mavericks could be occupational mavericks as well).

Practical constraints. In inventory research, samples are drawn from the real world, and the investigator has to work within practical constraints; that is, the samples cannot always be collected in precisely the preferred way. Simply to reach 400 bona fide actors, let alone persuade them to fill in a psychological test, would be a fair achievement, since there is no place to go to find a mailing list for that occupation. Theater programs or advertisements in *Variety* offer some possibilities, but thorny problems arise in ascertaining age, experience, and job satisfaction, not to mention the sample's willingness to cooperate. The same problems occur with many other occupations. Consequently, one takes one's data where one finds them, and the sampling methods used cannot always be described precisely. Sampling issues have often been overemphasized: the crucial issue is not the sampling method, but the characteristics of the final sample.

Reporting of return rates. One criticism leveled at earlier editions of the SVIB *Manual* is that the percent of returned forms for each occupational sample has not been reported. There are two reasons for the omission: First, in some cases the figure is not available. For example, if biologists are tested by handing out test booklets to everyone in sight at a national biological convention, what is the percent return? Second, the return rate is a meaningless number. If 1,000 forms are sent to entertainers featured in nightclub advertisements and only 100 are returned, and if, concurrently, 500 forms are sent to military officers through official channels and 450 are returned, does a comparison between the 10-percent and 90-percent returns say anything useful about the people who do or do not respond? Not likely. These results say more about the collection mechanism than about the people involved.

Quality of address lists. As noted above, many extraneous factors influence the percent usable response in an occupational sampling. The most important of these is the quality of the address list. If one is working with a professional organization with a well-established membership—an organization with annual dues, perhaps a professional journal, and an annual convention—then the quality of addresses will be high, and one can count on about a 50-percent return. But if the national organization is loose, the return will be much lower. (One address list included names that were 20 years out of date; some quiet investigation revealed that this organization benefited in lobbying with its state legislature by showing as large a membership as possible, and for this reason no one was ever removed from the roster.)

Quality of the final sample. Percent return, then, has practically nothing to do with the quality of the final sample. A low rate of return does not necessarily project a poor sample, nor does a 100-percent response guarantee a useful sample. The payoff lies in the *characteristics* of the sample, no matter how the people were surveyed; and in close attention to the issues of job satisfaction, experience, and "performing the occupation in the typical manner."

Some factors that do *not* relate to sample quality are race, geographic location, method tested (whether by mail or in person), and again, percentage return. Randomness, or representativeness, or precision in selection of the sample is not necessarily the best predictor of whether the sample will meet the criteria of experience, success, and satisfaction. In the end, the quality of the sample used for the construction of a scale is reflected in the validity data—the scale works, or it does not.

The particular characteristics of each SCII occupational sample, or criterion group, are reported in Appendix C.

The General Reference Sample: Men- or Women-in-General

A key feature of the Strong scoring system is the general reference sample, which is for all practical purposes *two* samples: Men-in-General (MIG) and Women-in-General (WIG). These samples are used to determine the popularity of each item across the general population—usually termed base-rate popularity—for comparison with the popularity of that item within a specific occupational sample. Those items that provoke one response from the occupational sample and another from the reference sample are the items used in that occupation's Occupational Scale.

Item popularity. The reference sample is necessary because the base-rate popularity varies considerably from item to item; to ignore this variance would be to add considerable error to the scales. For example, if the scoring system weighted items with respect only to their popularity within the various occupations, the most popular items would appear in most of the scales, and their discriminating power would be reduced or even nullified. Conversely, the relatively unpopular items would appear in so few scales as to be almost useless. Thus, using a reference sample to control for item popularity results in a scoring system that reacts more to differences between occupations than to similarities among them.

If this technique were not employed, the most obvious result would be the domination of the scales by a large, general "popularity" factor. The intercorrelations between the Occupational Scales can be used to identify "popularity" factors; if the correlations are all positive, the usual explanation is that no correction for item popularity was used.

Composition of the general reference samples. The composition of the reference samples is critical to the development of valid, useful scales. Conceptually, the two reference samples should be located at the intersection of all the dimensions within the domain of interests. Operationally, the goal is to select a sample that falls at the mean of all the item-response distributions, such as those shown in Chapter 3. To find such a sample for the earlier SVIB MIG and WIG samples, roughly 20 individuals were drawn from each of 50 occupations for each sex; thus each sample contained 1,000 individuals, one sample consisting of men who responded to the men's booklet, the other of women who responded to the women's booklet. (The precise composition of the two samples is described in the *Handbook for the SVIB*.)

When the two booklets were merged into the SVIB-SCII booklet in 1974, these two samples, though large and well selected, could no longer be used because neither of them had responded to all of the items in the combined booklet. But they were clearly the model to be emulated. Thus, in the development of the new SCII reference samples, the goal was to match the composition and characteristics of the old MIG and WIG samples—to generate new samples that had item-response percentages identical to those of the old samples on those items that were common to the old (SVIB) and new (SCII) booklets. The rationale was that if new samples could be matched with the old ones on the 250 common items, then the responses of the new samples to the 75 new items could be assumed to represent roughly the response percentages that the old, carefully selected samples would have given, had they responded to the new items. To achieve this matching, several hundred men and women were tested with the new inventory, wherever they could be found—in occupational groups, university classes, neighborhood clubs, among friends, friends of friends, schoolteachers, in the local Jaycees, Army Reserve units, and so forth. This diverse pool was fed into a computer that was programmed to select a sample randomly and compare it with the old in-general samples on the items to which both groups had responded (for the MIG, 254 items; for the WIG, 249 items); and to continue doing this until new samples matching the old had been found. Then, the assumption was made—in the absence of a more reasonable approach —that the percentage response of these new samples to the new SCII items was roughly what that of the former in-general samples would have been. The new samples became the reference samples, with the considerable advantage that item popularities for all items, based on the responses of samples almost identical to the previous MIG and WIG samples, are now available for both sexes.

The new samples, 300 males and 300 females, were designated the 1973 MIG and WIG samples. When combined, they were the 1973 General Reference Sample (GRS), and their utility has not diminished —they are the samples used in norming the 113 new Occupational Scales for the 1981 edition of the SCII. The mean age for the MIG is 33.4 years; for the WIG, 35.2 years. The mean educational level of both groups is two years beyond high school.

Scale Construction: Item Weights

Once an occupational sample is tested, the first step in item analysis is to compare the sample's item responses with those of the appropriate-sex reference sample. This is done by computing the percent of both samples answering "Like," "Indifferent," and "Dislike" to each of the 325 items, and then calculating the differences. The results for a given item might be as follows:

Sample	Item-response percentages			
	Like	Indifferent	Dislike	Total
Occupational	20	35	45	100
Reference	40	40	20	100
Differences	−20	−5	+25	0

The next step is to assign scoring weights to these differences, and the technique used to accomplish this has changed through the years. For earlier versions of the scales, E. K. Strong used variable weights based on the ratio of the criterion- and reference-sample response percentages. Essentially, he calculated the ratio for each difference by dividing the response percentage of the occupational sample by that of the reference sample. When the ratio was large, a large scoring weight was assigned to that response; smaller ratios were assigned smaller weights. (This is only an approximation of the technique; for a more precise description, see Strong, 1943.) One problem with this technique is that it treated a comparison between 2 and 4 percent in the same manner as a comparison between 20 and 40 percent, because it was based on the *ratio* of the response percentages rather than the *magnitude* of the differences.

For his first scales, developed in 1927, Strong used ±30 weights: the largest ratios were assigned scoring weights of 30 or −30; the smallest ones, a weight of 0. Such a large range of weights made scoring very difficult, and because he could find no benefit in a large weight range, Strong dropped his weights to ±15 in 1930, then ±4 in 1938. Finally, in 1966, Campbell converted the scoring weights completely to unit weights of +1, 0, or −1. Although the concept of variable weights—varying according to the size of the differences in response percentages—is intuitively appealing, empirical comparisons between variable weights and unit weights show the latter to be just as effective and sometimes better (as, for example, in cross-validation studies with new samples). Consequently, the SCII system continues to be based completely on unit weights.

Reliability versus validity. Even since unit weights were adopted, the system of selecting and weighting items has varied in its details, because empirical scale construction always involves a trade-off between item validity and scale reliability: emphasizing the former, which is directly related to scale validity, produces short scales; emphasizing the latter, which is based on test-retest correlations, produces long scales. The rela-

tive importance attached to the two factors has changed from time to time, depending on the bias of the test reviser. Thus, if scale validity is stressed, only those items showing large differences between the criterion and reference samples are weighted; if scale reliability is stressed, then as many "good" items as possible are weighted, even those of moderate or low validity, because longer scales are more stable over time than shorter scales are. Unfortunately, there is no automatic procedure by which to resolve this trade-off. Many statistics can be adduced to demonstrate the presence of the dilemma, but its resolution even in this, the most empirical of tests, must be to some extent arbitrary.

In the past, more consideration has been given to scale reliability than to scale validity; stability in the scores was deemed more important than accuracy. In the development of the SCII, the strategy shifted slightly toward giving each of these factors roughly equal weight. The general goal was to find, for each Occupational Scale, about 60 items showing a 16-percent or larger difference between the criterion and reference samples; scales of this length have good test-retest reliabilities, and items showing this great a difference (16 percent or more) provide valid scales that are usually resistant to cross-validation shrinkage—when applied to new samples, their power to discriminate persists.

Rules for item weighting. Item selection and weighting for the SCII Occupational Scales proceeded as follows:

1. For each item in the inventory, the criterion group's response percentage for each of the three alternatives ("Like," "Indifferent," "Dislike") was calculated. The analogous percentages for the reference sample, either male or female as appropriate, were also calculated, and then subtracted from the criterion group's percentages. The resulting differences were used to identify the discriminating items.

2. Typically, 60 to 70 items showing a minimum difference of 16 percent between the criterion and reference samples were found. If more were available, the minimum cutoff was raised to 19 percent, or 20, or 21, until the number of items had dropped to roughly 65. In no case was the minimum lowered below 16 percent. The minimum cutoff ("Min. percent diff.") and number of items used, for each scale, are shown in Tables 6-1 and 6-2.

3. After the items were thus identified, the "Like" or "Dislike" response choice that showed the larger difference ("Like," for example) was weighted +1 or −1, depending on the direction of the difference; the opposing response choice ("Dislike") was then automatically weighted in the opposite direction, even if the percent difference of that particular response was not above the minimum cutoff (that is, no matter how small the empirical difference). This technique, which assumes each item to be a miniature dimension, increases the reliability of the scale about .03-.04 cor-

relational points and does not affect validity (percent overlap) either way.

4. Once the "Like" and "Dislike" choices for an item had been weighted, the "Indifferent" response choice was also weighted, but only if the difference between the samples on that response was 10 percent or more; if the difference was positive, the "Indifferent" response was weighted +1, and if it was negative, it was weighted −1. For those scales where the "Like" and "Dislike" minimum cutoff percentages had been raised, the "Indifferent" cutoff for weighting was also raised; for example, where the former had been raised to 21, the latter was raised to 13.

Scale Characteristics

The number of items weighted, and the minimum response-percentage difference used, for each 1981 scale are shown in Table 6-1 (men) and Table 6-2 (women), along with the percent overlap between the criterion and reference samples on that scale (the calculation of percent overlap is explained below under "Concurrent Validity"). For comparison, the same information is shown for the 1974 scales. The most important columns are those showing percent overlap, since these figures indicate concurrent validity, that is, how well the scales separate the criterion and reference samples.

Because of the increase in the available item pool, the new scales are slightly longer, on the average, than the 1974 SCII scales. And because of the quality of the new criterion samples, the 1981 percent overlaps

are slightly lower (an average of about 3 percentage points), which is an improvement.

Tables 6-1, 6-2, and 6-3 also list the means and standard deviations for the MIG and WIG samples used to build the 1974 and 1981 Occupational Scales. If the scales are separating the occupational samples from the reference samples as they should, the MIG and WIG samples should score as low on the various 1981 SCII scales as they did on the 1974 scales. Comparisons of mean scores in Tables 6-1 and 6-2 indicate that standard scores for the MIG and WIG are actually lower on the 1981 scales than they were on the 1974 scales. To the extent they *are* lower, the 1981 scales are more powerful.

Table 6-3 also reports the differences between the MIG and WIG samples on all of the 1981 SCII Occupational Scales (thus the MIG and WIG samples are both scored on opposite-sex scales as well as same-sex scales). These differences demonstrate the normative problem in working with male and female samples; frequently women scored much higher on the male scales than the men did, and vice versa. For this reason, scales based on appropriate-sex samples are more useful for any given individual. Chapter 7 examines this issue more thoroughly.

Norming the Occupational Scales

Once the items were selected, the scales were normed by scoring the original occupational samples and using their raw-score means and standard deviations in the standard score conversion formula, yield-

TABLE 6-1

Scale Characteristics and Concurrent Validities (Percent Overlap) for the 1974 and 1981 SCII Men's Occupational Scales

Scale	1974 Scales (blanks: no scale available)					1981 Scales					Change in overlap
	Number of items	Min. percent diff.	MIG mean	S.D. MIG	Percent overlap	Number of items	Min. percent diff.	MIG mean	MIG S.D.	Percent overlap	
ACCOUNTANT	47	18	21.2	15.1	25	57	16	27.6	12.1	31	−6
ADVERTISING EXECUTIVE	55	20	29.6	13.5	39	55	20	29.6	13.5	39	0
AGRIBUSINESS MANAGER	76	20	21.7	19.3	33	76	20	21.7	19.3	33	0
AIR FORCE OFFICER	51	20	30.9	12.4	39	37	16	30.0	13.9	40	−1
ARCHITECT	42	18	20.8	14.7	24	68	18	23.4	13.4	25	−1
ARMY OFFICER	47	17	30.7	12.7	39	39	16	30.1	12.4	37	2
ART TEACHER						66	26	15.6	14.4	16	
ARTIST, COMMERCIAL						68	25	20.6	13.7	21	
ARTIST, FINE	50	30	25.2	13.4	29	69	29	19.8	14.1	21	8
BANKER	45	18	29.1	13.7	38	45	18	29.1	13.7	38	0
BEAUTICIAN						65	21	30.4	9.2	31	
BIOLOGIST	54	17	25.8	14.2	32	73	21	23.7	14.4	28	4
BUSINESS EDUCATION TEACHER	51	17	29.6	13.3	38	67	22	22.8	12.7	23	15
BUYER	43	18	25.0	18.2	38	43	18	25.0	18.2	38	0
CHAMBER OF COMMERCE EXECUTIVE	51	18	33.7	12.6	47	67	22	24.0	14.9	29	18
CHEMIST						61	22	20.5	17.3	28	
CHIROPRACTOR	29	16	34.5	11.4	47	29	16	34.5	11.4	47	0
COLLEGE PROFESSOR	46	17	36.1	12.3	54	46	17	36.1	12.3	54	0
COMPUTER PROGRAMMER	36	16	35.5	13.3	54	66	16	34.6	12.1	49	5
CREDIT MANAGER	45	20	30.5	13.6	41	62	17	32.9	14.4	48	−7

(Continued)

TABLE 6-1 (*continued*)

Scale	1974 Scales (blanks: no scale available)					1981 Scales					Change in overlap
	Number of items	Min. percent diff.	MIG mean	S.D. MIG	Percent overlap	Number of items	Min. percent diff.	MIG mean	MIG S.D.	Percent overlap	
Dentist	24	17	30.5	10.8	35	24	17	30.5	10.8	35	0
Department Store Manager	57	25	27.1	14.6	35	64	17	31.6	12.5	41	−6
Dietitian	48	17	31.4	9.9	35	55	16	31.1	10.5	36	−1
Elected Public Official						61	19	30.9	12.4	39	
Elementary Education Teacher	28	17	30.9	14.4	43	44	16	28.7	13.7	37	6
Engineer	42	18	36.3	12.7	55	68	18	28.4	14.6	38	17
English Teacher	42	18	30.0	13.6	40	42	18	30.0	13.6	40	0
Executive Housekeeper						58	16	34.3	10.4	44	
Farmer	51	30	24.5	15.0	31	70	22	31.8	11.5	40	9
Flight Attendant						63	22	31.8	9.8	36	
Foreign Language Teacher						62	22	27.3	10.2	26	
Forester	39	17	32.4	12.9	44	66	19	31.0	11.7	38	4
Geographer						69	19	23.6	13.7	27	
Geologist						65	22	25.6	14.4	32	
Guidance Counselor	52	18	28.9	13.0	36	52	18	28.9	13.0	36	0
Interior Decorator	59	25	24.1	8.9	17	59	25	24.1	8.9	17	0
Investment Fund Manager	47	17	30.3	11.2	35	47	17	30.3	11.2	35	0
IRS Agent						36	16	36.7	10.8	52	
Lawyer	44	17	31.1	13.2	42	57	16	32.0	13.3	44	−2
Librarian	50	17	23.6	15.0	29	62	21	28.6	11.9	33	−4
Life Insurance Agent	65	22	23.5	15.6	30	65	22	23.5	15.6	30	0
Marketing Executive						56	16	30.8	11.1	36	
Mathematician	50	24	23.4	15.0	29	50	24	23.4	15.0	29	0
Math-Science Teacher	37	17	33.0	13.5	47	37	17	33.0	13.5	47	0
Medical Technologist	39	17	24.6	14.0	29	39	17	24.6	14.0	29	0
Minister	52	20	23.5	13.3	26	52	20	23.5	13.3	26	0
Musician	21	16	34.9	12.5	50	72	19	29.7	12.2	36	14
Navy Officer	37	16	31.5	13.9	44	55	16	30.6	13.2	40	4
Nurse, Licensed Practical	64	19	28.8	8.7	26	64	19	28.8	8.7	26	0
Nurse, Registered	43	15	27.0	11.0	27	33	16	27.8	10.8	29	−2
Nursing Home Administrator						57	17	29.7	13.9	40	
Occupational Therapist						74	18	26.5	12.7	30	
Optometrist	34	16	31.1	12.7	41	32	16	28.8	13.1	36	5
Personnel Director	44	20	34.4	12.0	48	62	17	31.1	13.5	42	6
Pharmacist	42	18	28.5	13.1	35	39	16	27.7	11.5	30	5
Photographer	48	25	24.7	13.6	28	57	16	33.3	10.4	41	−13
Physical Education Teacher						63	18	18.6	14.0	19	
Physical Therapist	41	17	30.4	11.8	37	54	16	25.6	12.1	27	10
Physician	34	17	27.6	13.5	34	34	17	27.6	13.5	34	0
Physicist						64	25	15.1	19.4	24	
Police Officer	46	19	31.7	14.3	45	54	16	26.6	12.5	30	15
Psychologist	49	20	28.6	15.6	40	49	20	28.6	15.6	40	0
Public Administrator	41	18	34.9	12.4	50	65	19	28.7	15.2	40	10
Public Relations Director						73	23	23.2	14.9	28	
Purchasing Agent	40	18	35.2	15.0	56	47	16	33.8	13.0	48	8
Radiologic Technologist						45	16	27.3	11.9	30	
Realtor	54	18	31.1	15.5	46	54	18	31.1	15.5	46	0
Recreation Leader	55	20	27.6	15.3	38	65	16	32.0	12.8	43	−5
Reporter	57	20	27.7	14.0	35	70	19	25.2	15.4	33	2
Restaurant Manager						56	18	28.5	13.2	35	
School Administrator	43	18	30.1	14.4	42	65	18	32.4	12.4	43	−1
Skilled Crafts	50	23	27.8	16.0	39	50	23	27.8	16.0	39	0
Social Science Teacher	44	20	31.1	13.0	41	44	20	31.1	13.0	41	0
Social Worker	49	17	25.2	15.4	33	63	18	25.1	16.1	34	−1
Sociologist						71	21	23.3	16.9	32	
Special Education Teacher						62	16	27.6	15.7	38	
Speech Pathologist	54	17	29.9	15.1	42	54	17	29.9	15.1	42	0
Systems Analyst						40	16	31.1	13.7	43	
Veterinarian	63	18	22.6	13.0	23	63	18	22.6	13.0	23	0
Vocational Agriculture Teacher	55	23	20.0	17.2	27	55	23	20.0	17.2	27	0
YMCA Director						64	20	28.7	14.2	38	

TABLE 6-2

Scale Characteristics and Concurrent Validities (Percent Overlap) for the 1974 and 1981 SCII Women's Occupational Scales

Scale	1974 Scales (blanks: no scale available)					1981 Scales					Change in overlap
	Number of items	Min. percent diff.	WIG mean	WIG S.D.	Percent overlap	Number of items	Min. percent diff.	WIG mean	WIG S.D.	Percent overlap	
ACCOUNTANT	40	18	23.0	13.3	25	63	20	20.9	13.5	21	4
ADVERTISING EXECUTIVE	69	20	30.1	10.3	33	69	20	30.1	10.3	33	0
AIR FORCE OFFICER						66	18	25.1	10.7	23	
ARCHITECT						67	26	17.3	16.0	21	
ARMY OFFICER	41	17	30.5	12.7	39	68	18	28.7	10.3	29	10
ART TEACHER	46	17	19.8	17.6	27	46	17	19.8	17.6	28	−1
ARTIST, COMMERCIAL						68	27	20.1	14.6	22	
ARTIST, FINE	58	30	25.8	12.9	29	68	28	22.1	14.1	25	4
BANKER	47	18	30.0	11.4	35	47	18	30.0	11.4	35	0
BEAUTICIAN	53	21	30.5	12.4	38	64	19	28.4	14.4	38	0
BIOLOGIST						73	25	20.6	15.4	25	
BUSINESS EDUCATION TEACHER	46	20	21.6	13.0	22	63	23	21.0	12.8	20	2
BUYER	41	17	24.5	10.8	22	41	17	24.5	10.8	22	0
CHAMBER OF COMMERCE EXECUTIVE						62	20	27.9	11.2	30	
CHEMIST	51	25	12.3	20.8	22	67	26	15.6	17.8	22	0
CHIROPRACTOR						58	16	23.5	10.9	21	
COLLEGE PROFESSOR	60	18	34.9	12.5	50	60	18	34.9	12.5	50	0
COMPUTER PROGRAMMER	44	18	26.4	14.4	33	65	20	30.0	12.2	37	−4
CREDIT MANAGER	61	19	26.6	12.4	30	71	16	26.6	13.2	29	1
DENTAL ASSISTANT	43	17	30.1	14.1	41	63	16	31.0	13.0	41	0
DENTAL HYGIENIST	34	16	30.8	12.3	39	34	16	30.8	12.3	39	0
DENTIST	41	18	25.7	13.1	29	63	19	26.0	13.6	31	−2
DEPARTMENT STORE MANAGER	52	20	25.9	13.7	31	67	17	28.3	11.3	31	0
DIETITIAN	18	16	34.7	11.4	48	39	16	27.8	11.3	30	18
ELECTED PUBLIC OFFICIAL						61	20	26.9	13.5	33	
ELEMENTARY EDUCATION TEACHER	33	16	35.3	12.0	50	28	16	33.1	12.2	45	5
ENGINEER	39	18	23.5	15.1	29	69	25	22.1	14.6	26	3
ENGLISH TEACHER	43	17	32.1	14.0	46	43	17	32.1	14.0	46	0
EXECUTIVE HOUSEKEEPER	47	18	30.2	12.1	37	62	18	28.9	11.6	33	4
FARMER						66	18	33.4	10.5	42	
FLIGHT ATTENDANT	52	20	29.1	13.2	37	62	18	30.0	11.8	36	1
FOREIGN LANGUAGE TEACHER	30	16	32.9	13.5	47	39	16	27.9	12.8	33	14
FORESTER						70	23	20.9	14.4	23	
GEOGRAPHER						66	21	28.9	13.4	37	
GEOLOGIST						75	26	19.0	15.0	21	
GUIDANCE COUNSELOR	34	17	31.2	15.2	46	34	17	31.2	15.2	46	0
HOME ECONOMIST	39	17	26.8	15.4	36	72	18	24.9	13.3	28	8
INTERIOR DECORATOR	49	22	15.8	15.0	17	49	22	15.8	15.0	17	0
IRS AGENT						57	17	33.4	11.8	43	
LAWYER	53	18	28.4	14.7	38	62	23	23.5	15.0	29	9
LIBRARIAN	31	16	32.2	15.4	48	60	16	30.9	14.1	43	5
LIFE INSURANCE AGENT	65	23	23.3	12.1	23	65	23	23.3	12.1	23	0
MARKETING EXECUTIVE						69	22	23.7	11.4	22	
MATHEMATICIAN	55	25	20.3	15.8	25	55	25	20.3	15.8	25	0
MATH-SCIENCE TEACHER	54	18	32.3	11.2	40	54	18	32.3	11.2	40	0
MEDICAL TECHNOLOGIST	51	17	28.5	14.2	38	51	17	28.5	14.2	37	1
MINISTER						65	21	22.7	16.5	30	
MUSICIAN	21	16	34.9	12.2	50	63	16	31.7	12.1	41	9
NAVY OFFICER						65	18	29.0	10.5	31	
NURSE, LICENSED PRACTICAL	52	20	26.2	13.3	31	52	20	26.2	13.3	31	0
NURSE, REGISTERED	29	16	31.9	14.4	46	30	16	30.7	13.3	41	5
NURSING HOME ADMINISTRATOR						65	18	25.4	12.0	26	
OCCUPATIONAL THERAPIST	31	17	35.8	12.0	52	53	16	28.5	13.9	37	15
OPTOMETRIST	52	17	28.4	12.1	33	61	16	31.6	13.1	42	−9
PERSONNEL DIRECTOR						66	19	28.2	12.0	32	
PHARMACIST	39	17	28.6	13.2	36	65	16	30.8	11.3	37	−1
PHOTOGRAPHER						54	21	32.5	11.5	42	

(*Continued*)

TABLE 6-2 (*continued*)

Scale	1974 Scales (blanks: no scale available)					1981 Scales					Change in overlap
	Number of items	Min. percent diff.	WIG mean	WIG S.D.	Percent overlap	Number of items	Min. percent diff.	WIG mean	WIG S.D.	Percent overlap	
PHYSICAL EDUCATION TEACHER	39	17	25.0	14.3	30	62	19	23.3	12.5	24	6
PHYSICAL THERAPIST	31	17	35.8	13.4	55	45	16	27.9	14.4	37	18
PHYSICIAN	48	18	27.4	15.8	38	48	18	27.4	15.8	38	0
PHYSICIST	61	30	7.6	20.6	17	61	30	7.6	20.6	17	0
POLICE OFFICER						63	16	26.5	12.1	29	
PSYCHOLOGIST	53	25	22.5	17.4	32	53	25	22.5	17.4	32	0
PUBLIC ADMINISTRATOR						69	23	23.2	14.3	27	
PUBLIC RELATIONS DIRECTOR						69	25	21.4	14.3	24	
PURCHASING AGENT						62	19	26.6	12.4	30	
RADIOLOGIC TECHNOLOGIST	34	17	31.0	13.2	41	39	16	29.9	12.9	38	3
REALTOR						69	23	19.7	12.8	18	
RECREATION LEADER	42	18	34.0	11.6	46	63	18	31.0	12.2	39	7
REPORTER	58	20	30.1	12.9	39	69	19	25.3	15.6	34	5
RESTAURANT MANAGER						54	20	25.6	13.7	30	
SCHOOL ADMINISTRATOR						65	19	31.4	12.1	40	
SECRETARY	31	17	32.6	14.4	48	31	17	32.6	14.4	48	0
SOCIAL SCIENCE TEACHER	27	16	33.9	11.8	46	27	16	33.9	11.8	46	0
SOCIAL WORKER	26	17	29.9	16.4	45	63	16	31.3	15.2	46	−1
SOCIOLOGIST						71	23	21.7	16.7	29	
SPECIAL EDUCATION TEACHER						20	16	35.3	12.4	51	
SPEECH PATHOLOGIST	42	17	29.9	15.8	44	53	16	32.7	13.1	46	−2
SYSTEMS ANALYST						66	21	28.4	13.3	35	
VETERINARIAN	65	21	24.9	12.6	27	65	21	24.9	12.6	27	0
YWCA DIRECTOR	34	17	34.2	13.7	51	50	16	34.7	12.6	50	1

ing for the criterion sample a mean of 50 and a standard deviation of 10. All future individual scores are converted to this distribution for easy comparison.

Reliability

Test-retest statistics for the 1981 Occupational Scales are reported in Tables 6-4 and 6-5 for three samples tested and retested over two-week, thirty-day, and three-year periods. These are the same samples used to study the reliability of the General Occupational Themes (Table 4-3) and the Basic Interest Scales (Table 5-5); the samples are described on p. 32.

The median correlations over these three periods were .91, .89, and .87, respectively, slightly higher than the comparable statistics for the 1974 Occupational Scales; for example, the 1974 median correlation over three years was .85. The increase reflects the slightly greater length of the 1981 Occupational Scales.

The magnitude of the test-retest correlations and the stability of the means over the three testing periods demonstrate that the SCII scales are quite stable over short time periods. Over longer time periods, the stability will be somewhat less but still high.

Men's and Women's Occupational Scales

Until the development of the SCII, the two sexes were treated separately by the Strong; two booklets, two sets of scales and norms, and two different profiles were provided. In the SCII, only one booklet—a combination of the former two—is used, and the results for both sexes are furnished on the same profile form. But because men and women still respond differently to many items, as demonstrated by the data in Chapter 7, separate scales and norms for men and women remain necessary. The interpretation of opposite-sex scores is also affected by the way in which the SCII was developed. The best items were taken from each of the existing SVIB booklets and merged into the SCII booklet. Of the 325 items in the SCII, two—*City planner* and *Professional gambler*—were new in 1974, 180 are common to both of the earlier booklets, 74 appeared only in the men's booklet, and 69 appeared only in the women's booklet. Consequently, all but seven of the 1974 SCII men's Occupational Scales were based on the 254 items (180 + 74) from the men's booklet, and all but eight of the women's scales were based on the analogous 249 from the women's booklet; none of these 109 scales could be used to score the samples of the other sex, because the samples had been tested earlier with the older booklets. For the 1981 edition of the SCII, 127 of the 162 occupational criterion samples have been tested with the combined booklet (T325) and just 35 of the scales are based on items from only the men's booklet (20 scales) or the women's booklet (15 scales). Because all of the samples for the 35 remaining single-sex scales were collected since 1966, it was not necessary to collect new samples to ensure up-to-date scales;

TABLE 6-3

Means and Standard Deviations for the Women- and Men-in-General
Samples on the 1981 SCII Occupational Scales

| Scale | Sex | Women (N = 300) | | Men (N = 300) | | Difference (female − male) |
		Mean	S.D.	Mean	S.D.	
ACCOUNTANT	f	20.9	13.5	37.3	13.6	−16.4
ACCOUNTANT	m	22.4	10.4	27.6	12.1	−5.2
ADVERTISING EXECUTIVE	f	30.1	10.3	37.8	9.2	−7.7
ADVERTISING EXECUTIVE	m	33.3	12.8	29.6	13.5	+3.7
AGRIBUSINESS MANAGER	m	15.9	14.1	21.7	19.3	−5.8
AIR FORCE OFFICER	f	25.1	10.7	41.8	10.8	−16.7
AIR FORCE OFFICER	m	16.8	10.9	30.0	13.9	−13.2
ARCHITECT	f	17.3	16.0	33.3	13.0	−16.0
ARCHITECT	m	30.3	13.1	23.4	13.4	+6.9
ARMY OFFICER	f	28.7	10.3	43.4	9.6	−14.7
ARMY OFFICER	m	21.1	10.4	30.1	12.4	−9.0
ART TEACHER	f	19.8	17.6	13.9	15.6	+5.9
ART TEACHER	m	35.0	12.8	15.6	14.4	+19.4
ARTIST, COMMERCIAL	f	20.1	14.6	24.6	12.4	−4.5
ARTIST, COMMERCIAL	m	31.5	13.0	20.6	13.7	+10.9
ARTIST, FINE	f	22.1	14.1	28.6	12.1	−6.5
ARTIST, FINE	m	29.0	13.5	19.8	14.1	+9.2
BANKER	f	30.0	11.4	33.3	11.4	−3.3
BANKER	m	22.8	10.7	29.1	13.7	−6.3
BEAUTICIAN	f	28.4	14.4	26.8	13.3	+1.6
BEAUTICIAN	m	43.6	9.6	30.4	9.2	+13.2
BIOLOGIST	f	20.6	15.4	32.4	12.8	−11.8
BIOLOGIST	m	31.7	12.7	23.7	14.4	+8.0
BUSINESS EDUCATION TEACHER	f	21.0	12.8	21.8	12.8	−0.8
BUSINESS EDUCATION TEACHER	m	29.8	12.2	22.8	12.7	+7.0
BUYER	f	24.5	10.8	27.6	13.1	−3.1
BUYER	m	22.0	14.6	25.0	18.2	−3.0
CHAMBER OF COMMERCE EXECUTIVE	f	27.9	11.2	30.8	12.4	−2.9
CHAMBER OF COMMERCE EXECUTIVE	m	22.7	12.6	24.0	14.9	−1.3
CHEMIST	f	15.6	17.8	33.0	15.0	−17.4
CHEMIST	m	22.8	15.7	20.5	17.3	+2.3
CHIROPRACTOR	f	23.5	10.9	33.2	11.9	−9.7
CHIROPRACTOR	m	32.5	10.7	34.5	11.4	−2.0
COLLEGE PROFESSOR	f	34.9	12.5	41.6	10.5	−6.7
COLLEGE PROFESSOR	m	41.5	9.6	36.1	12.3	+5.4
COMPUTER PROGRAMMER	f	30.0	12.2	43.0	11.2	−13.0
COMPUTER PROGRAMMER	m	34.0	11.1	34.6	12.1	−0.6
CREDIT MANAGER	f	25.6	13.2	33.3	14.5	−7.7
CREDIT MANAGER	m	29.2	12.3	32.9	14.4	−3.7
DENTAL ASSISTANT	f	31.0	13.0	30.7	12.1	+0.3
DENTAL HYGIENIST	f	30.8	12.3	26.1	9.9	+4.7
DENTIST	f	26.0	13.6	38.5	11.5	−12.5
DENTIST	m	31.0	11.6	30.5	10.8	+0.5
DEPARTMENT STORE MANAGER	f	28.3	11.3	35.8	12.8	−7.5
DEPARTMENT STORE MANAGER	m	33.2	10.5	31.6	12.5	+1.6
DIETITIAN	f	27.8	11.3	32.1	10.3	−4.3
DIETITIAN	m	39.4	10.3	31.1	10.5	+8.3
ELECTED PUBLIC OFFICIAL	f	26.9	13.5	33.9	13.9	−7.0
ELECTED PUBLIC OFFICIAL	m	29.7	10.7	30.9	12.4	−1.2
ELEMENTARY EDUCATION TEACHER	f	33.1	12.2	21.9	11.9	+11.2
ELEMENTARY EDUCATION TEACHER	m	42.0	12.1	28.7	13.7	+13.3
ENGINEER	f	22.1	14.6	39.8	12.6	−17.7
ENGINEER	m	18.7	14.0	28.4	14.6	−9.7
ENGLISH TEACHER	f	32.1	14.0	23.2	14.2	+8.9
ENGLISH TEACHER	m	37.8	11.9	30.0	13.6	+7.8
EXECUTIVE HOUSEKEEPER	f	28.9	11.6	31.3	13.7	−2.4
EXECUTIVE HOUSEKEEPER	m	36.6	8.1	34.3	10.4	+2.3
FARMER	f	33.4	10.5	36.7	11.1	−3.3
FARMER	m	27.5	9.5	31.8	11.5	−4.3

(*Continued*)

TABLE 6-3 (*continued*)

| Scale | Sex | Women (N = 300) | | Men (N = 300) | | Difference (female − male) |
		Mean	S.D.	Mean	S.D.	
FLIGHT ATTENDANT	f	30.0	11.8	29.4	10.2	+0.6
FLIGHT ATTENDANT	m	43.9	9.2	31.8	9.8	+12.1
FOREIGN LANGUAGE TEACHER	f	27.9	12.8	20.4	11.4	+7.5
FOREIGN LANGUAGE TEACHER	m	43.7	8.4	27.3	10.2	+16.4
FORESTER	f	20.9	14.4	36.4	10.7	−15.5
FORESTER	m	28.9	11.3	31.0	11.7	−2.1
GEOGRAPHER	f	28.9	13.4	43.2	10.2	−14.3
GEOGRAPHER	m	31.4	11.5	23.6	13.7	+7.8
GEOLOGIST	f	19.0	15.0	35.0	12.7	−16.0
GEOLOGIST	m	26.3	13.3	25.6	14.4	+0.7
GUIDANCE COUNSELOR	f	31.2	15.2	26.1	15.2	+5.1
GUIDANCE COUNSELOR	m	30.5	11.9	28.9	13.0	+1.6
HOME ECONOMIST	f	24.9	13.3	16.1	11.6	+8.8
INTERIOR DECORATOR	f	15.8	15.0	14.6	11.9	+1.2
INTERIOR DECORATOR	m	36.8	10.2	24.1	8.9	+12.7
INVESTMENT FUND MANAGER	m	27.8	10.5	30.3	11.2	−2.5
IRS AGENT	f	33.4	11.8	43.1	11.3	−9.7
IRS AGENT	m	33.3	9.7	36.7	10.8	−3.4
LAWYER	f	23.5	15.0	37.7	12.7	−14.2
LAWYER	m	34.3	11.4	32.0	13.3	+2.3
LIBRARIAN	f	30.9	14.1	35.5	11.0	−4.6
LIBRARIAN	m	43.1	10.5	28.6	11.9	+14.5
LIFE INSURANCE AGENT	f	23.3	12.1	29.6	13.7	−6.3
LIFE INSURANCE AGENT	m	19.2	11.4	23.5	15.6	−4.3
MARKETING EXECUTIVE	f	23.7	11.4	35.3	10.5	−11.6
MARKETING EXECUTIVE	m	27.5	10.7	30.8	11.1	−3.3
MATHEMATICIAN	f	20.3	15.8	30.3	14.1	−10.0
MATHEMATICIAN	m	27.9	11.9	23.4	15.0	+4.5
MATH-SCIENCE TEACHER	f	32.3	11.2	38.4	11.0	−6.1
MATH-SCIENCE TEACHER	m	29.2	13.7	33.0	13.5	−3.8
MEDICAL TECHNOLOGIST	f	28.5	14.2	35.3	13.2	−6.8
MEDICAL TECHNOLOGIST	m	22.8	15.1	24.6	14.0	−1.8
MINISTER	f	22.7	16.5	22.6	15.2	+0.1
MINISTER	m	29.3	12.5	23.5	13.3	+5.8
MUSICIAN	f	31.7	12.1	28.6	11.3	+3.1
MUSICIAN	m	40.7	10.3	29.7	12.2	+11.0
NAVY OFFICER	f	20.0	10.5	43.9	9.5	−14.9
NAVY OFFICER	m	19.8	11.3	30.6	13.2	−10.8
NURSE, LICENSED PRACTICAL	f	26.2	13.3	20.4	10.4	+5.8
NURSE, LICENSED PRACTICAL	m	41.7	10.4	28.8	8.7	+12.9
NURSE, REGISTERED	f	30.7	13.3	31.1	12.3	−0.4
NURSE, REGISTERED	m	32.3	13.0	27.8	10.8	+4.5
NURSING HOME ADMINISTRATOR	f	25.4	12.0	28.8	14.2	−3.4
NURSING HOME ADMINISTRATOR	m	32.5	11.3	29.7	13.9	+2.8
OCCUPATIONAL THERAPIST	f	28.5	13.9	32.2	12.3	−3.7
OCCUPATIONAL THERAPIST	m	39.4	10.6	26.5	12.7	+12.9
OPTOMETRIST	f	31.6	13.1	43.8	11.6	−12.2
OPTOMETRIST	m	30.8	14.6	28.8	13.1	+2.0
PERSONNEL DIRECTOR	f	28.2	12.0	36.4	11.8	−8.2
PERSONNEL DIRECTOR	m	29.0	11.9	31.1	13.5	−2.1
PHARMACIST	f	30.8	11.3	39.8	11.0	−9.0
PHARMACIST	m	28.5	12.7	27.7	11.5	+0.8
PHOTOGRAPHER	f	32.5	11.5	38.7	9.2	−6.2
PHOTOGRAPHER	m	38.6	10.9	33.3	10.4	+5.3
PHYSICAL EDUCATION TEACHER	f	23.3	12.5	34.1	13.9	−10.8
PHYSICAL EDUCATION TEACHER	m	24.7	13.5	18.6	14.0	+6.1
PHYSICAL THERAPIST	f	27.9	14.4	33.1	12.0	−5.2
PHYSICAL THERAPIST	m	28.6	13.2	25.6	12.1	+3.0
PHYSICIAN	f	27.4	15.8	36.7	13.0	−9.3
PHYSICIAN	m	26.4	14.1	27.6	13.5	−1.2
PHYSICIST	f	7.6	20.6	25.1	18.0	−17.5

(*Continued*)

TABLE 6-3 (*continued*)

Scale	Sex	Women (N = 300)		Men (N = 300)		Difference (female − male)
		Mean	S.D.	Mean	S.D.	
PHYSICIST	m	14.6	17.1	15.1	19.4	−0.5
POLICE OFFICER	f	26.5	12.1	39.9	12.4	−13.4
POLICE OFFICER	m	21.5	11.7	26.6	12.5	−5.1
PSYCHOLOGIST	f	22.5	17.4	28.4	16.1	−5.9
PSYCHOLOGIST	m	34.1	13.7	28.6	15.6	+5.5
PUBLIC ADMINISTRATOR	f	23.2	14.3	35.7	11.4	−12.5
PUBLIC ADMINISTRATOR	m	31.6	14.1	28.7	15.2	+2.9
PUBLIC RELATIONS DIRECTOR	f	21.4	14.3	29.8	12.0	−8.4
PUBLIC RELATIONS DIRECTOR	m	30.3	13.7	23.2	14.9	+7.1
PURCHASING AGENT	f	26.6	12.4	38.4	14.2	−11.8
PURCHASING AGENT	m	26.8	10.7	33.8	13.0	−7.0
RADIOLOGIC TECHNOLOGIST	f	29.9	12.9	34.1	11.0	−4.2
RADIOLOGIC TECHNOLOGIST	m	32.4	13.6	27.3	11.9	+5.1
REALTOR	f	19.7	12.8	27.5	15.2	−7.8
REALTOR	m	22.4	10.7	31.1	15.5	−8.7
RECREATION LEADER	f	31.0	12.2	37.4	12.1	−6.4
RECREATION LEADER	m	33.4	10.9	32.0	12.8	+1.4
REPORTER	f	25.3	15.6	31.8	13.3	−6.5
REPORTER	m	37.8	11.8	25.2	15.4	+12.6
RESTAURANT MANAGER	f	25.6	13.7	34.5	15.6	−8.9
RESTAURANT MANAGER	m	28.8	10.8	28.5	13.2	+0.3
SCHOOL ADMINISTRATOR	f	31.4	12.1	36.7	11.9	−5.3
SCHOOL ADMINISTRATOR	m	32.2	10.7	32.4	12.4	−0.2
SECRETARY	f	32.6	14.4	26.3	11.2	+6.3
SKILLED CRAFTS	m	18.3	12.3	27.8	16.0	−9.5
SOCIAL SCIENCE TEACHER	f	33.9	11.8	32.9	13.2	+1.0
SOCIAL SCIENCE TEACHER	m	32.0	11.7	31.1	13.0	+0.9
SOCIAL WORKER	f	31.3	15.2	32.9	13.5	−1.6
SOCIAL WORKER	m	36.4	14.1	25.1	16.1	+11.3
SOCIOLOGIST	f	21.7	16.7	33.2	13.1	−11.5
SOCIOLOGIST	m	31.3	14.1	23.3	16.9	+8.0
SPECIAL EDUCATION TEACHER	f	35.3	12.4	29.2	12.4	+6.1
SPECIAL EDUCATION TEACHER	m	43.8	13.3	27.6	15.7	+16.2
SPEECH PATHOLOGIST	f	32.7	13.1	31.5	12.7	+1.2
SPEECH PATHOLOGIST	m	40.6	12.4	29.9	15.1	+10.7
SYSTEMS ANALYST	f	28.4	13.3	42.9	11.0	−14.5
SYSTEMS ANALYST	m	22.3	13.9	31.1	13.7	−8.8
VETERINARIAN	f	24.9	12.6	33.1	10.7	−8.2
VETERINARIAN	m	24.9	13.9	22.6	13.0	+2.3
VOCATIONAL AGRICULTURE TEACHER	m	9.7	13.5	20.0	17.2	−10.3
YWCA DIRECTOR	f	34.7	12.6	39.8	13.7	−5.1
YMCA DIRECTOR	m	32.5	11.4	28.7	14.2	+3.8

eventually, however, these occupations will be re-sampled to provide data for item selection from the entire item pool.

Ordering the Occupational Scales on the Profile

The Occupational Scales are ordered on the profile in the categories developed by John Holland for his occupational-classification system (see Chapter 4); the code letters used on the profile indicate the one, two, or three General Occupational Themes most closely associated statistically with each Occupational Scale.

Earlier groupings. Earlier forms of the Strong profile used occupational groups developed from the statistical relationships between the scales. Generally, scales were grouped together if they correlated .65 or above with each other, or if the criterion samples had standard-score means of 40 or higher on each other's scales. These groupings were not entirely satisfactory for a variety of reasons: some scales had only small correlations with other scales and could not be grouped with any others; some scales seemed to belong, statistically, to more than one group; some pairs of scales were asymmetrical (for example, veterinarians belonged with farmers, but farmers did not belong with veterinarians); and some groupings just did not seem reasonable (for example, the clustering of artists with the biological scientists). The most serious problem was the lack of a unifying theory to guide the grouping or to use in understanding the groups once they were formed.

Despite the attendant problems, the profile group-

TABLE 6-4

Two-Week and Thirty-Day Test-Retest Correlations for Scores on the 1981 SCII Occupational Scales

Scale	Sex	Test-retest correlation[a]	Two-week statistics (N = 106 women, 74 men)				Test-retest correlation[b]	Thirty-day statistics (N = 35 women, 67 men)			
			Test		Retest			Test		Retest	
			Mean	S.D.	Mean	S.D.		Mean	S.D.	Mean	S.D.
ACCOUNTANT	f	.93	24.75	14.47	24.69	14.31	.91	30.35	16.12	31.16	15.06
ACCOUNTANT	m	.92	21.47	11.45	21.23	11.23	.89	24.75	12.10	25.60	12.66
ADVERTISING EXECUTIVE	f	.89	32.58	9.22	31.66	9.44	.88	38.16	10.60	38.85	11.10
ADVERTISING EXECUTIVE	m	.91	30.44	12.55	30.99	12.82	.90	36.65	13.88	37.89	13.53
AGRIBUSINESS MANAGER	m	.93	17.10	12.81	17.64	13.10	.90	15.32	12.36	15.31	12.14
AIR FORCE OFFICER	f	.92	30.83	12.21	30.62	12.00	.92	37.65	12.79	38.53	13.06
AIR FORCE OFFICER	m	.85	17.96	11.54	19.47	11.65	.90	24.64	14.86	26.20	14.44
ARCHITECT	f	.94	22.89	16.60	22.07	17.11	.90	28.54	13.08	28.84	13.63
ARCHITECT	m	.91	26.91	13.29	26.77	13.76	.91	26.88	13.31	28.55	13.00
ARMY OFFICER	f	.91	32.57	10.82	33.84	11.44	.92	40.03	11.59	41.56	12.23
ARMY OFFICER	m	.86	20.62	10.54	21.87	11.47	.86	28.31	13.09	30.16	13.03
ART TEACHER	f	.91	14.05	17.29	16.37	18.01	.89	20.86	16.02	22.67	17.22
ART TEACHER	m	.95	26.73	15.32	27.39	15.44	.93	25.1	16.91	26.73	16.36
ARTIST, COMMERCIAL	f	.93	24.28	13.47	23.62	13.89	.87	27.24	12.31	27.76	13.00
ARTIST, COMMERCIAL	m	.92	28.94	14.04	28.44	14.30	.91	27.50	13.70	28.16	13.68
ARTIST, FINE	f	.91	26.85	13.53	25.51	14.44	.85	29.43	11.81	28.62	12.86
ARTIST, FINE	m	.91	28.10	13.98	27.06	15.20	.88	24.53	13.17	24.66	14.35
BANKER	f	.92	28.10	10.71	28.87	10.38	.89	29.31	9.53	30.31	10.01
BANKER	m	.89	21.35	11.75	21.96	11.48	.86	26.74	11.94	27.74	11.89
BEAUTICIAN	f	.93	32.70	12.53	32.20	13.27	.87	26.00	10.70	25.46	11.20
BEAUTICIAN	m	.95	38.85	11.52	39.63	11.49	.95	37.53	12.07	38.80	11.68
BIOLOGIST	f	.95	23.92	15.47	24.17	15.78	.92	26.62	12.95	26.70	12.81
BIOLOGIST	m	.92	26.58	12.26	25.88	12.82	.90	24.16	12.67	23.85	12.66
BUSINESS EDUCATION TEACHER	f	.93	18.03	12.52	18.82	12.84	.90	20.30	10.39	21.28	10.74
BUSINESS EDUCATION TEACHER	m	.93	22.69	12.80	24.03	13.82	.87	24.68	10.72	25.98	11.82
BUYER	f	.87	24.86	11.63	24.53	11.58	.82	26.17	10.92	27.17	10.77
BUYER	m	.89	19.93	14.71	20.85	15.33	.89	28.03	15.30	29.36	16.11
CHAMBER OF COMMERCE EXECUTIVE	f	.92	26.62	11.01	26.87	11.13	.91	32.17	11.18	33.27	11.41
CHAMBER OF COMMERCE EXECUTIVE	m	.92	19.03	12.10	19.60	12.88	.92	27.77	13.14	28.82	13.47
CHEMIST	f	.96	20.20	17.67	20.63	17.96	.92	25.16	15.77	25.94	15.55
CHEMIST	m	.92	18.03	14.12	18.19	14.84	.87	18.19	14.62	18.53	14.01
CHIROPRACTOR	f	.81	24.18	10.65	25.95	11.24	.80	29.04	10.25	30.89	10.45
CHIROPRACTOR	m	.82	32.76	10.32	34.07	11.86	.73	35.73	9.49	37.11	10.48
COLLEGE PROFESSOR	f	.92	35.34	10.44	34.97	10.45	.89	39.39	9.52	38.98	9.69
COLLEGE PROFESSOR	m	.89	39.28	9.33	38.43	10.02	.89	37.95	9.38	37.22	9.47
COMPUTER PROGRAMMER	f	.95	33.95	12.68	34.53	12.56	.93	37.44	12.06	38.10	11.96
COMPUTER PROGRAMMER	m	.92	34.90	9.93	34.99	10.35	.93	31.63	11.15	31.31	11.27
CREDIT MANAGER	f	.93	25.24	12.99	25.77	12.93	.89	30.14	13.45	31.09	13.56
CREDIT MANAGER	m	.91	27.77	12.09	29.17	12.92	.88	31.34	11.61	32.72	12.36
DENTAL ASSISTANT	f	.90	36.31	10.27	36.83	10.15	.91	28.94	10.91	29.59	11.27
DENTAL HYGIENIST	f	.86	31.44	12.20	32.31	12.15	.85	27.88	11.64	27.94	11.22
DENTIST	f	.94	29.99	14.60	30.87	14.81	.89	33.44	11.80	34.70	12.20
DENTIST	m	.85	31.30	11.54	31.52	11.91	.68	29.55	10.72	30.54	10.27
DEPARTMENT STORE MANAGER	f	.90	28.89	10.16	29.41	10.48	.92	36.37	11.96	37.54	12.81
DEPARTMENT STORE MANAGER	m	.93	31.16	9.73	31.40	9.97	.90	34.60	10.34	35.73	10.69
DIETITIAN	f	.78	27.22	9.92	26.80	10.56	.75	31.66	10.46	33.10	10.67
DIETITIAN	m	.90	32.30	11.34	33.32	11.93	.86	34.92	10.27	36.59	10.89
ELECTED PUBLIC OFFICIAL	f	.92	24.47	11.95	25.64	13.20	.90	35.25	12.45	36.33	13.38
ELECTED PUBLIC OFFICIAL	m	.91	26.04	10.05	26.74	10.85	.90	33.39	11.00	34.36	11.43
ELEMENTARY EDUCATION TEACHER	f	.90	25.81	13.42	26.14	14.19	.85	24.90	11.57	26.45	12.03
ELEMENTARY EDUCATION TEACHER	m	.89	34.65	13.82	36.56	14.77	.84	30.80	14.04	31.40	14.66
ENGINEER	f	.96	27.21	15.50	27.72	15.88	.92	33.07	13.62	34.09	13.77
ENGINEER	m	.93	19.07	12.91	20.18	13.82	.91	20.06	14.46	21.23	14.11
ENGLISH TEACHER	f	.94	23.06	14.15	23.92	14.94	.91	29.02	14.26	30.35	14.12
ENGLISH TEACHER	m	.94	31.78	13.32	32.84	13.74	.90	35.28	13.31	35.96	13.23
EXECUTIVE HOUSEKEEPER	f	.89	26.16	12.30	27.63	12.78	.85	28.70	10.81	30.35	11.14
EXECUTIVE HOUSEKEEPER	m	.88	32.05	9.22	32.82	9.60	.85	35.26	8.83	36.91	9.57

(*Continued*)

TABLE 6-4 (*continued*)

Scale	Sex	Two-week statistics (N = 106 women, 74 men)					Thirty-day statistics (N = 35 women, 67 men)				
		Test-retest corre-lation[a]	Test		Retest		Test-retest corre-lation[b]	Test		Retest	
			Mean	S.D.	Mean	S.D.		Mean	S.D.	Mean	S.D.
FARMER	f	.93	36.90	8.66	36.83	8.80	.90	31.46	8.28	31.13	8.10
FARMER	m	.92	32.05	10.24	31.20	10.91	.87	26.75	8.55	25.57	8.94
FLIGHT ATTENDANT	f	.91	32.25	10.36	33.03	11.05	.88	34.73	10.80	36.38	10.92
FLIGHT ATTENDANT	m	.94	38.62	11.46	39.38	12.03	.93	40.01	11.01	41.15	11.64
FOREIGN LANGUAGE TEACHER	f	.88	17.31	11.86	17.86	12.33	.85	26.07	11.93	26.17	12.83
FOREIGN LANGUAGE TEACHER	m	.96	33.17	11.65	33.31	12.18	.91	34.47	11.42	34.84	11.45
FORESTER	f	.95	28.68	16.28	28.99	15.97	.90	29.48	12.10	29.19	12.32
FORESTER	m	.91	30.41	11.13	30.01	11.74	.88	25.90	10.15	25.28	10.45
GEOGRAPHER	f	.95	33.33	13.70	32.93	13.58	.91	39.00	11.31	39.38	11.80
GEOGRAPHER	m	.86	23.09	11.57	22.33	11.55	.84	27.21	11.28	27.48	10.85
GEOLOGIST	f	.95	25.56	16.34	25.22	16.55	.92	28.54	13.43	28.28	14.04
GEOLOGIST	m	.91	27.08	13.33	26.45	14.46	.88	23.04	11.94	22.94	12.60
GUIDANCE COUNSELOR	f	.91	24.27	16.22	24.32	17.45	.83	29.88	13.23	30.68	14.97
GUIDANCE COUNSELOR	m	.93	27.60	13.90	27.72	14.59	.80	30.18	10.67	30.34	12.00
HOME ECONOMIST	f	.93	19.52	14.10	19.92	14.53	.91	19.12	12.40	19.99	13.13
INTERIOR DECORATOR	f	.88	11.40	13.22	10.82	13.78	.88	18.92	13.13	20.07	13.82
INTERIOR DECORATOR	m	.93	31.80	10.55	30.62	10.81	.92	31.57	11.27	31.58	11.44
INVESTMENT FUND MANAGER	m	.85	27.19	8.98	26.79	9.70	.84	32.61	11.76	32.78	11.74
IRS AGENT	f	.92	32.63	12.42	33.99	13.58	.86	41.21	12.25	42.39	12.29
IRS AGENT	m	.90	32.64	10.54	33.53	11.32	.84	36.25	9.59	38.04	10.45
LAWYER	f	.94	27.69	13.90	26.85	13.63	.93	36.45	14.73	36.92	15.70
LAWYER	m	.91	29.00	10.76	29.83	11.39	.93	36.86	12.54	37.54	12.47
LIBRARIAN	f	.91	26.68	11.40	26.51	11.11	.91	35.72	11.40	37.43	11.26
LIBRARIAN	m	.93	32.96	11.37	32.58	11.32	.93	36.07	11.37	36.44	11.19
LIFE INSURANCE AGENT	f	.91	22.16	11.06	23.81	12.30	.91	30.29	11.70	31.55	12.82
LIFE INSURANCE AGENT	m	.90	17.78	11.61	19.29	12.92	.88	24.40	12.09	26.10	13.00
MARKETING EXECUTIVE	f	.90	27.71	10.62	26.93	10.76	.89	34.67	11.92	35.35	12.79
MARKETING EXECUTIVE	m	.82	27.08	9.47	25.69	9.47	.81	33.85	11.06	33.62	11.92
MATHEMATICIAN	f	.92	21.75	13.68	21.27	14.25	.89	23.08	13.24	21.84	13.33
MATHEMATICIAN	m	.87	24.94	10.95	23.95	12.11	.87	23.54	11.65	22.86	11.60
MATH-SCIENCE TEACHER	f	.94	34.05	10.43	34.33	10.37	.92	32.21	11.49	31.91	11.40
MATH-SCIENCE TEACHER	m	.92	29.47	13.36	30.76	14.42	.86	28.17	13.71	29.44	14.34
MEDICAL TECHNOLOGIST	f	.93	30.05	13.34	31.22	14.58	.92	30.33	13.96	31.19	13.71
MEDICAL TECHNOLOGIST	m	.89	21.32	14.38	22.43	16.12	.86	21.12	14.66	22.83	15.21
MINISTER	f	.93	17.08	15.35	18.57	17.01	.86	25.67	13.92	27.21	15.04
MINISTER	m	.91	24.01	13.04	25.27	14.82	.85	27.12	12.08	28.09	12.81
MUSICIAN	f	.93	31.33	11.96	31.89	11.88	.90	33.22	10.96	34.62	10.89
MUSICIAN	m	.94	39.12	11.65	38.42	12.37	.92	35.81	12.09	35.94	11.81
NAVY OFFICER	f	.92	33.06	11.50	33.91	11.48	.92	39.72	11.44	41.45	11.64
NAVY OFFICER	m	.89	20.08	11.64	22.13	12.52	.88	25.92	14.37	27.81	14.41
NURSE, LICENSED PRACTICAL	f	.89	22.56	11.76	24.10	12.07	.89	19.11	11.29	20.23	12.09
NURSE, LICENSED PRACTICAL	m	.93	36.56	10.86	37.01	10.72	.90	32.05	9.85	32.66	10.57
NURSE, REGISTERED	f	.85	28.40	11.74	28.04	13.06	.84	33.95	11.81	32.89	12.30
NURSE, REGISTERED	m	.87	30.32	11.48	31.73	12.14	.84	29.16	12.18	30.16	12.88
NURSING HOME ADMINISTRATOR	f	.90	23.38	12.52	23.62	12.37	.87	29.09	11.39	30.36	12.20
NURSING HOME ADMINISTRATOR	m	.86	28.04	11.51	28.89	12.34	.84	33.02	10.22	34.98	11.74
OCCUPATIONAL THERAPIST	f	.90	29.09	12.81	28.79	13.46	.89	32.44	13.01	32.53	13.07
OCCUPATIONAL THERAPIST	m	.93	33.54	12.12	33.67	12.20	.93	32.24	14.64	33.25	13.90
OPTOMETRIST	f	.93	33.21	13.12	34.14	13.74	.90	38.97	12.02	40.08	12.11
OPTOMETRIST	m	.88	29.26	14.76	29.52	15.13	.82	29.51	13.26	29.70	12.80
PERSONNEL DIRECTOR	f	.92	28.03	10.76	28.60	11.34	.92	37.20	11.60	38.77	13.09
PERSONNEL DIRECTOR	m	.90	25.07	11.55	26.11	12.56	.86	34.10	11.22	35.30	12.39
PHARMACIST	f	.92	35.56	11.95	35.46	11.92	.90	34.46	11.82	35.06	11.01
PHARMACIST	m	.87	27.81	11.64	28.23	11.34	.80	26.92	12.39	27.46	11.69
PHOTOGRAPHER	f	.94	35.84	11.38	35.19	11.71	.89	39.28	9.53	39.63	10.24
PHOTOGRAPHER	m	.93	38.11	11.19	37.43	11.58	.93	37.67	11.94	38.13	11.47
PHYSICAL EDUCATION TEACHER	f	.92	30.90	12.52	32.12	12.22	.90	27.62	13.72	27.14	14.13
PHYSICAL EDUCATION TEACHER	m	.86	24.02	13.89	26.52	14.50	.82	18.26	13.77	19.28	14.53

(*Continued*)

TABLE 6-4 (*continued*)

Scale	Sex	Two-week statistics (N = 106 women, 74 men)					Thirty-day statistics (N = 35 women, 67 men)				
		Test-retest correlation[a]	Test		Retest		Test-retest correlation[b]	Test		Retest	
			Mean	S.D.	Mean	S.D.		Mean	S.D.	Mean	S.D.
PHYSICAL THERAPIST	f	.91	31.47	13.94	31.42	13.50	.86	31.13	12.82	31.04	12.32
PHYSICAL THERAPIST	m	.89	28.92	12.32	29.84	12.50	.85	25.44	13.65	26.47	12.92
PHYSICIAN	f	.94	28.06	15.31	28.39	15.73	.87	33.61	12.89	33.05	13.13
PHYSICIAN	m	.90	25.08	13.88	26.24	15.05	.78	26.42	12.31	26.43	12.47
PHYSICIST	f	.95	12.35	19.02	13.03	19.38	.91	16.43	17.98	16.81	17.65
PHYSICIST	m	.91	12.86	15.35	12.76	16.37	.88	11.67	15.29	11.78	15.13
POLICE OFFICER	f	.90	34.92	11.69	36.73	12.40	.87	37.58	12.96	39.56	14.32
POLICE OFFICER	m	.85	26.81	10.72	28.65	11.07	.84	24.49	12.61	26.61	13.10
PSYCHOLOGIST	f	.92	21.09	13.67	21.15	13.95	.85	29.44	12.37	29.99	12.32
PSYCHOLOGIST	m	.90	28.73	12.51	28.39	12.45	.89	33.57	12.94	34.20	12.83
PUBLIC ADMINISTRATOR	f	.94	25.40	12.28	25.19	12.21	.92	35.31	13.43	36.42	14.67
PUBLIC ADMINISTRATOR	m	.92	24.19	13.53	24.79	15.13	.88	34.26	13.32	36.03	13.86
PUBLIC RELATIONS DIRECTOR	f	.94	20.98	12.31	20.81	12.35	.91	31.25	13.56	32.72	14.14
PUBLIC RELATIONS DIRECTOR	m	.94	24.22	13.20	24.15	13.40	.94	30.82	15.10	31.52	14.83
PURCHASING AGENT	f	.89	27.82	12.00	29.68	13.35	.88	36.29	13.43	38.99	14.59
PURCHASING AGENT	m	.90	24.69	10.94	25.79	12.02	.87	33.18	11.77	34.71	12.40
RADIOLOGIC TECHNOLOGIST	f	.89	35.57	11.57	36.13	11.09	.88	30.22	12.87	31.14	12.73
RADIOLOGIC TECHNOLOGIST	m	.89	34.23	12.65	35.03	12.78	.90	27.26	14.15	27.71	13.47
REALTOR	f	.90	19.59	11.64	21.00	12.82	.91	27.86	13.27	29.90	14.43
REALTOR	m	.90	25.51	10.58	25.82	11.19	.91	28.94	11.68	29.23	12.12
RECREATION LEADER	f	.91	31.76	11.69	32.68	12.59	.86	39.15	10.68	40.26	11.91
RECREATION LEADER	m	.91	31.55	11.69	31.90	11.97	.88	35.24	10.23	35.96	10.89
REPORTER	f	.94	26.41	13.68	26.24	13.60	.93	34.15	13.85	35.44	14.76
REPORTER	m	.95	32.14	13.04	31.84	13.26	.94	32.67	13.94	33.14	13.81
RESTAURANT MANAGER	f	.88	24.62	13.06	25.73	13.65	.88	33.45	14.02	35.32	15.39
RESTAURANT MANAGER	m	.89	29.02	10.41	28.50	10.74	.87	30.07	10.65	30.49	11.01
SCHOOL ADMINISTRATOR	f	.92	28.41	11.04	29.55	12.51	.88	37.89	11.50	39.15	12.44
SCHOOL ADMINISTRATOR	m	.91	28.32	11.54	29.59	13.26	.84	33.94	10.47	35.14	11.64
SECRETARY	f	.92	30.24	12.44	30.30	12.44	.85	28.47	10.55	29.65	11.24
SKILLED CRAFTS	m	.93	24.24	13.36	24.55	13.55	.90	19.67	13.44	20.30	13.10
SOCIAL SCIENCE TEACHER	f	.89	28.79	11.59	29.01	12.70	.87	34.93	12.14	34.76	12.53
SOCIAL SCIENCE TEACHER	m	.93	30.34	12.07	31.05	13.46	.84	34.28	10.34	34.49	11.34
SOCIAL WORKER	f	.92	28.01	11.80	27.95	12.39	.88	38.03	12.10	38.67	12.87
SOCIAL WORKER	m	.93	29.83	14.86	29.11	15.12	.91	33.79	15.93	34.23	15.50
SOCIOLOGIST	f	.94	22.74	13.87	22.24	13.46	.92	31.64	13.18	31.77	13.16
SOCIOLOGIST	m	.92	22.75	13.26	23.14	12.98	.88	28.73	12.93	29.90	12.43
SPECIAL EDUCATION TEACHER	f	.88	33.62	13.46	34.49	14.34	.78	31.50	11.62	32.54	12.42
SPECIAL EDUCATION TEACHER	m	.91	35.32	16.57	37.44	17.97	.87	33.78	16.37	34.81	17.02
SPEECH PATHOLOGIST	f	.88	29.90	10.87	29.03	11.01	.85	36.16	11.24	36.09	11.59
SPEECH PATHOLOGIST	m	.91	33.02	12.95	33.64	14.45	.88	37.23	13.30	38.58	13.15
SYSTEMS ANALYST	f	.96	32.85	13.38	32.87	13.27	.92	38.32	12.05	38.83	12.05
SYSTEMS ANALYST	m	.90	20.48	12.29	21.29	12.49	.87	26.04	14.37	27.18	13.77
VETERINARIAN	f	.94	29.40	14.22	29.60	14.34	.89	28.64	10.69	28.93	10.52
VETERINARIAN	m	.91	25.65	14.00	26.13	13.69	.88	19.52	13.16	18.82	12.38
VOCATIONAL AGRICULTURE TEACHER	m	.88	13.28	13.96	14.08	14.50	.87	11.45	13.31	11.35	13.09
YWCA DIRECTOR	f	.90	32.55	12.93	34.24	14.64	.85	41.30	11.42	43.07	13.14
YMCA DIRECTOR	m	.92	28.94	13.46	29.20	14.53	.88	32.48	11.63	32.82	11.92

[a] Median correlation = .91.

[b] Median correlation = .89.

ings were useful in interpreting the profiles—they provided more focus than did no groupings at all. Instead of the sterile statement, "You have the interests of a physician," the groupings provided a broader interpretation, "You have interests similar to those of physicians and other biological scientists, such as ————." Although this approach was decidedly su-

perior to listing the scales alphabetically, it was not completely satisfactory, because the particular characteristics of each group were not well described.

New groupings. Because the SVIB profile groupings and Holland's occupational types were similar, his occupational-classification system offered some potential for improvement. And because Holland drew many

TABLE 6-5
Three-Year Test-Retest Correlations for Scores on the 1981 SCII Occupational Scales
($N = 65$ women, 75 men)

Scale	Sex	Test-retest correlation (median = .87)	Test		Retest	
			Mean	S.D.	Mean	S.D.
Accountant	f	.88	31.79	16.39	33.48	16.17
Accountant	m	.85	25.66	12.79	27.00	13.22
Advertising Executive	f	.84	35.99	10.52	37.34	11.05
Advertising Executive	m	.90	32.54	13.26	33.05	14.29
Agribusiness Manager	m	.89	16.95	14.42	17.23	14.80
Air Force Officer	f	.87	35.90	13.78	37.62	13.63
Air Force Officer	m	.84	24.75	14.39	27.00	14.10
Architect	f	.91	30.23	16.91	31.25	16.77
Architect	m	.89	30.37	14.44	31.74	14.41
Army Officer	f	.86	37.10	12.02	37.66	11.91
Army Officer	m	.79	26.46	12.34	27.53	12.16
Art Teacher	f	.86	18.80	16.59	18.81	16.92
Art Teacher	m	.93	26.58	17.90	26.66	17.83
Artist, Commercial	f	.87	26.07	14.31	27.08	14.87
Artist, Commercial	m	.89	28.77	14.72	29.31	14.89
Artist, Fine	f	.84	28.93	13.50	29.99	14.20
Artist, Fine	m	.86	27.29	15.07	27.77	15.40
Banker	f	.84	31.25	11.38	31.82	11.57
Banker	m	.81	25.74	13.08	26.46	12.95
Beautician	f	.85	25.27	12.48	25.76	12.29
Beautician	m	.93	36.37	12.07	36.89	11.99
Biologist	f	.92	30.69	16.15	31.30	15.86
Biologist	m	.90	30.58	14.79	31.51	14.14
Business Education Teacher	f	.86	20.29	11.98	20.77	12.47
Business Education Teacher	m	.84	25.20	12.48	25.25	12.52
Buyer	f	.76	24.34	11.09	26.13	10.68
Buyer	m	.85	22.65	15.75	22.38	16.30
Chamber of Commerce Executive	f	.88	28.07	11.75	29.78	12.40
Chamber of Commerce Executive	m	.89	22.45	14.05	23.86	14.70
Chemist	f	.92	29.24	19.13	29.78	18.82
Chemist	m	.92	26.51	17.91	27.14	18.17
Chiropractor	f	.75	31.69	11.22	33.38	11.65
Chiropractor	m	.71	34.00	9.71	33.66	10.88
College Professor	f	.90	41.97	11.12	42.52	10.87
College Professor	m	.89	40.83	10.95	41.06	10.86
Computer Programmer	f	.92	39.69	14.47	40.51	14.41
Computer Programmer	m	.93	36.17	13.23	36.38	13.90
Credit Manager	f	.88	28.41	13.98	29.57	13.97
Credit Manager	m	.83	29.97	13.08	30.64	13.52
Dental Assistant	f	.89	29.14	11.00	29.30	11.57
Dental Hygienist	f	.78	28.40	11.32	27.59	10.91
Dentist	f	.89	35.87	14.62	36.70	14.67
Dentist	m	.79	31.94	11.51	32.47	12.09
Department Store Manager	f	.87	32.62	12.68	33.29	12.28
Department Store Manager	m	.88	31.58	11.68	32.54	11.52
Dietitian	f	.69	32.39	10.60	33.92	10.51
Dietitian	m	.76	34.90	10.10	36.26	10.74
Elected Public Official	f	.89	30.62	13.07	31.49	13.86
Elected Public Official	m	.89	30.21	12.05	30.96	12.76
Elementary Education Teacher	f	.82	26.29	13.40	26.61	12.99
Elementary Education Teacher	m	.83	34.12	14.98	33.92	14.05
Engineer	f	.93	34.47	16.79	35.36	16.52
Engineer	m	.93	26.54	16.51	27.89	17.21
English Teacher	f	.88	28.22	14.83	28.16	15.46
English Teacher	m	.87	33.64	13.57	32.63	13.77
Executive Housekeeper	f	.82	28.50	11.84	30.12	11.75
Executive Housekeeper	m	.77	34.84	8.21	35.97	8.14
Farmer	f	.90	33.72	9.65	34.39	9.88
Farmer	m	.85	29.82	9.44	30.49	10.08

(*Continued*)

TABLE 6-5 (*continued*)

Scale	Sex	Test-retest correlation (median = .87)	Test		Retest	
			Mean	S.D.	Mean	S.D.
FLIGHT ATTENDANT	f	.86	30.00	10.77	30.26	11.34
FLIGHT ATTENDANT	m	.87	37.93	10.95	38.21	11.45
FOREIGN LANGUAGE TEACHER	f	.82	25.43	13.59	26.04	14.19
FOREIGN LANGUAGE TEACHER	m	.89	36.45	13.04	36.60	12.30
FORESTER	f	.93	31.61	16.07	31.88	15.70
FORESTER	m	.87	32.05	12.09	32.53	12.66
GEOGRAPHER	f	.90	40.30	14.07	40.75	13.66
GEOGRAPHER	m	.85	31.57	12.89	33.09	12.50
GEOLOGIST	f	.92	31.26	16.46	31.92	16.23
GEOLOGIST	m	.88	29.42	14.99	30.10	15.18
GUIDANCE COUNSELOR	f	.84	28.63	15.07	27.62	14.76
GUIDANCE COUNSELOR	m	.81	28.14	12.45	27.04	12.34
HOME ECONOMIST	f	.86	19.85	12.78	19.87	12.97
INTERIOR DECORATOR	f	.83	18.18	14.83	19.75	15.68
INTERIOR DECORATOR	m	.92	31.24	12.99	31.45	13.02
INVESTMENT FUND MANAGER	m	.80	31.64	11.20	32.67	12.05
IRS AGENT	f	.79	38.22	11.90	38.74	12.98
IRS AGENT	m	.80	34.24	10.56	34.68	11.33
LAWYER	f	.91	33.86	14.77	34.40	15.41
LAWYER	m	.89	35.04	12.58	35.71	12.28
LIBRARIAN	f	.86	37.17	11.63	39.20	12.30
LIBRARIAN	m	.92	37.64	13.47	39.14	12.87
LIFE INSURANCE AGENT	f	.87	26.04	13.12	26.46	13.49
LIFE INSURANCE AGENT	m	.85	20.50	13.61	21.29	13.98
MARKETING EXECUTIVE	f	.86	32.93	12.47	34.20	12.56
MARKETING EXECUTIVE	m	.80	32.45	11.23	33.86	12.35
MATHEMATICIAN	f	.91	28.96	16.30	29.14	16.25
MATHEMATICIAN	m	.89	28.26	14.19	29.30	14.44
MATH-SCIENCE TEACHER	f	.91	35.38	12.21	35.29	12.64
MATH-SCIENCE TEACHER	m	.88	32.43	14.06	31.78	15.08
MEDICAL TECHNOLOGIST	f	.88	33.53	14.97	33.62	15.81
MEDICAL TECHNOLOGIST	m	.84	25.11	14.89	24.94	16.60
MINISTER	f	.86	23.93	14.79	24.27	15.13
MINISTER	m	.81	25.37	13.34	24.98	13.19
MUSICIAN	f	.91	33.38	12.81	34.97	13.24
MUSICIAN	m	.91	37.16	13.21	37.53	12.98
NAVY OFFICER	f	.86	38.72	12.54	39.87	12.28
NAVY OFFICER	m	.84	26.58	13.24	27.63	13.37
NURSE, LICENSED PRACTICAL	f	.82	21.49	11.20	21.85	11.95
NURSE, LICENSED PRACTICAL	m	.87	33.06	11.31	33.54	10.88
NURSE, REGISTERED	f	.77	32.36	11.43	32.14	12.57
NURSE, REGISTERED	m	.81	29.56	11.09	29.18	11.74
NURSING HOME ADMINISTRATOR	f	.82	26.55	12.33	27.37	12.84
NURSING HOME ADMINISTRATOR	m	.82	29.70	12.42	30.72	12.53
OCCUPATIONAL THERAPIST	f	.84	33.02	13.47	33.76	14.25
OCCUPATIONAL THERAPIST	m	.87	33.68	13.76	33.59	13.33
OPTOMETRIST	f	.88	40.84	13.60	41.76	13.84
OPTOMETRIST	m	.81	32.16	13.43	32.20	14.85
PERSONNEL DIRECTOR	f	.87	33.30	11.76	34.50	12.91
PERSONNEL DIRECTOR	m	.84	30.44	12.35	31.35	12.89
PHARMACIST	f	.89	37.60	12.34	38.29	12.59
PHARMACIST	m	.85	29.22	11.20	29.39	12.32
PHOTOGRAPHER	f	.85	38.77	11.04	39.84	11.35
PHOTOGRAPHER	m	.88	37.49	12.14	39.01	12.41
PHYSICAL EDUCATION TEACHER	f	.90	28.38	14.58	27.63	14.90
PHYSICAL EDUCATION TEACHER	m	.81	20.63	13.06	19.84	13.92
PHYSICAL THERAPIST	f	.87	33.25	13.86	33.28	14.85
PHYSICAL THERAPIST	m	.86	27.96	12.37	27.26	13.20
PHYSICIAN	f	.89	35.69	15.02	35.89	14.78
PHYSICIAN	m	.82	29.25	13.61	29.23	13.91
PHYSICIST	f	.93	21.50	22.57	21.46	22.28

(*Continued*)

TABLE 6-5 (*continued*)

Scale	Sex	Test-retest correlation (median = .87)	Test		Retest	
			Mean	S.D.	Mean	S.D.
PHYSICIST	m	.92	19.03	19.49	19.42	19.04
POLICE OFFICER	f	.88	32.67	14.85	32.37	14.14
POLICE OFFICER	m	.86	23.10	13.68	23.15	13.00
PSYCHOLOGIST	f	.89	31.24	15.48	30.75	15.70
PSYCHOLOGIST	m	.86	34.38	13.84	34.67	13.93
PUBLIC ADMINISTRATOR	f	.89	31.99	13.45	33.28	14.43
PUBLIC ADMINISTRATOR	m	.87	31.19	13.53	32.03	13.97
PUBLIC RELATIONS DIRECTOR	f	.88	28.13	12.81	29.97	13.69
PUBLIC RELATIONS DIRECTOR	m	.91	27.27	15.28	28.66	15.90
PURCHASING AGENT	f	.84	32.58	12.95	33.24	13.25
PURCHASING AGENT	m	.80	31.68	11.07	32.46	12.29
RADIOLOGIC TECHNOLOGIST	f	.88	30.83	12.56	30.62	13.36
RADIOLOGIC TECHNOLOGIST	m	.88	29.63	12.82	29.31	13.62
REALTOR	f	.88	23.61	14.19	24.78	14.58
REALTOR	m	.90	25.09	13.57	25.15	13.16
RECREATION LEADER	f	.85	34.77	11.51	35.02	11.78
RECREATION LEADER	m	.85	31.69	11.85	31.97	11.40
REPORTER	f	.87	31.56	13.33	32.48	14.02
REPORTER	m	.89	32.68	14.42	33.14	14.52
RESTAURANT MANAGER	f	.80	30.67	13.65	31.95	14.39
RESTAURANT MANAGER	m	.83	28.37	11.65	29.36	11.60
SCHOOL ADMINISTRATOR	f	.85	34.57	11.01	34.90	11.98
SCHOOL ADMINISTRATOR	m	.82	31.90	11.18	32.14	11.52
SECRETARY	f	.87	26.42	12.41	26.92	12.26
SKILLED CRAFTS	m	.92	22.35	15.42	22.48	15.19
SOCIAL SCIENCE TEACHER	f	.84	32.48	12.24	31.99	12.34
SOCIAL SCIENCE TEACHER	m	.85	29.92	12.71	28.82	12.30
SOCIAL WORKER	f	.88	33.06	12.34	33.19	13.14
SOCIAL WORKER	m	.88	30.58	16.93	30.52	16.14
SOCIOLOGIST	f	.91	31.62	14.16	31.95	14.37
SOCIOLOGIST	m	.89	31.32	15.32	32.06	14.23
SPECIAL EDUCATION TEACHER	f	.83	30.58	13.37	29.60	12.80
SPECIAL EDUCATION TEACHER	m	.82	33.94	17.06	33.48	15.80
SPEECH PATHOLOGIST	f	.87	34.00	12.45	33.99	12.60
SPEECH PATHOLOGIST	m	.84	36.06	14.15	35.73	13.91
SYSTEMS ANALYST	f	.91	39.68	15.02	40.32	14.50
SYSTEMS ANALYST	m	.88	30.78	15.80	32.86	16.30
VETERINARIAN	f	.90	32.72	13.07	32.95	13.22
VETERINARIAN	m	.86	25.84	12.86	25.70	13.82
VOCATIONAL AGRICULTURE TEACHER	m	.85	13.43	15.19	13.13	15.78
YWCA DIRECTOR	f	.85	37.09	12.42	37.28	12.80
YMCA DIRECTOR	m	.86	28.54	12.88	28.48	12.55

of his ideas about occupational types from research on the Strong, the substantial overlap between the two systems comes as no surprise.

The major advantage of Holland's categories is that he paid more attention to the theoretical concerns of classification systems than did Strong. He constructed categories that were both exhaustive and mutually exclusive; and most important, he developed a rationale for his classification and described it at length (Holland, 1966, 1973). As discussed in Chapter 4, his descriptions of the six types were used to establish the General Occupational Theme scales, and the six themes were used as the basis for organizing the Occupational Scales on the 1974 and 1981 profiles.

Several kinds of information were used to arrive at the Holland classifications for the Occupational Scales.

The most important were the mean scores of the criterion samples on the six General Occupational Themes; next were the correlations between these Themes and the Occupational Scales; next were the correlations between the Occupational Scales and the Basic Interest Scales; and, finally, the correlations between the Occupational Scales themselves were considered.

Table 6-6 lists, for each occupational sample, the General Occupational Theme means and the correlations between the Themes and the 1981 Occupational Scales. Correlations for the men's Occupational Scales were calculated on a sample of 300 men, those for the women's on a sample of 300 women. Code types, as listed in Table 6-6, were then assigned to the Occupational Scales. Usually, only means of 53

TABLE 6-6

Data Used to Classify Occupational Scales: General Occupational Theme Scale Means and Correlations for Each Occupational-Scale Criterion Sample

| Scale | Sex | General Occupational Theme mean for each occupational sample | | | | | | Correlations between Theme scales and Occupational Scales (decimal points omitted) | | | | | | | | | | | | Code type |
| | | | | | | | | Calculated on 300 women | | | | | | Calculated on 300 men | | | | | | |
		R	I	A	S	E	C	R	I	A	S	E	C	R	I	A	S	E	C	
ACCOUNTANT	f	46	49	49	44	50	57	20	18	−29	−35	14	44	20	−01	−54	−44	24	43	C
ACCOUNTANT	m	53	50	44	47	52	56	−01	−22	−41	03	36	67	16	−26	−45	−01	57	65	C
ADVERTISING EXECUTIVE	f	43	46	57	45	51	46	−16	−10	31	−37	06	−37	−33	−15	12	−31	05	−32	AE
ADVERTISING EXECUTIVE	m	50	50	54	50	55	46	−16	−09	64	18	32	−27	−29	00	65	31	24	−19	AE
AGRIBUSINESS MANAGER	m	60	46	38	48	61	58	02	−36	−69	08	36	56	40	−45	−70	02	58	54	ERC
AIR FORCE OFFICER	f	53	50	51	46	50	52	40	27	05	−28	18	08	34	−07	−36	−37	26	18	RC
AIR FORCE OFFICER	m	60	52	44	48	53	53	50	29	−19	06	31	41	61	−02	−40	05	52	53	RC
ARCHITECT	f	53	53	57	41	46	46	32	45	29	−52	−32	−34	12	29	01	−67	−44	−38	AIR
ARCHITECT	m	51	52	55	43	46	46	19	29	56	−44	−48	−43	07	34	52	−36	−53	−40	AIR
ARMY OFFICER	f	53	52	53	49	52	53	59	41	16	14	42	25	55	11	−15	10	54	42	RC
ARMY OFFICER	m	60	52	44	49	53	54	36	26	−02	34	51	42	43	05	−25	32	59	55	RC
ART TEACHER	f	50	51	58	50	52	45	23	30	79	11	02	−30	09	35	77	29	−09	−25	A
ART TEACHER	m	51	48	59	48	47	42	−22	−07	70	05	−14	−48	−28	10	76	21	−27	−42	A
ARTIST, COMMERCIAL	f	47	49	60	43	45	40	−04	13	53	−40	−26	−63	−31	11	41	−39	−46	−73	A
ARTIST, COMMERCIAL	m	51	48	58	41	45	41	−25	−10	60	−31	−40	−68	−37	07	65	−17	−52	−68	A
ARTIST, FINE	f	45	49	59	39	44	38	−09	09	37	−57	−44	−68	−32	02	20	−58	−59	−76	A
ARTIST, FINE	m	50	50	58	38	42	38	−26	−08	42	−48	−61	−76	−40	07	45	−38	−72	−77	A
BANKER	f	49	46	45	49	53	61	02	−21	−48	09	43	80	20	−28	−52	00	57	77	CE
BANKER	m	51	49	53	49	55	58	−09	−25	−34	11	54	58	10	−36	−41	10	68	55	CE
BEAUTICIAN	f	44	42	49	48	52	51	−37	−75	−51	−09	13	15	09	−75	−59	−13	35	21	E
BEAUTICIAN	m	50	47	53	46	54	48	−32	−43	35	13	34	−06	−06	−21	50	33	39	04	EA
BIOLOGIST	f	52	60	54	44	42	46	45	70	14	−32	−40	−16	17	62	04	−46	−58	−23	I
BIOLOGIST	m	54	59	50	44	43	46	12	51	17	−29	−66	−33	−18	47	27	−25	−79	−41	I
BUSINESS EDUCATION TEACHER	f	45	43	47	54	55	65	−08	−37	−39	31	61	68	20	−36	−40	36	77	73	CES
BUSINESS EDUCATION TEACHER	m	52	46	44	54	59	64	−11	−35	−19	46	66	65	16	−26	−07	56	76	68	CES
BUYER	f	49	46	48	50	56	54	−13	−29	−31	28	65	58	17	−37	−46	18	74	55	EC
BUYER	m	50	48	46	53	63	55	−12	−32	00	37	83	42	17	−30	−12	37	89	50	EC
CHAMBER OF COMMERCE EXECUTIVE	f	42	43	50	49	49	56	−26	−39	−10	15	69	38	01	−43	−25	20	78	51	EC
CHAMBER OF COMMERCE EXECUTIVE	m	51	46	48	49	55	52	−15	−21	18	37	66	18	−04	−24	09	46	68	30	E
CHEMIST	f	53	61	53	44	44	50	52	74	15	−27	−23	01	32	63	−07	−44	−34	02	IR
CHEMIST	m	56	62	49	44	44	49	34	74	14	−19	−44	−01	02	72	20	−25	−59	−09	IR
CHIROPRACTOR	f	49	52	53	50	51	50	51	48	13	03	21	16	58	18	−11	06	49	39	IRE
CHIROPRACTOR	m	55	54	47	54	55	52	35	44	25	54	53	26	33	30	20	60	60	36	IRE
COLLEGE PROFESSOR	f	48	56	55	47	44	47	23	58	27	−33	−44	−33	−16	53	17	−44	−68	−41	IA
COLLEGE PROFESSOR	m	47	55	55	48	44	48	02	45	35	−34	−69	−48	−35	43	40	−29	−83	−55	IA
COMPUTER PROGRAMMER	f	51	55	52	44	47	53	55	62	03	−33	−13	18	40	48	−21	−53	−20	15	IRC
COMPUTER PROGRAMMER	m	58	55	46	44	48	53	39	36	−21	−34	−46	20	28	35	−14	−51	−50	06	IRC
CREDIT MANAGER	f	44	46	49	50	55	60	−02	−21	−42	16	64	73	21	−31	−50	12	75	71	CE
CREDIT MANAGER	m	56	49	44	51	58	58	19	−17	−29	38	70	79	39	−25	−28	35	84	74	CE

(Continued)

TABLE 6-6 (continued)

| Scale | Sex | General Occupational Theme mean for each occupational sample | | | | | | Correlations between Theme scales and Occupational Scales (decimal points omitted) | | | | | | | | | | | | Code type |
| | | | | | | | | Calculated on 300 women | | | | | | Calculated on 300 men | | | | | | |
		R	I	A	S	E	C	R	I	A	S	E	C	R	I	A	S	E	C	
DENTAL ASSISTANT	f	45	48	50	52	50	52	−01	−32	−49	08	10	38	41	−34	−57	01	38	43	C
DENTAL HYGIENIST	f	51	54	49	50	51	47	19	30	−09	28	05	09	26	44	06	26	00	03	IR
DENTIST	f	51	56	53	46	47	48	64	73	23	−21	−16	−04	54	62	07	−32	−14	00	IR
DENTIST	m	54	56	48	51	50	50	33	55	15	05	−15	−02	30	52	24	11	−04	01	IR
DEPARTMENT STORE MANAGER	f	44	45	53	49	58	52	−11	−24	05	11	74	27	13	−32	−20	16	82	41	E
DEPARTMENT STORE MANAGER	m	52	47	46	48	60	52	−34	−56	−09	18	67	27	02	−48	−15	26	80	38	E
DIETITIAN	f	47	51	50	50	50	51	31	48	−04	15	37	33	42	22	−24	07	49	42	EC
DIETITIAN	m	55	51	46	51	55	55	13	06	−02	54	62	56	33	09	07	61	69	61	ECR
ELECTED PUBLIC OFFICIAL	f	47	49	54	51	54	51	12	23	38	34	55	06	00	11	23	47	59	21	E
ELECTED PUBLIC OFFICIAL	m	52	48	48	51	56	49	−14	−04	32	39	55	03	−09	−03	20	48	57	22	E
ELEMENTARY EDUCATION TEACHER	f	45	45	53	52	50	52	−19	−39	−02	38	38	31	13	−32	03	50	45	41	S
ELEMENTARY EDUCATION TEACHER	m	56	50	47	53	52	52	16	−09	−00	50	09	11	27	00	22	54	08	13	S
ENGINEER	f	56	57	51	43	47	50	66	67	19	−26	−12	01	57	52	−10	−42	−15	06	RI
ENGINEER	m	60	57	45	44	48	51	61	62	−08	−23	−25	22	58	46	−23	−34	−19	22	RI
ENGLISH TEACHER	f	45	48	54	52	52	49	−16	05	62	26	25	−23	−40	18	69	31	03	−16	A
ENGLISH TEACHER	m	51	51	54	57	52	49	−04	08	68	40	23	−25	−32	13	73	45	−03	−26	AS
EXECUTIVE HOUSEKEEPER	f	49	47	51	54	54	57	20	−09	−18	50	66	65	45	−21	−26	51	77	66	CER
EXECUTIVE HOUSEKEEPER	m	58	49	45	52	55	54	19	−01	−03	58	64	56	47	−09	−11	59	70	62	CER
FARMER	f	50	43	47	49	51	54	00	−43	−74	−11	04	42	33	−52	−76	−16	32	40	RC
FARMER	m	61	46	38	43	51	51	−01	−31	−73	−46	−29	13	29	−41	−79	−46	01	13	R
FLIGHT ATTENDANT	f	46	47	57	50	53	45	−04	−19	39	23	52	−10	−01	−15	34	30	53	−02	EA
FLIGHT ATTENDANT	m	51	50	55	50	54	47	−10	−13	51	40	49	07	−01	14	70	49	38	09	EA
FOREIGN LANGUAGE TEACHER	f	43	46	56	53	50	49	−17	−02	42	23	24	−16	−30	10	50	42	14	02	A
FOREIGN LANGUAGE TEACHER	m	49	48	54	52	49	49	−30	−10	49	27	00	−22	−37	14	69	35	−18	−15	A
FORESTER	f	55	53	52	46	45	49	62	64	16	−25	−30	−10	50	43	−08	−38	−30	−15	RI
FORESTER	m	60	51	42	45	48	50	26	09	−37	−44	−54	−07	29	−04	−42	−52	−43	−16	R
GEOGRAPHER	f	50	54	52	44	47	49	35	53	25	−42	−23	−25	05	41	−01	−60	−43	−28	I
GEOGRAPHER	m	52	54	48	44	46	48	−11	28	27	−35	−47	−35	−49	29	33	−33	−71	−41	I
GEOLOGIST	f	53	58	53	42	43	46	35	56	15	−46	−41	−30	09	39	−12	−64	−55	−33	IR
GEOLOGIST	m	56	58	48	41	43	45	13	32	−00	−57	−75	−37	−09	32	05	−59	−83	−47	IR
GUIDANCE COUNSELOR	f	48	51	51	58	53	53	01	28	33	67	45	15	−14	32	40	73	25	12	SEC
GUIDANCE COUNSELOR	m	54	51	44	62	55	56	11	11	09	80	61	44	13	06	11	82	57	41	SCE
HOME ECONOMIST	f	48	46	49	55	54	52	−09	−33	−19	43	56	42	30	−33	−25	53	69	51	ES
INTERIOR DECORATOR	f	45	47	56	44	55	45	−11	−01	58	−30	02	−39	−09	−03	43	−18	06	−30	AE
INTERIOR DECORATOR	m	47	47	56	47	53	46	−60	−44	35	−14	03	−32	−50	−27	46	02	−01	−31	AE
INVESTMENT FUND MANAGER	m	49	52	49	47	52	50	−36	−17	17	−31	14	−20	−42	−04	14	−24	10	−15	EI
IRS AGENT	f	46	51	52	51	53	58	36	36	07	35	68	62	31	22	−06	32	71	73	CE
IRS AGENT	m	54	51	45	50	54	57	23	03	−08	46	69	73	27	−05	−10	48	73	71	CE
LAWYER	f	45	51	56	45	49	46	08	28	39	−20	06	−32	−28	17	24	−23	−12	−35	AI

(Continued)

TABLE 6-6 (continued)

| Scale | Sex | General Occupational Theme mean for each occupational sample | | | | | | Correlations between Theme scales and Occupational Scales (decimal points omitted) | | | | | | | | | | | | Code type |
| | | R | I | A | S | E | C | Calculated on 300 women | | | | | | Calculated on 300 men | | | | | | |
								R	I	A	S	E	C	R	I	A	S	E	C	
Lawyer	m	52	50	50	47	50	47	−07	10	56	19	22	−33	−37	16	58	21	01	−30	AI
Librarian	f	47	49	56	46	48	51	04	27	41	−36	−03	−19	−30	26	36	−47	−32	−22	A
Librarian	m	49	50	55	46	46	50	−36	06	54	−13	−27	−40	−57	23	66	−07	−50	−36	A
Life Insurance Agent	f	44	49	53	52	63	52	02	07	21	41	76	26	11	−05	04	51	82	43	E
Life Insurance Agent	m	52	49	45	53	64	51	06	−06	10	53	77	33	19	−15	−05	52	84	44	E
Marketing Executive	f	45	50	54	44	53	51	−02	15	20	−35	11	−16	−21	02	−09	−40	04	−13	EI
Marketing Executive	m	51	52	48	46	54	50	−23	−03	28	−18	10	−28	−40	−01	18	−08	05	−22	EI
Mathematician	f	49	58	48	43	40	48	22	51	04	−39	−51	−17	−07	48	−05	−48	−66	−22	I
Mathematician	m	50	58	50	45	43	47	03	45	17	−43	−63	−32	−27	47	21	−40	−75	−39	I
Math-Science Teacher	f	54	56	45	49	47	54	45	39	−45	02	−03	61	50	28	12	−09	10	58	IRC
Math-Science Teacher	m	57	58	46	55	45	52	64	84	10	17	−13	23	43	80	12	10	−19	21	IRS
Medical Technologist	f	57	60	48	48	45	51	58	75	−05	01	−14	25	51	69	−12	−10	−12	26	IR
Medical Technologist	m	55	59	47	54	51	54	55	78	10	26	00	30	42	74	08	18	−05	33	IR
Minister	f	47	50	58	60	46	45	23	46	59	50	31	−03	−05	39	60	64	20	02	SA
Minister	m	52	54	51	61	54	52	18	38	49	73	43	17	−02	34	55	76	31	20	SIE
Musician	f	44	50	60	46	46	45	−06	17	65	−39	−30	−59	−30	31	67	−34	−50	−56	A
Musician	m	50	50	57	43	46	43	−25	01	54	−40	−55	−64	−40	22	62	−28	−65	−62	A
Navy Officer	f	53	50	54	47	50	51	61	42	14	−11	24	17	58	13	−24	−21	35	35	R
Navy Officer	m	61	53	45	49	52	53	73	51	02	25	27	43	75	20	−23	23	51	54	RC
Nurse, Licensed Practical	f	55	54	53	53	47	55	28	27	−14	50	19	45	44	28	01	49	32	53	RIC
Nurse, Licensed Practical	m	52	52	48	53	51	52	−17	−22	−21	41	17	30	00	−17	08	48	25	32	S
Nurse, Registered	f	47	51	54	54	49	47	31	58	38	46	11	−16	11	40	34	60	18	−04	SI
Nurse, Registered	m	56	54	47	51	50	49	38	36	13	45	21	27	33	37	−01	42	11	21	IRS
Nursing Home Administrator	f	44	47	50	52	54	56	−02	−09	−12	39	73	48	18	−23	−28	38	82	59	EC
Nursing Home Administrator	m	55	49	46	53	57	54	07	−04	05	63	72	46	22	−14	−02	61	80	54	ECS
Occupational Therapist	f	50	51	54	53	47	45	53	64	51	10	−17	−40	39	51	44	26	−20	−29	RAS
Occupational Therapist	m	57	52	52	53	48	45	15	27	50	33	−14	−34	04	33	61	41	−27	−31	RAS
Optometrist	f	48	54	51	48	49	51	59	78	12	−15	−06	14	54	64	−08	−24	06	27	IR
Optometrist	m	55	55	46	47	50	50	39	60	09	02	−28	−01	28	66	28	−03	−20	−01	IR
Personnel Director	f	45	47	53	50	54	52	04	07	23	23	65	20	05	−08	−02	35	72	38	E
Personnel Director	m	55	50	46	53	56	52	07	07	25	55	69	29	10	02	14	62	68	41	E
Pharmacist	f	46	54	50	47	49	51	34	48	−24	−36	−23	16	27	28	−41	−57	−15	14	I
Pharmacist	m	54	54	44	48	54	51	27	34	−21	29	19	32	40	21	−25	25	43	41	IE
Photographer	f	48	48	58	44	48	44	−00	12	49	−49	−26	−61	−23	05	33	−52	−39	−66	A
Photographer	m	56	53	53	44	50	45	−19	−16	55	−40	−33	−72	−24	−06	57	−29	−38	−63	A
Physical Education Teacher	f	52	49	48	56	49	52	46	06	−43	31	11	34	60	−13	−46	33	39	35	SR
Physical Education Teacher	m	56	50	44	56	51	50	22	03	−13	54	15	24	40	06	05	62	28	26	SR
Physical Therapist	f	49	52	52	52	46	46	55	60	15	04	−22	−12	47	40	10	08	−14	−14	IR
Physical Therapist	m	58	55	47	52	49	48	50	45	03	35	−07	13	46	39	12	37	03	07	IR

(Continued)

TABLE 6-6 (*continued*)

Scale	Sex	General Occupational Theme mean for each occupational sample						Correlations between Theme scales and Occupational Scales (decimal points omitted)												Code type
								Calculated on 300 women						Calculated on 300 men						
		R	I	A	S	E	C	R	I	A	S	E	C	R	I	A	S	E	C	
PHYSICIAN	f	52	59	49	49	43	46	41	79	21	−13	−33	−18	15	78	17	−20	−41	−19	IR
PHYSICIAN	m	55	60	51	53	48	49	48	80	24	11	−18	−06	22	81	37	12	−22	−04	IR
PHYSICIST	f	51	61	53	42	41	48	47	70	13	−27	−34	−04	22	64	−02	−40	−48	−07	IR
PHYSICIST	m	57	62	50	41	42	47	31	60	11	−34	−62	−18	−02	57	14	−41	−74	−27	IR
POLICE OFFICER	f	49	48	52	50	51	50	32	06	03	31	53	21	39	−06	−10	25	59	28	RE
POLICE OFFICER	m	58	49	44	50	52	49	26	−16	17	30	24	17	41	−21	−12	27	39	19	RE
PSYCHOLOGIST	f	46	60	55	54	47	45	23	65	49	−09	−15	−31	−18	66	46	−13	−45	−35	IAS
PSYCHOLOGIST	m	49	58	53	53	47	48	09	53	62	07	−06	−33	−34	57	65	09	−42	−38	IAS
PUBLIC ADMINISTRATOR	f	47	50	55	46	50	51	11	30	37	−11	18	−18	−15	16	18	−08	13	−11	EA
PUBLIC ADMINISTRATOR	m	53	52	52	51	51	52	07	30	58	39	41	00	−20	31	59	50	20	02	CA
PUBLIC RELATIONS DIRECTOR	f	42	46	58	46	52	46	−02	15	50	−05	23	−28	−29	02	33	02	17	−21	AE
PUBLIC RELATIONS DIRECTOR	m	48	47	54	47	52	46	−38	−28	46	16	27	−32	−49	−15	51	28	15	−24	AE
PURCHASING AGENT	f	49	47	53	49	58	55	26	08	08	26	85	49	38	−13	−17	25	89	59	EC
PURCHASING AGENT	m	57	50	45	49	58	55	25	18	11	39	77	53	34	01	−12	39	82	65	EC
RADIOLOGIC TECHNOLOGIST	f	49	50	50	51	50	50	33	18	−36	14	00	28	56	09	−47	−07	17	37	R
RADIOLOGIC TECHNOLOGIST	m	57	54	46	49	50	50	23	24	−23	15	−12	23	41	25	−19	08	−01	29	RI
REALTOR	f	44	44	52	49	61	52	−01	−07	15	25	77	25	16	−20	−08	34	85	43	E
REALTOR	m	53	48	42	51	63	53	−04	−39	−38	−29	77	46	28	−40	−46	19	86	52	E
RECREATION LEADER	f	50	49	55	56	52	49	24	28	44	46	48	02	15	15	25	60	55	17	SRE
RECREATION LEADER	m	54	48	47	53	52	50	−11	−25	17	52	53	07	−04	−25	12	64	52	11	SRE
REPORTER	f	45	48	58	47	48	44	06	21	57	−09	03	−47	−35	13	51	−06	−18	−52	A
REPORTER	m	49	48	54	46	46	46	−38	−20	56	−02	−14	−53	−62	01	65	05	−40	−51	A
RESTAURANT MANAGER	f	48	48	50	49	55	55	13	04	03	22	80	52	27	−14	−20	25	87	57	EC
RESTAURANT MANAGER	m	53	46	44	46	57	52	−30	−64	−21	00	49	22	12	−58	−35	04	69	32	E
SCHOOL ADMINISTRATOR	f	46	50	54	56	54	52	15	23	37	47	59	14	03	13	24	59	58	30	SE
SCHOOL ADMINISTRATOR	m	56	52	47	57	56	56	16	16	22	72	67	35	16	09	17	79	63	44	SE
SECRETARY	f	49	45	48	51	52	57	−25	−66	−30	13	40	48	12	−60	−27	17	63	53	C
SKILLED CRAFTS	m	61	51	42	49	52	52	47	05	−45	−29	−24	23	66	−13	−56	−26	06	28	R
SOCIAL SCIENCE TEACHER	f	49	48	50	53	53	53	00	18	31	49	41	07	−24	16	37	56	26	09	SEC
SOCIAL SCIENCE TEACHER	m	52	49	45	60	56	53	−03	−18	14	68	61	24	−04	−20	18	74	54	24	SEC
SOCIAL WORKER	f	44	49	56	54	50	46	00	24	51	32	29	−24	−36	20	51	49	10	−22	SA
SOCIAL WORKER	m	51	50	51	56	49	47	−28	−09	42	48	32	−19	−23	37	75	57	11	−17	SA
SOCIOLOGIST	f	46	57	56	47	45	47	22	56	42	−08	−08	−24	−24	54	36	−12	−37	−33	IA
SOCIOLOGIST	m	50	56	53	48	45	48	13	57	64	02	−18	−26	−32	57	68	00	−57	−33	IA
SPECIAL EDUCATION TEACHER	f	45	48	54	56	51	51	−02	00	24	72	48	14	04	02	31	79	46	25	S
SPECIAL EDUCATION TEACHER	m	56	50	50	56	52	49	06	−05	19	75	36	14	17	11	41	49	24	12	S
SPEECH PATHOLOGIST	f	42	50	45	54	49	46	−20	18	46	32	21	−36	−36	20	44	49	10	−21	SA
SPEECH PATHOLOGIST	m	52	53	52	52	49	47	04	34	51	51	17	−24	−23	37	75	57	−05	−16	SA
SYSTEMS ANALYST	f	51	56	53	44	48	53	50	65	18	−33	−15	03	27	55	−05	−51	−25	02	IRC
SYSTEMS ANALYST	m	57	56	46	44	50	54	45	54	00	−15	05	49	35	48	−17	−33	03	50	IRC
VETERINARIAN	f	52	55	51	43	45	46	43	57	11	−41	−39	−21	23	45	−01	−58	−43	−26	IR
VETERINARIAN	m	58	54	43	46	49	48	26	22	−24	−17	−39	−06	37	15	−21	−22	−23	−09	RI
VOCATIONAL AGRICULTURE TEACHER	m	61	53	40	57	57	57	55	12	−47	32	32	54	69	−14	−54	29	52	53	RCE
YWCA DIRECTOR	f	47	48	53	57	52	52	21	19	27	63	73	33	20	06	13	71	74	44	SE
YMCA DIRECTOR	m	53	49	47	60	56	52	−04	19	19	77	56	28	01	−10	16	83	58	29	SE

or higher were considered in the coding, but a few samples had no means that high; usually, *all* means of 53 or higher were reflected in the coding, but some samples had as many as four or five high means.

The hexagonal arrangement. After the codes had been assigned, the Occupational Scales were ordered to conform to the Holland hexagon. Most of the Occupational Scales fell into code types that ordered themselves reasonably around the perimeter of the hexagon—which demonstrates, again, the close fit between Holland's system and the SCII data. Only nine of the 162 Occupational Scales—m PHARMACIST (IE), m INVESTMENT FUND MANAGER (EI), f and m MARKETING EXECUTIVE (EI), m PUBLIC ADMINISTRATOR (CA), f and m PHYSICAL EDUCATION TEACHER (SR), f and m RECREATION LEADER (SRE)—were assigned to unexpected categories represented by the diagonals of the hexagon (that is, IE or EI, AC or CA, and SR or RS). A few occupations, notably m INVESTMENT FUND MANAGER and f DIETITIAN, had no high mean scores, which probably means that these occupations are not psychologically homogeneous. The remainder of the occupations, the vast majority, clustered neatly into the designated code types.

Interpretive value of code types. The code types and their ordering on the profile aid in profile interpretation. Clusters of identical code types, such as the RC cluster containing AIR FORCE, ARMY, and NAVY OFFICER, help draw attention to the similarities between occupations. Comparisons between similar code types, such as EC and CE—the former including BUYER, PURCHASING AGENT, CHAMBER OF COMMERCE EXECUTIVE, and RESTAURANT MANAGER, the latter including BANKER, CREDIT MANAGER, and IRS AGENT—draw attention to the nuances often separating closely related occupations. Respondents should therefore be encouraged to compare their highest one, two, or three General Occupational Theme scores (depending on the point spread of the scores) with the various possible combinations of the codes for these Themes.

The interpretive value of the codes is discussed at length in Chapter 10.

Occupations not listed on the profile. The occupations listed in Table 6-6 are only those that were used to develop empirical scales; consequently their number is restricted. Many other occupational samples have been collected over the years, but for a variety of reasons they were not used to construct Occupational Scales, usually because they were too small but occasionally for other reasons, such as a close intuitive and statistical relationship with some other occupation already on the profile. Although these samples have not proved to be appropriate for scale construction, they can nonetheless provide useful data. Their mean scores are especially useful, since samples used for the calculation of mean scores need not be as stringently selected as those used to establish item-scoring weights. All of these samples were scored on the General Occupational Themes and assigned a code type.

They are listed, along with the occupations accorded Occupational Scales on the profile, in Appendix B, ordered according to the Holland classification system. Counselors and their clients should refer to this appendix for further information on the classification of occupations.

Concurrent Validity

Concurrent validity is the power of a scale to discriminate between people concurrently in different occupations. Two types of validity information are relevant: first, the contrast between the criterion (occupational) samples and the reference (MIG or WIG) samples; second, the mean scores of occupations on each other's scales.

Percent overlap. The contrast between the criterion and reference samples is usually expressed in terms of *percent overlap,* a statistic suggested by Tilton (1937). This statistic, which ranges from zero to 100 percent, gives the percentage of scores in one distribution (criterion sample) that are matched by scores in another distribution (reference sample). If the scale discriminates perfectly between the two samples, so that their distributions are entirely separated, the overlap is zero percent; if the scale does not discriminate at all and the two distributions are identical, the overlap is 100 percent.

Although the percent overlap can be calculated by actually counting the overlapping scores and converting the resulting figure to a percentage, Tilton provides a table that permits the calculation of this statistic by using the means and standard deviations of the two samples in the formula

$$Q = \frac{M_1 - M_2}{(SD_1 + SD_2)/2}$$

where M_1 and M_2 are the two mean scores and SD_1 and SD_2 are the two standard deviations. The index Q is used to enter Tilton's overlap table (Table 6-7) to determine the percent overlap of the two distributions. The use of this formula assumes that the two distributions are normally distributed, although we have found from experience that the formula is quite robust even with skewed distributions.

The Q index is essentially a measure of the number of standard-deviation units separating the two distributions; as such, it reflects the magnitude of the difference, not simply statistical rarity. Table 6-7 shows the amount of separation, in terms of standard-deviation units, that is associated with various levels of percent overlap. For example, a Q index of 2.00, associated with a percent overlap of about 32, represents a separation of two standard deviations between the distributions, an enormous separation by the usual standards of psychological research. For some perspective with other measures, it is worth noting that two standard deviations correspond roughly to differences of 30 IQ points, or 6 inches in height, or 1.8 GPA units

TABLE 6-7
Tilton Percent–Overlap Table
(See text for derivation of Q index)

Q	Percent overlap	Q	Percent overlap	Q	Percent overlap	Q	Percent overlap
0.00	100	0.63	75	1.35	50	2.30	25
0.02	99	0.66	74	1.38	49	2.35	24
0.05	98	0.69	73	1.41	48	2.40	23
0.08	97	0.72	72	1.44	47	2.45	22
0.10	96	0.74	71	1.48	46	2.51	21
0.12	95	0.77	70	1.51	45	2.56	20
0.15	94	0.80	69	1.54	44	2.62	19
0.18	93	0.82	68	1.58	43	2.68	18
0.20	92	0.85	67	1.61	42	2.74	17
0.23	91	0.88	66	1.65	41	2.81	16
0.25	90	0.91	65	1.68	40	2.88	15
0.28	89	0.94	64	1.72	39	2.95	14
0.30	88	0.96	63	1.76	38	3.03	13
0.33	87	0.99	62	1.79	37	3.11	12
0.35	86	1.02	61	1.83	36	3.20	11
0.38	85	1.05	60	1.87	35	3.29	10
0.40	84	1.08	59	1.91	34	3.39	9
0.43	83	1.11	58	1.95	33	3.50	8
0.46	82	1.14	57	1.99	32	3.62	7
0.48	81	1.17	56	2.03	31	3.76	6
0.51	80	1.20	55	2.07	30	3.92	5
0.53	79	1.23	54	2.12	29	4.11	4
0.56	78	1.26	53	2.16	28	4.34	3
0.58	77	1.29	52	2.21	27	4.65	2
0.61	76	1.32	51	2.25	26	5.15	1

Source: J. W. Tilton, "The Measurement of Overlapping," *Journal of Educational Psychology*, 28: 656–60.

(on a four-point scale), or the difference between the 16th and 86th percentiles.

Percent overlaps for the SCII Occupational Scales are given in Table 6-1 (men's scales) and in Table 6-2 (women's scales). The median overlap for both the men's and the women's scales is 34 percent. This degree of overlap is associated with a Q index of roughly 1.91, which means that the scales are separating the criterion samples from the reference samples by about two standard deviations, on the average. The best scale in this respect is the male ART TEACHER scale, which has an overlap of only 16 percent (Q index = 2.81) between the criterion sample and the MIG; the best female scales are PHYSICIST and INTERIOR DECORATOR, which have an overlap of only 17 percent (Q index = 2.74) between each criterion sample and the WIG. The poorest scale is the male COLLEGE PROFESSOR scale, which has an overlap of 54 percent (Q index = 1.23) between the criterion sample and the MIG sample, indicating that the COLLEGE PROFESSOR criterion sample is less homogeneous than the other samples—one intuitively senses this to be the case—and therefore harder to separate from the reference sample.

This wide range of percent overlap indicates that the scales vary considerably in their validities. Scales with the highest validities (the lowest overlaps) are usually those for occupations that are tightly defined and quite distinct from most other occupations, as is the case with artists, physicists, chemists, and interior decorators. Scales with low validities (high overlaps)

are usually those for occupations that are not as well defined, or where the occupational samples were tested with earlier forms of the SVIB. For the latter samples, item data are available only for the smaller pool of overlapping items (that is, items appearing in both the SCII and the older SVIB booklets).

Mean scores for other occupations. Another important type of concurrent-validity information is the mean scores of the occupational samples on each other's scales. Because these data are so voluminous, they are not included in this *Manual;* a table of mean scores for 162 occupational samples on 162 scales would have to include 26,244 numbers.

The mean scores for the SCII scales follow the same pattern as the earlier SVIB means, which are reported in the *Handbook for the SVIB.* Mean scores for the various occupations on a given Occupational Scale tend to be normally distributed around the General Reference Sample mean, and range roughly across 30 to 40 scale points, that is, three to four standard deviations. Some related occupations score almost as high on each other's scales as they do on their own—in a few particular cases, even a few points higher. The latter case can happen when members of occupation A respond more positively to the set of items comprising the occupational scale for occupation B than do even the members of occupation B. Such instances are rare, and occur only in occupations with strong overlapping interests, such as artists and architects.

Predictive Validity

The predictive validity of an Occupational Scale is the scale's power to distinguish between people who will eventually enter different occupations—to distinguish, for example, between students who will become bankers and those who will become artists and farmers. This is an important attribute, because the inventory is generally used to help make long-term decisions; thus it is important that there be data to support the long-range predictive power of these scales.

Strong's studies of validity. The SVIB has a long history of research on predictive validity, beginning with E. K. Strong's attempts in the 1930's. He believed intensely in the value of empirical data, and very early he began collecting longitudinal data to use in studying the practical usefulness of his inventory. During the year following initial publication of the inventory (1927), Strong administered it to the senior class at Stanford University; five years later he asked these students, in a survey, which occupations they had entered, to determine if the inventory had accurately predicted their career choices. The results were published in the *Journal of Educational Psychology* in 1935 under the title, "Predictive Value of the Vocational Interest Test" (Strong, 1935). In this report (p. 334), Strong grappled (as every investigator has since) with the issue of what constitutes predictive validity:

Determination of the validity of a vocational test is fraught with many difficulties. What should be the criterion? At first thought "final vocational choice" appears to be the only ultimate criterion in guidance. But ... one cannot assume that every man [or woman] eventually enters the occupation for which he [or she] is best fitted. If this were true there would be no great need for vocational tests. ... Because final occupational choice cannot be accepted as a perfect criterion, it necessarily follows that a vocational test which correlates perfectly with final occupational choice is as faulty as the present system of finding one's livelihood.

This fact is of crucial importance in understanding why the SVIB, or the SVIB-SCII, or any other interest inventory, cannot, by the nature of the problem, approach perfect predictive validity.

Strong concluded, however, that a substantial relationship should exist between scores on his test and eventual occupational choice, and he argued that the following four propositions, if true, would constitute persuasive evidence of high validity:

1. People continuing in occupation X should obtain higher interest scores on the scale for X than they do on scales for any other occupations.

2. Interest scores *on scale* X should be higher for people continuing in occupation X than for people in occupation Y.

3. Interest scores *on scale* X should be higher for people continuing in occupation X than for people who change from X to occupation Y.

4. People changing from occupation Y to occupation X should score higher on the X scale *prior to the change* than they scored on the Y scale.

Strong used the results of his five-year follow-up of Stanford seniors to evaluate the inventory on these four propositions and concluded, as summarized in the 1938 *Manual* for the Strong: "The first three propositions are true with respect to averages but, of course, there were some individual exceptions. ... The fourth proposition is approximately true."

Several years later Strong studied the predictive validity of the test for these students and several hundred of their peers (combined *N*: 524) over a longer time period and reported the results in his book *Vocational Interests 18 Years After College* (Strong, 1955). In general, his results supported the propositions he had advanced 20 years earlier. Strong attempted to quantify his findings by using expectancy ratios and "percent accuracy." His calculations have been questioned—more is said about that in the following paragraphs—but the general pattern of his results showed substantial agreement with his earlier work.

Validity studies since Strong. Following Strong's lead, a number of other investigators have conducted studies of the validity of the inventory over long time periods. The usual paradigm is to test a group of students, lay the data away, let several years pass, locate the students, ascertain their current occupations (and their perseverance, satisfaction, and success in those occupations), then study the degree of correspondence between their earlier scores and their current occupations. Several such studies are reported in the 1971 *Handbook*; the basic finding of these studies is that there is a substantial relationship between high scores on the Occupational Scales and eventual occupation entered. Depending on how the hit rate is calculated, between one-half and three-fourths of all college students enter occupations that are predictable from their earlier scores, assuming that a relatively loose definition of occupation is used—for example, if "social scientist" is used as the criterion category, instead of more specific occupational categories such as psychologist, sociologist, anthropologist, or economist.

The level of accuracy is influenced, as one might suppose, by various external factors. McArthur (1954), for example, showed that Harvard students from homes of high socioeconomic status (and private schools) are less predictable than are other Harvard students (those from public schools): the former are more likely to enter occupations dictated by the family fortunes, such as banking or trusteeships, than they are to follow their own interests—sometimes, according to McArthur's observations, to the considerable detriment of their occupational satisfaction. Trimble (1965), in a study of former St. Louis high school students, showed that the inventory works best in predicting occupational choice when the occupation selected is one of those listed on the profile, and that the test does less well in predicting "related" occupations. Campbell (1966a) showed that predictability is higher for students who have well-defined interest patterns, an outcome that also appeared in Strong's 18-year follow-up of Stanford students. Brandt and Hood (1968), using the files of the Counseling Service at the University of Iowa, demonstrated that students with severe emotional problems are less predictable than normal students. Harmon (1969) has provided evidence showing that, for women making a career commitment outside of the home, measured interests are as predictive of career choices as they are for men.

In general, these studies support Strong's original proposition that measured interests are predictive of occupational choice; they extend his original work by documenting situations in which the predictive validity is higher or lower than average.

But the precise derivation of Strong's "hit ratios" is a bit difficult to follow, and as Dolliver (1969) complained, the figures are misleading. Dolliver questioned Strong's conclusion, based on the results of his 18-year follow-up of Stanford students (Strong, 1955), that there are 3.6 to 1 odds for a man's entering an occupation where he has a high score, and 5 to 1 odds against his entering an occupation where he scored low.

In a refreshing (and rare) extension of the critic's usual role, Dolliver himself grappled with the problem of how best to report the results of an SVIB predictive-validity study (Dolliver et al., 1972). He and two of his associates, James Irvin and Stephen Bigley, searched the files of the University of Missouri Testing and Counseling Service for SVIBs completed at least nine years earlier and found 1,000 men who had been tested, on the average, 12 years earlier. They managed to collect follow-up data from 130 of them who were in occupations for which the SVIB has a corresponding Occupational Scale. (They actually received data from 220 men; 90 were in occupations with no SVIB scale.) Using classification methods developed by McArthur (1954), they classified these men into three categories according to the predictive level of their earlier scores: Good Hits, Poor Hits, and Clean Misses.

Their results are reported in Table 6-8, a table adapted from their report, which includes the results from several of the predictive-validity studies just discussed. The data in the first row of Table 6-8 were taken from Strong's 18-year follow-up of Stanford students: Good Hits were those with standard scores of 45 or above on the scale for the occupation they ultimately entered; Poor Hits were standard scores of 40-44; and Clean Misses were scores of 39 or below. As mentioned above, McArthur (1954) split his sample of Harvard students into students from private and public high schools. Trimble (1966) separated his sample into two subgroups: one in occupations for which matching, or direct, scales were available, a second in occupations for which related scales had to be used. Brandt and Hood (1968) studied two groups, normal and deviant (so classified on the basis of their MMPI profiles).

Scanning the table gives a general picture of the level of predictive accuracy one can expect: the Good Hit rate centers around 50 percent, from McArthur's high of 61 percent to Dolliver's low of 42 percent. The results, though ranging over 20 percentage points, are *relatively* consistent, especially given the variability in age of the subjects when tested, purpose of testing, specific techniques of investigators, percent of earlier sample reassessed, and variability of classification techniques. All things considered, the hit rate looks to be about 50 percent.

In an extension of this work, Dolliver and Kunce (1973) identified another source of error in validity studies that depend on following up individuals over time—that is, the characteristics of people who choose not to cooperate with the researcher. They asked the question, "Who drops out of an SVIB follow-up study?" then answered it using data from the original testing of these dropouts. "We found those in intellectual occupations and those with the most accurate SVIB results show greater likelihood of dropping out. . . . Those for whom the [earlier] SVIB was most accurate did not make themselves available for further study." Their data thus suggest that the level of predictive accuracy reported by follow-up studies is a conservative estimate of true validity.

Dolliver's conclusions about predictive accuracy are worth stating here, both because he has given consid-

TABLE 6-8

Dolliver's Summary of SVIB Predictive-Validity Studies: Percentages of Sample Falling in Three Hit Categories

Study[a]	N	Study span (years)	Good hits (above 44)	Poor hits (40-44)	Clean misses (below 40)
Strong (direct scale)	524	18	48%	18%	34%
McArthur (total sample)	60	14	45	20	35
McArthur (public school)	31	14	61	13	26
Trimble (total sample)	177	10	44	15	41
Trimble (direct scale)	120	10	49	17	34
Brandt and Hood (total sample)	259	7	47	20	33
Brandt and Hood (normals)	129	7	56	16	28
Dolliver et al. (total sample)	130	12	42	12	46

[a] See text for an explanation of the parenthetical qualifications.

erable thought to this issue and because he comes to the topic as critic, unencumbered with the rose-colored glasses that test authors are prone to use in describing the validity statistics of their inventories. Dolliver et al. (1972) said (and all italics are in the original):

Data gathered in this study and the summary of results from other studies indicate that the "3.6-to-1" statement [of E. K. Strong's] is an overstatement. The best estimate seems to be that a score of 45 or higher (A— score), one of several, would be predictive of the occupation entered for somewhat less than 50 percent of the subjects over long periods of time. Thus, statements about SVIB A scores would be accurate and easily understood if the wording were changed to *the chances are about 1-to-1 that a man would end up in an occupation for which he received an A score.* The "5-to-1" statement [of E. K. Strong's] regarding SVIB C scores [30 and below] seems an *under-statement.* . . . A more accurate statement regarding C scores would be that *the chances are about 8-to-1 that a person will not end up in an occupation for which he received a C score.*

All of these studies were based on initial and follow-up testing with the older forms of the SVIB. A recent study by Spokane (1979) examined the predictive validity of the SCII for college women and men over a 3½-year span. Excellent predictive validity was found for 42.5 percent of the females and 59.3 percent of the males. Thus, SCII predictive-validity hit rates compare favorably with the older SVIB hit rates, which averaged around 50 percent. Spokane also found that students who stated interests consistent with their measured interests reported higher levels of job satisfaction.

Predictive accuracy among black students. Racial differences in interests have not been a problem with interest inventories, for no such differences have been identified. An important study of predictive accuracy for blacks tested with the earlier SVIB Occupational

Scales was reported by Borgen and Harper (1973). They compared predictive accuracy for white and black students who had been winners of the National Achievement and National Merit Scholarships and concluded that "membership in career groups was predicted at least as well for these able blacks as it was for the whites." Nor is that finding restricted to high academic achievers: in a study of vocational high school students, Barnette and McCall (1964) reported no differences between blacks and whites.

Predictive validity and the Basic Interest Scales. Another study related to the predictive validity of the Occupational Scales was published by Johnson and Johansson (1972). They reanalyzed data from earlier studies of male students who had had high scores on either the Life Insurance Agent or Physicist scales. Ten years later, about 75 percent of these students were in occupations related to their earlier profiles. But what was more revealing was that whether a student with a high score on an Occupational Scale went directly into that occupation or into a related occupation was influenced considerably by his score on the appropriate Basic Interest Scale. For example, a student with a high score on the Life Insurance Agent scale and a high score on the Sales Basic Interest Scale was likely to become a salesman; another student, with the same score on the Life Insurance Agent scale but a *low* score on the Sales scale (which meant that his common interests with salesmen were in areas other than sales), was more likely to enter a related occupation, such as public relations or advertising.

The principal result of their study was to show that the more consistency there is between scores on the Occupational Scales and scores on the Basic Interest Scales, the more specific (and more confident) the counselor can be in predicting outcomes from the profile. Chapter 5 discusses the issue of consistency (or inconsistency) further.

Unpredictable Scales

One embarrassment in working with empirical scales is that they do not always behave predictably. If several scales are constructed under precisely the same rules for item selection, weighting, and norming, then the scales should operate in similar fashion—yet often they do not. Their validities, as measured by percent overlap between samples, sometimes vary markedly; their reliabilities also vary, though they are usually more consistent, given equal scale length, than are the validities. When this variation between scales of similar items is combined with the variations created by differing numbers of items per scale and differing levels of item validity, the range in characteristics across the total set of scales is large.

The most noticeable variation from one Occupational Scale to another is in the population mean—that is, the average score earned on an Occupational Scale by people not in that occupation. In every form of the inventory, there have been scales with uncomfortably high population means. On the 1938 men's form, for example, it was the Farmer scale—over 50 percent of high school senior boys scored at or above the mean of farmers. Other problem scales were the Real Estate Salesman scale, which had the greatest overlap with Men-in-General of any scale on the profile, and Musician-Performer, a scale on which the majority of liberal arts students scored high. On the 1946 women's form, it was the Elementary School Teacher, Secretary, and Housewife scales; high scores for young women were common on these scales. On the 1966 men's form, the Physical Therapist and Computer Programmer scales showed many more high scores than the other scales, and on the 1969 women's form, the same was true for the Army Officer and Navy Officer scales. Much of what is known as "shrewd, clinical interpretive skill" comes from knowing about and having a reasonable explanation for these high population means.

Though good counselors learn to overcome, and even profit by, these aberrations, we should not forget that that is exactly what they are—aberrations. We do not intend that the scales behave differently; they just do, and we have to learn to deal with their idiosyncrasies. Why scales with apparently similar items have different scale characteristics is something that remains unexplained.

CHAPTER SEVEN

Merging of the Men's and Women's Forms

The SVIB-SCII is the first form of the Strong to be designed for use by both men and women. Historically, beginning with the men's form published in 1927 and the women's in 1933, the interests of the two sexes have been analyzed separately. Two reasons may be cited for Strong's decision to make that enduring distinction: first, the item responses of men and women were demonstrably different in the 1930's; second, the employment patterns of men and women differed markedly, not only in the large number of women in the housewife-mother role but also in the radically different distribution of the sexes in many occupations. Given these two factors, the provision of a single inventory seemed inappropriate.

For nearly four decades, dissatisfaction with this system was minimal, though Strong himself was always eager for women to undertake research on the women's form. For its part, the counseling profession never really settled upon a rationale for handling the two forms: some counselors, for example, used the men's form with career-oriented women. Moreover, the dual system was cumbersome: for example, a researcher testing a group of 20 men and 20 women was forced to choose among giving everybody one form, eliminating one sex from the sample, or using two different forms with two small subsamples.

More profound concerns began to emerge in the 1960's. As attention focused on the inequalities of the sex roles, and as pressures increased on institutions and programs that were continuing to separate the sexes artificially, the necessity and wisdom of two separate systems was questioned more often, and more vigorously.

One of the main goals in developing the SCII, then, was to eliminate completely any differential treatment of the sexes. This has proved difficult, since men and women continue to respond differently to the individual inventory items.

Differences Between Men and Women

Men and women, *on the average*, report somewhat different interests; no one who works closely with the results from interest inventories can avoid coming to that conclusion. That fact must be handled carefully, however, when working with any single individual, for he/she can easily fall outside of the averages; the existence of average differences is no justification for limiting the options of either sex, because the overlap is so large that the ranges are almost identical.

The problem confronting those responsible for interest inventories is how to work with the differences that do occur—so that the unique qualities of every individual of either sex can be addressed by the scoring system—without using the group differences to restrict the choices of any one person.

The nature of the difference. Men and women differ substantially in their responses to many inventory items. Specifically, the response differences between the Men- and Women-in-General samples are 16 percent or larger on 149 of the items. Because the importance attached to any particular response is a direct function of the frequency of that response among various samples—the criterion samples, the reference samples, and the Special Scale normative samples—these differences between men and women become a major factor in determining how the data from any single individual are to be analyzed.

For example, the item *Interior decorator* is marked "Like" by a substantial majority of women (67 percent of the Women-in-General sample) though by only a minority of men (28 percent of the Men-in-General sample). Consequently, when a woman gives this response, she is not telling us anything very useful; she is responding in a way typical of most women, and we have made only minimal progress toward understanding her occupational interests. But when a man responds "Like," he has chosen an unusual response, one suggesting that he, unlike most men, has interests in common with men in such occupations as interior decoration, art, and architecture. Because of these patterns, the sex of the respondent must be considered when the answer sheet is scored.

Teenage sex differences. Differences between the sexes in vocational interests appear early; in fact, they overwhelm all other considerations in the vocational musings of grade-school children. Data illustrating this point are listed in Table 7-1, which reports the most popular occupations, in terms of percent "Like" responses to particular items, for the boys and girls in a typical eighth-grade class tested in 1972 with the SCII. Obviously, sex role was the most important ingredient in their responses. Only one occupational

TABLE 7-1

Popular Occupations Among Male ($N = 81$) and
Female ($N = 76$) Eighth-Graders

Occupation item	Percentage "Like"		
	Girls	Boys	Difference
Occupations marked "Like" by more than half of the boys			
Auto racer	24%	65%	41
Jet pilot	22	57	35
Cartoonist	61	57	−4
Professional athlete	45	53	8
Inventor	17	51	34
Occupations marked "Like" by more than half of the girls			
Children's clothes designer	76%	14%	62
Interior decorator	68	21	47
Fashion model	66	11	55
Costume designer	64	13	51
Flight attendant	64	20	44
Actor/Actress	63	33	30
Home economics teacher	61	12	49
Cartoonist	61	57	4
Elementary school teacher	61	26	35
Nurse's aide/Orderly	59	10	49
Manager, child care center	58	11	47
Dressmaker/Tailor	57	15	42
Photographer	56	34	22
Manager, women's style shop	55	10	45
Waiter/Waitress	55	16	39
Artist	54	35	19
Typist	53	9	44

item, *Cartoonist*, appeared on both lists; every other occupation among the popular items has a strong sex-role identification.

Adult sex differences. Differences between the sexes diminish with age but never become trivial. An example of an item showing differences over all ages is given in Table 7-2, which lists the response data for several samples to the item *Operating machinery*. These are samples of convenience, and are used only for illustrative purposes; the first four comparisons, in particular, are between small samples and must be viewed with caution. (As explained in more detail in Chapter 3, item-response comparisons are more valid and more stable when the samples contain at least 200 individuals.)

The first sample is an eighth-grade class from a typical suburban school. The second is a ninth-grade class from a slightly more rural setting. The third consists of 112 National Merit Scholarship finalists from Kansas. The fourth is 42 pairs of husbands and wives who were tested during the preliminary tryout of the new inventory. The fifth is Strong's original Men- and Women-in-General samples collected during the 1930's and 1940's. The sixth is the SVIB Men- and Women-in-General samples tested during the 1960's. The seventh is the SCII Men- and Women-in-General samples (the General Reference Sample), tested in the 1970's.

The response percentages listed in Table 7-2 show that the male-female difference on this item, reported in the last column for each sample, was relatively constant over all samples. Although the percentages vary

from sample to sample, generally about half of the males, compared with a fifth of the females, answered "Like." The smallest difference, that between the small samples of National Merit Scholarship winners, is attributable to the low response among the males.

The strong and consistent male-female difference in mechanical interests is shown graphically in Fig. 7-1, which plots the distribution of "Like" percentages to the item *Operating machinery* for over 400 occupational samples. Male samples are distinguished graphically from female samples. The distributions overlap considerably, but the separation between the sexes is obvious. The samples with the highest and lowest percentages for each sex, listed at the top of the table, are interesting.

This figure, incidentally, is another illustration of the varied popularity of items over many occupations (see Chapter 3). The range of percent "Like" responses was from 4 percent (Christian education directors) to 97 percent (farmers).

Sex differences within the same occupation. Although male-female differences are obvious when general male groups are compared with general female groups, one might suppose that such differences do not appear when men and women in the same occupation

TABLE 7-2

Item-Response Comparisons to the Item *Operating machinery*
for Seven Pairs of Male-Female Samples

Sample	Response	N and response percentage		
		Males	Females	Difference
Eighth-graders	N	81	76	
(Mahtomedi, Minn.,	Like	33%	14%	19
1972)	Indifferent	32	28	4
	Dislike	35	58	−23
Ninth-graders	N	91	108	
(Stillwater, Minn.,	Like	62%	14%	48
1972)	Indifferent	25	32	−7
	Dislike	13	54	−41
National Merit	N	75	37	
Scholarship winners	Like	24%	14%	10
(Kansas, 1973)	Indifferent	40	45	−5
	Dislike	36	41	−5
Husbands and wives	N	42	42	
(1972)	Like	52%	14%	38
	Indifferent	24	36	−12
	Dislike	24	50	−26
Men- and Women-in-	N	500	500	
General (1938, 1946)	Like	54%	27%	27
	Indifferent	26	34	−8
	Dislike	20	39	−19
Men- and Women-in-	N	1,000	1,000	
General (1969)	Like	42%	26%	16
	Indifferent	34	32	2
	Dislike	24	42	−18
General Reference	N	300	300	
Sample (1973)	Like	47%	23%	24
	Indifferent	34	36	−2
	Dislike	19	41	−22

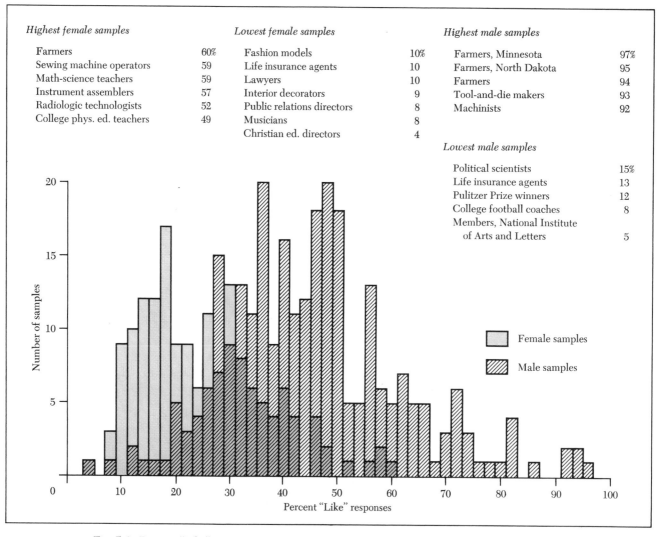

Fig. 7-1. Percent "Like" responses to the item *Operating Machinery* for 438 occupational samples

are compared. Table 7-3 demonstrates that the differences persist. These data consider men and women in the same occupation, contrasting their responses to those items showing large differences between men- and women-in-general. Twelve pairs of samples, all of them collected for this revision of the SCII, were selected, with each of the six Holland types represented by two pairs of samples. The samples were large and well selected: each individual had had at least two years of experience; all reported that they liked their work; and, wherever appropriate, all had the necessary degree or certification in their field.

These samples can be used to determine whether the contrasts in interests between men and women disappear when samples from the same occupation are compared. There are three possibilities:

1. Men and women in the same occupation have the same interests.

2. They have different interests, but the differences are specific to each occupation.

3. They have different interests, and the differences are constant across all occupations.

To study this point, the ten SCII items that Men-in-General prefer more often than Women-in-General (26-percent or greater difference) and the ten items that Women-in-General prefer more often than Men-in-General (34-percent or greater difference) are listed in Table 7-3. The percentages in the table indicate the contrast between the male and female occupational samples in their percentage "Like" responses to these items. For example, the first number in the first row shows the MIG-WIG comparison on the item *Decorating a room with flowers*, a 57-percent difference (70 percent of the women versus 13 percent of the men responded "Like"). The numbers in the succeeding columns report the analogous figures for male and female

TABLE 7-3

SCII Items Showing Large Response Differences Between Men and Women in the Same Occupations

(Percentage difference between the two sexes in "Like" response to the designated item)

Item	MIG vs. WIG	Farmers	Police officers	Physical therapists	Physicists	Musicians	Photographers	Elementary education teachers	Social workers	Chamber of Commerce executives	Personnel directors	Accountants	Credit managers	Average of 12 samples
Items favored by women														
Decorate a room with flowers	57%	56%	65%	62%	39%	57%	53%	60%	56%	37%	56%	49%	56%	54%
Sewing	50	55	33	51	38	47	33	45	38	52	36	47	46	43
Costume designer	42	36	43	34	25	43	36	43	32	38	40	37	46	38
Preparing dinner for guests	42	56	32	43	32	23	29	34	34	37	32	33	43	36
Family pages in the newspaper	40	52	35	39	24	38	28	47	30	45	34	35	39	37
Interior decorator	39	47	48	42	25	38	26	46	40	42	40	45	45	40
Florist	36	49	37	37	16	35	31	42	36	32	25	24	27	33
Trying new recipes	36	60	34	36	32	24	28	38	41	41	36	39	36	37
Author of children's books	34	41	21	32	9	26	33	22	20	16	27	19	19	24
Dressmaker/Tailor	34	43	30	30	21	26	15	30	27	34	20	25	38	28
Items favored by men														
Industrial arts	39%	18%	16%	24%	11%	1%	18%	28%	16%	13%	23%	13%	36%	18%
Popular mechanics magazines	37	42	38	38	37	27	36	41	34	30	36	21	40	35
Mechanical engineer	32	40	26	21	8	15	19	28	16	14	21	15	25	21
Enjoy tinkering with small hand tools	31	25	29	22	26	29	21	41	26	33	36	21	41	29
Sports pages in the newspaper	31	29	39	46	25	26	18	38	37	34	38	46	41	35
Have mechanical ingenuity	27	35	21	6	16	21	20	18	16	12	17	5	21	17
Boxing	26	18	38	23	10	23	16	23	18	20	30	20	16	21
Building contractor	26	34	31	16	19	5	15	30	16	28	26	18	22	22
Electronics technician	26	23	20	28	11	21	19	21	14	5	11	6	15	16
Manufacturer	26	30	18	31	23	10	23	24	18	52	28	25	34	26

farmers, male and female police officers, and so forth. The last number shows the average difference for this item across the twelve samples. The figures in the first and last columns are in most cases quite similar, differing by only 4 or 5 percentage points.

These data indicate that the differences in interests between men and women are relatively constant across all occupations in all of the Holland-code areas; no occupation is free of them, nor does any occupation studied have any novel pattern of differences that does not appear in other occupations.

The data in Table 7-3, then, clearly show that sex cannot (or should not) be ignored in norming interest inventories. No matter how samples are selected, men and women respond differently to some items. To ignore this fact would be to introduce unnecessary error variance. Somehow, our methods of analysis must accommodate these differences without penalizing either sex.

Sex differences over time. Differences between the sexes in vocational interests may be diminishing, in response to the growing awareness that many aspects of traditional sex roles are arbitrary. That possibility can be studied empirically, using data from the archives at the Center for Interest Measurement Research. Male and female samples from five occupations, tested during the 1930's, are available for comparison with similar samples from the 1960's and 1970's; Table 7-4 reports the results.

Four items showing male-female response differences were used, two chosen more often by men (*Repairing electrical wiring* and *Expressing judgments publicly, regardless of what others say*) and two chosen more often by women (*Decorating a room with flowers* and *Regular hours for work*). For each item, the percentage of each male and female sample responding "Like" is listed in the table, as well as the difference between the two. These four items were not selected in an attempt to exaggerate differences; they were chosen because they are typical of male-female high-contrast items. Of the 20 comparisons (four items over five occupations), 13 show larger differences in the 60's than in the 30's. In general, the gap between men and women on these items was at least as great as and

TABLE 7-4

Male-Female Response Differences on Selected SCII Items:
1930's vs. 1960's vs. 1970's Samples
(Percent of each sample responding "Like")

Occupation	Sample	Decorating a room with flowers			Regular Hours for work			Repairing electrical wiring			Expressing judgments publicly		
		Male	Female	Difference	Male	Female	Difference	Male	Female	Difference	Male	Female	Difference
Artists	1930's	42%	87%	−45	39%	63%	−24	29%	17%	+12	38%	32%	+6
	1960's	31	80	−49	29	48	−19	24	11	+13	60	40	+20
	1970's	34	73	−39	15	25	−10	23	15	+8	51	45	+6
Lawyers	1930's	21	79	−58	57	59	−2	31	23	+8	55	49	+6
	1960's	9	63	−54	30	40	−10	32	8	+24	66	49	+17
	1970's	15	62	−47	27	29	−2	31	16	+15	60	62	−2
Life insurance agents	1930's	34	85	−51	49	56	−7	35	15	+20	41	32	+9
	1960's	14	76	−62	14	26	−12	31	8	+23	56	38	+18
	1970's	12	71	−59	14	17	−3	33	9	+24	50	44	+6
Reporters	1930's	30	83	−53	47	72	−25	22	12	+10	56	38	+18
	1960's	12	78	−66	24	36	−12	25	9	+16	68	49	+19
	1970's	16	69	−53	36	38	−2	18	12	+6	62	51	+11
YMCA-YWCA staff	1930's	31	92	−61	55	60	−5	50	23	+27	37	21	+16
	1960's	10	70	−60	36	33	+3	40	20	+20	35	38	−3
	1970's	14	70	−56	29	42	−13	34	17	+17	47	38	+9

perhaps greater in the 1960's than it was in the 1930's. Data for the 1970's samples indicate differences comparable to those in the 1930's, suggesting a slight trend toward reduced male-female differences. But certainly, the differences have not disappeared; until they do, the major research effort should be directed toward developing a system that accommodates the contrasts.

Item changes over time. Although the main purpose of preparing Table 7-4 was to study male-female differences over time, the arrangement of the data also permits analysis of the change in popularity for each of the four items. Each had a different pattern. The first, *Decorating a room with flowers*, showed a mild decrease in popularity over time, roughly 10 percentage points among both men and women. The second, *Regular hours for work*, showed a marked decrease in popularity in both sexes, with differences between the 1930's and 1970's samples amounting to 25 or 35 percent, a considerable shift. The third, *Repairing electrical wiring*, showed little change for either sex. The fourth, *Expressing judgments publicly, regardless of what others say*, showed a sizable increase, especially among the male samples.

Such changes in item responses over time, which are reported in greater detail in the *Handbook for the SVIB*, demonstrate why psychological tests must be renormed periodically.

Constructing the SCII Occupational Scales

In recent years, several experimental methods of Occupational Scale construction were studied to further

knowledge about the best possible procedures for measuring the interests of women and men (Hansen, 1976). All of the methods begin with one of two approaches. One approach assumes that occupationally relevant sex differences exist, and that the best technique is separate-sex scale construction that provides a male and a female scale for each occupation. The other approach assumes that the sex differences in interests documented in previous sections of this chapter are irrelevant to interest measurement, and that the preferred technique is the development of combined-sex scales that differentiate people in the same occupation from people-in-general.

Separate-sex approach, two methods. Method 1 is the empirical-scale-construction technique used with the Strong for the past 54 years; the method involves contrasting criterion subjects, all of the same sex and same occupation, with an in-general sample of the same sex. Method 2, a modification of the separate-sex construction technique, was developed to eliminate items that differentiate women from men. Johansson and Harmon (1972) distinguished between valid and nonvalid sex-differentiating items: items that differentiated men-in-general from women-in-general were defined as nonvalid discriminators; but items differentiating women from men in the same occupation were defined as valid discriminators. They suggested, as has Rayman (1976), that when nonvalid sex-differentiating items are eliminated, women and men should score similarly on the resulting scales, and also that scales developed on that basis should be more

TABLE 7-5

Tilton Percent-Overlap Statistics for the Experimental Scales

(See Table 6-7 and associated text)

Experimental method	Method number	Sex of scale	Occupational Scale (sex indicated in column 3)											
			Radiologic Technologist		Physicist		Librarian		Social Worker		Personnel Director		Credit Manager	
			Q	%Ov	Q	%Ov	Q	%Ov	Q	%Ov	Q	%Ov	Q	%Ov
Separate sexes, biased items retained	1	f	1.76	38	2.77	17	1.59	43	1.48	46	1.97	32	2.10	30
Separate sexes, biased items eliminated	2	f	1.69	40	2.50	21	1.36	50	1.42	48	1.78	37	1.98	32
Separate sexes, biased items retained	1	m	2.07	30	2.38	23	1.96	33	1.91	34	1.61	42	1.40	48
Separate sexes, biased items eliminated	2	m	1.96	33	2.14	28	1.66	41	1.66	41	1.45	47	1.41	48
Combined sexes, biased items retained	3	—	1.83	36	2.51	21	1.69	40	1.52	45	1.52	45	1.55	45
Combined sexes, biased items eliminated	4	—	1.78	38	2.27	26	1.36	50	1.36	50	1.52	45	1.45	47

valid and reliable than those developed using Method 1.

Combined-sex approach, two methods. Method 3 is an extension of Method 1 that uses the entire SCII item pool (325 items) to build the best possible scale, using combined-sex criterion and contrast samples. Method 4 also develops a combined-sex scale, but, like Method 2, eliminates nonvalid sex-differentiating items from the available SCII item pool.

Studies examining the four experimental methods. All four of the experimental methods were explored in a study by Hansen (1976), who used criterion samples of female and male sociologists; Methods 1, 3, and 4 were studied by Webber and Harmon (1978), who used criterion samples of female and male veterinarians and life insurance agents.

Both studies found, for all of the methods, that results vary depending on the sex and occupation of the criterion group. To summarize: Hansen found that the method that produced the most valid scale for female sociologists was Method 1 (separate sexes, biased items retained) or Method 4 (combined sexes, biased items eliminated); and that the most valid scale for male sociologists was Method 1. Webber and Harmon found that the most valid scales for both female veterinarians and female life insurance agents were developed using Method 3 (combined sexes, biased items retained); and that the most valid scales for both male veterinarians and male life insurance agents were developed using Method 1. No particular pattern is evident in these results, except perhaps that Method 2 is not represented in any of the "best" characterizations.

Hansen also examined the item overlap of the separate-sex male and female scales developed with Method 1 (biased items retained) and Method 2 (biased items eliminated). She found that for the sociologists only 27 percent of the items on the female and male scales (Method 1) were identical. Eliminating the sex-biased items (Method 2) increased the item overlap for the separate-sex scales, but still only 41 percent of the items were shared. The non-overlapping items, according to Johansson and Harmon (1972), reflect real occupational differences between men and women in sociology.

Tables 7-5 and 7-6 present data derived from the application of the four experimental methods to additional occupations. The occupations were selected to represent each of the six Holland types and are presented in the tables in RIASEC order. In all instances the samples are large, well-selected groups composed of people who said that they like their work, were at least 25 years old, and had been in the occupation for at least three years. Although half of the occupations have traditionally been entered more often by women, and half more often by men, all six occupations have been open to both men and women for a sufficient number of years to ensure the measurement of interests that truly represent the occupations.

Table 7-5 summarizes the Tilton percentage-overlap validities for the six occupations (see Chapter 6 for a thorough discussion of the Tilton overlap statistics). The criterion groups used in calculating the overlap percentages were, for the female scales, the female criterion samples and the WIG; for the male scales, the male criterion samples and the MIG; and, for the combined scales, the male and female criterion samples and the General Reference Sample. *For every occupation the best scale for at least one of the two sexes was the scale developed using Method 1.* For example, Method 1 produced the most valid scale for male radiologic technologists, female physicists, male librarians, male social workers, male and female personnel directors, and female credit managers. In most of the instances where Method 1 was the most successful for one sex, Method 3 was the most successful for the opposite sex. Thus, Method 3 worked best (produced the

TABLE 7-6

Shared and Unshared Items on Matched Male and Female Occupational Scales for Two Methods of Scale Construction

	Scale-construction method													
Occupational Scale (sex as indicated in column heads)	Method 1 (Separate sexes, biased items retained)							Method 2 (Separate sexes, biased items eliminated)						
	Items on female scale only		Items on male scale only		Items on both male and female scales		Total shared	Items on female scale only		Items on male scale only		Items on both male and female scales		Total shared
	N	%Ov	N	%Ov	N	%Ov		N	%Ov	N	%Ov	N	%Ov	
RADIOLOGIC TECHNOLOGIST	16	26%	23	38%	22	36%	61	6	19%	13	42%	12	39%	31
PHYSICIST	27	30	30	33	34	37	91	15	19	16	20	49	61	80
LIBRARIAN	39	39	41	40	21	21	101	12	21	24	42	21	37	57
SOCIAL WORKER	35	36	35	36	28	28	98	26	33	21	27	32	40	79
PERSONNEL DIRECTOR	32	34	28	30	34	36	94	22	33	13	20	31	47	66
CREDIT MANAGER	36	37	26	26	36	37	98	21	26	25	31	35	43	81

most valid scales) for female radiologic technologists, male physicists, female librarians, female social workers, and male credit managers. In no instance was either Method 2 or Method 4, both of which eliminate sex-differentiating items, the technique that produced the most valid scale. Table 7-6 illustrates the large percentages of items that differentiate men from women in the same occupation *even after nonvalid sex-differentiating items* (those with large WIG and MIG differences) *are eliminated*. Although the percent of overlapping items on the separate female- and male-normed scales does increase, the overlap generally remains less than 50 percent, leaving a sizable number of items that represent valid sex differences in interests within an occupation.

As these data demonstrate, developing a strategy for the construction of empirical Occupational Scales is a complicated issue. What works best (is most valid) for one occupation may be the least valid for another. But if users are to accept and understand the results on the Occupational Scales, the same method of scale construction must be used for both sexes and all occupations. To mix the modes of scale construction would lead to unimaginable confusion. Thus, because combined-sex construction is not the most *valid* approach for most occupations, and because combined-sex scales are often less *reliable* than separate-sex scales, single-sex construction continues to be the strategy used to develop the SCII Occupational Scales. Moreover, Method 1 (biased items retained) is superior to Method 2 (biased items eliminated) because Method 1 takes advantage of *all* the differences in interests between people in an occupation and people not in the occupation, whereas Method 2 (and 4) ignores those differences that are sex-related.

Intuitively, scale constructors would expect these results, but of course only the results of careful studies can validate the intuition.

Using Opposite-Sex Scales

The results of constructing separate-sex scales can be studied by inspecting occupations for which scales for both sexes are available. These scales are listed in Table 7-7, along with the results from the General Reference Samples of 300 women and 300 men. The critical issue is whether the two scales for each occupation (for example, male and female ELEMENTARY TEACHER) perform equally well with either sex, or whether the scales perform better when used with the appropriate sex. (The third possibility, that the scales perform *better* when used for the *opposite* sex, was not considered; but as the data demonstrate, that is not the case.) The data most useful in answering the question are the mean differences listed in Table 7-7. If the scales perform equally well with both sexes, those differences should be roughly zero. They are not; they are mostly negative, showing that each sex usually scores lower on its own scale than on the scale for the other sex. *Assuming that low scores are good*—because low scores indicate good separation between the General Reference Sample and the occupational samples—the differences show that the appropriate-sex scale is usually superior. Empirical scales developed on male samples work better for men; those developed on female samples work better for women.

This conclusion does not always hold, since the item-by-item sex differences influence each scale differently. Although the influence is not consistent, the tendency is for men to score higher on those pairs of scales dominated by traditionally "male" items and for women to score higher on those pairs dominated by traditionally "female" items. "Male" and "female," here, refer to items showing large differences in popularity between men- and women-in-general. Consequently, on scales such as ARMY OFFICER and MEDICAL TECHNOLOGIST, men ("men-in-general sample," in the table) have higher means than women, on both men's *and* women's scales; whereas on scales such as MUSICIAN and ART TEACHER, women ("women-in-general sample") have higher means than men, again on both men's and women's scales.

This relationship leads to complexity in the interpretation of Occupational Scales developed for men and women who are in occupations stereotypically

TABLE 7-7
Women- and Men-in-General Mean Scores on, and Correlations Between, the 77 Pairs of Women's and Men's Occupational Scales

Scale	Women-in-General				Men-in-General			
	Correlation between m and f scales	Mean score on female scale	Mean score on male scale	Mean difference	Correlation between m and f scales	Mean score on male scale	Mean score on female scale	Mean difference
ACCOUNTANT	.66	21	22	−1	.71	28	37	−9
ADVERTISING EXECUTIVE	.63	30	33	−3	.55	30	38	−8
AIR FORCE OFFICER	.67	25	17	+8	.74	30	42	−12
ARCHITECT	.69	17	30	−13	.58	23	33	−10
ARMY OFFICER	.82	29	21	+8	.84	30	43	−13
ART TEACHER	.75	20	35	−15	.79	16	14	+2
ARTIST, COMMERCIAL	.78	20	32	−12	.78	21	25	−4
ARTIST, FINE	.82	22	29	−7	.81	20	29	−9
BANKER	.74	30	23	+7	.76	29	33	−4
BEAUTICIAN	.48	28	44	−16	.21	30	27	+3
BIOLOGIST	.79	21	32	−11	.75	24	32	−8
BUSINESS EDUCATION TEACHER	.92	21	30	−9	.89	23	22	+1
BUYER	.74	24	22	+2	.79	25	28	−3
CHAMBER OF COMMERCE EXECUTIVE	.81	28	23	+5	.81	24	31	−7
CHEMIST	.84	16	23	−7	.78	20	33	−13
CHIROPRACTOR	.60	24	32	−8	.61	34	33	+1
COLLEGE PROFESSOR	.82	35	42	−7	.83	36	42	−6
COMPUTER PROGRAMMER	.67	30	34	−4	.76	35	43	−8
CREDIT MANAGER	.85	26	29	−3	.86	33	33	0
DENTIST	.64	26	31	−5	.60	30	38	−8
DEPARTMENT STORE MANAGER	.80	28	33	−5	.89	32	36	−4
DIETITIAN	.50	28	39	−11	.54	31	32	−1
ELECTED PUBLIC OFFICIAL	.88	27	30	−3	.93	31	34	−3
ELEMENTARY EDUCATION TEACHER	.59	33	42	−9	.66	29	22	+7
ENGINEER	.82	22	19	−3	.85	28	40	−12
ENGLISH TEACHER	.87	32	38	−6	.88	30	23	+7
EXECUTIVE HOUSEKEEPER	.87	29	37	−8	.90	34	31	+3
FARMER	.81	33	28	+5	.86	32	37	−5
FLIGHT ATTENDANT	.78	30	44	−14	.70	32	29	+3
FOREIGN LANGUAGE TEACHER	.69	28	44	−16	.73	27	20	+7
FORESTER	.52	21	29	−8	.64	31	36	−5
GEOGRAPHER	.64	29	31	−2	.51	24	43	−19
GEOLOGIST	.77	19	26	−7	.81	26	35	−9
GUIDANCE COUNSELOR	.78	31	30	+1	.77	29	26	+3
INTERIOR DECORATOR	.62	16	37	−21	.65	24	15	+9
IRS AGENT	.79	33	25	+8	.78	37	43	−6
LAWYER	.70	24	34	−10	.71	32	38	−6
LIBRARIAN	.58	31	43	−12	.60	29	36	−7
LIFE INSURANCE AGENT	.89	23	19	+4	.95	24	30	−6
MARKETING EXECUTIVE	.84	24	28	−4	.79	31	35	−4
MATHEMATICIAN	.83	20	28	−8	.85	23	30	−7
MATH-SCIENCE TEACHER	.68	32	29	+3	.62	33	38	−5
MEDICAL TECHNOLOGIST	.90	28	23	+5	.88	25	35	−10
MINISTER	.85	23	29	−6	.89	24	23	+1
MUSICIAN	.83	32	41	−9	.90	30	29	+1
NAVY OFFICER	.71	29	20	+9	.76	31	44	−13
NURSE, LICENSED PRACTICAL	.73	26	42	−16	.65	29	20	+9
NURSE, REGISTERED	.55	31	35	−4	.57	27	31	−4
NURSING HOME ADMINISTRATOR	.82	25	32	−7	.87	30	29	+1
OCCUPATIONAL THERAPIST	.65	28	39	−11	.74	26	32	−6
OPTOMETRIST	.65	32	31	+1	.66	29	44	−15
PERSONNEL DIRECTOR	.87	28	29	−1	.88	31	36	−5
PHARMACIST	.51	31	28	+3	.39	28	40	−12
PHOTOGRAPHER	.76	32	39	−7	.72	33	39	−6
PHYSICAL EDUCATION TEACHER	.77	23	25	−2	.70	19	34	−15
PHYSICAL THERAPIST	.79	28	29	−1	.82	26	33	−7
PHYSICIAN	.82	27	26	+1	.79	28	37	−9
PHYSICIST	.88	8	15	−7	.87	15	25	−10
POLICE OFFICER	.70	26	22	+4	.79	27	40	−13

(Continued)

TABLE 7-7 (*continued*)

	Women-in-General				Men-in-General			
Scale	Correlation between m and f scales	Mean score on female scale	Mean score on male scale	Mean difference	Correlation between m and f scales	Mean score on male scale	Mean score on female scale	Mean difference
PSYCHOLOGIST	.87	22	34	−12	.85	29	28	+1
PUBLIC ADMINISTRATOR	.75	23	32	−9	.64	29	36	−7
PUBLIC RELATIONS DIRECTOR	.72	21	30	−9	.78	23	30	−7
PURCHASING AGENT	.88	27	27	0	.89	34	38	−4
RADIOLOGIC TECHNOLOGIST	.86	30	32	−2	.75	27	34	−7
REALTOR	.68	20	22	−2	.83	31	28	+3
RECREATION LEADER	.73	31	33	−2	.82	32	37	−5
REPORTER	.68	25	38	−13	.74	25	32	−7
RESTAURANT MANAGER	.56	26	29	−3	.78	28	34	−6
SCHOOL ADMINISTRATOR	.84	31	32	−1	.87	32	37	−5
SOCIAL SCIENCE TEACHER	.65	34	32	+2	.69	31	33	−2
SOCIAL WORKER	.76	31	36	−5	.85	25	33	−8
SOCIOLOGIST	.83	22	31	−9	.77	23	33	−10
SPECIAL EDUCATION TEACHER	.73	35	44	−9	.77	28	29	−1
SPEECH PATHOLOGIST	.80	33	41	−8	.76	30	32	−2
SYSTEMS ANALYST	.78	28	22	+6	.78	31	43	−8
VETERINARIAN	.60	25	25	0	.65	23	33	−10
YWCA/YMCA DIRECTOR	.80	35	32	+3	.87	29	40	−11

associated with the opposite sex—for example, the scales for male ART TEACHER and female ARMY OFFICER. Because these scales are dominated by items favored by the opposite sex, opposite-sex samples tend to score higher than appropriate-sex samples. The net effect at the individual level is that virtually everyone scores higher on some of the scales for the other sex than he/she does on any of the scales for his/her own sex.

The soundest conclusion to be drawn from the data in Table 7-7 is that, where possible, Occupational Scales should be developed in pairs, one for men, one for women, and this has been the primary goal for the 1981 SVIB-SCII.

Profiling the Results

To provide a system that recognizes sex differences yet does not penalize either sex, separate scales have been maintained for the two sexes in the 1981 revision of the SCII. Scales for both men and women have been developed for 77 of the 85 occupations represented on the profile, and everyone is scored on all scales.

There were two possible approaches to profiling the Occupational Scales: (1) score each person only on scales developed for his or her own sex, or (2) score each person on all scales, regardless of the individual's sex. The data in Table 7-7 indicate that from a purely technical standpoint the best way to profile the results would be to report only the male-scale scores for men and only the female-scale scores for women. When scales such as INTERIOR DECORATOR show a 9-point difference between men's and women's scales in the male sample and a 21-point difference in the female sample, the two scales cannot be considered interchangeable. However, since one of the chief goals in the develop-

ment of this edition of the Strong was to encourage both women and men to consider occupations heretofore dominated by the other sex, our resolution to this dilemma on the SCII has been to score everyone on every scale. Although this approach does increase the problems of interpretation, it also offers the individual a maximum of information, and encourages each person to at least ponder the similarity, or lack of it, between her/his interests and those of men and women in a wide range of occupations.

The problems encountered in furnishing the respondent with scores on both same-sex and opposite-sex scales without misinterpretation are substantial, and accommodations have been made on the profile to help make interpretation more accurate. First, interpretive comments on the General Occupational Themes and Basic Interest Scales, based on the repondent's sex and on the distributions for that sex, are printed out on the profile. Second, the norms for each sex on each of the General Occupational Themes and Basic Interest Scales are printed on the profile. Third, the Occupational Scale scores are presented on the profile in both numerical and graphic manner. The intent is to make all of the scores available, while at the same time providing the appropriate normative information for each sex.

Conclusions

The data in this chapter document clearly that:

1. Men and women, on the average, respond differently to almost half of the inventory items.

2. The size of the differences is considerable.

3. The differences do not disappear when only men and women who have made the same occupational choice are compared.

4. The differences have not lessened appreciably since 1930.

5. Attempts to develop combined-sex scales appear to be premature, and the validity of these scales varies from occupation to occupation.

6. Empirical scales constructed on the basis of same-sex criterion and reference samples work better (are more valid) than scales based on opposite-sex samples.

The emphasis in this chapter has been on male-female response differences. A statement of policy is therefore appropriate at this point: these differences should in no way be used to discriminate against, repress, or embarrass any individual of either sex. Women with mechanical interests, no matter how common or rare they are, should have the same range of options open to them as do men with similar interests; analogously, men with domestic or artistic interests should not find their way barred by either formal or informal barriers. People should be allowed to follow their own inclinations; no societal need requires that individuals be limited to arbitrary occupational sex roles.

Yet the data in this chapter also demonstrate that the route to *equal* treatment is not necessarily through *identical* treatment, for identical treatment of groups that are dissimilar will not have identical impact. Thus, separate scales and separate norms are necessary, but we must be certain that they are used as a means of expanding options, not of limiting them.

CHAPTER EIGHT

The Special Scales

The Special Scales are extreme examples of the empirical approach that dominated the early history of the Strong. Each Special Scale is composed of items selected strictly according to a statistical criterion, just as the items in the Occupational Scales are selected.

Academic Comfort Scale

This scale was initially labeled ACADEMIC ACHIEVEMENT; then, when experience indicated that this was not quite the scale's flavor, the name was changed to ACADEMIC ORIENTATION. Further experience indicates that the score is most closely associated with degree of comfort in being in an academic setting, hence the second and, one hopes, the last name change.

Constructing the AC scale. The predecessors of the ACADEMIC COMFORT scale were originally constructed by comparing the item responses of good and poor students at the University of Minnesota's College of Science, Literature, and the Arts; because men and women were scored on separate inventories, the result was separate male and female scales. The single scale for the 1974 SCII was constructed by using items that were common to the previous SVIB men's and women's ACADEMIC ACHIEVEMENT scales and that had survived the screening for the merged booklet. Because all of the items on the scale are included in all three booklets, every sample in the Strong archives that responded to any of these booklets can be scored on this scale. The items that are weighted positively cover a wide range of academic topics, with emphasis on the arts and sciences. Items weighted negatively are fewer in number, with no particular common theme, except for minor clusters of sales and blue-collar items.

Norming the AC scale. The earlier forms of the scale were normed by scoring samples of liberal arts college graduates and setting their mean equal to 50. On scales developed in that fashion, samples of Ph.D.s usually scored around 60.

For the SCII AC scale, samples of Ph.D.s were used as the normative groups, since several good samples were available (the scale has not been renormed for the 1981 revision). For the men, the criterion sample of college professors ($N = 421$) was used; for the women, the criterion samples of psychologists ($N = 275$) and mathematicians ($N = 119$) were used. The raw-score means and standard deviations of these three samples were averaged (although, because they were within 2 points of each other, the effect of averaging was slight), and the results were used in a raw-score-to-standard-score conversion formula that places these samples at a standard-score mean of 60 and standard deviation of 10. The item-selection and scale-norming process was successful; both male and female occupational samples scored at virtually the same level on the SCII scale as they did on the earlier versions of the scale.

One potential complication was that the earlier scale norms might have been quite different for men and women. Because the sexes had never been combined on this scale, there was no way of knowing if one sex had "greater" academic interests than the other. If they did, then men and women from the same occupation would score differently on this scale. As the data in Table 8-1 demonstrate, men and women in 24 of the 77 pairs of matched-sex occupational samples differed by one-half standard deviation or more; in 53 pairs, they differed less, but almost all of the female samples showed more academic interest than the male samples did.

No particular characteristic distinguishes the occupations with large (± 5) male-female differences from those occupations showing only minor differences. Perhaps this is simply a manifestation of a common observation: that women are usually more comfortable in classroom settings than men. In any event, the sizable differences appeared in less than one-third of the occupations.

Data on the 1973 MIG and WIG samples show that the 300 women scored higher than the 300 men did, with means of 48.3 to 43.8, respectively, indicating that the general sample of women was more academically oriented than the analogous sample of men. The two standard deviations were 14.0 and 15.7, respectively, much larger than the 10.0 of the scale-standardization sample—which is good, because diversity in the reference samples is desirable.

AC scale validity. Table 8-2 lists mean AC scores for 198 occupational samples; these data constitute the validity foundation for this scale. The rank-ordering of the scale means is reassuringly sensible. Occupations requiring a high level of academic training—biologists, chemists, physicists, psychologists, mathematicians,

TABLE 8-1

Mean Scores of Female vs. Male Occupational Samples on the ACADEMIC COMFORT Scale

Occupational sample	Female mean	Male mean	Difference	Occupational sample	Female mean	Male mean	Difference
Accountants	46	42	+4	Mathematicians	61	60	+1
Advertising executives	44	44	0	Math-science teachers	54	52	+2
Air Force officers	48	43	+5	Medical technologists	56	55	+1
Architects	53	47	+6	Ministers	56	52	+4
Army officers	47	45	+2	Musicians	52	47	+5
Art teachers	49	46	+3	Navy officers	48	46	+2
Artists, commercial	47	43	+4	Nurses, licensed practical	49	48	+1
Artists, fine	49	48	+1	Nurses, registered	52	49	+3
Bankers	41	41	0	Nursing home administrators	44	40	+4
Beauticians	35	38	−3	Occupational therapists	49	46	+3
Biologists	65	61	+4	Optometrists	53	48	+5
Business education teachers	41	39	+2	Personnel directors	44	41	+3
Chamber of Commerce executives	39	37	+2	Pharmacists	53	47	+6
Chemists	65	62	+3	Photographers	45	42	+3
Chiropractors	50	46	+4	Physical education teachers	45	43	+2
College professors	60	59	+1	Physical therapists	52	48	+4
Computer programmers	53	48	+5	Physicians	59	59	0
Credit managers	42	39	+3	Physicists	64	61	+3
Dentists	54	51	+3	Police officers	44	39	+5
Department store managers	41	36	+5	Psychologists	61	58	+3
Dietitians	50	45	+5	Public administrators	50	50	0
Elected public officials	49	42	+7	Public relations directors	46	44	+2
Elementary education teachers	44	44	0	Purchasing agents	42	41	+1
Engineers	54	51	+3	Radiologic technologists	47	45	+2
English teachers	50	51	−1	Realtors	39	34	+5
Executive housekeepers	43	40	+3	Recreation leaders	47	41	+6
Farmers	38	33	+5	Reporters	49	48	+1
Flight attendants	42	43	−1	Restaurant managers	44	34	+10
Foreign language teachers	52	52	0	School administrators	51	46	+5
Foresters	53	45	+8	Social science teachers	48	42	+6
Geographers	55	54	+1	Social workers	50	47	+3
Geologists	59	56	+3	Sociologists	60	56	+4
Guidance counselors	51	43	+8	Special education teachers	46	45	+1
Interior decorators	42	42	0	Speech pathologists	50	50	0
IRS agents	49	42	+7	Systems analysts	54	49	+5
Lawyers	52	47	+5	Veterinarians	54	46	+8
Librarians	52	53	−1	YW/YMCA directors (1974-81)	46	41	+5
Life insurance agents	45	38	+7	Women-/Men-in-general	48	44	+4
Marketing executives	48	44	+4				

college professors, physicians—scored the highest, all in the high 50's or low to middle 60's. At the bottom of the distribution, with means more than three standard deviations lower, were occupational samples with much lower requisite educational levels — farmers, beauticians, florists, realtors, and sewing machine operators. When occupations such as these can be spread apart by three standard deviations, the scale is clearly related to educational level. Of course, this scale is not a measure of ability, but only of interests, although interests are probably as important as ability if a student is to persist to the end of graduate training.

Correlations of AC scores with grades usually range between .10 and .30. Correlations of this magnitude, indicating that the level of the score is only slightly related to grades, have been found at the University of Massachusetts, the United States Military Academy, Pennsylvania State University, and the University of California (Berkeley), as well as the University of Minnesota.

Yet, mean scores for students entering these institutions vary widely, in meaningful ways. Students entering Minnesota junior colleges have average scores of about 30-35. Freshmen at Pennsylvania State University and the University of Massachusetts have average scores of about 40-45. Freshmen entering the University of Minnesota College of Liberal Arts average about 46. Students entering the University of California (Berkeley) and Dartmouth College average about 45-50, and entering freshmen at Harvard University average 55-60. These are large differences, and, again, the rank order is eminently reasonable, suggesting that the student's score has some relationship to the institution entered.

AC scale reliability. Test-retest statistics for the AC scale over 14-day, 30-day, and 3-year intervals are pre-

TABLE 8-2

Mean Scores on the ACADEMIC COMFORT Scale for 198 Occupational Samples

Scale mean	Sample	Scale mean	Sample
65	Biologists f, Chemists f	45	Dental hygienists f, Funeral directors f, Life insurance agents f, Photographers f, Physical education teachers f; Army officers m, Dietitians m, Foresters m, Mental health workers m, Radiologic technologists m, Special education teachers m
64	Physicists f		
63			
62	Chemists m		
61	Mathematicians f, Psychologists f; Biologists m, Physicists m		
60	College professors f, Sociologists f; Mathematicians m	44	Advertising executives f, Elementary education teachers f, Restaurant managers f, Nursing home administrators f, Personnel directors f, Police officers f; Advertising executives m, Elementary education teachers m, Marketing executives m, Public relations directors m
59	Geologists f, Physicians f; College professors m, Physicians m		
58	Language interpreters f; Psychologists m		
57			
56	Medical technologists f, Ministers f; Geologists m, Sociologists m	43	Army noncommissioned officers f, Dental assistants f, Executive housekeepers f, Nightclub entertainers f; Air Force officers m, Commercial artists m, Flight attendants m, Guidance counselors m, Physical education teachers m, Vocational agriculture teachers m
55	Geographers f; Medical technologists m		
54	Dentists f, Engineers f, Math-science teachers f, Systems analysts f, Veterinarians f; Geographers m		
53	Architects f, Computer programmers f, Foresters f, Marine officers f, Optometrists f, Pharmacists f; Librarians m	42	Credit managers f, Flight attendants f, Home economics teachers f, Interior decorators f, Purchasing agents f, Stockbrokers f; Accountants m, Broadcasters m, Elected public officials m, Interior decorators m, IRS agents m, Photographers m, Social science teachers m
52	Foreign language teachers f, Lawyers f, Librarians f, Musicians f, Nurses f, Physical therapists f; Foreign language teachers m, Math-science teachers m, Ministers m		
51	Guidance counselors f, School administrators f; Dentists m, Engineers m, English teachers m, Food scientists m, Priests m	41	Bankers f, Business education teachers f, Department store managers f, Navy noncommissioned officers f; Bankers m, Industrial arts teachers m, Personnel directors m, Purchasing agents m, Recreation leaders m, YMCA directors m
50	Cartographers f, Chiropractors f, Dietitians f, English teachers f, Public health nurses f, Public administrators f, Social workers f, Speech pathologists f; Public administrators m, Speech pathologists m	40	Executive housekeepers m, Highway Patrol officers m, Nursing home administrators m, Stockbrokers m
		39	Agribusiness managers f, Chamber of Commerce executives f, Realtors f, Secretaries f; Auto sales dealers m, Business education teachers m, Credit managers m, Police officers m, Retail clerks m
49	Art teachers f, Fine artists f, Elected public officials f, IRS agents f, Licensed practical nurses f, Occupational therapists f, Reporters f; Registered nurses m, Systems analysts m		
48	Air Force officers f, Christian education directors f, Marketing executives f, Navy officers f, Social science teachers f; Fine artists m, Cartographers m, Computer programmers m, Licensed practical nurses m, Optometrists m, Physical therapists m, Reporters m	38	Farmers f, Telephone operators f; Beauticians m, Life insurance agents m
		37	Buyers m, Chamber of Commerce executives m, Sales managers m, Skilled crafts m
		36	Department store managers m, Nursery managers m
		35	Beauticians f, Instrument assemblers f, Retail clerks f; Funeral directors m
47	Army officers f, Commercial artists f, Occupational health nurses f, Radiologic technologists f, Recreation leaders f; Architects m, Lawyers m, Marine officers m, Musicians m, Pharmacists m, Social workers m	34	Realtors m, Restaurant managers m
		33	Sewing machine operators f; Dairy processing managers m, Farmers m
		32	
		31	Agribusiness managers m, Grain elevator managers m
46	Accountants f, Broadcasters f, Mental health workers f, Public relations directors f, Special education teachers f, YWCA directors f; Art teachers m, Chiropractors m, Investment fund managers m, Navy officers m, Occupational therapists m, School administrators m, Veterinarians m	30	
		29	Farm supply managers m
		28	Corrections officers m
		27	
		26	Florists m

sented in Table 8-3, along with similar data on the INTROVERSION-EXTROVERSION scale, which is discussed in the next section of this chapter. (The samples used to calculate these statistics are described on p. 32.) As the data in Table 8-3 indicate, the AC scale is stable over both short and long time periods, with test-retest correlations of .91 to .85 and test-retest means within a point of each other.

Interpreting the AC scale. Scores on the AC scale should be interpreted as the name implies: as an indication of the degree to which the respondent is comfortable in academic settings. High scores will be found among people who are well educated or who intend to become well educated; low scores will be found among those who are uncomfortable in academic settings and who find intellectual exercises boring.

TABLE 8-3

Test-Retest Statistics over 14-Day, 30-Day, and 3-Year
Intervals for the ACADEMIC COMFORT and
INTROVERSION-EXTROVERSION Scales

Scale	Test-retest correlation	Test		Retest	
		Mean	S.D.	Mean	S.D.
14-day interval ($N = 180$)					
ACADEMIC COMFORT	.91	39	15.4	40	16.6
INTROVERSION-EXTROVERSION	.91	53	12.3	52	13.8
30-day interval ($N = 102$)					
ACADEMIC COMFORT	.86	46	13.5	46	13.5
INTROVERSION-EXTROVERSION	.90	39	12.0	38	12.0
3-year interval ($N = 140$)					
ACADEMIC COMFORT	.85	49	13.7	49	14.3
INTROVERSION-EXTROVERSION	.82	51	11.5	52	12.0

Most people with advanced degrees will score high on this scale; high school dropouts will score low. Those who drop out of college will also score low, though not as low as high school dropouts.

College and university students who have high scores on this scale will normally be doing well in school and will usually report satisfaction with their educational experience, though they may be dissatisfied with specific factors, such as individual teachers or courses. In contrast, students with low scores will frequently be doing poorly and will usually be thinking about dropping out of school and looking for outside activities. Their dissatisfaction is generally diffuse, likely to be directed toward the entire educational experience.

Most graduate students score at least 50 on the AC scale, with the majority scoring between 55 and 60. Students seeking advanced degrees who score low (40 and below, for example) usually report that they view their education as a means to an end, as a necessary hurdle to be cleared on the way to the career they are seeking; they are seldom enchanted with the academic nature of their study. When queried about their similarity or dissimilarity with other students in their program, they report themselves to be less concerned with the academic and more concerned with the practical nature of their education than are their classmates. These generalizations vary from program to program—even the most academically oriented business school student scores lower than the average student in the philosophy department, which is to be expected in light of the item content of the scale. Still, the overall trends are consistent.

As Chapter 10 illustrates, this scale and the INTROVERSION-EXTROVERSION scale are particularly useful to the counselor at the outset of the interview when a good preliminary working impression of the client is needed.

Introversion-Extroversion Scale

The INTROVERSION-EXTROVERSION (IE) scale is another special scale retained from the earlier form of the Strong because it proved useful in understanding a person's pattern of interests. Psychologists have long realized the importance of the introversion-extroversion dimension, and this dimension continually reasserts itself in research studies.

Scores on the IE scale reflect the person's interest in being alone, as opposed to working closely with other people. High scores are earned by introverts, people who would rather work with things or ideas; low scores are earned by extroverts, people who enjoy working with others, especially in social-service settings.

The IE scale appears on the SCII profile for two reasons: first, the scale is clinically helpful, since the score gives a quick index of the person's attitude toward working with others; second, the validity statistics, as reported below, demonstrate that the IE scale successfully discriminates between people-oriented occupations and non-people-oriented occupations.

Constructing the IE scale. The original scales were constructed by comparing the SVIB item responses of MMPI-defined extroverts with those of MMPI-defined introverts among the student body of the University of Minnesota; separate scales were developed for the male and female booklets. Details are reported in the *Handbook for the SVIB*.

The single IE scale for the 1974 SCII was constructed by using the items that had survived the screening for the merged booklet. Again, as with the ACADEMIC COMFORT scale, only those items common to both the former male (Form T399) and female (Form TW398) booklets were used, so that all of the occupational-criterion groups could be scored on the new scale.

Norming the IE scale. The 1974 IE scale was normed by using information generated by the earlier SVIB scales (the scale has not been renormed for the 1981 revision). A wide range of both male and female occupational samples had been scored on the SVIB scales, and their means are presented in the *Handbook*. As usual, the IE means formed a reasonably normal curve, but the male samples distributed around a standard score of 44 on the men's scale and the women's samples distributed around a standard score of 50 on the women's scale. Because the scales for women and men were separate, no direct comparison was possible, and one could not say whether the 6-point difference in means reflected a "true" sex difference on the introversion-extroversion dimension or whether the two scales were not equivalent. As discussed below, data from the SCII IE scale suggest that the latter explanation is the more reasonable.

The intent in norming the 1974 scale was to locate a standard score of 50 in the middle of the curve, halfway between the extroversion and introversion extremes. To ensure this, three samples of each sex with mean scores on the earlier scales falling at the peak of a bell-shaped distribution were selected as the norming samples. Three samples of each sex, rather than one, were used to protect the norming from any potential disruption created by the unknown idiosyncrasies of a single sample. The samples selected, their means on the older scales, and their raw-score statis-

tics on the new scale are listed in Table 8-4. The raw-score means and standard deviations of these six samples, on the new scale, were averaged, and these data were then used in the usual raw-score-to-standard-score conversion formula. The net effect was to convert the scores into a distribution with a population mean of about 50, the most extroverted occupations averaging about 40, and the most introverted about 60.

Female samples scored on the older women's IE scale and on the SCII IE scale compare very well; most of the samples had mean scores on the new scale within 2 or 3 points of their mean score on the earlier scale. For the male samples scored on the older men's scale and on the SCII scale, however, the differences were larger and more consistent; most of the male samples scored 4 to 6 points higher on the SCII scale than they did on the older scale (see the 1974 *Manual*). These results answer a question posed earlier in this chapter: the data on the new scale indicate that

TABLE 8-4

Normative Samples for the Introversion-Extroversion Scale

Normative sample	N	Earlier scale Mean	1974 scale (raw scores) Mean	S.D.
Male samples				
Investment managers	237	44	10.5	13.1
Purchasing agents	164	44	8.6	14.5
Vocational agriculture teachers	395	44	7.8	13.7
Female samples				
Business education teachers	300	50	6.5	13.7
Home economics teachers	373	50	5.8	13.1
Registered nurses	263	50	7.9	13.2

TABLE 8-5

Mean Scores of Female vs. Male Occupational Samples on the Introversion-Extroversion Scale

Occupational sample	Female mean	Male mean	Difference	Occupational sample	Female mean	Male mean	Difference
Accountants	53	50	+3	Mathematicians	58	58	0
Advertising executives	47	56	−9	Math-science teachers	56	53	+3
Air Force officers	50	51	−1	Medical technologists	56	53	+3
Architects	55	54	+1	Minister	42	42	0
Army officers	47	49	−2	Musicians	52	53	−1
Art teachers	50	50	0	Navy officers	50	50	0
Artists, commercial	52	54	−2	Nurses, licensed practical	52	50	+2
Artists, fine	55	57	−2	Nurses, registered	47	51	−4
Bankers	51	50	+1	Nursing home administrators	45	45	0
Beauticians	52	50	+2	Occupational therapists	50	49	+1
Biologists	57	56	+1	Optometrists	53	53	0
Business education teachers	50	49	+1	Personnel directors	44	44	0
Chamber of Commerce executives	46	41	+5	Pharmacists	54	53	+1
Chemists	56	56	0	Photographers	50	51	−1
Chiropractors	49	48	+1	Physical education teachers	51	49	+2
College professors	52	52	0	Physical therapists	52	51	+1
Computer programmers	58	58	0	Physicians	53	51	+2
Credit managers	48	48	0	Physicists	58	59	−1
Dentists	54	53	+1	Police officers	45	48	−3
Department store managers	47	48	−1	Psychologists	47	47	0
Dietitians	50	48	+2	Public administrators	45	43	+2
Elected public officials	40	41	−1	Public relations directors	43	43	0
Elementary education teachers	52	51	+1	Purchasing agents	45	46	−1
Engineers	54	56	−2	Radiologic technologists	52	53	−1
English teachers	47	44	+3	Realtors	42	48	−6
Executive housekeepers	47	48	−1	Recreation leaders	42	44	−2
Farmers	54	60	−6	Reporters	46	48	−2
Flight attendants	46	44	+2	Restaurant managers	47	48	−1
Foreign language teachers	49	50	−1	School administrators	41	43	−2
Foresters	54	56	−2	Social science teachers	47	44	+3
Geographers	52	53	−1	Social workers	45	44	+1
Geologists	56	58	−2	Sociologists	47	48	−1
Guidance counselors	44	45	−1	Special education teachers	48	47	+1
Interior decorators	50	49	+1	Speech pathologists	45	46	−1
IRS agents	46	49	−3	Systems analysts	53	53	0
Lawyers	45	45	0	Veterinarians	58	57	+1
Librarians	50	52	−2	YW/YMCA directors (1974-81)	43	42	+1
Life insurance agents	40	41	−1	Women-/Men-in-General	50	50	0
Marketing executives	47	47	0				

TABLE 8-6

Mean Scores on the INTROVERSION-EXTROVERSION Scale for 200 Occupational Samples

Scale mean	Sample	Scale mean	Sample
60	Farmers m	49	Chiropractors f, Foreign language teachers f, Retail clerks f; Army officers m, Business education teachers m, Interior decorators m, IRS agents m, Occupational therapists m, Physical education teachers m
59	Sewing machine operators f; Physicists m, Skilled crafts m		
58	Computer programmers f, Mathematicians f, Physicists f, Veterinarians f; Computer programmers m, Geologists m, Mathematicians m	48	Credit managers f, Dental hygienists f, Night club entertainers f, Special education teachers f; Chiropractors m, Credit managers m, Department store managers m, Dietitians m, Executive housekeepers m, Funeral directors m, Investment fund managers m, Police officers m, Realtors m, Reporters m, Restaurant managers m, Sociologists m
57	Biologists f; Fine artists m, Veterinarians m		
56	Chemists f, Geologists f, Instrument assemblers f, Math-science teachers f, Medical technologists f; Advertising executives m, Biologists m, Cartographers m, Chemists m, Engineers m, Foresters m		
		47	Advertising executives f, Army officers f, Department store managers f, English teachers f, Executive housekeepers f, Marketing executives f, Occupational health nurses f, Registered nurses f, Psychologists f, Restaurant managers f, Social science teachers f, Sociologists f; Marketing executives m, Psychologists m, Special education teachers m
55	Architects f, Fine artists f, Cartographers f; Grain elevator managers m, Nursery managers m		
54	Dentists f, Engineers f, Farmers f, Foresters f, Navy noncommissioned officers f, Pharmacists f, Telephone operators f; Architects m, Commercial artists m, Corrections officers m, Dairy processing managers m, Industrial arts teachers m		
		46	Chamber of Commerce executives f, Christian education directors f, Flight attendants f, Funeral directors f, IRS agents f, Reporters f; Broadcasters m, Buyers m, Marine officers m, Priests m, Purchasing agents m, Retail clerks m, Speech pathologists m
53	Accountants f, Agribusiness managers f, Optometrists f, Physicians f, Systems analysts f; Agribusiness managers m, Dentists m, Florists m, Geographers m, Math-science teachers m, Medical technologists m, Musicians m, Optometrists m, Pharmacists m, Radiologic technologists m, Systems analysts m		
		45	Lawyers f, Nursing home administrators f, Police officers f, Public administrators f, Purchasing agents f, Social workers f, Speech pathologists f; Guidance counselors m, Lawyers m, Mental health workers m, Nursing home administrators m
52	Commercial artists f, Beauticians f, College professors f, Dental assistants f, Elementary education teachers f, Geographers f, Language interpreters f, Musicians f, Licensed practical nurses f, Physical therapists f, Radiologic technologists f, Secretaries f; College professors m, Farm implement managers m, Farm supply managers m, Librarians m	44	Guidance counselors f, Mental health workers f, Personnel directors f; English teachers m, Flight attendants m, Personnel directors m, Recreation leaders m, Social science teachers m, Social workers m
		43	Broadcasters f, Marine officers f, Public relations directors f, YWCA directors f; Public administrators m, Public relations directors m, School administrators m
51	Bankers f, Home economics teachers f, Public health nurses f, Physical education teachers f; Air Force officers m, Elementary education teachers m, Highway Patrol officers m, Registered nurses m, Photographers m, Physical therapists m, Physicians m	42	Ministers f, Realtors f, Recreation leaders f, Stockbrokers f; Ministers m, YMCA directors m
		41	School administrators f; Chamber of Commerce executives m, Elected public officials m, Life insurance agents m, Sales managers m
50	Air Force officers f, Art instructors f, Army noncommissioned officers f, Business education teachers f, Dietitians f, Interior decorators f, Librarians f, Navy officers f, Occupational therapists f, Photographers f; Accountants m, Army noncommissioned officers m, Art instructors m, Bankers m, Beauticians m, Food scientists m, Foreign language teachers m, Navy officers m, Licensed practical nurses m, Vocational agriculture teachers m	40	Elected public officials f, Life insurance agents f
		39	Auto sales dealers m
		38	Stockbrokers m

the differences on the older scales between the male and female distribution means were due to lack of equivalence in the norms, not to some difference between the sexes on the introversion-extroversion dimension. On the 1974 scale, where a direct comparison can be made, the sexes have similar scores.

This point is made even more strikingly by the data presented in Table 8-5, which lists the mean scores for male and female samples from the same occupations. The differences are minimal; all but five pairs of the 77 pairs of means are within 3 points of each other. Women have a slight—very slight—tendency to score more in the extroverted direction, but the differences

between women and men in the same occupations are trivial compared to the much larger differences between occupations.

The scores of the 1973 MIG and WIG samples on the IE scale were essentially identical: the 300 women averaged 50.5, with a standard deviation of 11.4; the 300 men averaged 50.2, with a standard deviation of 12.2.

IE scale validity. Table 8-6 lists mean IE scores for 200 occupational samples. The samples are spread over a range of about two standard deviations. Occupations at the high or introverted end of the distribution—in the upper 50's and low 60's—are those that work with things and ideas, such as farmers, skilled crafts, sewing machine operators, physicists, mathematicians, and computer programmers. Occupations at the low or extroverted end of the distribution—in the low 40's and high 30's—are those that work with people, such as stockbrokers, auto sales dealers, life insurance agents, elected public officials, school administrators, sales managers, and Chamber of Commerce executives.

IE scale reliability. Test-retest statistics for the IE scale over 14-day, 30-day, and 3-year intervals are presented in Table 8-3, along with similar data for the ACADEMIC COMFORT scale. (The samples used to calculate these statistics are described on p. 32.) As the data in Table 8-3 indicate, the IE scale is stable over both short and long time periods, with test-retest correlations of .91 to .82 and test-retest means within a point of each other.

Interpreting the IE scale. A person's score on the IE scale reflects her/his interest in being alone, as opposed to working closely with people: high scores are earned by introverts, people who would rather work with things or ideas; low scores are earned by people who enjoy working with others, especially in sales and social service.

Students with high scores—60 or over—are frequently shy; often they feel great discomfort in any social setting, and they may even find it hard to talk with a counselor in a private office. Many such students express dissatisfaction with their lack of social ease and want to change. Others are comfortable with that aspect of themselves and seek a career that will allow them to remain in the background of public attention.

Quite often, adults who appear to be outgoing and socially adept score high, toward the introverted end, on the IE scale; the test appears to have "missed." Interview inquiries in such cases frequently reveal that these people do indeed see themselves as introverts, but for some practical reason, they have learned to exhibit extroverted behavior—"to close more sales, to get reelected, to keep the office going." Such people usually report that their extroversion operates in relatively short bursts of a few hours or perhaps a day or two; then, they retreat to regenerate their capacity for that behavior. The extroversion skills seem to form with age; this pattern of introverted score and extroverted skill is seldom seen among students.

Students with low scores—40 or under—usually converse easily, and are often among the leaders of their peer groups because of their eagerness to assume substantial social responsibility. Such students frequently are involved in clubs or organizations and many times take leadership roles. Adults with low scores on the IE scale are usually active in community activities or professional organizations.

Most people are located between the two extremes, and their more moderate IE scores suggest only trends in these directions.

As mentioned above, this scale and the ACADEMIC COMFORT scale are particularly useful to the counselor at the outset of the interview. Chapter 10 elaborates on this and several other aspects of the interpretation of these scales.

CHAPTER NINE

The Administrative Indexes

The SVIB-SCII Administrative Indexes are routine clerical checks performed by computer on each answer sheet to make certain that nothing has gone awry during the administration, completion, or processing of the answer sheet. The indexes examine three statistics: total responses, infrequent responses, and the percentages of "Like," "Indifferent," and "Dislike" responses. (How the three are used in interpreting the profile is discussed at length in Chapter 10.)

Total Responses Index

The first of these indexes, TOTAL RESPONSES (TR), is the number of item responses read by the computer from the answer sheet. The SCII inventory has 325 items; thus if every item was answered, the number printed on the profile should be 325. Occasionally, the marks on the answer sheet will be too light, and the computer will not pick up all of the responses. Or, the person taking the SCII may overlook a section of items, or neglect to complete the inventory. A few answers may be omitted without appreciably affecting the scoring, but if the TR index drops below about 310, the counselor should check the answer sheet to see what happened.

Infrequent Responses Index

The INFREQUENT RESPONSES (IR) index is based on response choices that are selected infrequently, and is used basically to identify answer sheets that may be marked incorrectly. The item weights are assigned so that any respondent selecting several uncommon choices will receive a low score on the index; if the respondent marks more unusual items than the average person does, the score becomes negative. This inverse-weighting technique was employed to simplify the use of the index by counselors and other users. All that needs to be remembered is that if the index is a negative number, there is likely to be a problem somewhere.

To develop this index, the item-response percentages of the General Reference Sample (GRS) were scanned to locate items that were chosen infrequently. One important criterion in selecting SCII items was that they be neither extremely popular nor extremely unpopular; thus, not many of the items that survived the item screening were selected infrequently by the total GRS sample. However, when the male and female GRS samples were separated, several items appeared for which the response rate was 6 percent or less; these items became the INFREQUENT RESPONSES indexes, one index for each sex.

Each item-response choice on the two IR indexes was weighted -1, and the GRS samples, along with several other samples, were scored on the scales. The results for each sample are presented in Table 9-1. Among the women, almost everyone selected six or fewer of the infrequent response items. Thus, for women, six infrequent responses were set as the acceptable number of atypical responses. The analogous figure for men is 11. Almost anyone who chooses more of these responses has given an inordinately large number of infrequent responses. Such cases should be scrutinized carefully to make certain that no problems occurred during test administration or scoring.

In practice, each respondent is given a constant on this index—women 6 points, men 11—and 1 point is subtracted from this constant for each infrequent response selected. The result is printed on the profile as the IR score; the highest possible score for women is 6; for men, it is 11.

The IR can indicate the presence of a problem, but it cannot specify which of many possible circumstances is responsible. In one case successfully flagged by this index, the respondent became confused on the answer sheet, skipped a number, and answered the remainder of the items in the wrong spaces on the answer sheet. In another case, a job applicant who was irritated that she had to take the inventory filled it in randomly. In still another case, an individual tried to fool the system—"just to see what would happen," he said—by marking choices reflecting the exact opposite of his true feelings.

When the index is negative, some confusion has probably occurred, and each case should be checked on its own merits. Occasionally no problem exists; the respondent simply has unique interests. That in itself is useful information.

LP, IP, DP Indexes

The LP, IP, and DP indexes show the percent of "Like," "Indifferent," and "Dislike" responses selected in each section of the inventory. These figures reflect

TABLE 9-1

Score Distributions on the Male and Female
INFREQUENT RESPONSE Indexes for Several Samples

Female samples on the female index

Raw score (before constant is added)	General Reference Sample (N=300)	Miscellaneous sample No. 1 (N=201)	Miscellaneous sample No. 2 (N=106)	Eighth-grade students (N=76)	College professors (N=400)
−7				1	
−6				0	
−5	1	1	1	13	+
−4	1	2	4	8	1
−3	5	5	2	11	2
−2	9	9	7	22	4
−1	24	26	19	20	10
0	59%	55%	68%	25%	25
					58%
Mean	0.7	0.8	0.6	2.0	0.7
S.D.	1.0	1.1	1.1	1.8	1.1

Male samples on the male index

Raw score (before constant is added)	General Reference Sample (N=300)	Miscellaneous sample No. 1 (N=200)	Miscellaneous sample No. 2 (N=56)	Eighth-grade students (N=81)	Agri-business managers (N=408)
−13		1			+
−12	+	0			+
−11	0	0		1	+
−10	1	1	2	1	0
−9	0	0	0	1	1
−8	+	0	0	0	+
−7	0	0	2	1	+
−6	1	1	0	5	1
−5	1	1	4	7	3
−4	3	4	4	6	3
−3	6	6	11	11	7
−2	9	8	11	26	11
−1	17	18	25	19	20
0	63%	63%	43%	21%	54%
Mean	0.9	0.9	1.4	2.4	1.2
S.D.	1.7	1.7	2.0	2.3	2.1

(NOTE: A plus mark indicates a value less than 1 percent.)

something of the respondent's response style in filling in the inventory.

Normal response ranges. Means and standard deviations on the LP, IP, and DP indexes for each section of the SCII booklet are given in Table 9-2 for a sample of 300 men and 300 women. These figures show the normal ranges for each section. Although response percentages vary some from section to section, the means average about 40 and the standard deviations about 15. Scores for most respondents will fall between the mean and ± 2 standard deviations, that is, between 10 and 70 percent. Consequently, a "10-70" boundary is sufficient for most interpretive purposes. Indexes within this range are normal and can be accepted without further thought. If response percentages fall outside of these limits, the interpretation of certain portions of the profile may have to be modified, as discussed below.

High LP's. A high percentage of "Like" responses for the entire inventory—for example, 75 percent or higher over several sections—will be reflected in the level of scores on the General Occupational Themes and the Basic Interest Scales; a large number of them will be high. This occurs because these scales assign positive weights only to the "Like" response (in contrast to the Occupational Scales, which also weight the "Dislike" position positively, depending on the direction of the difference between the criterion and reference samples). Although these scores are accurate—they reflect what the respondent says he/she likes—the interpretation of the profile needs to be modified somewhat. For example, if scores on 15 or 16 Basic Interest Scales are over 60, then the definition of a high score, usually regarded as any score over 58, needs to be altered for this individual. In such cases, only the three to five highest scores should be considered "high."

No single characteristic describes all persons with high LP's, but some combination of the adjectives "enthusiastic," "curious," "shallow," "unfocused," "energetic," and "manic" will fit many of them.

High DP's. Conversely, if the "Dislike" response percentage is high over several sections of the booklet, the General Occupational Theme and Basic Interest Scale scores will be low, and the above comments need to be reversed.

Persons with high DP's tend to fall into two categories. One category includes those people with an intense occupational focus—they mark almost everything "Dislike" because they are interested in a single area, such as art, or science, or mechanics. The other category includes those who have few "Likes" in the world and who find virtually everything repugnant.

TABLE 9-2

Means and Standard Deviations on the LP, IP, and DP
Indexes for 300 Men and 300 Women

Booklet section	Sex	Response-percentage index[a]					
		LP		IP		DP	
		Mean	S.D.	Mean	S.D.	Mean	S.D.
I. Occupations	Men	28	12	31	14	41	17
	Women	30	13	29	16	41	17
II. School subjects	Men	41	17	33	15	26	16
	Women	45	15	29	15	26	15
III. Activities	Men	37	16	34	15	28	14
	Women	41	14	29	14	29	13
IV. Amusements	Men	38	16	34	15	28	16
	Women	41	14	29	14	30	14
V. Types of people	Men	38	20	41	20	21	15
	Women	43	19	38	19	18	14
VI. Preference between two activities	Men	39	12	22	15	38	10
	Women	40	10	23	15	37	10
VII. Characteristics	Men	56	18	22	15	21	14
	Women	47	18	22	14	30	17

[a] For some sections of the booklet, the three response patterns are labeled differently.

TABLE 9-3

Mean "Like" Response Percentages for Female and Male Occupational Samples

Mean "Like" percent	Occupational samples	Mean "Like" percent	Occupational samples
47	Marine officers f	37	Broadcasters f, Chamber of Commerce executives f, Credit managers f, Dental assistants f, Dentists f, Engineers f, Lawyers f, Librarians f, Photographers f, Retail clerks f, Systems analysts f; Army officers m, Business education teachers m, Chamber of Commerce executives m, Elected public officials m, Industrial arts teachers m, IRS agents m, Registered nurses m, Public relations directors m, Recreation leaders m
46			
45	Auto dealers m		
44			
43	Ministers f, School administrators f		
42	Elected public officials f, Funeral directors f, Life insurance agents f, Recreation leaders f; Marine officers m		
41	Executive housekeepers f, Occupational health nurses f, YWCA directors f; School administrators m, Stockbrokers m	36	Biologists f, Chemists f, Computer programmers f, Foresters f, Musicians f, Pharmacists f; Art instructors m, Credit managers m, Department store managers m, Elementary education teachers m, Foreign language teachers m, IRS agents m, Marketing executives m, Licensed practical nurses m, Physical therapists m, Sociologists m, Speech pathologists m
40	Army officers f, Flight attendants f, IRS revenue officers f, Navy officers f, Registered nurses f, Purchasing agents f; Mental health workers m, YMCA directors m		
39	Agribusiness managers f, Chiropractors f, Food service managers f, Foreign language teachers f, IRS agents f, Mental health workers f, Nursing home administrators f, Personnel administrators f, Physical education teachers f, Public administrators f, Public health nurses f, Public relations directors f, Realtors f, Sociologists f, Special education teachers f; Executive housekeepers m, Flight attendants m, Public administrators m	35	Architects f, Cartographers f, Farmers f, Geographers f, Veterinarians f, Air Force officers m, Beauticians m, IRS tax auditors m, Lawyers m, Peace officers m, Physical education teachers m
		34	Accountants f, Beauticians f, Fine artists f, Geologists f, Physicists f; Accountants m, Architects m, Chemists m, Commercial artists m, Computer programmers m, Engineers m, Food service managers m, Funeral directors m, Librarians m, Musicians m, Optometrists m, Pharmacists m, Photographers m, Radiologic technologists m
38	Advertising executives f, Air Force officers f, Artists f, Business education teachers f, College professors f, Department store managers f, Dietitians f, Elementary education teachers f, Home economics teachers f, IRS revenue agents f, IRS tax auditors f, Marketing executives f, Occupational therapists f, Physical therapists f, Police officers f, Radiologic technologists f, Reporters f, Social workers f, Speech pathologists f, Stockbrokers f; Dietitians m, Navy officers m, Nursing home administrators m, Occupational therapists m, Personnel administrators m, Purchasing agents m, Retail clerks m, Social workers m, Special education teachers m	33	Agribusiness managers m, Biologists m, Cartographers m, Computer programmers m, Correctional officers m, Physicists m, Reporters m, Veterinarians m
		32	Dairy processing managers m, Elevator managers m, Fine artists m, Foresters m, Geographers m
		31	Geologists m, Nursery managers m

The two types present two very different counseling tasks: the first is no problem, because the person is already committed passionately to a fixed course; the second, however, is a formidable challenge, because the person systematically rejects virtually every choice offered.

High IP's. Occasionally a respondent will check "Indifferent" to a large majority of items in the booklet. These people usually report considerable vocational confusion or, sometimes, generalized apathy. The inventory cannot be much help in such cases—if a young person has no consistent themes within his or her interests, the inventory cannot manufacture them. Some psychologists have found it helpful to have such a person retake the inventory, stressing that the "Indifferent" response should be avoided. No empirical study has been made of the value of scores under such instructions, but adopting this approach at least helps to break the counseling impasse.

Extreme cases. The LP, IP, and DP percentages can

provide other useful information, especially when percentages are either extremely high or extremely low. Profiles with one or more percentages below 10 or over 70 should be studied carefully, for they can provide clues for further exploration by the counselor. For example, an occasional student answers "Dislike" to virtually every occupation in the first section of the booklet, while at the same time giving a fairly normal number of L's, I's, and D's to the remaining sections of the booklet; such an unusual response pattern should be noted by the counselor and explored with the student. In other cases, students may answer "Dislike" to most of the school subjects, suggesting another fruitful area of discussion for the counselor and client.

Differences between occupations. The range of LP, IP, and DP scores among occupational samples is substantial. Mean LP scores for 159 occupational samples are reported in Table 9-3. Occupations attracting outgoing, lively, physically active people—such as flight attendants, military officers, recreation leaders, and salespersons—have high LP scores, averaging around 41 percent. Occupations attracting people with intensely focused interests—such as artists, scientists, and writers—have lower LP scores, around 33 percent. In general, the female occupational samples have slightly higher average "Like" response percentages than the male samples do.

LP intercorrelations. The intercorrelations between the LP indexes for the seven sections of the booklet are given in Table 9-4. (The correlations for the IP and DP indexes, not given, are similar in pattern to those for the LP index.) Correlations among the first five sections of the booklet, all of which contain only L-I-D items, run about .65, indicating a fair consistency among people in the number of "Like" responses given from section to section in the booklet.

The correlations for section VI are smaller than are the correlations for sections I-V. In section VI, "Preference Between Two Activities," the respondent can choose either the item on the left or the one on the right, or mark in the middle, indicating that often the items are equal in attraction. This forced-choice item format controls any tendency for response set, but it also makes statistical analysis more difficult, because the individual's response depends on a combination of attraction or aversion to the two choices offered in an item. If the alternatives in this section were realigned in new item combinations, activities formerly rejected by particular respondents might be selected, and vice versa.

LP, IP, and DP scores for section VI, "Preference Between Two Activities," are presented on the profile, along with scores for the other six sections, to provide counselor and client with complete information, and to allow determination of the response percentage for the entire profile. But the left and right choices in section VI do not reflect a systematic arrangement of items, or two poles of a psychological characteristic. For example, responses on the left are not weighted as extrovert items, nor are responses on the right

TABLE 9-4

Intercorrelations of the LIKE PERCENTAGE Indexes for the Seven Sections of the SCII Booklet

(Figures above the diagonal based on sample of 300 women; those below on sample of 300 men)

Booklet section	Booklet section						
	I	II	III	IV	V	VI	VII
I. Occupations		.55	.70	.61	.44	.16	.30
II. School subjects	.65		.62	.59	.45	.18	.38
III. Activities	.74	.60		.71	.52	.12	.42
IV. Amusements	.69	.66	.74		.56	.18	.37
V. Types of people	.51	.47	.59	.59		.16	.31
VI. Preference between two activities	.22	.16	.15	.20	.18		.19
VII. Characteristics	.42	.36	.56	.51	.41	.24	

weighted as introvert items, or vice versa. Occasionally, extremely high LP scores on other sections of the inventory will be accompanied by high IP, or equal, scores on the "Preferences" items. This pattern often reflects the response pattern of an individual who is unwilling to reject anything.

The correlations for the final section, "Your Characteristics," are also smaller, averaging about .35.

The correlations in Table 9-4 indicate a mild tendency for people to adopt the same response strategy over various sections of the booklet, though this tendency is not particularly strong. As demonstrated earlier by Figs. 3-1, 3-2, 3-3, and 7-1, the most important determinant of response is item content. Note in particular that correlations of about .65 do not mean that 42 percent of the variance ($.65 \times .65$) is accounted for by the yea-sayer/nay-sayer phenomenon. For that to be the case, the individual's responses would have to be independent of content, and they clearly are not. What the correlation of .65 indicates is that people do differ in the number of "Likes," "Indifferents," and "Dislikes" they choose, and that they are consistent over a variety of inventory sections.

CHAPTER TEN

Interpreting the Results

This chapter is intended to help the counselor understand how to interpret the scores on the SVIB-SCII profile, and how to guide the student or counselor in making use of the profile. The first sections discuss the specifics of interpretation: what to do first, what to talk about on the profile, what conclusions to draw. The final section of the chapter presents case studies of both typical and unusual profiles, as further illustration of how interpretation proceeds.

Although the profile may seem complex at first, you will find—with a profile in front of you to refer to—that it soon makes sense. After you have examined an actual case in detail with the help of the *Manual*, and perhaps three or four more to cover particular points, you will find the explanation and interpretation of the profile flowing easily, leaving you more time to work with the particular concerns of the individual student. For the first case, however, careful study of this chapter is essential.

The interpretive remarks in the chapter assume that the counselor is familiar with the preceding chapters of this *Manual*, and with the remarks on the reverse side of both the student's and counselor's copies of the profile (pp. 17 and 18).

Pre-Test Orientation

Generally, the SCII should be administered in the larger context of career planning; no one should be asked, out of the blue, to sit down and begin marking an answer sheet. An orientation is required, and the character and extent of the orientation will vary as the situation permits or demands. The remarks made at that point need not—in many cases, should not—be extensive. What is said may also depend on special circumstances: in individual testing, the counselor might perceive an excess of skepticism or apprehension; in another case, a sense of competition (where, for example, students are seeking entrance to medical school) may call for discouragement of "look-good" test-taking strategies. If students are filling in the inventory as part of a college orientation session in a large group, the test administrator will have less opportunity to explain the inventory in detail and answer questions than is the case in the usual counseling setting; at the same time, in large group or classroom settings, more visual aids can be used, and the orientation time available per student can be used more efficiently.

At a minimum, anyone filling in the inventory should be told that it is designed to help people make occupational decisions by identifying patterns in their likes and dislikes, and by showing how these patterns compare with those of people in a wide range of occupations.

Sitting Down with the Profile

In preparation for profile interpretation, the following points should be stressed to the counselee:

First, career planning should not be done randomly. People should take some initiative in planning their careers; in particular they should use the best data available to make their decisions.

Second, this inventory will provide some useful information, but that information should not be followed blindly; other data about abilities, experiences, and motivations should also be considered.

Third, career planning is a lifelong activity, not the work of a single afternoon. The information provided by the inventory should be used in long-range planning, now and in the years to come; it should not be used to make one-time decisions about the immediate future.

In these preliminary discussions, the inventory should also be demystified. The counselor or other test administrator should remind the client that the test is not a magic crystal ball, that it cannot solve problems, that it cannot "tell them what they should be"— it can only provide information. The general nature of the test and its results might be described thus:

"This test is basically a questionnaire that asks for your reaction to a wide range of occupations, school subjects, and various activities. Your answers will be scanned by a computer, which will compare them with the answers of people already employed in a wide range of jobs, and the results will tell you something about how you compare with them in what you say you like and dislike. The test won't tell you what to do; it can't mysteriously show you some place where you will be happy and successful. It will only give you some detailed information about yourself and how your vocational interests compare with those of others."

Interpreting the Profile

Ideally, the counselor will have studied the profile at some length before the client arrives for the interview. If this can be managed, the counselor's task will be eased: the interpretation is likely to be more accurate, and the client will be more confident of the entire procedure. Certainly, preparation is warranted until the counselor builds some familiarity with the SCII. In practice, however, preparation is often a luxury, and the counselor must build an impression of the client as the interview proceeds.

Whether prepared or not, the counselor should begin with the Administrative Indexes and the Special Scales; they can be important to the validity of the interpretation and the success of the interview.

The Administrative Indexes. The first numbers to look at on the profile are the scores on the Administrative Indexes; these are designed to detect problems in test administration and scoring. *If they indicate problems, the remainder of the profile is suspect.*

The TOTAL RESPONSES index reports how many pencil marks the computer picked up from the answer sheet. Since the inventory has 325 items, and since each one requires a single response, the number reported for this index should be 325 or close to it. Generally, the SCII scoring routine is not notably affected by a few missing responses. But if more than 10 percent (32) of the responses are missing, something must be done. If the answer sheet is available, it should be examined; in some cases, making heavier marks and then rescoring (through the computer) solves the problem. More often, the person must be retested—when several responses are omitted, it is usually because the person overlooked a block of questions in the booklet, perhaps an entire column or section.

The next index to examine is the INFREQUENT RESPONSES index. This is a measure of the number of highly unusual responses that the person made to the inventory; it is arranged so that the figure reported will be negative if the person picked an unusually high number of atypical responses. When it is negative, some checking should be done; until a reasonable explanation is found, the profile should be treated skeptically. Usually, some specific explanation emerges: for example, the person inadvertently skipped a number on the answer sheet; or the person failed to take the task seriously and filled in the answer sheet randomly; or the person tried some unusual test-taking strategy.

The remaining Administrative Indexes—the LP, IP, and DP response indexes—indicate, for each section of the booklet, how the person distributed his or her responses over the "Like," "Indifferent," and "Dislike" choices. These figures can be clinically useful, though in practice they have been found to be subject to considerable overinterpretation. In large samples, the average response percentages are roughly as follows:

Inventory section	LP	IP	DP
Occupations	30%	30%	40%
School Subjects			
Activities			
Amusements	40	30	30
Types of People			
Preferences			
Characteristics	50	30	20

(These figures are only rough averages to keep in mind during counseling sessions; accurate means and standard deviations for these percentages are given in Table 9-2.)

People filling in the inventory's answer sheet deviate a great deal from these averages, but the deviations are rarely troublesome; the SCII scoring techniques are quite robust in the face of substantial individual differences. If the figures fall between roughly 10 and 70, all is well, and the numbers warrant no further attention. But if some numbers fall outside of these limits, some useful clinical information may be gained by studying them, and perhaps from talking to the client about them.

If the numbers are high—80 or 90 percent, for example—this may tell you something about the client that is not apparent anywhere else on the profile. For example, if he or she has picked that many "Likes" in any of the sections, that suggests a high level of activity preference, perhaps even a manic state. The explanation will vary from person to person, and the counselor should look for supporting clinical data. If, for example, a woman has marked "Like" to 85 percent of the occupations, that suggests she is not being very discriminating in what she says she likes. If a high percentage of "Likes" appears in the section on school subjects, it tells you that she really thrives in the school environment; if, in contrast, the percentage of "Likes" in that section is low—for example, 5 percent or so—that tells you something else about how she feels toward school. A high percentage of "Likes" in the "Types of People" section suggests that she is unconditionally accepting of other people—an observation perhaps worth some discussion in the counseling interview.

The last section of the booklet, "Characteristics," offers a list of activities, and the person is asked for a self-evaluation in these activities. The average person answers "Yes" (I can do it) to about half of these items. Many counselors have found it useful to consider this section a crude measure of self-esteem. If, for example, a young man marks considerably fewer than 50 percent of these items "Yes," it suggests that he is being hard on himself. But if he marks a great many of them "Yes" (roughly 80 percent or more), it means that he has an optimistic view of his own abilities. In general, optimism is a healthy sign, and a high percentage is no cause for concern; indeed, one component of whether the young man can tackle something or not is surely whether he thinks he can.

Occasionally, profiles appear with a very low "Like" percentage (LP) in one or several categories. This can indicate one of two situations: one is among the easiest possible counseling cases, the other is among the hardest. A person with a very low average on the LP indexes is either (1) highly focused, likes only one kind of activity, and rejects everything else; or (2) likes nothing and has rejected all options. In the former case, counseling is easy. The one area the person has focused on will be evident from the rest of the profile—for example, one or two related Basic Interest Scales will be high, everything else will be low—and the counseling can focus on where that person can find a job, or, more generally, a career that will provide an outlet for these interests. The pattern of interests will be clear; the task is to find the outlet. Compared to other counseling situations, this one is easy.

The other possibility indicated by a low average of the LP's is that the person reports very few likes because he or she does not like to do anything. Usually such a person is passive, apathetic, and confused. A low, unfocused LP index indicates, at best, occupational confusion, and, at worst, considerable personal distress or apathy, perhaps a sense of hopelessness and even desperation, one of the most difficult situations the counselor will confront.

An interest inventory cannot be much help to such a person, except to alert the counselor to the situation. No data exist that can suggest specific directions or even general orientations for the person who has rejected everything on the inventory. The counselor can do one of three things, or all of them—one specific, one general, one therapeutic—and it may make sense to defer the choice until discussion of the remainder of the profile has yielded stronger impressions of the client.

The *specific* suggestion is to have the client fill in the SCII again, this time with a definite set toward marking more activities "Like." The counselor might say:

"Why don't you fill this in again, this time forcing yourself to mark more things 'Like.' Try to mark at least a third of the answers 'Like.' Let's just experiment, to see if any useful trends emerge."

A profile generated in this manner should be interpreted carefully. No data exist on such cases to determine whether this approach is valid. If a meaningful profile results—and "meaningful" implies both internal consistency and reasonableness when compared with other information available on the client—then the results can be used for counseling. If the profile remains suspect—either because there is still no clear-cut pattern or because the pattern appears unreasonable in the context of the other available information (as when a highly intellectual pattern emerges for someone with a low achievement background and anti-school history)—then the profile should be ignored. This interest inventory simply cannot help in such cases.

The *general* suggestion to someone with no focused pattern of interests goes something like this:

"The results of this inventory do not show any clear-cut pattern of interest for you. The inventory isn't magic—it can't show something that isn't there. These results suggest that you haven't accumulated enough occupational familiarity or experience to have a good idea about what you would like or dislike. Your major goal now should be to get out and learn more about the world—to find out what appeals to you and what you find boring or distasteful. You need some experience."

This suggestion is most often directed at young people; it would normally be inappropriate for adults, except in those cases where the person had followed an unusually restricted life style. For adults with unclear profiles, the counselor will probably need to consider some combination of this general suggestion and the following therapeutic one.

The *therapeutic* suggestion has the counselor tackling the underlying causes of the confused profile in whatever style feels most comfortable with this particular client. A direct approach, for example, would be to say something like this:

"Your profile shows no clear-cut pattern—no predominant, strong interests in any special area. That suggests you are floundering, and we ought to talk about whether that is accurate and what can be done about it. Perhaps you need to focus your interests artificially in one direction for a while, to see what happens. Pick whatever area you would like to learn more about, seek out other people in that area, get some experience, see what happens. Perhaps you'll hit on something that interests you, perhaps you won't. If you don't, try another area. I suggest you force yourself to concentrate in some particular area, so that you can get a better idea about what you like and dislike. Probably you've been uncomfortable about your lack of focus, and you simply need to tackle that issue head-on."

Again, no hard data exist to document the usefulness of the approach, but at least it gives a positive direction to the counseling.

In another vein, one sometimes sees a profile with low "Indifferent" percentages (IP) for various sections of the booklet. This can be interpreted either as a person with firm, resolute ideas about his or her preferences, or as someone who is overly structured, even rigid. A low IP, taken alone, constitutes insufficient data from which to draw solid conclusions, but it does alert the counselor to see if a pattern of inflexible opinions emerges elsewhere in the client.

Everything in the preceding discussion about the LP, IP, and DP indexes (other than the figures for population averages) is based on clinical experience. Counselors should compare their own experiences with these indexes and learn what they can from working with them. One tendency is to overinterpret them, however, and counselors should be careful not to develop, and then confirm, hypotheses solely on the basis of these data. The percentages provide useful information about a person's test-taking strategy, but how that translates into real-world behavior is not firmly established.

The Special Scales. The next step in working with the profile is to look at the Special Scales. These are generally useful in learning something about the client's overall orientation; more specifically, they can tell you something about what is likely to happen in the counseling session.

The Introversion-Extroversion (IE) score is a good predictor of how the interview will go, since it measures, to some extent, the person's sociability. The scale is normed so that the average person scores about 50, with "introverts" averaging about 60 and "extroverts" about 40. High scores, 60 and above, indicate social introversion.

People with scores in the high range—around 60—are not particularly talkative. They do not volunteer much information, and are not likely to ask many questions; the counselor will have to supply the conversational momentum.

If the score is even higher—65 to 75—the conversation may be strained. The client will probably be monosyllabic, ill at ease, and uncommunicative.

Scores higher than 75 are rare, and indicate a substantial level of discomfort in most new social settings, including the counseling interview. The counselor will have to take a great deal of initiative just to keep the interchange going. Again, these are only averages; individual cases may surprise you.

Low scores on the IE scale—40 or below—indicate a person relatively comfortable in social settings, and the interview will probably flow smoothly; the lower the score, the more this will be true. Anyone with a score of 35 or below will be talkative. People with even more extreme scores—those in the 20's—will carry, even dominate, the conversation; the counselor will have only to respond, or to ask a few guiding questions.

But this scale, like any scale, can be overinterpreted. It can also lead to self-fulfilling prophecies: "This score says this person is an introvert, so I shall treat him like an introvert—and, sure enough, he doesn't have much to say." Caution is merited before settling on any rigid expectations.

The ACADEMIC COMFORT (AC) scale is a rough index of the degree of comfort that a person feels, or might feel, in an academic environment, especially a high-quality liberal-arts-and-science university environment. Because so much career counseling revolves around the amount and kind of education the person is pursuing or contemplating, this score is frequently useful in understanding how the person views the academic experience. Average scores by educational level are distributed roughly as follows:

Educational level	AC score
Ph.D. recipients	60
M.A. recipients	55
B.A. recipients	50
College dropouts	30
People who never entered college	25
High school dropouts	20

As teenagers, people generally score about 10 points lower on this scale than they will as adults.

If the AC scale is high—50 or above—the person will probably be intellectually curious about the profile and interested in the rationale behind the test and his or her scores. If the scale is low—30 or below—the person will be more practical and just want a quick, straightforward summary of the results, not a discussion of the technical details.

The counselor must stress continually to the client

that the AC scale *is not a measure of abilities,* that it is simply a measure of interest in academic pursuits: some people with high scores will not do particularly well at the university level, though they will probably enjoy it; some low scorers will earn advanced degrees, though they will usually report that the university is not where they would enjoy spending much more time.

In any case, people with high scores—55 or above—should be encouraged to pursue some kind of postgraduate work. Clinical experience suggests that people with high scores who do not continue their education will always wish they had. High scorers should be told something like this:

"Look, you like the academic world; you are comfortable around the world of ideas, you like studying, you like learning, you like being around professors and students. Somehow, you need to arrange your life so that some part of it revolves around the academic environment. Go back to school, or go on and get that graduate degree. If you don't, you'll always wish you had."

People need legitimate encouragement early if they are to avoid eventual bitterness or despair.

Inevitably, you will find people in academic settings with low AC scores; for them, it is important to emphasize that the scale is not a measure of ability, but rather a measure of comfort in the situation. The figures cited above are, after all, only averages. Still, people who are in academic settings will be at least mildly disturbed by a low score, and we have found it useful to say things such as:

"You have a low score on this scale, and yet you are going after a Ph.D. [or M.A. or L.L.B., or whatever]. I suspect you are in school simply to get a union card, to gain the credentials that will allow you to do the job you want to do, to climb the ladder to the next rung. You are not here because of any great love of learning. You probably think professors are impractical, unrealistic people who have little idea of what the real world demands, and you probably want to get out of here as fast as the requirements will allow. Is that about right?"

Invariably, this appraisal strikes a familiar note with these people. They should not necessarily be discouraged from seeking further education, but you should point out to them that they will probably continue to feel a bit out of place in the academic environment. You should also point out that *there is nothing wrong with that;* indeed, some people are relieved to learn that this tension will (or does) exist—in some way the phenomenon is easier to understand and accept once it has been confirmed in this "scientific" manner.

Coding the Profile

With some practice, it takes only a few moments to glance over the Administrative Indexes and Special Scales and develop an impression of how the person answered the inventory and thus how he or she might react to the interview. Very often what the client volunteers in your discussion of the Administrative Indexes and Special Scales will offer useful confirmation or modification of that impression. You can then move on to study other areas of the profile, both to determine the main patterns in the person's interests and to establish the basic code type of the profile—in terms of the six General Occupational Themes.

The General Occupational Themes. The coding process begins with the General Occupational Themes. For each theme, the computer prints a numerical score and a comment on the profile; of these, the latter is more important, since it interprets how the person scored in relation to others of the same sex.

A useful mnemonic in working with these themes is RIASEC, which combines the first letters of the six themes. In that order, the six themes can be characterized by the following shorthand descriptions:

R — REALISTIC
  outdoors, technical, mechanical interests
I — INVESTIGATIVE
  scientific, inquiring, analytical interests
A — ARTISTIC
  dramatic, musical, self-expressive interests
S — SOCIAL
  helping, guiding, group-oriented interests
E — ENTERPRISING
  entrepreneurial, persuasive, political interests
C — CONVENTIONAL
  methodical, organized, clerical interests

To the right of each theme's numerical score, the computer prints one of the following seven interpretive comments; each corresponds to a particular percentile band, as indicated:

Comment	Percentile
Very high	94th and above
High	85th to 93rd
Moderately high	70th to 84th
Average	31st to 69th
Moderately low	16th to 30th
Low	7th to 15th
Very low	6th and below

The percentile bands were established—one for each sex, since the sexes respond in markedly different fashion—by using the means and standard deviations of the MIG and WIG components of the General Reference Sample. Each band covers about one-half standard deviation, except for the Average band, which covers one full standard deviation centered on the mean; thus, anyone who scores within one-half standard deviation either way from the mean will fall into the Average band.

To introduce the themes to the client, the counselor can say something like this:

"Research has shown that the world of occupations can be divided into six general areas; on the profile, these six areas are called General Occupational Themes. The first, the REALISTIC theme, covers the gen-

eral area of mechanics, the outdoors, and technical and engineering work. The second, INVESTIGATIVE, includes scientific jobs, generally those jobs that 'investigate' various phenomena, problems, or processes. The third, ARTISTIC, characterizes jobs such as artist, interior decorator, musician, and actor. The fourth, SOCIAL, covers occupations in which people work closely with others in a helping way, such as counseling or social work. The fifth, ENTERPRISING, includes jobs in which people make good use of persuasion, such as sales, public relations, and legal or political work. The sixth theme, CONVENTIONAL, includes jobs in which the work is carefully organized, such as accounting and clerical occupations. The numerical scores printed out by the computer next to the six themes give you some idea of how your interests in these areas compare with those of other people, and the statements printed next to the numbers show how your scores compare to those of others of your sex (men and women tend to score differently on these scales). It's useful to pick out the one, two, or three highest scores to indicate your code type. In your case, that would be EI. When we go over the rest of the profile, we'll see that this code type helps us to understand all your other scores. It's also useful to see which General Themes you scored low on; we'll keep *that* in mind, too, when we go over the rest of the profile. Incidentally, the average person scores about 50 on each theme, and about two-thirds of people in general fall between 40 and 60; so 40 is a low score, and 60 is high."

In interpreting the General Theme scales, a useful approach is to circle the asterisks that are plotted for scales that have interpretive comments given as either "Very high" or "Very low." If there are no "Very highs" or "Very lows," circle the "Highs" and "Lows." If there are none of them either, circle the "Moderately highs" and "Moderately lows." In brief, highlight the extremes. Then, working only with the high scores, write on the profile (with a heavy pencil or magic marker) the one, two, or three letters that capture the strongest themes, and write them in order of dominance. For example, if the profile has "Very high" after the E-Theme and "High" after the I-Theme, and no other "Very high" or "High" scores, write the letters EI boldly across the Themes portion of the profile. If there are two "Highs," look at the numerical scores to see which is higher and write the letters in the appropriate order. And if there is only one "High," write just that letter.

The purpose of this step is to generate a one-, two-, or three-letter code type, using the General Occupational Themes. This code type affords further interpretive power, as we shall see below. The idea of circling the "Lows" is to point out to the person some areas of interest that do *not* characterize him or her. Frequently it serves to accent "Highs" by contrast; for example: "Your low score on REALISTIC tends to support your high score on SOCIAL—you really do like people better than machines."

The Basic Interest Scales. The next step in organizing the client's profile pattern is to look at the Basic Interest Scales in the same manner. Again, circle the "Highs" and "Lows." Usually, the "Highs" cluster in one or two of the RIASEC areas; using these concentrations, write boldly across the Basic Interest Scale portion of the profile the appropriate one-, two-, or three-letter code type, using your judgment to decide on rank order. If, for example, the two highest scores are PUBLIC SPEAKING and LAW/POLITICS, and the next two are MATHEMATICS and SCIENCE, the code type would be EI.

While doing this, you can explain to the client the meaning of the Basic Interest Scales, using words something like these:

"Each of these scales is concerned with just one topic—AGRICULTURE, NATURE, SCIENCE, ART, TEACHING, an so forth. The scales identify the specific areas where your interests are strong or weak. High scores mean strong interest. As you can see from your profile, you have your highest scores on the PUBLIC SPEAKING and LAW/POLITICS scales, which are in the ENTERPRISING theme; and your next highest scores on the MATHEMATICS and SCIENCE scales, which are in the INVESTIGATIVE theme. I'll circle these high scores so that they stand out, and I'll put a big EI in a circle to indicate that your highest scores are in the ENTERPRISING and INVESTIGATIVE areas. (Notice that this corresponds to the high scores you had on the General Themes themselves.) Your lowest scores are on MILITARY ACTIVITIES, ADVENTURE, and WRITING. Again, I'll circle those scores so that they stand out.

"Now let's go over the other Basic Interest scores in detail."

The counselor and student should look over the Basic Interest Scales together, at least glancing at each one, because these scales are the easiest to interpret. Their meaning is clear, and the character of each is well captured by its name.

The Occupational Scales. The next step in the process of highlighting the patterns in the person's profile is to study the scores on the Occupational Scales, looking again for the high scores—40 and over. Circle the three or four highest scores by locating the asterisks in the "Very similar" or "Similar" columns. If the client has no "Very similar" or "Similar" scores, locate the asterisks in the "Moderately similar" column. Then circle the code types for these occupations; these appear on the profile just to the left of the Occupational Scale titles. Usually, the code types you circle will show some similarity—they will be listed close to each other—and by inspecting all of them you can come up with a summary one-, two-, or three-letter code type to write in big letters somewhere on the profile in the Occupational Scale score section.

The Occupational Scales tie the client's pattern of interests into the working world; a high score—which is plotted graphically in the "Moderately similar," "Similar," or "Very similar" columns—indicates that the

person's interests match those of people happily employed in that occupation.

Pointing out the lowest scores is also useful. Though it may not serve much of a counseling function—the person is well aware that he/she has no interest in those areas—it does serve a useful function in raising the credibility of the test. For example, pointing out to hard-driving executives that the computer says they are not at all like artists or interior decorators reassures them that the test works.

The counselor and student should work together in trying to find a common element among the high scores. The following is an example, based on fictitious scores, of what a counselor might say:

"The Occupational Scale scores show how your interests compare with those of people actually working in these occupations. If you have a high score on any of these, it will be plotted in the 'Moderately similar,' 'Similar,' or 'Very similar' columns. A score in this range indicates that your likes and dislikes are similar to those of people happily employed in that occupation.

"To the left of each scale is a code, given in one, two, or three letters; the code uses the letters of the General Occupational Themes—these over here—to indicate the strongest themes in that occupation. Usually, your high scores will be on Occupational Scales that are characterized by some of the same themes. In your case, for example, you have high scores on the PHARMACIST (IE), ELECTED PUBLIC OFFICIAL (E), and MARKETING EXECUTIVE (EI) scales. The ENTERPRISING theme runs through all of these—and this pattern corresponds to the pattern we saw earlier among your scores on the General Occupational Themes and the Basic Interest Scales.

"By looking at your scores on the Occupational Scales, and tying in your other results, we can get a better picture of the part of the working world you'd be happy in."

Frequently the student will want to focus on one or two specific Occupational Scales for further discussion. That is perfectly appropriate, and the counselor should be prepared to do that. Concurrently, the counselor should be gently persistent in pointing out the underlying themes, and how these specific occupations fit into them.

Settling on a final code type. At this point, you will have three code types written somewhere on the profile: one for the General Occupational Themes, one for the Basic Interest Scales, and one for the Occupational Scales. Look at all three of these and choose an overall summary by using your clinical judgment. Use not only the three code types you have listed but such other clues as you might find on the profile. Explain what you are doing—the better the student understands how this code type was derived, the better he or she will be able to use it in searching out appropriate occupational material.

Once you have settled on the final code type, the next step is to explain to the client the characteristics of that code type, and this can be done best by referring once again to the Basic Interest Scales and the Occupational Scales. For example, you might say:

"Using all the scales in this inventory, we've established your overall code type as EI, a combination of the ENTERPRISING and INVESTIGATIVE interest patterns. First, we saw that your highest General Occupational Theme scores were in the ENTERPRISING and INVESTIGATIVE themes. Then we saw that these were supported by your high scores on the Basic Interest Scales, PUBLIC SPEAKING and LAW/POLITICS, on the one hand, and MATHEMATICS and SCIENCE, on the other. By looking at the Occupational Scales, we can see which occupations share these interests with you. These three, for example. . . ."

Searching Out Further Possibilities

The next step in profile interpretation is to help the person understand where people with his or her particular code type tend to settle in the occupational world. This can be done by referring to the profile, paying particular attention to those occupations that have the same code type—in this case, EI—anywhere within their code types. You should begin with those occupations coded specifically EI, and then work through anything beginning with EI; next switch to the IE occupations; and finally go to those with EI or IE in the second and third positions. By this time both counselor and counselee should understand the general pattern that is emerging. Then you can both speculate about other occupations, not given on the profile, that might fall in this segment of the world of work.

The next step in this occupation-seeking stage is to consult Appendix B of this *Manual* (or *The Occupations Finder,* Holland, 1976), which lists many more occupations and their code types. With the use of this listing, a large group of possible EI occupations can be constructed; the counselee might be encouraged to assemble this grouping by him-/herself.

Since the main purpose of this inventory is to stimulate the counselees to consider occupations that may match their interests, and to help them find further pathways for exploration, these occupation-seeking steps should proceed in ways that maximize the number of opportunities actively considered. In particular, the counselees should be encouraged to consider relevant occupations they may not have considered before because of lack of exposure, or because of some misconception of the nature of an occupation, or preconception that the occupation was not open to them—perhaps on grounds of sex, social class, or ethnic background. Emphatically, clients should be encouraged to consider all relevant occupations.

Although little is known about how a person's patterns of vocational interests are initially formed, it seems likely that the major influence is past experience. If that experience has been limited, the resulting patterns of interests may be constricted. Consequently, every client, no matter what his or her age or specific situation, should be encouraged to engage in wideranging vocational exploration, and to gain a broad range of experience.

The counselor might consider saying something like the following, by way of emphasizing this point:

"This inventory can give you some useful ideas about occupations you might consider, but you should not depend upon it entirely in considering what new directions you might take. The results presented on the profile are determined by what you said your interests were, and your interests have probably been greatly influenced by the experiences you have had. What this means is that if you have had no experience in specific areas—say art or public speaking or agriculture—you may not know whether you would like the activities involved or not. For this reason, you should be alert for opportunities to try out activities that are still unfamiliar to you. In particular, you might consider learning about occupations that have until now been restricted to members of the opposite sex. Historically, some occupations have been open mainly to men, others mainly to women. For example, most young women have not considered teaching vocational agriculture; most young men have not considered home economics. But sexual barriers in occupations are falling now, and all occupations are open to members of both sexes. Be certain that you give some attention to the new ones that may be opening up for you."

Information about occupations can be found in many places, especially in the booklets put out by trade or professional organizations. A comprehensive, succinct source of information about occupations is the *Occupational Outlook Handbook,* published regularly by the U.S. Department of Labor. Once given some help in finding such sources, students will often seek out further information and resources on their own.

Case Studies

Following is a series of case studies. The cases were selected to demonstrate a variety of common profile characteristics.

To illustrate one important point—that successful people in the same occupation can have a wide range of profile patterns—seven profiles from the same occupation, life insurance underwriter, have been included; these people, all of whom are spectacularly successful in their work, show both a common ENTERPRISING theme in their interests and a wide divergence in their other interests. A point that must constantly be stressed in working with people and their profiles is that occupational stereotyping is misleading; though occupations do indeed have common themes within them, the opportunity for variety is substantial, and in fact, varied interests within occupations is the norm, not an exception. These seven cases document that point.

Because of space limitations, the following pages do not reproduce the complete profile for each case study. Instead, the highlights of the profiles are reported in Tables 10-1 to 10-17; the tables include:

1. All six General Occupational Theme scores. Scanning these six scores is the best way to get a quick overview of the entire profile.

2. Several of the highest and lowest Basic Interest Scale scores. Listing these scores affords a quick impression of the person's stronger likes and aversions.

3. The highest and lowest Occupational Scale scores. The highest ones identify occupations where the person's interests are likely to accord best with job demands; the lowest ones show those occupational situations where the person would feel most uncomfortable.

4. Scores on the ACADEMIC ORIENTATION (ACADEMIC COMFORT) and INTROVERSION-EXTROVERSION scales. As discussed above, these scores give a quick preview of how the counseling interview will go.

5. The percentage of "Yes" responses to the Characteristics section of the test booklet. This figure provides a crude index of how the person relates his/her capabilities to the capabilities of people in general. (The final three profiles replace this score with the Total "Like" Response percentage.)

6. Response percentages on other sections of the test booklet when these are outside the normal limits.

Each profile has been coded, using the convenient shorthand categories of the six Holland occupational themes. In each case, the overall profile code is based on a combination of the interim codes emerging from scores on the three different types of scales: the General Occupational Themes, the Basic Interest Scales, and the Occupational Scales. Usually, the convergence of the three code-type decisions is substantial; when they deviate, some discretion is necessary to arrive at the overall coding. That process is discussed for each profile; how the interim and final coding should proceed is discussed in general terms in the preceding pages.

The first 14 cases were scored on the 1974 Occupational Scales, and are given here exactly as they were in the 1977 edition (the Second Edition) of the *Manual for the SVIB-SCII*; at that time the ACADEMIC COMFORT (AC) scale was called ACADEMIC ORIENTATION (AOR). The last three cases have been scored on the 1981 scales; they differ from the others in some particulars.

Cases A through G: Successful Life Insurance Underwriters. The seven men in cases A through G are all startlingly successful life insurance salesmen. In a setting where $1 million in annual sales is considered outstanding, they consistently sell three or four times that amount. Last year the group aggregate was something in excess of $40 million; by any standard, they are all-stars. I met and tested them as part of their study-group activity on personal career development.

These men live throughout the country; no two of them are from the same city. For several years, they have been meeting for three or four days annually (usually in some lush watering spa for the idle rich) for personal and professional reasons. They use this time to keep each other informed of new developments in

their businesses, to exchange hints, leads, and gossip, and to relax. They have become warm friends and act both as innovative stimulators for each other and as important sources of personal support when tension is high and failure looms. I suspect they are a more important resource for each other than they realize, both in the positive, motivating sense and in the emotional, supportive sense.

One of the reasons they have such a firm relationship is, as we shall see, the strong common theme that runs through their vocational interests, that is, an emphasis on ENTERPRISING activities; still, the diversity among them is equally interesting.

Case A. The profile for Case A, summed up in Table 10-1, is dominated by ENTERPRISING interests; among the General Occupational Themes, that is the only elevated score—a 62, which qualifies as "Moderately high"

TABLE 10-1
Case A

GENERAL OCCUPATIONAL
THEMES

R	47	Moderately low
I	47	Average
A	36	Moderately low
S	46	Average
E	62	Moderately high
C	41	Moderately low

Ⓔ

HIGH BASIC INTEREST SCALES

R	Military Activities	73
E	Sales	70
R	Adventure	63
R	Nature	61
E	Merchandising	61
R	Agriculture	58

ⓇⒺ

LOW BASIC INTEREST SCALES

A	Writing	30
A	Art	37
S	Religious Activities	37
I	Science	39
S	Social Service	39
C	Office Practices	40
A	Music/Dramatics	41

FIVE HIGHEST
OCCUPATIONAL SCALES

SEC	Personnel Director	53
EI	Investment Fund Manager	52
ECR	Realtor	51
ES	Life Insurance Agent	49
ES	Sales Manager	49

FIVE LOWEST
OCCUPATIONAL SCALES

ⒺⓈ

A	Librarian	−4
IR	Physical Scientist	−1
IRC	Medical Technologist	4
IAS	Psychologist	8
A	Artist	9

overall code Ⓔ

Academic Orientation	32
Introversion-Extroversion	43
Percentage Yes: Characteristics	50

in the comparison rankings. The other Theme scores are average or low; using the Theme scores, then, this profile would be coded "E."

Among the Basic Interest Scales, the high scores are on scales in the ENTERPRISING and REALISTIC clusters. Because of the support for them elsewhere on the profile, the ENTERPRISING scores (SALES and MERCHANDISING) are probably more meaningful than the REALISTIC scores (MILITARY, ADVENTURE, NATURE, and AGRICULTURE), particularly because the MECHANICAL ACTIVITIES score is so low. The REALISTIC interests probably derive from an orientation toward adventure, risk, the novelty of the outdoors, rather than a love of working with one's hands. This person probably has fantasies about owning his own ranch, living in the mountains, and participating in lots of rugged outdoors activities, but in fact probably does not (and will not) actually engage in the many messy REALISTIC activities, such as greasing the tractors or slogging through the rain to feed the cattle, that are the day-to-day chores in such settings, especially in light of the ENTERPRISING, people-oriented nature of the remainder of the profile. If the MECHANICAL ACTIVITIES score were even average, this man might well get into something like farming as a sideline endeavor, but with the strong rejection of machinery reported here, that is only a faint possibility.

His low Basic Interest Scale scores show a strong rejection of art and social activities, and his low score on the OFFICE PRACTICES scale suggests that the area of his occupation that he least appreciates—and had better have someone else help him with—is the paperwork: the forms, the reports, the routine of business.

Working strictly from the Basic Interest Scales, one would classify this profile as RE.

The highest Occupational Scale scores for Case A carry various code types, but again, E is the major theme, with some support for S; the low scores show a rejection of artistic and scientific activities.

Using the Occupational Scales alone, we would likely assign person A the code type ES.

Combining the three classifications—E from the General Occupational Themes, RE from the Basic Interest Scales, and ES from the Occupational Scales—leads to an overall classification of E. This assignment is also supported by the score of 43 on the INTROVERSION-EXTROVERSION scale, which is in the extroverted direction. Because the extroverted end of the IE scale reflects more "social service" extroversion than "sales/persuasion" extroversion, the score of 43 for person A is probably an underrepresentation of his actual interest in working with others face-to-face. Meeting him supports that conclusion: he is an outgoing fellow, though probably oriented more toward his own business success than toward helping others solve their particular difficulties—except as those difficulties may involve insurance.

The AOR score of 32 is in the general range of most sales personnel, and indicates a distaste for academic

activities. This person is not likely to seek further academic training and, in fact, is probably skeptical of the activities of most academicians, seeing them as too impractical or unrealistic for his tastes.

Overall, this is a profile of an outgoing, sales-oriented, rugged realist with a considerable propensity for risk-taking, an aversion to science and the arts, and a predilection for making money, which he is doing.

Case B. The General Occupational Themes on this profile (Table 10-2) show an ENTERPRISING-ARTISTIC (EA) pattern, with a strong rejection of the REALISTIC theme. This is the pattern of a liberal-arts-educated businessman, someone interested in the cultural as well as business activities in his community—and one who has absolutely no interest in working outdoors or with his hands.

TABLE 10-2
Case B

GENERAL OCCUPATIONAL
THEMES

R	34	Very low
I	42	Moderately low
A	56	Moderately high
S	42	Moderately low
E	62	Moderately high
C	43	Moderately low

HIGH BASIC INTEREST SCALES

E	Sales	70
E	Public Speaking	65
E	Law/Politics	59
E	Merchandising	59

LOW BASIC INTEREST SCALES

R	Nature	26
S	Domestic Arts	27
I	Medical Service	33
R	Agriculture	39
C	Office Practices	39
R	Adventure	40
I	Science	41
I	Medical Science	41
S	Athletics	41
R	Mechanical Activities	42

SIX HIGHEST
OCCUPATIONAL SCALES

AE	Advertising Executive	54
EI	Investment Fund Manager	53
ES	Chamber of Commerce Exec.	49
AE	Interior Decorator	48
ES	Life Insurance Agent	47
E	Lawyer	47

FIVE LOWEST
OCCUPATIONAL SCALES

RSE	Highway Patrol Officer	4
RES	Police Officer	4
R	Skilled Crafts	5
I	Veterinarian	8
RC	Farmer	8

Overall code

Academic Orientation	38
Introversion-Extroversion	40
Percentage Yes: Characteristics	50

TABLE 10-3
Case C

GENERAL OCCUPATIONAL
THEMES

R	65	High
I	45	Moderately low
A	36	Moderately low
S	64	High
E	77	Very high
C	62	High

HIGH BASIC INTEREST SCALES

E	Sales	76
R	Military Activities	76
R	Adventure	71
S	Athletics	68
S	Domestic Arts	66
E	Law/Politics	64
E	Business Management	64
E	Public Speaking	63
R	Agriculture	62
C	Office Practices	62
E	Merchandising	61
I	Mathematics	61

LOW BASIC INTEREST SCALES

A	Art	34
A	Writing	36

SEVEN HIGHEST
OCCUPATIONAL SCALES

ES	Life Insurance Agent	60
ESR	Chiropractor	56
ECR	Realtor	55
SEC	Personnel Director	54
SEC	Recreation Leader	54
ES	Sales Manager	54
C	Accountant	54

FIVE LOWEST
OCCUPATIONAL SCALES

A	Librarian	−5
ARI	Architect	−4
IR	Physical Scientist	−3
I	Biologist	−2
A	Artist	3

Academic Orientation	31
Introversion-Extroversion	31
Percentage Yes: Characteristics	64

Among the Basic Interest Scales, the E theme dominates; SALES, PUBLIC SPEAKING, LAW/POLITICS, and MERCHANDISING are the only scales with scores in the high range. Although scores on some of the ARTISTIC Basic Interest Scales are above average, none are high. The occupational focus of this man is obvious—a pure ENTERPRISING type.

The low Basic Interest scores are on those scales in the REALISTIC, INVESTIGATIVE, and CONVENTIONAL themes. The two low SOCIAL scales—ATHLETICS and DOMESTIC ARTS—are not really pure "social" scales; for this person especially, low scores on them probably represent something other than "anti-social" interests. The rejection of ATHLETICS is probably associated with

the rejection of other outdoors scales, such as NATURE (where he has a very low score of 26), AGRICULTURE, and ADVENTURE; the rejection of DOMESTIC ARTS is probably a reflection of a strong male-oriented, professional role: "People who make money don't keep house." Thus, he is probably more socially oriented than these two low scores indicate.

On the Occupational Scales, the ENTERPRISING theme continues to dominate, with the ARTISTIC trend showing up again in high scores on the ADVERTISING EXECUTIVE and INTERIOR DECORATOR scales. The other high scores include the LIFE INSURANCE AGENT scale and others characterized by verbal fluency and assertiveness—INVESTMENT FUND MANAGER, CHAMBER OF COMMERCE EXECUTIVE, and LAWYER. Because of his outgoing nature and concern for organized power—as demonstrated by his LAW/POLITICS and LAWYER scores—this person has probably fantasized about returning to law school some day, and has certainly fantasized about entering politics. The latter possibility, given his age, is still open to him.

The IE score of 40, toward the extroverted end, suggests that person B is outgoing and easy to talk with. That score also meshes well with the overall ENTERPRISING-ARTISTIC pattern of the profile.

The AOR score of 38 is modest; this person is not particularly academically oriented, even though he is quite artistically oriented. He would enjoy the arts end of academia, but not the science. He is probably not oriented toward graduate school, and his interest in further professional training likely extends only to practical seminars. There is a possibility that this AOR score is somewhat "too low"; because the SALES and BUSINESS MANAGEMENT items are weighted negatively on that scale, this person has lost many points in the AOR scoring, yet the remainder of the profile suggests a fairly intellectual orientation.

In the Characteristics section of the inventory, he responded "Yes" 50 percent of the time, the population average; his sense of self-esteem can be seen as comfortable.

Overall, this is the profile of an outgoing, enterprising, cosmopolitan, concert-attending professional businessman with some strong political interests, an aversion to getting his hands dirty or being cold and wet in the great outdoors, and some literary and artistic aspirations (perhaps hidden from his colleagues). He lives in a cosmopolitan, urban center on the Eastern seaboard, which is more appropriate for him than some wide-open western setting, such as Abilene or Cheyenne.

Case C. Person C (Table 10-3) has a profile that suggests lots of energy—even, one suspects, frantic energy. His IE score of 31 is that of a highly extroverted person; he is probably the focus of action in most of his family and social groups, for he also answered "Like" to 61 percent of the School Subjects section, 84 percent of the Activities section, and 96 percent of the Types of People section. He likes everything, maybe a bit indiscriminately. His personal style parallels his test-taking choices; he is outgoing, affable, generous, expansive—in a sense, a salesman's salesman. He could probably sell anything to anyone; at least he would enjoy trying.

His AOR score of 31 indicates that he is not particularly interested in the world of abstract ideas—he wants action—and his percentage "Yes" score of 64 in the Characteristics section shows that he is confident he can induce action.

Because this person marked "Like" to so many activities, his scores on the General Occupational Themes and Basic Interest Scales are elevated. Thus, one has to evaluate these scores a bit differently: high scores have to be higher before they can be considered important.

On the General Occupational Themes, he had one "Very high" score (ENTERPRISING) and three "Highs" (REALISTIC, SOCIAL, and CONVENTIONAL). Since scores on the last three were all of about the same magnitude, they should all be represented in the coding, yielding ERSC, even though four-letter codes are usually unwieldy.

Person C's high scores on the Basic Interest Scales are concentrated in the ENTERPRISING-REALISTIC areas. The high score on SALES (76) is supported by the other high scores on LAW/POLITICS, BUSINESS MANAGEMENT, PUBLIC SPEAKING, and MERCHANDISING. There is nothing about the enterprising way of life that this person dislikes; and his score of 62 on the OFFICE PRACTICES scale suggests that he even attends to his paperwork with some relish—if he finds time to get to it.

The other high Basic Interest scores indicate that this person enjoys the robust outdoor life; he scored uncommonly high on MILITARY ACTIVITIES (76), ADVENTURE (71), and ATHLETICS (76). His high score (66) on DOMESTIC ARTS is a bit unusual, and probably suggests some story, such as that he learned to cook while putting himself through school, or his father owned a restaurant, or he prepares elaborate meals for visitors. Though this score probably does not have much occupational relevance for this person, it yields an insightful question for the counselor to pursue in understanding the man's approach to life.

There are two low scores in the ARTISTIC area, demonstrating that even people who, like this person, appear to like everything have some clusters of substantial aversions.

Working with the Basic Interest Scales, we would again be prompted to give this profile a four-letter code, the same one generated from the General Occupational Themes—ERSC.

The highest Occupational Scale score—a very high 60—is on the LIFE INSURANCE AGENT scale; again, person C comes across as the classic salesperson. His other high Occupational Scales are on people-oriented, practical, social, doer scales. The high scores span the four themes again, though from the Occupational Scales alone the ordering would probably be ESCR.

Combining the three codes from the different types

TABLE 10-4
Case D

GENERAL OCCUPATIONAL
THEMES

R	58	Average
I	53	Average
A	35	Low
S	66	Very high
E	66	High
C	48	Average

ES or SE

HIGH BASIC INTEREST SCALES

E	Sales	72
R	Military Activities	69
E	Business Management	68
R	Agriculture	68
S	Religious Activities	66
E	Public Speaking	63
S	Athletics	63
I	Medical Science	61
E	Law/Politics	58

ERS

LOW BASIC INTEREST SCALES

| A | Art | 28 |
| A | Writing | 32 |

FIVE HIGHEST
OCCUPATIONAL SCALES

SEC	Personnel Director	58
RI	Forester	57
ES	Life Insurance Agent	56
SCE	School Superintendent	56
ECR	Agribusiness Manager	56

SEC

FIVE LOWEST
OCCUPATIONAL SCALES

A	Librarian	−5
IR	Physical Scientist	1
I	Mathematician	2
ARI	Architect	3
A	Artist	6

Overall code ES

Academic Orientation	36
Introversion-Extroversion	43
Percentage Yes: Characteristics	57

of scales, the final coding for this profile would be ERSC.

Overall, this is a profile of an energetic, outgoing, continually on-the-move salesman, probably a person with lots of stories and jokes, and the style to tell them. He undoubtedly spends most of his time with others, dislikes being alone, likes to be active. He probably takes on too much in his life, and because he likes everything he undoubtedly has trouble setting priorities. Nonetheless, he is in the right job: his high activity level produces a good income and great satisfaction.

Case D. Case D's profile (Table 10-4) shows a wide range of interests. Among the General Occupational Themes, he has a very high SOCIAL score and a high ENTERPRISING score. In addition, his REALISTIC score, though within the average range, is 58, just below the high range. On the strength of the Themes scores, his code type would be either ES or SE.

The breadth of his interests is demonstrated in the

Basic Interest Scales, where he has nine scores in the "High" or "Very high" range. These scores are distributed over the ENTERPRISING, REALISTIC, and SOCIAL areas, with one lone INVESTIGATIVE scale—MEDICAL SCIENCE—also high. Someone with this many high scores is usually energetic in several areas, and may in fact find it a bit difficult to be intensely focused in any one place. One thing that can be certain, because of the high ENTERPRISING and SOCIAL interests, is that the person enjoys being with people, usually in a helpful relationship, but also in a business relationship. His score of 43 on the IE scale, toward the extroverted end, supports this conclusion.

The one area he clearly finds unappealing is ART. The Basic Interest scores suggest an ERS code type.

The high Occupational Scale scores are basically on people-oriented occupations, with the possible exception of FORESTER. Although this person has a strong

outdoor orientation, it probably will remain an avocational interest for him, not a vocational pursuit. For this person, the interest has had some concrete influence on his life ways: he has moved from a large, metropolitan city to a more lusty, outdoor-oriented western city.

His AOR score of 36 suggests that he will not seek out further academic training.

His percentage "Yes" on the Characteristics section of the booklet—57 percent—is slightly above average, indicating (on this crude measure, at least) a comfortable level of self-esteem.

This profile describes a person earning a living in the life insurance business, heavily involved in community activities in an outdoor-oriented society, and quite successful and happy in this situation.

Case E. Case E (Table 10-5) is similar to Case D, but with two important differences: first, E's REALISTIC and CONVENTIONAL scores are higher; second, his SOCIAL score is lower. Both of them have the high ENTERPRISING scores typical of this group.

Case E, compared to Case D, is more practical, more inclined toward mechanical and outdoor activities, and more comfortable with paperwork. But both of them are basically salesmen, interested in persuasive activities.

Like Case D, Case E has a broad range of interests, as reflected in his Basic Interest Scale scores. The life insurance business is a good pursuit for his SALES, BUSINESS MANAGEMENT, and OFFICE PRACTICES interests, and he uses his avocational pursuits as an outlet for the outdoors and adventuresome areas of his interests, though the latter probably figures also in his willingness to take risks in promoting or closing sales. Case E, with a profile code of ERC on all sections of the profile, comes across as an enterprising, practical, organized fellow.

On the Occupational Scales, Case E's profile shows a varied high-score group, with business the only common theme, and with a couple of rather different occupations included—FORESTER and SOCIAL SCIENCE TEACHER. The ENTERPRISING, REALISTIC, and CONVENTIONAL themes run through these occupations but not in a completely consistent manner. This man probably feels tugged in opposing directions; on the one hand, he would like to be running an organized office; on the other is his inclination to be outside working with his hands, with his sleeves rolled up.

His AOR score of 38 suggests that he avoids the academic world. His IE score of 46 is only mildly in the extroverted area, which probably reflects his low level of interest in working with people in social-service activities.

His relatively low percentage "Yes" in Characteristics—29 percent—indicates that he was rather hard on himself in evaluating his own abilities, particularly given his level of professional success. In a counseling session, I would probably call this to his attention and suggest that he was being unduly demanding of himself, that he had not adequately acknowledged what he had achieved and was capable of achieving.

TABLE 10-5
Case E

GENERAL OCCUPATIONAL
THEMES

R	63	Moderately high	
I	48	Average	(ERC)
A	43	Average	
S	49	Average	
E	65	High	
C	62	High	

HIGH BASIC INTEREST SCALES

E	Sales	65
R	Agriculture	65
S	Athletics	64
E	Business Management	63
R	Adventure	59
R	Nature	58
I	Medical Science	58
E	Merchandising	58
C	Office Practices	58

(ERC)

LOW BASIC INTEREST SCALES

A	Music/Dramatics	37
S	Religious Activities	37
A	Art	40
S	Teaching	40

FIVE HIGHEST
OCCUPATIONAL SCALES

ERC	Purchasing Agent	53
CE	Banker	50
RI	Forester	48
ECS	Credit Manager	47
SEC	Social Science Teacher	46

(ERC)

FIVE LOWEST
OCCUPATIONAL SCALES

IR	Physical Scientist	−1
I	Biologist	3
ARI	Architect	6
I	Mathematician	8
A	Photographer	11

Overall code (ERC)

Academic Orientation	38
Introversion-Extroversion	46
Percentage Yes: Characteristics	29

Case F. Case F (Table 10-6) continues the ENTER-PRISING theme but differs slightly from the other cases in this series in having a stronger SOCIAL orientation. The two high General Occupational Themes—ENTERPRISING and SOCIAL—suggest a code of ES. (Because the scores are tied, the coding could as well be SE, but the remainder of the profile indicates that ES is clearly more appropriate.) Both the INVESTIGATIVE and REALISTIC themes are low, the latter very low.

Among the Basic Interest Scales, the ENTERPRISING theme continues strong, with high scores on SALES, MERCHANDISING, LAW/POLITICS, and PUBLIC SPEAKING—a consistent outgoing, extroverted pattern; on the basis of these scales, we would code this profile E.

Incidentally, when a profile shows a lone high score on a single Basic Interest Scale, as this one does on the MILITARY ACTIVITIES scale, the explanation is usually idiosyncratic; the person has scored high for some reason peculiar to that specific area. Which is to say that

unless high scores on the Basic Interest Scales cluster in some manner, *they should be interpreted gingerly.* In this case, for example, the person would probably report that he had a great time in the military, that the years thus spent had been a good time in his life; perhaps he has even remained active in military-reserve affairs. But when the MILITARY ACTIVITIES score is unsupported by any of the adjacent REALISTIC scales, it is probably more indicative of nostalgia than any concerted interest in the activities of the military, and it should be treated as such.

(The MILITARY ACTIVITIES scale is indeed one of the most homogeneous Basic Scales; every item in the scale employs the words "soldiers" or "military": *Be a military officer, Drill in a military company, Work with military personnel,* etc. When people score high on this scale, they have consistently reacted favorably to specifically military activities.)

This interpretation of person F's response to military items is corroborated by his lowest scores on the Basic Interest Scales, which include a collection of INVESTIGATIVE, REALISTIC, and CONVENTIONAL scales. Because these three themes constitute the code type for ARMY OFFICER, RIC, we must suppose that this person would not really enjoy being an Army officer—he just enjoys his memories.

The other interesting low score, on the RELIGIOUS ACTIVITIES scale, is noteworthy because the SOCIAL General Theme on this profile is high, suggesting some inconsistency. The single low score may be a rejection of traditional religious trappings in an otherwise highly developed social conscience, an interpretation that fits with my perception of this person. He spends a great deal of time in community service activities for the handicapped but, in fact, little time in organized religion.

The E theme, with variations, continues among the Occupational Scales; the five highest scores here are on scales variously coded E, AE, ES, EI, and ECS. The occupations involved—LAWYER, ADVERTISING EXECUTIVE, CHAMBER OF COMMERCE EXECUTIVE, INVESTMENT FUND MANAGER, and BUYER—all entail high-level persuasion and administrative planning; all require verbal fluency and assertiveness; all emphasize organizational leadership.

The IE score of 40 is well into the extroverted end of the dimension and accords well with the overall E pattern.

The percentage "Yes" of 64 on the Characteristics section is relatively high, indicating that this person has a healthy sense of confidence in his abilities, which again fits well with the ENTERPRISING theme. He likes to make things happen and is confident that he can.

The AOR score of 28 is low, indicating substantial distaste for academic settings. Part of the low score can be attributed to the strong rejection of scientific activities, and Case F is a living example of the common antithesis between sales and scientific interests. When he comes into contact with traditional academic types,

TABLE 10-6
Case F

GENERAL OCCUPATIONAL
THEMES

R	32	Very low
I	39	Low
A	53	Average
S	58	Moderately high
E	58	Moderately high
C	44	Moderately low

(ES)

HIGH BASIC INTEREST SCALES

E	Sales	65
E	Merchandising	62
E	Law/Politics	62
E	Public Speaking	59
R	Military Activities	59

(E)

LOW BASIC INTEREST SCALES

I	Medical Science	29
I	Medical Service	33
S	Religious Activities	35
I	Science	36
R	Mechanical Activities	37
C	Office Practices	37
R	Nature	42

FIVE HIGHEST
OCCUPATIONAL SCALES

E	Lawyer	55
AE	Advertising Executive	54
ES	Chamber of Commerce Exec.	53
EI	Investment Fund Manager	52
ECS	Buyer	52

(E)

FIVE LOWEST
OCCUPATIONAL SCALES

IRC	Medical Technologist	−2
I	Veterinarian	−1
R	Skilled Crafts	2
RC	Farmer	6
RSE	Highway Patrol Officer	8

Overall code (E)

Academic Orientation	28
Introversion-Extroversion	40
Percentage Yes: Characteristics	64

TABLE 10-7
Case G

GENERAL OCCUPATIONAL
THEMES

R	54	Average
I	40	Low
A	61	High
S	53	Average
E	67	High
C	45	Average

HIGH BASIC INTEREST SCALES

E	Sales	68
E	Public Speaking	67
E	Business Management	63
E	Law/Politics	61
A	Art	61
A	Writing	60
A	Music/Dramatics	59
S	Athletics	59

LOW BASIC INTEREST SCALES

I	Science	36
I	Medical Service	38
C	Office Practices	41

SIX HIGHEST
OCCUPATIONAL SCALES

E	Lawyer	56
ES	Chamber of Commerce Exec.	54
SEC	Personnel Director	53
ES	Sales Manager	52
SCE	Public Administrator	52
AE	Advertising Executive	51

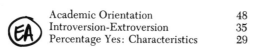

FIVE LOWEST
OCCUPATIONAL SCALES

IRC	Medical Technologist	5
IR	Physical Scientist	7
I	Mathematician	8
R	Skilled Crafts	8
RC	Farmer	12

Overall
code

	Academic Orientation	48
	Introversion-Extroversion	35
	Percentage Yes: Characteristics	29

he is almost certain to find them impractical, unrealistic, and too slow-moving for his tastes.

Overall, person F's profile is that of an enterprising, energetic person with stronger social concerns than the average salesman, someone more concerned with organizational leadership than the average enterprising type. He is practical, friendly, and organization-oriented, and he finds great satisfaction in making things happen.

Case G. This case (Table 10-7) concludes our look at these life insurance underwriters. He continues the EN-TERPRISING theme, but he differs in having a strong AR-TISTIC theme, as well. This general interest in art, music, drama, and literature pulls him more toward the academic world than his colleagues are, and probably more in the direction of the generally educated executive, as reflected by the EA code type.

Among the Basic Interest Scales, his four top scores

are all in the ENTERPRISING area, strongly suggesting that this theme will dominate his occupational world, since its pursuits require a great deal of time and energy. His next highest scores are all in the ARTISTIC area, but these interests are not likely to be indulged in his occupation—unless he can find, for example, an outlet in the advertising or media worlds. Consequently, the ARTISTIC interests probably dominate his hobbies and spare time (though he has indicated a considerable interest in athletics, as well). Because of this combination of ENTERPRISING and ARTISTIC interests, he would be eminently suited for fund-raising drives for museums or symphony orchestras.

He rejected SCIENCE and OFFICE PRACTICES; the latter suggests he finds the paperwork associated with the insurance practice to be simply a necessary evil.

His five highest Occupational Scales again reflect a broad orientation. He has common interests with lawyers, Chamber of Commerce executives, and public administrators, as well as with advertising executives, one of the chief occupations where the ARTISTIC and EN-TERPRISING themes go hand in hand.

His AOR score of 48 predicts that he would find the university campus a relatively comfortable place. His IE score of 35 is well toward the extroverted area, suggesting he is comfortable working with people and would normally carry the conversational momentum. His friends would probably describe him as outgoing, affable, talkative, and energetic.

His percentage "Yes" in the Characteristics section—29 percent—is surprisingly low, both because of the scores elsewhere on the profile and because of this man's outstanding occupational success. Perhaps he has some misgivings about his own talents; or, because he typically deals with very competent people, he may be comparing himself against a difficult benchmark. Because people need to feel good about themselves, I would suggest to him that—given his accomplishments—he allow himself a more charitable evaluation of his own abilities.

Because of Case G's stronger artistic and academic orientation—only Case B in this group approaches him on either count—he may go farther up the managerial ladder than his companions, who will, for the most part, stay in direct sales. The profile also predicts a considerable amount of community involvement in the cultural areas; because in most cities those involvements are in the "country club" set, this person is probably established among the so-called pillars of the community. Given his experience and his outgoing nature, he could probably accomplish almost any reasonable thing he set out to do in community programs.

Summary: Cases A through G. The preceding profiles illustrate two important general points: first, among people happily and successfully employed in the same occupation, a common general theme is usually found; second, even though the general theme dominates, there is always considerable variety in the secondary themes, variety that leads to a diversity of work styles, living situations, and avocations. The people within an occupation are usually more aware of the variety among them than of the general theme they share; a common response to a request to study an occupational group is, "You won't find anything similar about us—we're all so different." The profiles suggest why this is so.

Cases H and I. The remaining profiles in this chapter have been selected to illustrate other important points. Cases H (Table 10-8) and I (Table 10-9) are included because they continue the ENTERPRISING theme, but with some interesting variations. Both are handsome, fluent, politically oriented people. One is from the North, one is from the South; one is black, the other white. One has a law degree and career ambitions, and is currently in a high-level administrative post in one of our larger cities; the other is liberal-arts educated, married to a busy professional, expending a considerable amount of energy in raising a family, and dabbling in politics on the side. Both are women, and both appear to find their lives happy and useful.

Case H. Case H, whose profile is summarized in Table 10-8 and who has the stronger, more dominant ENTERPRISING theme of the two, is—for want of a better categorization—a homemaker. Her IE score, 42, shows a fair amount of extroversion; her AOR score, 37, suggests that she is not particularly anxious to go back to school. Though her energy level and outgoing nature will lead her into a wide range of activities, the activities will probably be in the business or political arenas. Her two highest scores on the Basic Interest Scales, on LAW/POLITICS and BUSINESS MANAGEMENT, and her highest Occupational Scale scores, on LAWYER, LIFE INSURANCE SALES, ADVERTISING EXECUTIVE, and ARMY OFFICER (which, for women, is essentially a managerial scale), support that prediction.

Her percentage "Yes" of 57 on the Characteristics section is slightly above average, showing that she is comfortable with her own abilities.

Two of her lowest Basic Interest Scale scores—TEACHING and DOMESTIC ARTS—suggest that she will be increasingly eager to get out of the house as her children grow up. Her other two low Basic Interest scores—AGRICULTURE and NATURE—indicate that she will look elsewhere than the great outdoors for excitement.

Because she lives in a relatively affluent setting, with many extracurricular options open to her, and because she energetically makes things happen in her life, she has not experienced the corrosive despair that many women in her age bracket and marital status feel when they perceive time passing and their occupational horizons shrinking. Whether the future will continue to provide enough opportunities for her imagination and energy is an issue that she and her husband should be dealing with now, while some flexibility is possible.

She might move more actively into politics—already active on the local level, she could escalate into the

TABLE 10-8
Case H

GENERAL OCCUPATIONAL
THEMES

R	39	Moderately low
I	50	Average
A	52	Average
S	41	Low
E	60	High
C	54	Moderately high

HIGH BASIC INTEREST SCALES

E	Law/Politics	69
E	Business Management	69
E	Sales	63
E	Merchandising	61
E	Public Speaking	61

LOW BASIC INTEREST SCALES

S	Teaching	31
R	Nature	35
R	Agriculture	36
S	Domestic Arts	39
I	Mathematics	41
I	Science	43
I	Medical Service	43

FIVE HIGHEST
OCCUPATIONAL SCALES

AE	Advertising Executive	59
E	Lawyer	59
ES	Life Insurance Agent	57
RE	Army Officer	55
EC	Buyer	52

FIVE LOWEST
OCCUPATIONAL SCALES

IR	Chemist	3
I	Physical Scientist	4
CRI	Licensed Practical Nurse	9
ESC	Home Economics Teacher	10
I	Mathematician	12

Overall code

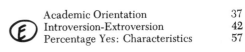

Academic Orientation	37
Introversion-Extroversion	42
Percentage Yes: Characteristics	57

regional or national level—or she might well take advantage of her husband's substantial cash flow to consider opening her own business. Of course, there is always the possibility that she will simply go the bridge-and-country-club route, luxuriating in a comfortable, cosmopolitan life style. If she does that, she will likely wake up one day and wonder where her life has gone.

Case I. The profile for this case (Table 10-9) has a broad focus, with high scores on the ARTISTIC, SOCIAL, and ENTERPRISING themes; thus far, the third of these has guided her career.

Her IE score of 33, well down toward the extroverted end of the scale, reflects both her outgoing nature and her social-service concern. Her AOR score of 48 is roughly what one would expect in a law school graduate, which she is. Given the strong business trend in her interests, this score is quite high. (The SCII items dealing with business are weighted negatively on the

TABLE 10-9
Case I

GENERAL OCCUPATIONAL
THEMES

R 46 Average
I 51 Average
A 67 Very high
S 57 Moderately high
E 60 High
C 45 Moderately low

HIGH BASIC INTEREST SCALES

E	Merchandising	69
A	Music/Dramatics	68
E	Law/Politics	67
E	Public Speaking	67
A	Art	67
A	Writing	59
S	Social Service	59

LOW BASIC INTEREST SCALES

R	Mechanical Activities	40
I	Medical Service	40
C	Office Practices	40
I	Science	41
I	Medical Science	41

FIVE HIGHEST
OCCUPATIONAL SCALES

SEC	Social Science Teacher	53
A	Reporter	52
E	Lawyer	52
SER	Recreation Leader	49
AS	English Teacher	49

FIVE LOWEST
OCCUPATIONAL SCALES

I	Physical Scientist	−8
IR	Chemist	4
RC	Instrument Assembler	8
IR	Dental Hygienist	9
I	Mathematician	12

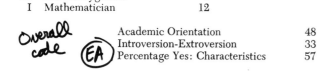

Academic Orientation	48
Introversion-Extroversion	33
Percentage Yes: Characteristics	57

AOR scale; consequently, anyone with business interests is, in a sense, penalized on this scale, not because of any intent on the test author's part, but because the norm group of successful academics was somewhat anti-business.)

Case I's artistic interests are expressed mainly in her avocational pursuits, though they may influence her somewhat in the way she chooses to allocate the public resources in her charge, which are considerable. I hope so.

Her future ambitions are focused in the political arena, and her high scores on LAW/POLITICS, PUBLIC SPEAKING, even MERCHANDISING, augur well for her enjoying the activities necessary to rise in that culture. Her high Occupational Scale scores—SOCIAL SCIENCE TEACHER, LAWYER, REPORTER—all knit together the image of someone on her feet, talking, writing, persuading others about social issues.

Her percentage "Yes" on the Characteristics section is 57—somewhat above average, indicating a comfortable self-concept. (Once again, this is at best a crude measure, and should not be taken too seriously. This case is a good example: in person, this woman exudes massive self-confidence, much more so than would be predicted by the relatively mild percentage of 57.)

This woman is on her way up the political ladder; given a few breaks, in a few years she will be running for Congress, and she has already set her sights even higher.

Cases J and K. These cases also make an interesting contrast, for they represent two different types of teenage profiles; both are from 16-year-old high school girls. Person J shows no strong interests in anything; her General Occupational Themes are all low, as are her Basic Interest Scale scores, with the interesting exception of the ADVENTURE scale. Person K, in contrast, shows a substantial scattering of interests all over the profile—a high level of interest, but a lack of focus. Both are counseling challenges.

Case J. Person J (Table 10-10) is the more demanding case. Her interest profile is that of a teenager saturated with apathy and boredom. Little interests her, less excites her. She marked "Like" to only 5 percent of the occupations (in contrast to a population average of roughly 30 percent); nor did the School Subjects section or the Activities section elicit many more "Likes."

The fact that she did not answer "Like" to many items does not in itself mean that the Occupational Scale scores will be low, for people with few interests—in the sense of answering "Like" infrequently—can have high Occupational Scale scores if the pattern of "Dislikes" resembles a pattern found in some particular occupation. But for person J, that was not the case. Even her aversions failed to cluster. Her score on BEAUTICIAN was the only high score, and in the absence of any supporting pattern, this score should not be taken too seriously.

Her AOR is very low—22. Most assuredly, she does not enjoy school, or at least its academic component, and she will probably have trouble with college. Because she is from a high-socioeconomic-level family, she will be pressured into entering college, but unless she radically changes her attitude it will not be a successful experience for her.

Her IE score of 65 is far in the introverted direction, which predicts she will be relatively uncommunicative in the counseling interview.

Her combination of limited interests, minimal academic drive, and introversion produces a challenging counseling case. For such people, the SCII cannot help much. It is not a crystal ball that can look beneath boredom, apathy, or lack of experience to see some hidden rough-cut diamond. Until this person finds something to motivate her, standardized instruments cannot help.

My inclination would be to say something like this to this person: "The inventory doesn't show any strong

TABLE 10-10
Case J

GENERAL OCCUPATIONAL
THEMES

R	30	Very low
I	36	Low
A	41	Low
S	29	Very low
E	37	Low
C	37	Low

HIGH BASIC INTEREST SCALES

| R | Adventure | 59 |

LOW BASIC INTEREST SCALES

S	Domestic Arts	31
E	Business Management	32
E	Law/Politics	33
E	Public Speaking	33
S	Social Service	33
R	Mechanical Activities	33
R	Nature	35
A	Art	37
S	Religious Activities	37
S	Teaching	38
R	Military Activities	41
I	Medical Science	41
E	Sales	42

HIGHEST
OCCUPATIONAL SCALES

| CRE | Beautician | 47 |
| | (No other "similar" scores) | |

FIVE LOWEST
OCCUPATIONAL SCALES

A	Art Teacher	−8
ESC	Home Economics Teacher	−5
SEC	Guidance Counselor	−3
S	Social Worker	−2
S	Director, Christian Education	−2

Overall code
none

Academic Orientation	22
Introversion-Extroversion	65
Percentage Yes: Characteristics	21

Responses to other inventory items:

Section	L	I	D
Occupations	5	13	82
School Subjects	14	42	44
Activities	8	43	49
Amusements	18	28	49
Types of People	21	42	33

patterns in your interests. You are going to have to live awhile, try out more things, seek more experience, probe new environments, search out interesting people in a wide range of settings to talk to—in general, grow up and out. The lack of any pattern here suggests that you are fairly passive in your approach to the world. You need to get tuned in, turned on. Take some initiative for generating new experiences, read more books and magazines, search out some hobbies, try a few jobs, build yourself a focus. No one is going to come along and drop a future in your lap; you're going to have to create it." Whatever a counselor can say to fire up such

a person might be helpful; nondirective "uh-uhs" probably will not.

This teenager will probably lead her parents through some trying times; the only thing that excites her is adventure, and she is young and pretty enough to find that in abundance. In counseling this young woman, I would raise gently the issue of prudence, but I would be realistic about the impact, or lack of it, that I or any other counselor can have in such cases.

Case K. Person K (Table 10-11), also a 16-year-old female, is another story entirely. Her range of interests is so broad, yet so traditional, that her major problem will be to expand her horizons to include new possibilities, and then to focus on one of those possibilities.

Among her General Occupational Themes, the ARTISTIC and SOCIAL themes are high, arguing for a code type of AS. The others are in the average range; none are low.

TABLE 10-11
Case K

GENERAL OCCUPATIONAL
THEMES

R	44	Average
I	51	Average
A	64	High
S	58	Moderately high
E	49	Average
C	48	Average

HIGH BASIC INTEREST SCALES

A	Music/Dramatics	69
A	Art	67
R	Nature	67
R	Agriculture	67
I	Medical Service	62
A	Writing	62
S	Teaching	62
S	Religious Activities	62
S	Domestic Arts	62

LOW BASIC INTEREST SCALES

E	Law/Politics	38
R	Mechanical Activities	40
E	Business Management	41

FIVE HIGHEST
OCCUPATIONAL SCALES

RIA	Occupational Therapist	51
IRS	Physical Therapist	49
A	Musician	49
SI	Registered Nurse	49
SC	Elementary Teacher	49

FIVE LOWEST
OCCUPATIONAL SCALES

I	Physical Scientist	−4
ECS	Credit Manager	9
S	Social Worker	9
CE	Business Education Teacher	10
IR	Chemist	11

Overall code

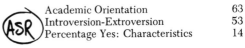

Academic Orientation	63
Introversion-Extroversion	53
Percentage Yes: Characteristics	14

On her Basic Interest Scales, she has high scores in four of the six clusters—A, R, I, and S—with the ARTISTIC scales all high. Her breadth of interests, as demonstrated by these scores, should give her many options to consider in future experiences and training.

Her pattern of scores does suggest that she is well socialized into the "typical teenage girl" pattern, and that is probably worth some attention in the counseling interview. The high scores on TEACHING, RELIGIOUS ACTIVITIES, and DOMESTIC ARTS scales are what used to be called the "premarital pattern," typical of young women whose major goal in life is to find a husband, get married, and raise children. The high score on the MEDICAL SERVICE scale, indicative of nursing interests, fits into that pattern also.

Her high scores on the Occupational Scales are a continuation of this "traditional teenager" syndrome, with high scores in the paramedical, teaching, and artistic areas. And because, as her exposure to the world broadens, her interests may expand, she should be encouraged not to focus too strongly on these scores until she learns more about other options that are open to her. Although she is now a traditional 16-year-old, she may eventually be a broadened, restless, nontraditional 36-year-old, especially given her energy level; the time to start providing some increased options to that 36-year-old is now, not later when she is burdened by children, a house, and a husband.

With the changing role of women in our society, this young woman should have her options expanded. She should be encouraged to consider a wider range of occupational choices than she currently is. For example, along with nursing, she might well consider medical school. Given the average level of scientific interests on her profile, she will not think very seriously about either, but the point is that she should not restrict herself to the traditional female roles in whatever area she is considering.

A counselor might mention the statistics of women in the labor force—that almost half of married women work, that most mothers live at least half of their life *without* children in the home, that a career is a stabilizing influence in one's life, that there are many ways to make a useful, satisfying contribution, and raising children is only one of them. In general, the counselor should help raise her consciousness about the changing roles of women in our society.

Because this young woman has a high score on the AOR scale—63—she will undoubtedly seek, and probably enjoy, higher education. Initially, she should probably seek a liberal-arts education, at least until her focus of interests sharpens; she needs more exposure, more confidence in herself. As indicated by her low percentage of "Yes" responses on Characteristics—14—she does not have much faith in her abilities, and she needs time and maturation to overcome that.

The first place to explore further opportunities for her is in the ARTISTIC areas, since those are her strongest interests. These careers depend on artistic skills—drawing, singing, dancing, playing an instrument, writing, acting—and if she is not already far along in developing these talents, she must decide if she is willing to make the necessary commitment to become really proficient in one of them, proficient enough at least to teach, if not to perform. Perhaps, once she has gained some experience and exposure, other avenues in the artistic world will become visible to her. At the moment, her goal should be to accumulate experience, skills, and a broader exposure. Because she is energetic, imaginative, and eager, this should not be a problem. In fact, because she is young, enthusiastic, interested in many things, and a good student, with some learning and planning time ahead of her, her options are many, her future bright.

Cases L and M. Cases L and M have been included here both as interesting case studies in themselves and to demonstrate the robustness of the scoring procedures in the presence of novel test-taking strategies; both of these people were decisive in the extreme, almost systematically avoiding the "Indifferent" response category when responding to the test booklet.

Case L (Table 10-12) is an academic administrator; Case M (Table 10-13) is a corporate executive. Both are high-energy extroverts with a diverse scattering of interests across several areas. Both are outspoken, with firm ideas; on some issues, their colleagues would likely describe them as opinionated, a characteristic probably related to their extremely low percentages of "Indifferent" responses. Case M chose the middle response position less than 5 percent of the time, and not at all in the School Subjects, Activities, and Characteristics sections. Case L was even more extreme, never using the "Indifferent" response in the last six sections of the booklet, and only 8 percent of the time in the first section. For the most part, either they liked something or they did not. They were decisive.

But despite their superficial similarity in personality characteristics and their markedly similar, if deviant, response style, the two profiles show some important differences.

Case L, the academic administrator—specifically, a psychologist and head of the department—is an IA type, heavy on the arts and science but with a smattering of communication interests. The profile shows the typical "intellectual" rejection of the CONVENTIONAL and REALISTIC areas; the exceptions here, the high scores on the ADVENTURE and NATURE scales, probably reflect more an outdoors orientation than a solid pattern of vocational interests.

The high AOR score—67—reflects the academic involvement; the low IE score—32—reflects the outgoing, affable nature that succeeds well in administration, though the absence of any middle response to most items could reflect a rigidity troublesome to the administrative process. The charitable interpretation would be firm-mindedness.

TABLE 10-12
Case L

GENERAL OCCUPATIONAL
THEMES

R	30	Very low
I	59	Moderately high
A	67	Very high
S	54	Average
E	48	Average
C	37	Low

HIGH BASIC INTEREST SCALES

E	Law/Politics	66
A	Art	64
E	Public Speaking	63
A	Writing	62
S	Teaching	62
A	Music/Dramatics	61
R	Adventure	59
S	Athletics	59
R	Nature	58

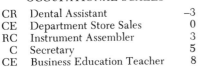

LOW BASIC INTEREST SCALES

R	Agriculture	30
R	Mechanical Activities	32
I	Medical Service	33
S	Religious Activities	33
C	Office Practices	36
R	Military Activities	41
E	Sales	41
E	Business Management	41

FIVE HIGHEST
OCCUPATIONAL SCALES

IAS	Psychologist	64
E	Lawyer	61
IS	Speech Pathologist	57
SEC	Guidance Counselor	57
SEC	Social Science Teacher	55

FIVE LOWEST
OCCUPATIONAL SCALES

CR	Dental Assistant	−3
CE	Department Store Sales	0
RC	Instrument Assembler	3
C	Secretary	5
CE	Business Education Teacher	8

overall code

Academic Orientation	67
Introversion-Extroversion	32
Percentage Yes: Characteristics	79

Responses to other inventory items:

Section	L	I	D
Occupations	40	8	52
School Subjects	64	0	36
Activities	61	0	39
Amusements	46	0	54
Types of People	58	0	42
Preferences	53	0	47
Characteristics	79	0	21

Case M, the corporate executive, has a profile saturated with the ENTERPRISING, SOCIAL, and ARTISTIC General Occupational Themes, with an overwhelming flavor of extroversion. The profile shows an enormously high percentage of "Like" responses. Still, the low scores on a few Basic Interest Scales—MATHEMATICS, SCIENCE,

and MILITARY ACTIVITIES—show that the responses were not made indiscriminately; some activities were consistently less appealing to this person than others.

The range of high scores on the General Occupational Themes and the Basic Interest Scales, coupled with the high percentage of "Like" responses and the very extroverted score on the IE scale—23—suggest a certain

TABLE 10-13
Case M

GENERAL OCCUPATIONAL
THEMES

R	53	Moderately high
I	46	Average
A	67	Very high
S	70	Very high
E	73	Very high
C	43	Moderately low

HIGH BASIC INTEREST SCALES

A	Music/Dramatics	73
E	Public Speaking	71
E	Merchandising	70
S	Social Service	69
E	Law/Politics	69
E	Business Management	68
A	Art	68
A	Writing	66
E	Sales	66
S	Religious Activities	66
S	Teaching	64
R	Nature	63
S	Domestic Arts	61

LOW BASIC INTEREST SCALES

I	Mathematics	31
I	Science	36
R	Military Activities	41

FIVE HIGHEST
OCCUPATIONAL SCALES

SE	YWCA Staff	65
SER	Recreation Leader	62
ESA	Flight Attendant	58
A	Art Teacher	57
ES	Life Insurance Agent	55

FIVE LOWEST
OCCUPATIONAL SCALES

I	Physical Scientist	−25
I	Mathematician	−18
IR	Chemist	−14
IRC	Computer Programmer	−3
IR	Engineer	6

Overall code

Academic Orientation	38
Introversion-Extroversion	23
Percentage Yes: Characteristics	86

Responses to other inventory items:

Section	L	I	D
Occupations	69	3	28
School Subjects	56	0	44
Activities	71	0	29
Amusements	67	8	26
Types of People	83	8	8
Preferences	43	23	33
Characteristics	86	0	14

PROFILE— STRONG VOCATIONAL INTEREST BLANK —FOR MEN (Form T399)

1968 BASIC INTEREST SCALES

SCALE	PLOTTED SCORE
PUBLIC SPEAKING	46
LAW/POLITICS	39
BUSINESS MANAGEMENT	35
SALES	42
MERCHANDISING	37
OFFICE PRACTICES	40
MILITARY ACTIVITIES	50
TECHNICAL SUPERVISION	27
MATHEMATICS	61
SCIENCE	63
MECHANICAL	50
NATURE	54
AGRICULTURE	56
ADVENTURE	53
RECREATIONAL LEADERSHIP	40
MEDICAL SERVICE	56
SOCIAL SERVICE	56
RELIGIOUS ACTIVITIES	45
TEACHING	50
MUSIC	64
ART	67
WRITING	58

DOUBLE LINE = AVERAGE SCORE FOR 650 52-YEAR-OLD MEN

Non-Occupational Scales 1968

AACH	66
DIV	55
MFII	46
MO	25
OIE	53
OL	54
SL	43
AR	46

Administrative Indices 1968

TR	396
UNP	8
FC	4
LP	22
IP	30
DP	48

1968 OCCUPATIONAL SCALES 1968

	OCCUPATION	STD. SCORE		OCCUPATION	STD. SCORE
I	DENTIST	52	VI	LIBRARIAN	33
	OSTEOPATH	45		ARTIST	44
	VETERINARIAN	39		MUSICIAN PERFORMER	44
	PHYSICIAN	53		MUSIC TEACHER	22
	PSYCHIATRIST	28	VII	C.P.A. OWNER	29
	PSYCHOLOGIST	29	VIII	SENIOR C.P.A.	26
	BIOLOGIST	55		ACCOUNTANT	14
II	ARCHITECT	40		OFFICEWORKER	16
	MATHEMATICIAN	34		PURCHASING AGENT	14
	PHYSICIST	38		BANKER	15
	CHEMIST	48		PHARMACIST	26
	ENGINEER	42		FUNERAL DIRECTOR	21
III	PRODUCTION	19	IX	SALES MANAGER	13
	ARMY OFFICER	10		REAL ESTATE SALESMAN	22
	AIR FORCE OFFICER	27		LIFE INS. SALESMAN	20
IV	CARPENTER	30	X	ADVERTISING MAN	35
	FOREST SERVICE MAN	26		LAWYER	33
	FARMER	42		AUTHOR-JOURNALIST	40
	MATH SCIENCE TEACHER	32	XI	PRESIDENT-MFG.	21
	PRINTER	39		SUPP. OCCUPATIONAL SCALES	
	POLICEMAN	24		CREDIT MANAGER	12
V	PERSONNEL DIRECTOR	15		CHAMBER OF COM. EXEC.	21
	PUBLIC ADMINISTRATOR	14		PHYSICAL THERAPIST	37
	REHABILITATION COUNS.	14		COMPUTER PROGRAMMER	33
	YMCA STAFF MEMBER	15		BUSINESS ED. TEACHER	15
	SOCIAL WORKER	11		COMMUNITY REC. ADMIN.	9
	SOCIAL SCIENCE TEACHER	6			
	SCHOOL SUPERINTENDENT	5			
	MINISTER	22			

NON-OCCUPATIONAL SCALES: AACH   AR   DIV   MFII   MO   OIE   OL   SL

ADMINISTRATIVE INDICES: TR   UNP   FC   LP   IP   DP

Fig. 10-1. Profile of Case N, 1971 testing, as reproduced in Campbell (1971), p. 300

franticness; this is probably a person who is running in all directions, who has many projects going at once, who revels in a feeling of involvement in many areas, who complains about not having time alone while continuing to accept new appointments and responsibilities. In short, this is the profile of an overcommitted executive, the so-called Type A, with both high success potential and high heart-attack potential.

Both of these cases are women. Case L, the academic administrator, is well characterized by the SCII profile; her highest score is on PSYCHOLOGIST—which she is—and she also scored high (50) on the COLLEGE PROFESSOR scale, which reassured her. Further, her other high scores look reasonable. Case M is not so well served by the SCII profile, for her major constellation of interests resembles that of men in hard-driving business settings such as Advertising Executive (where she had a score of 64), Chamber of Commerce Executive (62), and Personnel Director (64)—and for these occupations it has not yet been possible to amass female samples of sufficient size to establish the interest patterns of women so employed. Here is an example of the occasional case where the counselor might well dwell on the scales for the opposite sex. There is little risk of misinterpretation; the dominant enterprising extroversion is abundantly clear.

This woman is living out her interests, perhaps too successfully; she describes her life with words such as "fascinating," "stressful," "successful," and "frantic." Where the balance should be drawn between "fascinating" and "frantic" is a question she must grapple with personally; here the counselor, besides simply discussing the direction she might go, should also point out that time and energy are finite, and that setting some priorities for her future involvements might be the most important outcome of a career-planning session.

Case N. This case has been included to give some developmental flavor; this is the profile of a 17-year-old boy whose earlier SVIB profile, produced when he was 10, was used as a case study in the *Handbook for the Strong Vocational Interest Blank* (Campbell, 1971). The comparison of profiles over a crucial 7-year developmental period is instructive, to see both how the boy has changed (or, more accurately, has remained stable) and how the test has changed.

Figure 10-1 shows the SVIB profile as it appeared in 1971, with this student's scores; although the profile is slightly stylized for purposes of reproduction in the *Handbook*, the basic layout here reflects, for all practical purposes, what the earlier version looked like. Note that separate forms for men and women were still being used in 1971.

Following is the text of the profile interpretation as it appeared in the 1971 *Handbook*:

The SVIB should typically not be used by students under 15 or 16, and probably not even with immature youths at those ages. Yet these ages are only guidelines; if a student can handle the vocabulary, and if he is cognizant of the world of work, then some information can be gained from looking at his SVIB scores. To pressure young boys and girls into premature career choices, or even to suggest indirectly that they must have a choice is not wise, I think; they need time to stare at clouds, and throw stones in lakes, and pretend that their last name is Bernhardt, or Namath, or Armstrong. Still, some fascinating information can be gained by looking at SVIB profiles from young students.

The figure shows the profile for a 10-year-old boy, a fifth-grader. He is a "typical" little boy, with scuffed sneakers, a long history of cuts and abrasions, and an almost perfect record of losing his father's tools. He is also bright, with excellent reading skills; most of his standardized test scores are at the ninth- and tenth-grade levels. He had no trouble reading the Strong, though his attention span was not sufficient to complete it in one sitting; he worked over the booklet in spare moments over several days.

His results document what his parents attest to—that he

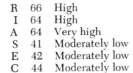

TABLE 10-14
Case N

GENERAL OCCUPATIONAL THEMES

R	66	High
I	64	High
A	64	Very high
S	41	Moderately low
E	42	Moderately low
C	44	Moderately low

HIGH BASIC INTEREST SCALES

R	Adventure	71
R	Mechanical Activities	68
I	Science	68
R	Nature	65
A	Writing	65
A	Music/Dramatics	64
I	Mathematics	63
R	Military Activities	62
R	Agriculture	58
A	Art	58

LOW BASIC INTEREST SCALES

E	Business Management	35
E	Merchandising	37
C	Office Practices	40
S	Teaching	40
E	Sales	41

FIVE HIGHEST OCCUPATIONAL SCALES

IR	Engineer	57
IRC	Computer Programmer	54
IRS	Math-Science Teacher	53
IA	College Professor	53
RIC	Cartographer	52

FIVE LOWEST OCCUPATIONAL SCALES

ECS	Buyer	−6
ECR	Agribusiness Manager	−3
CE	Banker	1
C	Accountant	3
ES	Sales Manager	3

 overall code (RIA)

Academic Orientation	62
Introversion-Extroversion	50
Percentage Yes: Characteristics	43

is fascinated by science. His highest scores on the Basic Interest Scales fell into two areas: math-science and the arts (music, art, and writing). This pattern is typical of academically oriented scientists, and the strong rejection of the scales at the top of the profile, especially the business activities, also supports that pattern of interests.

The same pattern appeared, as it should, among the Occupational Scales; the high scores were in Groups I and II, the sciences, with some moderately high ones in Groups VI and X, the art-oriented occupations. The lowest scores were in Groups VIII and III, the business and technical-supervisory occupations; the Group V scores—public administration and social service occupations—were also low.

All of this was summed up in the Academic Achievement scale score—66, quite high for a college student, let alone a ten-year-old—and this score, particularly in concert with the rest of the profile, strongly suggests that the boy is destined for some type of academic-intellectual-scientific career.

There was no particular purpose in giving him the inventory, simply curiosity on his part and his parents'. What was accomplished was that the three of them had, so they reported, a fascinating two-hour conversation about the role of work in an individual's life, and about the possible different styles of life. His father commented later, "We talked about things that I never knew he was interested in, and he had insights that I never imagined him capable of." Clearly, the most important end served was family communication.

This knowledge of the boy's interests, by itself, does not provide any direct answers to the parents' questions of how he should be treated with respect to career development. Two extreme viewpoints could be adopted by his parents: they could recognize that the boy is a bookish, scholarly dreamer who should be allowed to pursue his interests unimpeded; or they could conclude, "Well, his preferences will ensure his education in those areas; what we should do is lean on him to ensure some breadth and diversity in his life by acquainting him with shop work, athletic activities, and some business philosophy."

In this particular family, the mother opts for the former, the father for the latter—the future should be interesting.

Seven years later, the form of the profile has changed markedly, but the boy has not, at least in his inventoried interests. As the summary of his profile in Table 10-14 shows, he is still a science-oriented academician, and still strongly rejects business, in both its ENTERPRISING and its CONVENTIONAL aspects. His AOR score remains high—62—though interestingly not quite as high as it was at age 10—66. His current IE score of 50 is close to the earlier score of 53. The one area of substantial change is the rugged, outdoors, realistic scales—during these 7 years, his scores on the ADVENTURE, MECHANICAL ACTIVITIES, and NATURE scales have jumped about 15 points. Along with the scholarly bookishness, there is now a robustness.

Some contrasts, regrettably, cannot be made: the General Occupational Themes were not on the profile in 1971, and the Basic Interest and Occupational Scales were not arranged in the six Holland categories. The Basic Interest Scales were simply arranged in order of their intercorrelations, and the Occupational Scales were grouped in the clusters developed earlier by E. K. Strong; these clusters, based solely on scale intercorrelation, were useful but not as theoretically informative as the Holland types. A wider variety of Special Scales was reported on the earlier SVIB profile; many of them have been dropped for reasons reported elsewhere in this *Manual*. The Administrative Indexes have been expanded to include LP, IP, and DP percentages for each section of the booklet, because these percentages have so often proved to be clinically useful.

In any event, this 17-year-old boy continues to excel in the classroom, especially in mathematics. He is test-bright, with a College Board total of 1720, and a CEEB Math Achievement II score of 800. He has been admitted to an excellent engineering school and plans to concentrate on electrical engineering and computers. His interests range broadly through science and the arts, and he has a special love for the rugged outdoors, having

done a great deal of wilderness canoeing, backpacking, and rock-climbing. Like the 10-year-old, he still has scuffed sneakers and an unbroken record of losing the family tools. The stability of his interests is dramatic—

TABLE 10-15
Case O

GENERAL OCCUPATIONAL THEMES

R	54	Moderately high
I	64	Very high
A	61	High
S	32	Very low
E	35	Very low
C	38	Low

HIGH BASIC INTEREST SCALES

I	Medical Science	High	63
A	Music/Dramatics	High	64
I	Mathematics	High	61
I	Science	High	59
R	Mechanical Activities	High	58
R	Nature	Mod. high	58
R	Adventure	High	57

LOW BASIC INTEREST SCALES

S	Religious Activities	Very low	33
C	Office Practices	Very low	36
S	Social Service	Very low	37
E	Sales	Very low	37
E	Business Management	Low	37
S	Domestic Arts	Very low	40

HIGHEST OCCUPATIONAL SCALES

I	Geographer	67
IRC	Systems Analyst	63
IR	Optometrist	62
IR	Dentist	61
IR	Physician	61
I	Biologist	61
IAS	Psychologist	60
IRC	Computer Programmer	59
I	Pharmacist	58
RI	Forester	58
IR	Chemist	57
A	Musician	57
A	Photographer	56
IA	College Professor	56
EI	Marketing Executive	55
R	Navy Officer	55
E	Public Administrator	50
RC	Army Officer	50

LOWEST OCCUPATIONAL SCALES

CES	Business Education Teacher	−1
C	Secretary	5
ES	Home Economics Teacher	8
EC	Buyer	10
RIC	Licensed Practical Nurse	12
EC	Nursing Home Administrator	12

Academic Comfort	63
Introversion-Extroversion	57
Total Like Response Percentage	41

demonstrating, in this case at least, that many adult interests are already well-formed by age 10.

Cases O, P, and Q. These three women have one important interest in common—they like to be in charge of other people. Even though their fields differ, within their particular areas they like to be in positions of authority. On all three profiles, this interest is reflected in high scores on the ARMY OFFICER scale. Officers in the military necessarily assume leadership positions, and that role is reflected in the items that differentiate experienced Army officers from people-in-general.

Cases O and P show strong scientific interests, and Case Q's profile reflects administrative and social interests. All three were scored on the 1981 scales.

TABLE 10-16
Case P

GENERAL OCCUPATIONAL THEMES

R	58	High
I	68	Very high
A	48	Moderately low
S	42	Low
E	40	Moderately low
C	51	Average

HIGH BASIC INTEREST SCALES

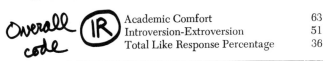

I	Science	Very high	64
I	Medical Science	High	63
R	Military Activities	Very high	62
R	Mechanical Activities	High	62
I	Mathematics	High	61

LOW BASIC INTEREST SCALES

S	Athletics	Low	34
S	Religious Activities	Low	37
E	Sales	Very low	37
S	Social Service	Low	41
S	Domestic Arts	Low	44

HIGHEST OCCUPATIONAL SCALES

IR	Physician	66
IRC	Systems Analyst	65
I	Geographer	65
IR	Optometrist	63
IR	Dentist	63
IRC	Computer Programmer	62
IA	College Professor	60
IR	Medical Technologist	58
RC	Army Officer	56
A	Photographer	51
EC	Dietitian	50

LOWEST OCCUPATIONAL SCALES

ES	Home Economics Teacher	4
CES	Business Education Teacher	8
C	Secretary	9
S	Elementary Teacher	11
E	Beautician	12

Academic Comfort		63
Introversion-Extroversion		51
Total Like Response Percentage		36

Overall code

TABLE 10-17
Case Q

GENERAL OCCUPATIONAL THEMES

R	53	Moderately high
I	50	Average
A	65	Very high
S	57	Moderately high
E	65	Very high
C	47	Average

HIGH BASIC INTEREST SCALES

A	Music/Dramatics	Very high	68
E	Business Management	Very high	68
R	Nature	Very high	67
E	Law/Politics	Very high	66
E	Merchandising	Very high	65
R	Agriculture	Very high	65
A	Writing	High	63
E	Public Speaking	High	61
S	Teaching	Mod. high	60

LOW BASIC INTEREST SCALES

C	Office Practices	Mod. low	40
I	Science	Mod. low	41

HIGHEST OCCUPATIONAL SCALES

SRE	Recreation Leader	62
SA	Social Worker	61
SE	School Administrator	61
SE	YWCA Director	60
SA	Speech Pathologist	59
A	Reporter	58
SEC	Guidance Counselor	56
SEC	Social Science Teacher	55
E	Personnel Director	54
AE	Lawyer	54
E	Public Administrator	54
SA	Minister	54
RC	Army Officer	53
A	English Teacher	53
AE	Public Relations Director	52
A	Foreign Language Teacher	48

LOWEST OCCUPATIONAL SCALES

IR	Physicist	6
E	Beautician	10
I	Mathematician	12
C	Dental Assistant	18
IRC	Math-Science Teacher	18

Academic Comfort		58
Introversion-Extroversion		31
Total Like Response Percentage		60

Overall code

The profile for **Case O** (Table 10-15) is an INVESTIGATIVE-ARTISTIC one, with moderately high interests in the REALISTIC area, and a clearly defined rejection of the SOCIAL, ENTERPRISING, and CONVENTIONAL themes. The pattern of INVESTIGATIVE and REALISTIC General Theme and Basic Interest Scale scores is one often seen in people with scientific interests. The high ARTISTIC score indicates additional interests in cultural activities and, along with the AC score of 63, a leaning toward academic environments.

Her intense science interests and love for theater and music are reflected also by the Basic Interest Scales. The high score on Nature reflects her interest in a limited amount of gardening and camping and canoeing. Her high Adventure score is related to a passion for travel (paradoxically, she has a distaste for flying!); within the confines of her career she organizes her life to take advantage of travel opportunities, and she is a frequent participant in international professional meetings.

Case O is a psychologist working in a university environment, and for the past few years she has been in charge of a large research project. This interest in being in charge of other people is reflected in her high score on the Army Officer scale (50). But she is not interested in performing those same supervisory tasks in a business environment, as exhibited by her low Enterprising scores and low scores on the associated Basic Interest Scales.

Case P is another woman with scientific interests— the Investigative-Realistic combination. She also shares Case O's academic interests (AC = 63), but has only an average interest in the artistic area, as reflected by her General Theme and Basic Interest Scale scores. The high Academic Comfort score is especially noteworthy for this woman, since she has been out of the academic world for about 20 years. (Typically, AC scores become lower the longer one is away from an academic environment.)

Her college major was in medical technology, still one of her high-score occupations—her highest score is Physician (66), an occupation she regrets she did not pursue. She did teach bacteriology and microbiology at a liberal arts college for about 10 years (College Professor, 60).

She satisfies her intellectual and academic interests by embarking on vocational opportunities that require new knowledge but that are not necessarily in the field of science, her primary interest. For example, she serves on the board of directors for one of the major U.S. bank systems and recently served as arbitrator

for school board contract negotiations that had been stalemated for over a year. She also works as a food editor (Dietitian, 50) and photographer (Photographer, 51) for her local newspaper.

Her high Army Officer score (56) reflects, as it did for Case O, a preference for being in charge of others.

Case Q is the profile for a woman who by her own admission wants her tomatoes to grow in straight rows (Agriculture, 65; Nature, 67; Army Officer, 53). Her highest General Theme scores are in the Enterprising and Artistic areas.

To date, her occupational activities have focused both on Teaching (60), in an Artistic field, and on her Social interests (moderately high General Theme score), in combination with the Enterprising theme. She had a double-major undergraduate degree in German and Education, with a minor in English. Since then, she has taught German to high school students (Foreign Language Teacher, 48); held the chair of the language department; and served as dean of the high school (notice the high scores on Business Management, School Administrator, and Public Administrator). She has also taught English to high school students (English Teacher, 53) and obtained her master's degree in guidance and counseling and worked as a high school counselor (Guidance Counselor, 56).

Case Q responded "Like" to a high percentage of items, and the variety of positions she has held during the last 12 years (including two interruptions for maternity leave) confirms this positive approach to a variety of activities within the ESA area.

The case studies presented here are illustrative of certain kinds of profiles, but every profile remains essentially unique, and the most sophisticated interpretation of a wide range of profiles emerges only from study of the *Manual*, from an understanding of the psychometric principles and technical details involved, and from working with dozens of cases to grasp the "feel" of working with individual profiles.

Appendixes

Correlation with NIE's "Guidelines for Assessment of Sex Bias and Sex Fairness in Career Interest Inventories"

In 1975, the National Institute of Education, an agency of the U.S. Department of Health, Education, and Welfare, published a set of "Guidelines for Assessment of Sex Bias and Sex Fairness in Career Interest Inventories" (see Diamond, 1975). These guidelines are reproduced here in italic type; following each is a description, in roman type, of the steps taken in the SVIB-SCII to meet these guidelines.

I. The Inventory Itself

A. The same interest inventory form should be used for both males and females unless it is shown empirically that separate forms are more effective in minimizing sex bias.

A. The SCII uses the same booklet and report form (profile) for both men and women.

B. Scores on all occupations and interest areas covered by the inventory should be given for both males and females, with the sex composition of norms—that is, whether male, female, or combined-sex norms—for each scale clearly indicated.

B. On all of the scales on the profile, scores are given for all respondents, whether male or female. In some cases, the respondent is scored against a combined-sex sample; in some, against both single-sex and combined-sex samples, by means of separate scores; and in others, only against people of his or her own sex. In each case, the composition of the norm group or groups is clearly indicated.

C. Insofar as possible, item pools should reflect experiences and activities equally familiar to both females and males. In instances where this is not currently possible, a minimum requirement is that the number of items generally favored by each sex be balanced. Further, it is desirable that the balance of items favored by each sex be achieved within individual scales, within the limitations imposed by validity considerations.

C. The SCII items are equally familiar to both sexes, since they comprise relatively common occupations, activities, school subjects, and the like.

The items for the SCII were selected from the combined item pools of the earlier men's and women's booklets. The factors considered in item selection are discussed in detail in Chapter 3 of this *Manual*. The most important factor is item validity—that is, whether or not the items discriminate between people in different occupations.

The SCII consists of 325 items. Of these, 30 are forced-choice items—such as "Choose the item on the left or the item on the right"—where the concept of popularity is irrelevant. Of the remaining 295 items, seven (2 percent) show no differences between the Men-in-General and Women-in-General samples, 133 items (45 percent) draw the "Like" response more often from men than from women, and 155 items (53 percent) are favored more often by women.

The same trend can be seen in the items showing the greatest differences between the sexes. Only 26 items have a 30-percent difference or more, a *very* large difference; of these, five are favored more by men, 21 more by women. To the extent that the inventory is biased at the item level, it is biased slightly in favor of women.

Because the items are reasonably well-balanced overall in terms of popularity between the sexes, no attempt has been made to assure balance in each individual scale. Instead, the items selected for each scale are the items that are most valid for that scale. In general, the Occupational Scales are fairly well-balanced; in those scales, men are compared with men, women with women, and the sex differences are minimized. Both the General Occupational Themes and the Basic Interest Scales are unisex; that is, men and women respond to the same scale items and are scored against the combined MIG-WIG reference sample (see Chapters 3 and 4 for a complete explanation of the reporting of these scales).

D. Occupational titles used in the inventory should be presented in gender-neutral terms (for example, letter carrier instead of mailman), or both male and female titles should be presented (for example, actor/actress).

D. All SCII items are presented in gender-neutral terms.

E. Use of the generic "he" or "she" should be eliminated throughout the inventory.

E. The words "he" and "she" do not appear in the inventory, or on any of the answer sheets or profiles.

II. Technical Information

A. Technical materials provided by the publisher should describe how and to what extent these guidelines have been met in the inventory and supporting materials.

A. This Appendix is a discussion of how the guidelines are met by the SCII. Other chapters and sections of this *Manual,* as well as the remarks on the profile, address the same issues.

B. Technical information should provide the rationale for either separate scales by sex or combined-sex scales (for example, critical differences in male-female response rates that affect the validity of the scales versus similarity of response rates that justify combining data from males and females into a single scale).

B. Chapter 7 of this *Manual* is devoted entirely to a discussion of the rationale for using separate Occupational Scales for men and women; essentially, it presents data showing how the sexes differ in item responses, reports how these differences are accommodated, and discusses research on combined-sex scale construction.

C. Even if it is empirically demonstrated that separate inventory forms are more effective in minimizing sex bias, thus justifying their use, the same vocational areas should be indicated for each sex.

C. The SCII does not use separate inventory forms.

D. The sex composition of the criterion and norm groups should be included in descriptions of these groups. Furthermore, reporting of the scores for one sex on scales normed or constructed on the basis of data from the other sex should be supported by evidence of validity—if not for each scale, then by a pattern of evidence of validity established for males and females scored on pairs of similar scales (male-normed and female-normed for the same occupation).

D. The sex composition of the SCII criterion and norm groups is included in the group descriptions (Appendix C) and on p. 48 of this *Manual.*

The validity of each scale rests upon the availability of empirical data. Research has demonstrated that scales valid for males are not as valid for females, and vice versa (Chapter 7). Therefore, all but eight of the 162 Occupational Scales are in matched pairs; that is, for each of 77 occupations there is a scale based on a female-normed sample and a scale based on a male-normed sample. The other eight occupations (four female and four male) are represented by a scale normed on only one of the sexes (for example, female HOME ECONOMICS TEACHER and male AGRIBUSINESS MANAGER). Every effort was made to obtain criterion samples for the development of matching scales for these eight occupations, to no avail; and if we are to offer any useful scale at all for these occupations, these efforts will have to suffice for now. With proper reporting, these scales can be used without discriminating effect. Where samples of adequate size *could* be assembled, in the research for the 1981 revision, a new scale was developed for the sex that had not previously been normed—for example, male BEAUTICIAN and female AIR FORCE OFFICER.

Scores on scales developed for the opposite sex do seem to be valid in a rank-order sense. For example, women who score high on a male scale are more interested in that occupation than women who score low on the same scale. Problems of interpretation remain,

but they are eased by scoring everyone on all of the scales on the profile, and by using the entire profile to verify patterns of occupational interests. This approach meets the guidelines' suggestion of presenting all scale scores, and experience to date indicates that the approach is adequate.

In addition, the profile emphasizes the General Occupational Themes and Basic Interest Scales, which are identical for both sexes (see the closing comment at section I, paragraph C, above). Through them, counselors can help clients understand better the meaning of the empirically derived Occupational Scales.

E. Criterion groups, norms, and other relevant data (for example, validity, reliability, item-response rates) should be examined at least every five years to determine the need for updating. New data may be required as occupations change or as sex and other characteristics of persons entering occupations change. Test manuals should clearly label the date of data collection for criterion or norm groups for each occupation.

E. The SVIB has undergone constant evolution since it was first published in 1927, and it continues to evolve. Major revisions of various portions of the system occurred in 1933, 1938, 1966, 1969, 1974, and 1981. In addition, new scales have been added regularly, and older ones dropped or modified. This *Manual* reports the dates of all data collection and norm-group establishment (see Appendix C and p. 48 of this *Manual*). Research continues, on a sustained, systematic basis, to develop new criterion groups, new norms, new male/female matched-scale pairs, and the bases for combined groups and scales. In general, however, the characteristic patterns of interests in occupations seem to change very little over time (see Campbell, 1971, p. 315).

F. Technical materials should include information about how suggested or implied career options (such as options suggested by the highest scores on the inventory) are distributed for samples of typical respondents by each sex.

F. This *Manual* reports the distributions of scores for both Men- and Women-in-General on all scales, which is the information necessary to know the frequencies of suggested options for each sex.

G. Steps should be taken to investigate the validity of interest inventories for minority groups (differentiated by sex). Publishers should describe comparable studies and should clearly indicate whether differences were found between groups.

G. The data that are available suggest that the issue of differences between ethnic groups in measured interests is unimportant. For example, Barnette and McCall (1964) found no ethnic differences in measured interests between the races among boys in craft-type curricula in New York schools; Borgen and Harper (1973) found no ethnic differences in measured interests among National Merit Finalists; and

Whetstone and Hayles (1975, p. 109) concluded: "The difference in the effectiveness of using the SVIB with black college men and with white college men appears to be small (if any)."

In an interesting unpublished 1967 study of 13,000 North Carolina high school students—split roughly 55-45 between ninth and twelfth graders, roughly 50-50 male-female, and roughly 20-80 black-white—students filled in a long biographical inventory concerned with two measures of interest, reading and science. Highly significant differences were found between the sexes on both scales, but no significant differences were found between the blacks and the whites. The figures for the twelfth graders were not quite as startlingly identical as those for the ninth graders were, but the same general pattern held—no important, consistent racial differences. In this study, as in every other study known to us, the data suggest that sex is an important issue in the norming of measures of interest, but that race is not.

III. Interpretive Information

A. The user's manual provided by the publisher should describe how and to what extent these guidelines have been met in the inventory and the supporting materials.

A. This Appendix to the *Manual* describes how the guidelines have been met in the SCII materials.

B. Interpretive materials for test users and respondents (manuals, profiles, leaflets, etc.) should explain how to interpret scores resulting from separate or combined male and female norms or criterion groups.

B. The interpretive materials given in this *Manual* in various chapters (particularly Chapter 10 and p. 71 of Chapter 6), as well as the comments on the reverse sides of the student's and counselor's copies of the profile, discuss the interpretation of scales based on combined-sex samples (the General Occupational Themes and Basic Interest Scales) and separate-sex samples (the Occupational Scales).

C. Interpretive materials for interest-inventory scores should point out that the vocational interests and choices of men and women are influenced by many environmental and cultural factors, including early socialization, traditional sex-role expectations of society, home-versus-career conflict, and the experiences typical of women and men as members of various ethnic and social-class groups.

C. This has been done on the back of the profile and in Chapter 10.

D. Manuals should recommend that the inventory be accompanied by orientation dealing with possible influences of factors in C above on men's and women's scores. Such orientation should encourage respondents to examine stereotypic "sets" toward activities and occupations and should help respondents to see that there is virtually no activity or occupation that is exclusively male or female.

D. This has been done in Chapter 10.

E. Interpretive materials for inventories that use homogeneous scales, such as health or mechanical, should encourage both sexes to look at all career and educational options, not just those traditionally associated with their sex group, within the broad areas in which their highest scores fall.

E. The appropriate comments appear both on the reverse side of the profile and in Chapter 10.

F. Occupational titles used in the interpretive materials and in the interpretation session should be stated in gender-neutral terms (for example, letter carrier instead of mailman) or both male and female titles should be presented (for example, actor/actress).

F. All occupational titles in the SCII booklet, *Manual*, and interpretive materials are given in gender-neutral terms.

G. The written discussions in the interpretive materials (as well as all inventory text) should be stated in a way that overcomes the impression now embedded in the English language that (a) people in general are of the male gender and (b) certain social roles are automatically sex-linked.

G. The general use of "he" and "his," or any suggestion that all people are male, has been avoided. The writing has been screened carefully to eliminate obvious or subtle sex-linked themes.

H. The user's manual (a) should state clearly that all jobs are appropriate for qualified persons of either sex, and (b) should attempt to dispel myths about women and men in the world of work that are based on sex-role stereotypes. Furthermore, ethnic occupational stereotypes should not be reinforced.

H. This *Manual* states that all jobs are appropriate for qualified persons of either sex. Ethnic occupational stereotypes are not mentioned in any way.

I. The user's manual should address possible user biases in regard to sex roles and to their possible interaction with age, ethnic group, or social class, and should caution against transmitting these biases to the respondent or reinforcing the respondent's own biases.

I. This issue is addressed in Chapter 7 and in Chapter 10; both chapters emphasize the benefits of full occupational exploration for both sexes. The inventory has long been used with people of all ages and all social classes, and no reports of bias on these dimensions have ever been noted.

J. Where differences in validity have been found between dominant and minority groups (differentiated by sex), separate interpretive procedures and materials should be provided that take these differences into account.

J. No differences have been found between dominant and minority groups in vocational interests; consequently, separate materials are not necessary.

K. Interpretive materials for respondent and user should encourage exploratory experiences in areas where interests have not had a chance to develop.

K. This *Manual* (especially Chapter 10) and the interpretive comments on the reverse side of the profile emphasize the need for such exploratory experiences.

L. Interpretive materials for persons reentering paid employment or education and persons changing careers or entering postretirement careers should give special attention to score interpretation in terms of the effects of years of stereotyping and home-career conflict, the norms on which the scores are based, and the options such individuals might explore on the basis of current goals and past experiences and activities.

L. Special interpretive comments for reentering people and for others seeking second careers can be found in Chapter 10.

M. Case studies and examples presented in the interpretive materials should represent men and women equally and should include but not be limited to examples of each in a variety of nonstereotypic roles. Case studies and examples of mature men and women and of men and women in different social classes and ethnic groups should also be included where applicable.

M. The case studies in Chapter 10 include men and women equally. Social class and ethnic representation have not been specially treated, since there are no data suggesting that these characteristics are related to SCII scores.

N. Both user's manuals and respondent's materials should make it clear that interest-inventory scores provide only one kind of helpful information, and that this information should always be considered together with other relevant information—skills, accomplishments, favored activities, experiences, hobbies, influences, other test scores, and the like—in making any career decision. However, the possible biases of these variables should also be taken into consideration.

N. For years, the SVIB-SCII *Manual* and its predecessors have emphasized that the inventory should not be used blindly, and that other information should also be used in making occupational decisions. The same warnings appear in this *Manual* and in all of the other interpretive materials.

Occupations and Their Code Types

The list of occupations that follows is designed for use with the six General Occupational Theme scales scored on the profile of the SVIB-SCII. Each occupation has been assigned a code type indicating the theme or themes that most strongly characterize it. For example, the occupation machine shop supervisor has been given the code type RCS, indicating that the three themes REALISTIC, CONVENTIONAL, and SOCIAL, in that order, are descriptive of that occupation. If an occupational sample scored high on a single theme, the code type assigned to that sample is the single letter for that theme; if two themes, then two letters; and if three, then three.

The six themes can be visualized as occupying the extremities of a hexagon, as shown below, and ordered around the edges so that adjacent themes are the most closely related and those directly across the hexagon are the least closely related.

REALISTIC (R)   INVESTIGATIVE (I)

CONVENTIONAL (C)   ARTISTIC (A)

ENTERPRISING (E)   SOCIAL (S)

The occupations are ordered in the list according to their code types. The list begins with the codes dominated by the REALISTIC theme and proceeds clockwise around the hexagon.

The code type for each occupation was derived either by testing people in that occupation to see which of the themes they scored highest on (see Table 6-6 for data on specific occupations) or by asking people of known code types which occupations they liked. Thus, the list includes only those occupations for which empirical data are available.

Because the samples were classified by sex, and because the sexes sometimes showed substantial differences on these themes, an "m" or "f" is given after each occupation to indicate the sex that that code type is based on: "(f,m)" when the two sexes in a given occupation are of the same code type, and "(f)" or "(m)" when data are available on only one sex. When the two sexes in an occupation are of different code types, each is listed at its appropriate code location, and at each location a cross-reference to the code type for the other sex is given—for example, "(f; m = SEI)."

These code types should be seen only as guidelines: they were assigned on the basis of the best available statistics, and they usually accord well with common sense; but they are based only on averages and should be treated as such. Occasionally, quirks appear, and the user must understand that not all of the problems of occupational classification have been solved. In particular, not all people in any one occupation are alike; though the code types of people working together usually are similar, many people (even many who are contentedly employed) have code types other than the one listed for their occupation.

Another common source of confusion is the information from men and women in the same occupation; sometimes the two groups have the same code type, sometimes they do not. Among pharmacists, for example, men most often fit the IE code type, that is, the INVESTIGATIVE-ENTERPRISING pattern, whereas women pharmacists most often fit the I, INVESTIGATIVE, pattern. Evidently, male pharmacists are more often involved in the *retailing* aspects of pharmacy, as reflected by their E code, whereas female pharmacists are more often engaged in the *laboratory* aspects, as reflected in their I code. Analogous sex differences appear in other occupations, too, and to the extent that they are reflected by General Occupational Themes, they are reported in the following list.

When working with an individual profile, it is useful to focus on those sections of the list that correspond to the respondent's highest scores on the General Occupational Themes. For example, if the respondent scored highest on the ENTERPRISING, SOCIAL, and CONVENTIONAL themes, those sections of the list dealing with the E, S, and C themes in all of their various combinations—ESC, ECS, SEC, CES, ES, CE, SE, and so forth—should be scanned for ideas. The sequence of the occupations in the list puts related code types near each other on the list (and because of the circularity of the hexagon arrangement, the code types at the beginning and end of the list are also closely related). The list thus identifies areas and specific occupations the user can give more attention to.

More information on the General Occupational Themes is given in Chapter 4 and on the back of the respondent's copy of the profile. (See also Chapter 10.)

RC	Air Force officer	(f,m)
RC	Army officer	(f,m)
RC	Drafting technician	(m; f=AR)
RC	Farmer	(f; m=R)
RC	Instrument assembler	(f,m)
RC	Navy enlisted personnel	(f,m)
RC	Navy officer	(m; f=R)
RC	Prison warden	(m)
RCS	Machine shop supervisor	(m)
RCS	Vocational agriculture teacher	(f; m=RCE)
RCE	Highway Patrol officer	(f; m=RSE)
RCE	Vocational agriculture teacher	(m; f=RCS)
RSE	Athletic director	(f; m=E)
RSE	County sheriff	(m)
RSE	Highway Patrol officer	(m; f=RCE)
RSE	Marine officer	(m; f=RSI)
RE	Building contractor	(m)
RE	Police officer	(f,m)
RE	Professional athlete	(f; m=ER)
RE	Secret service agent	(m; f=ER)
RSC	City or state employee	(m; f=SC)
RSI	Cabinetmaker	(m)
RSI	Marine officer	(f; m=RSE)
RS	Industrial arts teacher	(m)
RAS	Occupational therapist	(f,m)
R	Carpenter	(m)
R	Cartographer	(m; f=RI)
R	Corrections officer	(f,m)
R	Electrician	(m)
R	Farmer	(m; f=RC)
R	Forest ranger	(m)
R	Forester	(m; f=RI)
R	Navy officer	(f; m=RC)
R	Radiologic technologist	(f; m=RI)
R	Rancher	(m)
R	Skilled crafts	(f,m)
R	Tool-and-die maker	(m)
RI	Auto mechanic	(m)
RI	Cartographer	(f; m=R)
RI	Engineer	(f,m)
RI	Civil engineer	(f,m)
RI	Mechanical engineer	(f,m)
RI	Forester	(f; m=R)
RI	Machinist	(m)
RI	Merchant Marine officer	(m)
RI	Petroleum engineer	(m)
RI	Pilot	(m; f=ERI)
RI	Radiologic technologist	(m; f=R)
RI	Veterinarian	(m; f=IR)
RIC	Licensed practical nurse	(f; m=S)
IR	Animal husbandry professor	(m)
IR	Astronaut	(m)
IR	Chemist	(f,m)
IR	Dental hygienist	(f,m)
IR	Dentist	(f,m)
IR	Electronics technician	(m; f=I)
IR	Chemical engineer	(f,m)
IR	Electrical engineer	(f,m)
IR	Geologist	(f,m)
IR	Inventor	(m; f=IA)
IR	Laboratory technician	(f,m)
IR	Medical technologist	(f,m)
IR	NASA scientist	(m)
IR	Optometrist	(f,m)
IR	Physical therapist	(f,m)
IR	Physician	(f,m)

IR	Physicist	(f,m)
IR	Surgeon	(f,m)
IR	Urologist	(m)
IR	Veterinarian	(f; m=RI)
IRS	Math-science teacher	(m; f=IRC)
IRS	Osteopath	(m)
IRE	Chiropractor	(f,m)
IRE	Food scientist	(m)
IRC	Computer programmer	(f,m)
IRC	Math-science teacher	(f; m=IRS)
IRC	Systems analyst	(f,m)
IC	Computer operator	(m; f=C)
IE	Pharmacist	(m; f=I)
I	Biologist	(f,m)
I	Electronics designer	(m)
I	Electronics technician	(f; m=IR)
I	Geographer	(f,m)
I	Internist	(m)
I	Mathematician	(f,m)
I	Pathologist	(m)
I	Pediatrician	(m)
I	Pharmacist	(f; m=IE)
I	Experimental psychologist	(f,m)
I	Scientific researcher	(f,m)
I	Social scientist	(m; f=AI)
I	Technical writer	(f,m)
IS	Hospital supervisor	(m)
IS	Registered nurse	(m; f=SI)
IS	Educational psychologist	(f,m)
ISA	Clinical psychologist	(f,m)
IA	Astronomer	(m)
IA	College professor	(f,m)
IA	Economist	(m)
IA	Inventor	(f; m=IR)
IA	Language interpreter	(f,m)
IA	Scientific illustrator	(f)
IA	Sociologist	(f,m)
IAS	Psychiatrist	(f,m)
IAS	Psychologist	(f,m)
AIS	Orchestra conductor	(m)
AI	Social scientist	(f; m=I)
AI	Anthropologist	(m)
AI	Ballet dancer	(m; f=AE)
AI	Landscape gardener	(f; m=AR)
AI	Lawyer	(f,m)
AI	Sculptor	(m; f=AE)
AIR	Architect	(f,m)
AR	Drafting technician	(f; m=RC)
AR	Landscape gardener	(m; f=AI)
A	Art museum director	(f,m)
A	Art teacher	(f,m)
A	Commercial artist	(f,m)
A	Fine artist	(f,m)
A	Author	(f,m)
A	Broadcaster	(f,m)
A	English teacher	(f; m=AS)
A	Entertainer	(f,m)
A	Foreign language teacher	(f,m)
A	Librarian	(f,m)
A	Musician	(f,m)
A	Opera singer	(f,m)
A	Photographer	(f,m)
A	Poet	(f,m)
A	Reporter	(f,m)
AE	Advertising executive	(f,m)
AE	Ballet dancer	(f; m=AI)

AE	Children's clothes designer	(f)	E	Athletic director	(m; f=RSE)
AE	Costume designer	(f)	E	Beautician	(f; m=EA)
AE	Fashion model	(f)	E	Chamber of Commerce executive	(m; f=EC)
AE	Florist	(m; f=EA)	E	Department store manager	(f,m)
AE	Illustrator	(f)	E	Elected public official	(f,m)
AE	Interior decorator	(f,m)	E	Foreign correspondent	(f)
AE	Public relations director	(f,m)	E	Funeral director	(m; f=EC)
AE	Sculptor	(f; m=AI)	E	Life insurance agent	(f,m)
AS	English teacher	(m; f=A)	E	Personnel director	(f,m)
AS	Music teacher	(m; f=SA)	E	Public administrator	(f; m=CA)
SA	Mental health worker	(m; f=SE)	E	Realtor	(f,m)
SA	Minister	(f; m=SIE)	E	Restaurant manager	(m; f=EC)
SA	Music teacher	(f; m=AS)	E	Retailer	(f,m)
SA	Social worker	(f,m)	E	Sports reporter	(m)
SA	Speech pathologist	(f,m)	E	Traveling salesperson	(m)
SA	Writer, children's books	(f)	E	Waitress	(f)
SI	Registered nurse	(f; m=IS)	E	Women's style shop manager	(f)
SI	Student personnel worker	(m)	ER	Auctioneer	(m)
SIE	Minister	(m; f=SA)	ER	Dancing teacher	(f)
S	Director, Christian education	(f)	ER	Nursery manager	(m)
S	Elementary education teacher	(f,m)	ER	Professional athlete	(m; f=RE)
S	Licensed practical nurse	(m; f=RIC)	ER	Secret service agent	(f; m=RE)
S	Playground director	(m; f=SRE)	ERA	Stockbroker	(f; m=EC)
S	Priest	(m)	ERI	Pilot	(f; m=RI)
S	Public health nurse	(f,m)	ERS	Farm employment manager	(m)
S	Special education teacher	(f,m)	ERC	Agribusiness manager	(m; f=EC)
SR	Physical education teacher	(f,m)	ECR	Dietitian	(m; f=EC)
SRE	Agricultural extension agent	(m)	ECR	Factory manager	(m)
SRE	Playground director	(f; m=S)	ECR	Farm supply manager	(m)
SRE	Recreation leader	(f,m)	ECR	Ready-to-wear sales	(m; f=EC)
SE	Football coach	(m)	ECS	Auto sales dealer	(m)
SE	Juvenile parole officer	(m)	ECS	Hotel manager	(f,m)
SE	Labor arbitrator	(m)	ECS	Nursing home administrator	(m; f=EC)
SE	Manager, child care center	(m)	ECS	Retail clerk	(m; f=EC)
SE	Mental health worker	(f; m=SA)	ECS	Travel bureau manager	(f; m=ESC)
SE	School administrator	(f,m)	EC	Agribusiness manager	(f; m=ERC)
SE	Vocational counselor	(f)	EC	Appliance sales	(m)
SE	YMCA director	(m)	EC	Buyer	(f,m)
SE	YWCA director	(f)	EC	Chamber of Commerce executive	(f; m=E)
SC	Airline ticket agent	(m)	EC	Corporation executive	(m)
SC	City or state employee	(f; m=RSC)	EC	Corporation lawyer	(f,m)
SC	Teaching nun	(f)	EC	Dietitian	(f; m=ECR)
SCE	Guidance counselor	(m; f=SEC)	EC	Funeral director	(f; m=E)
SCE	High school counselor	(m)	EC	Manufacturer	(m)
SCE	Rehabilitation counselor	(m)	EC	Nursing home administrator	(f; m=ECS)
SEC	Guidance counselor	(f; m=SCE)	EC	Purchasing agent	(f,m)
SEC	Home economics teacher	(m; f=ES)	EC	Ready-to-wear sales	(f; m=ECR)
SEC	Social science teacher	(f,m)	EC	Restaurant manager	(f; m=E)
ESC	Employment manager	(m; f=CSE)	EC	Retail clerk	(f; m=ECS)
ESC	Receptionist	(f)	EC	Stockbroker	(m; f=ERA)
ESC	Travel bureau manager	(m; f=ECS)	EC	Wholesaler	(m)
ES	Computer sales	(f; m=EI)	CE	Banker	(f,m)
ES	County extension agent	(m)	CE	Certified public accountant	(f,m)
ES	Encyclopedia sales	(m)	CE	Courtroom stenographer	(f)
ES	Home economics teacher	(f; m=SEC)	CE	Credit manager	(f,m)
ES	Industrial sales	(m)	CE	Department store sales	(f,m)
ES	Occupational health nurse	(f)	CE	IRS agent	(f,m)
ES	Sales manager	(f,m)	CE	Office worker	(f)
ES	TV announcer	(f,m)	CES	Business education teacher	(f,m)
EI	Computer sales	(m; f=ES)	CES	Office manager	(m; f=C)
EI	Investment fund manager	(m)	CSE	County welfare worker	(m)
EI	Marketing executive	(f,m)	CSE	Employment manager	(f; m=ESC)
EA	Beautician	(m; f=E)	CS	Bank cashier	(m; f=C)
EA	Flight attendant	(f,m)	CA	Public administrator	(m; f=E)
EA	Florist	(f; m=AE)	C	Accountant	(m,f)
EA	Professional dancer	(f)	C	Bank cashier	(f; m=CS)

C	Bookkeeper	(f,m)		C	Secretary	(f)
C	Computer operator	(f; m=IC)		C	Statistician	(f,m)
C	Dental assistant	(f)		CR	Sewing machine operator	(f,m)
C	Hospital records clerk	(f)		CR	Telephone operator	(f; m=CER)
C	IRS tax auditor	(f,m)		CRE	Army non-commissioned officer	(f,m)
C	Office clerk	(f,m)		CRE	Elevator manager	(m)
C	Office manager	(f; m=CES)		CER	Dairy processing manager	(m)
C	Printer	(m)		CER	Executive housekeeper	(f,m)
C	Production manager	(m)		CER	Telephone operator	(m; f=CR)
C	Proofreader	(f)				

Descriptions of the Occupational Criterion Groups

The samples described below are the samples upon which the current SVIB-SCII Occupational Scales are based. All of the scales were developed at the Center for Interest Measurement Research (CIMR), at the University of Minnesota. The largest men's and women's samples are *Minister* m (498 *N*) and *College Professor* f (400 *N*); the smallest, *Licensed Practical Nurse* m (100 *N*) and *Restaurant Manager* f (92 *N*); and the mean size for all samples is 248.13 *N*. Of the 162 samples, 36 were tested before 1973, 110 since 1975; none were tested before 1966. The men's and women's samples having the highest mean age are *Banker* m (49.0) and *Interior Decorator* f (52.0); the lowest, *Flight At-*

tendant m (28.4) and *Forester* f (26.6); and the mean age for all samples is 39.25. The men's and women's samples having the highest mean years of education are *Biologist* m (21.7) and *Sociologist* f (21.4); the lowest, *Skilled Crafts* m (11.6) and *Licensed Practical Nurse* f (11.7). The men's and women's samples with the most mean years experience in their occupations are *Farmer* m (24.4), *Banker* f (23.0), and *Interior Decorator* f (23.0); the lowest, *Flight Attendant* m (4.0) and *Forester* f (3.4); and the mean for all samples is 12.19 years. In all, 40,197 people are included in the samples that follow.

The notation "n/a" indicates "not available."

Scale/sample	N	Year tested	Mean age	Mean years education	Mean years experience	Composition and comments
ACCOUNTANT (f)	294	1977	36.6	16.3	11.3	Members, American Institute of Certified Public Accountants. 75% completed BA degrees, 15% MA. Tested with the help of G. Perkins.
ACCOUNTANT (m)	317	1977	38.9	16.5	14.6	Members, American Institute of Certified Public Accountants. 76% completed BA degrees, 16% MA. Tested with the help of G. Perkins.
ADVERTISING EXECUTIVE (f)	215	1973	39.0	14.9	13.0	Advertising executives listed in *Standard Directory of Advertising Agencies*, 1973, with emphasis on agency executives. 29% completed BA degrees, 6% MA. Sample included media directors and buyers, creative directors, art directors, production directors, research directors, account executives, client service directors, and broadcasting directors.
ADVERTISING EXECUTIVE (m)	228	1968	41.0	15.1	14.5	Account executives listed in *Standard Directory of Advertising Agencies*, June 1968.
AGRIBUSINESS MANAGER (m)	332	1972	48.0	n/a	19.2	Elevator managers, implement dealers, farm service supply managers, dairy processing plant managers, and nursery managers from Minnesota, North Dakota, and South Dakota. Tested with the help of L. G. Wagner.
AIR FORCE OFFICER (f)	234	1979	32.3	17.0	8.7	Roster of commissioned officers provided by the Defense Manpower Data Center, Department of Defense. 52% completed BA degrees, 47% MA. Rank: lieutenant (4%), captain (77%), major (11%), lt. colonel (8%), colonel (1%).
AIR FORCE OFFICER (m)	292	1979	37.5	16.0	14.3	See women's sample above. 35% completed BA degrees, 60% MA. Rank: lieutenant (2%), captain (39%), major (25%), lt. colonel (21%), colonel (13%), higher (1%).
ARCHITECT (f)	206	1979	40.3	18.1	15.0	Roster from 44 state registration boards, obtained with the assistance of the National Council of Architectural Registration Boards. 71% completed BA degrees, 22% MA. Areas of specialty included housing (26%), institutional (21%), commercial (15%), and a combination (24%).
ARCHITECT (m)	207	1979	40.5	17.7	15.5	See women's sample above. 72% completed BA degrees, 15% MA. Areas of specialty included institutional (30%), commercial (27%), housing (16%), and a combination (16%).

Scale/sample	N	Year tested	Mean age	Mean years education	Mean years experience	Composition and comments
ARMY OFFICER (f)	285	1979	32.2	16.8	7.9	57% completed BA degrees, 35% MA. Rank: warrant officer (4%), lieutenant (19%), captain (59%), major (14%), lt. colonel (3%), colonel (1%).
ARMY OFFICER (m)	309	1979	36.8	16.9	13.5	See women's sample above. 11% had some college education, 42% completed BA degrees, and 44% MA. Rank: warrant officer (12%), lieutenant (3%), captain (31%), major (23%), lt. colonel (23%), colonel (7%), higher (1%).
ART TEACHER (f)	359	1967	46.0	16.6	10.0	From names supplied by the National Art Education Association, plus certified teachers in *Iowa Educational Directory*.
ART TEACHER (m)	303	1978	40.2	19.2	14.9	Members, National Art Education Association. 15% completed BA degrees, 64% MA, 19% PhD.
ARTIST, COMMERCIAL (f)	123	1979	35.2	16.1	11.0	Artists working for agencies and studios listed in *The Creative Black Book 1979*, a national directory of art services. 26% had taken art courses not leading to a degree, 50% completed BA degrees, 10% MA. 41% were freelance artists, 22% were employed by a studio, and 17% worked for a combination of employers.
ARTIST, COMMERCIAL (m)	199	1979	38.8	16.2	15.5	See women's sample above. 27% had taken art courses not leading to a degree, 47% completed BA degrees, 6% MA. 39% were freelance artists, 23% were employed by a studio, 10% by an advertising agency, and 15% worked for a combination of employers.
ARTIST, FINE (f)	247	1979	44.4	17.6	17.0	Names selected from *Who's Who in American Art*, 1978. 18% had taken art courses not leading to a degree, 25% completed BA degrees, 42% MA. 58% were freelance artists, 15% were employed by educational institutions, and 22% worked for a combination of employers.
ARTIST, FINE (m)	204	1979	43.4	18.0	20.7	Names selected from *Who's Who in American Art*, 1978. 13% had taken art courses not leading to a degree, 15% completed BA degrees, 55% MA. 39% were freelance artists, 39% were employed by educational institutions, and 15% worked for a combination of employers.
BANKER (f)	271	1968	49.0	13.0	23.0	Members, National Association of Bankwomen. Sampled proportionately by job title from overall roster.
BANKER (m)	171	1968	49.0	14.7	24.3	National sample of bank presidents and vice-presidents from a listing of bankers provided in *Martindale-Hubbell Law Directory*, 1968.
BEAUTICIAN (f)	103	1979	37.7	13.1	14.3	From listings of state licensing boards of Alaska, Georgia, Illinois, Iowa, Michigan, Minnesota, South Dakota, Utah, and Wisconsin. 93% attended cosmetology schools. Major activities included hair dressing (64%), management and supervision (10%), and a combination (22%).
BEAUTICIAN (m)	186	1975-1979	37.2	13.8	14.4	See women's sample above. 84% attended cosmetology schools. Major activities included hair dressing (61%), management and supervision (18%), and a combination (14%).
BIOLOGIST (f)	207	1975	42.5	21.1	12.7	Members, American Institute of Biological Sciences. 34% were in teaching, 24% in research, and 37% in a combination of activities.
BIOLOGIST (m)	209	1975	43.6	21.7	15.5	Members, American Institute of Biological Sciences. 30% were in teaching, 46% in a combination of teaching, research, and administration.
BUSINESS EDUCATION TEACHER (f)	420	1978	38.3	18.0	11.4	Members, National Business Education Association; all were secondary school teachers. 31% completed BA degrees, 66% MA.
BUSINESS EDUCATION TEACHER (m)	232	1978	38.8	18.5	13.2	Members, National Business Education Association; all were secondary school teachers. 15% completed BA degrees, 78% MA, 5% PhD.
BUYER (f)	204	1967	34.0	12.4	13.0	Heads of merchandise departments, nearly all in department stores.
BUYER (m)	176	1969	42.0	14.0	15.8	National sample of department-store buyers listed in *Sheldon's Retail Directory of the United States* (1969).
CHAMBER OF COMMERCE EXECUTIVE (f)	211	1979	45.8	13.4	7.4	Members, American Chamber of Commerce Executives (ACCE), and names selected from *Johnson's World Wide Chamber of Commerce Directory*. 67% had high school diplomas, 12% completed BA degrees.

Scale/sample	N	Year tested	Mean age	Mean years education	Mean years experience	Composition and comments
CHAMBER OF COMMERCE EXECUTIVE (m)	290	1978	42.7	15.9	12.4	See women's sample above. 9% had high school diplomas, 61% completed BA degrees, 10% MA.
CHEMIST (f)	260	1978	37.9	20.9	11.0	Members, American Chemical Society, all with PhD degrees. 43% were in research, 26% in teaching, and 14% in a combination of activities; 60% were employed by educational institutions, and 22% by industry.
CHEMIST (m)	278	1978	41.0	20.6	15.1	See women's sample above. 47% were in research, 18% in administration, 14% in teaching, and 17% in some combination of these activities; 52% were employed by industry, 35% by educational institutions.
CHIROPRACTOR (f)	205	1979	43.0	17.9	14.5	Rosters obtained from the American Chiropractic Association, the International Chiropractors Association, and *Digest of Chiropractic Economics*. 90% were self-employed or in partnerships; the remainder were employed by clinics, educational institutions, or a combination.
CHIROPRACTOR (m)	378	1969	44.0	16.4	16.0	National sample from membership lists of state associations of Chiropractors. Collected with the assistance of J. V. Durlacher, D.C., Assistant Director of Admissions, Palmer College of Chiropractic.
COLLEGE PROFESSOR (f)	400	1972	49.0	19.6	17.0	From college-catalog faculty listings and from rosters of samples tested previously with the SVIB. Heterogeneity sought with respect to academic area, type of institution, and location; criteria of selection included high academic rank and level of education. 1% completed less than MA degree, 22% MA, 77% PhD or equivalent. Area of specialization: business and law (9%), linguistics (7.5%), mathematics (6.8%), physical sciences (12%), biomedical sciences (9.5%), medical services (10.3%), social services and education (9.8%), social sciences (10.5%), art, music, and literature (13%), miscellaneous (11.8%).
COLLEGE PROFESSOR (m)	421	1969	n/a	n/a	n/a	National sampling from 37 disciplines; compiled in 1969 from data collected by CIMR since 1966.
COMPUTER PROGRAMMER (f)	243	1975	33.0	15.7	6.9	Rosters provided by the Society for Data Processors and write-in responses to articles in *Computerworld;* those selected for criterion sample spent at least 50% of their time programming, 13% had high school diplomas, 54% completed BA degrees, 14% MA. 71% worked in business-related areas, 14% in scientific areas, and 5% in educational areas.
COMPUTER PROGRAMMER (m)	203	1979	34.3	15.6	8.6	See women's sample above. Those selected for criterion sample spent at least 50% of their time programming. 25% had high school diplomas, 42% completed BA degrees, 12% MA. 76% worked in business-related areas, 7% in educational areas, and 3% in scientific areas.
CREDIT MANAGER (f)	192	1973-1975	45.6	13.1	11.2	Members, North Central Credit and Financial Management Association, and the Midwest Credit Managers Association.
CREDIT MANAGER (m)	199	1975	41.9	15.1	12.9	Members, North Central Credit and Financial Management Association.
DENTAL ASSISTANT (f)	207	1979	32.8	13.7	8.7	Members, American Dental Association, participants in a 1978 Annual Dental Assistants seminar held in Minnesota, and write-in responses to articles in *The Explorer*, a publication of the National Association of Dental Assistants. 30% had high school diplomas, 16% completed associate degrees, 45% had certificates in dental assisting. 76% were employed by private clinics, 14% by educational institutions.
DENTAL HYGIENIST (f)	394	1969	n/a	n/a	n/a	Tested through the California State Board of Dental Examiners with the help of H. Tschida. All licensed, in active practice, and with over 3 years' experience.
DENTIST (f)	240	1979	38.3	20.2	12.2	Members, American Dental Association, and the Association of Women Dentists. 68% were in general practice, 29% in a specialty area. Employment: self-employed or in partnership in a clinic (66%), educational institutions (8%), government agencies (4%), and a combination (15%).

Scale/sample	N	Year tested	Mean age	Mean years education	Mean years experience	Composition and comments
DENTIST (m)	232	1969	45.0	19.1	17.4	Practitioners and educators from 1968 directory of the American Dental Association. Tested with assistance of L. Meskin.
DEPARTMENT STORE MANAGER (f)	166	1979	35.8	14.5	8.1	Obtained with the assistance of the National Retail Merchants Association, the Minnesota Retail Merchants Association, and by contacting nationwide Yellow Page listings. 28% had high school diplomas, 20% had some college, 9% completed associate degrees, 34% BA. Major activities included financial records (18%), personnel management (16%), customer contact (11%), inventory control (10%), and a combination (36%).
DEPARTMENT STORE MANAGER (m)	200	1979	40.5	15.2	14.7	See women's sample above. 19% had high school diplomas, 21% some college, 49% completed BA degrees. Major activities included keeping financial records (16%), inventory control (11%), personnel management (10%), and a combination (49%).
DIETITIAN (f)	225	1979	37.8	17.5	11.2	Obtained with the assistance of the American Dietetic Association; all were practicing, registered dietitians. 52% completed BA degrees, 44% MA. 32% were employed by hospitals, 15% by government, 14% by educational institutions, and 12% were self-employed; major activities included administration and management (33%), consulting (21%), teaching (21%), and a combination (16%).
DIETITIAN (m)	200	1973-1977	35.1	17.7	8.5	See women's sample above. 45% completed BA degrees, 34% MA, 9% PhD. 31% were employed by hospitals, 19% by educational institutions, and 14% by government; major activities included administration and management (69%), teaching (9%), consulting (6%), and a combination (10%).
ELECTED PUBLIC OFFICIAL (f)	219	1978	48.3	15.5	6.4	Rosters provided by the National Women's Education Fund, including state legislators, state-wide constitutional office-holders, and members of the House of Representatives; and a 1976 list of city and county officials from *Women in Public Office: A Biographical Directory and Statistical Analysis.* 23% had high school diplomas, 39% completed BA degrees, 16% MA. 39% were employed in other occupations while they held office.
ELECTED PUBLIC OFFICIAL (m)	200	1973-1979	46.3	16.3	8.4	The 1973 participants were members of the 93rd U.S. Congress, tested by R. Willow. Others were selected from *State Elective Officials and the Legislatures,* 1977, published by the Council of State Governments. 20% had high school diplomas, 30% completed BA degrees, 26% law degrees, 13% MA, and 6% PhD. 67% were employed in other occupations while they held office.
ELEMENTARY EDUCATION TEACHER (f)	250	1978	36.8	17.5	10.6	From a commercially compiled national listing. 62% completed BA degrees, 37% MA. 97% were employed in public schools; 27% taught more than one grade.
ELEMENTARY EDUCATION TEACHER (m)	249	1979	35.5	17.9	10.9	From a commercially compiled national listing, and members of the Minneapolis State Board of Education. 52% completed BA degrees, 43% MA. 96% were employed in public schools; 22% taught 5th grade, 35% 6th grade, and 25% more than one grade.
ENGINEER (f)	201	1978	32.9	17.5	8.5	From the American Institute of Chemical Engineers, the Institute of Electrical and Electronics Engineers, the American Society of Civil Engineers, and the American Society of Mechanical Engineers; names selected in proportion to membership of each organization. 55% completed BA degrees, 34% MA, 9% PhD. 27% were employed by engineering firms, 32% by industry, and 20% by government; major activities included development and design (43%), administration (10%), and a combination (19%).
ENGINEER (m)	228	1978	40.9	17.8	16.4	See women's sample above. 48% completed BA degrees, 37% MA, and 17% PhD. 48% were employed by industry, 22% by engineering firms, and 12% by government; major activities included development and design (43%), administration (24%), and a combination (18%).
ENGLISH TEACHER (f)	352	1967	41.0	16.4	12.0	Drawn from Minnesota, Iowa, and Colorado; within each state, an attempt was made to balance samples between urban and rural areas.
ENGLISH TEACHER (m)	223	1968	35.0	17.0	10.2	From a directory of high school teachers provided by the Minnesota State Department of Education.

Scale/sample	N	Year tested	Mean age	Mean years education	Mean years experience	Composition and comments
EXECUTIVE HOUSEKEEPER (f)	200	1979	44.7	13.1	8.4	From subscribers to *Executive Housekeeper*, a publication for housekeeping managers of hospitals, hotels/motels, nursing homes, and educational institutions. 43% had high school diplomas, 9% completed associate degrees, 9% BA. 52% were employed by hospitals, 16% by nursing homes, and 13% by hotels/motels; major activities included personnel management (45%), safety and sanitation (11%), and a combination (36%).
EXECUTIVE HOUSEKEEPER (m)	206	1979	42.4	13.8	9.0	See women's sample above. 54% had high school diplomas, 18% completed associate degrees, 18% BA. 63% were employed by hospitals, 12% by nursing homes, and 8% by educational institutions; major activities included personnel management (48%), safety and sanitation (11%), and a combination (30%).
FARMER (f)	207	1977	40.8	13.3	17.7	National sample collected through write-in responses to articles in rural or farm-directed publications, and with the assistance of organizations such as the American National Cowbelles, Washington State Dairy Wives, United Farm Wives, Wisconsin State Grange, California Women for Agriculture, and Indiana Women in Agriculture. 58% had high school diplomas, 23% completed BA degrees. Women selected for sample spent about the same amount of time managing their farms (32 hours per week) as they did managing their homes (37 hours per week), and most of their farm management time was in outdoor work, as opposed to accounting and bookkeeping. Major farm products included dairy (41%), grain (36%), and livestock (18%).
FARMER (m)	200	1979	40.8	13.4	24.4	National sample from names provided by participants in the female sample, write-in responses to articles in agricultural magazines, and with the assistance of the Minnesota Agricultural Extension Service. 59% had high school diplomas, 23% completed BA degrees. They averaged 65 hours per week in farm management, and 8 hours per week in home management; 75% of work time was spent outdoors. Major farm products included grain (33%), dairy (27%), and livestock (24%).
FLIGHT ATTENDANT (f)	286	1979	30.5	14.4	8.7	From Ozark Air Lines, Trans World Airlines, Western Airlines, Eastern Airlines, Braniff International, and Delta Air Lines. 55% had high school diplomas, 12% completed associate degrees, 29% BA. They averaged 76 hours of flight time per month.
FLIGHT ATTENDANT (m)	201	1979	28.4	15.4	4.0	See women's sample above. Additional assistance from the Association of Flight Attendants. 35% had high school diplomas, 48% completed BA degrees. They averaged 80 hours of flight time per month.
FOREIGN LANGUAGE TEACHER (f)	315	1978	37.5	18.3	11.6	Members, American Council on the Teaching of Foreign Languages. 35% completed BA degrees, 64% MA. 91% were employed by secondary schools.
FOREIGN LANGUAGE TEACHER (m)	251	1979	38.8	19.2	13.4	Members, American Council on the Teaching of Foreign Languages, and Minnesota teachers. 25% completed BA degrees, 71% MA. 92% were employed by secondary schools.
FORESTER (f)	165	1979	26.6	17.2	3.4	Members, Society of American Foresters. 76% completed BA degrees, 22% MA. 57% were employed by government, 26% by industry. The largest area of specialization was timber management (42%); the remainder included land and fire management, and other areas.
FORESTER (m)	298	1979	38.9	17.1	14.3	Members, Society of American Foresters. 67% completed BA degrees, 23% MA, 9% PhD. 54% were employed by government, 29% by industry. The largest area of specialization was timber management (28%); the remainder included fire, land, and recreation management, and other areas.
GEOGRAPHER (f)	187	1979	38.5	19.4	11.5	Members, Association of American Geographers. 15% completed BA degrees, 43% MA, 40% PhD. 54% were employed by educational institutions, 26% by government, and 10% by private industry; major activities included teaching (41%), research/field work (22%), administrative (11%), and a combination (15%). Areas of specialty included physical/environmental (26%), urban/economic (24%), and cultural (18%).

Scale/sample	N	Year tested	Mean age	Mean years education	Mean years experience	Composition and comments
GEOGRAPHER (m)	277	1979	40.7	20.6	14.9	Members, Association of American Geographers. 3% completed BA degrees, 14% MA, 81% PhD. 81% were employed by educational institutions, 11% by government; major activities included teaching (51%), administrative (15%), research/field work (13%), and a combination (20%). Areas of specialty included urban/economic (26%), physical/environmental (24%), and cultural (16%).
GEOLOGIST (f)	203	1979	35.4	19.2	9.9	From the *Geological Society of America Directory*, 1978. 23% completed BA degrees, 47% MA, 30% PhD. 36% were employed by government, 27% by educational institutions, and 26% by private industry; major activities included research and exploration (59%), teaching (13%), and a combination of activities (12%).
GEOLOGIST (m)	242	1979	39.4	19.9	15.0	From the *Geological Society of America Directory*, 1978. 12% completed BA degrees, 36% MA, 52% PhD. 39% were employed by educational institutions, 30% by private industry, and 24% by government; major activities included research and exploration (41%), teaching (22%), administrative (12%), and a combination (18%).
GUIDANCE COUNSELOR (f)	347	1967	48.0	17.5	9.0	Members, National Association of School Counselors. Data gathered with the assistance of G. Blanton and J. Francis.
GUIDANCE COUNSELOR (m)	203	1967	37.0	18.0	5.0	From membership of Iowa Personnel and Guidance Association. Data gathered with the assistance of H. B. Engen.
HOME ECONOMICS TEACHER (f)	312	1979	38.3	17.7	12.3	Members, American Home Economist Association. 51% completed BA degrees, 47% MA. 86% were employed by elementary or secondary schools.
INTERIOR DECORATOR (f)	172	1966	52.0	14.7	23.0	Certified members, American Association of Interior Decorators.
INTERIOR DECORATOR (m)	192	1967	46.0	15.2	19.7	National sample, members of American Institute of Interior Design.
INVESTMENT FUND MANAGER (m)	237	1969	40.0	16.9	13.2	Portfolio managers (registered members, New York Stock Exchange) participating in Institutional Investors Seminar, New York, January 1969. Data collected with the assistance of H. Fiske.
IRS AGENT (f)	300	1976	37.8	n/a	5.1	Data gathered with the assistance of G. Kaufman, Internal Revenue Service. Sample consists of three equal groups: tax auditors, who consult with taxpayers and explain issues that do not involve accounting; revenue officers, who explain to taxpayers their delinquent tax obligations, and collect unpaid taxes; and revenue agents, who, as professional accountants, examine the books of individuals or corporations to determine their federal tax liability.
IRS AGENT (m)	300	1976	37.4	n/a	8.3	See women's sample above.
LAWYER (f)	273	1977	32.8	19.2	5.9	From *Martindale-Hubbell Law Directory*, 1976, 1977. Areas of practice included corporate law, criminal law, divorce, work in government agencies, legal research, and general practice.
LAWYER (m)	213	1977	37.1	19.4	10.5	From *Martindale-Hubbell Law Directory*, 1976, 1977. Areas of practice included corporate law, criminal law, work in government agencies, tax law, general practice.
LIBRARIAN (f)	280	1977	37.6	17.7	9.9	Members, American Library Association. 92% completed MA degrees or higher. 43% were employed by community or county, 30% by colleges or universities, and 9% by high schools.
LIBRARIAN (m)	315	1977	39.1	18.4	11.6	Members, American Library Association. 98% completed MA degrees or higher. 46% were employed by colleges or universities, 37% by community or county libraries.
LIFE INSURANCE AGENT (f)	214	1973	45.4	n/a	10	National sampling of holders of the American College of Life Underwriters certificate. All indicated connection with sales activities. Data collected with the assistance of R. Andrulis.
LIFE INSURANCE AGENT (m)	264	1973	43.6	n/a	14	See women's sample above.

Scale/sample	N	Year tested	Mean age	Mean years education	Mean years experience	Composition and comments
MARKETING EXECUTIVE (f)	207	1979	32.8	17.0	7.5	Members, American Marketing Association. 43% completed BA degrees, 45% MA. 52% reported research as their major activity; the remainder included planning, advertising administration, and product management.
MARKETING EXECUTIVE (m)	309	1979	37.9	17.8	11.5	Members, American Marketing Association. 27% completed BA degrees, 66% MA. 40% reported research as their major activity; the remainder included administration, planning, product management, advertising, and sales.
MATHEMATICIAN (f)	119	1966	49.0	20.0	20.0	From *Directory of American Mathematical Society,* 1966. PhDs.
MATHEMATICIAN (m)	223	1969	43.0	19.7	16.0	National sample from *American Men of Science,* 1968. PhDs.
MATH-SCIENCE TEACHER (f)	308	1967	44.0	16.5	15.0	Members of women teachers' groups in Minnesota, Iowa, and Colorado; within each state, an attempt was made to balance samples between urban and rural areas.
MATH-SCIENCE TEACHER (m)	463	1968	29.9	17+	5.3	From National Science Foundation science-institute courses. Collected by W. J. Lonner and S. E. Williamson.
MEDICAL TECHNOLOGIST (f)	345	1967	39.0	15.8	14.0	National sample from American Society of Medical Technologists.
MEDICAL TECHNOLOGIST (m)	252	1968	37.0	15.9	12.2	Members, American Society of Medical Technologists. Data collected with the assistance of S. Friedheim, Executive Director, ASMT.
MINISTER (f)	250	1977	34.8	19.7	5.8	Collected with the cooperation of the Midwest Career Development Center. 95% were employed by churches; 90% served as pastors, 4% as chaplains. 6% had completed Bachelor of Divinity degrees, 78% Master of Divinity, and 6% Doctor of Divinity.
MINISTER (m)	498	1969	43.9	20.0	13.4	Protestant ministers from 13 denominations. Collected by D. Hultgren.
MUSICIAN (f)	209	1979	35.4	16.7	14.4	Members of musician's unions in Milwaukee, San Francisco, Fort Worth, Atlanta, St. Louis, Denver, and Minneapolis; and from national write-in response to articles in musician's publications. 23% had high school diplomas, 40% completed BA degrees, 24% MA. 94% had had private instruction; of these, the average was 13 years. 22% were employed in other occupations simultaneously. Data collected with the assistance of L. Harmon.
MUSICIAN (m)	228	1979	34.2	16.0	16.3	See women's sample above. 34% had high school diplomas, 30% completed BA degrees, 14% MA. 86% had had private instruction; of these, the average was 8 years. 31% were employed in other occupations simultaneously. Data collected with the assistance of L. Harmon.
NAVY OFFICER (f)	282	1979	32.0	16.8	9.2	Roster of commissioned officers provided by the Defense Manpower Data Center, Department of Defense. 62% completed BA degrees, 33% MA. Rank: lieutenant (67%), lt. commander (21%), commander (9%), captain (3%).
NAVY OFFICER (m)	298	1979	37.6	17.1	14.4	See women's sample above. 48% completed BA degrees, 37% BA. Rank: lieutenant (31%), lt. commander (30%), commander (26%), captain (13%).
NURSE, LICENSED PRACTICAL (f)	222	1967	51.0	11.7	15.0	National sample, members of American Federation of Licensed Practical Nurses.
NURSE, LICENSED PRACTICAL (m)	100	1973	37.8	12+	11.0	Selected from list of nurses obtained from state associations and state boards of examiners. All had at least a high school diploma.
NURSE, REGISTERED (f)	291	1977	38.9	17.4	14.8	Sample drawn from various state nursing associations, hospitals, medical offices, and individual contacts. 8% completed RN degrees, 25% BA, 59% MA, and 8% PhD. 44% were employed by schools of nursing, 33% by hospitals; major activities included teaching (41%), administration (35%), and applied areas (14%). Data collected with the assistance of C. Merkle.
NURSE, REGISTERED (m)	291	1973	35.8	16+	10.0	From list of registered nurses obtained from state associations and state boards of examiners. All had at least an RN degree. Most frequently represented specialties were anaesthesiology, administration, surgery, psychiatry, and teaching; 34% of the sample were in the armed forces.

Scale/sample	N	Year tested	Mean age	Mean years education	Mean years experience	Composition and comments
Nursing Home Administrator (f)	215	1979	43.6	14.5	9.4	From a list of administrators of nursing homes approved by the Veterans Administration. 43% had high school diplomas, 13% associate degrees, 17% BA. Data collected by A. René.
Nursing Home Administrator (m)	300	1979	39.9	15.9	9.1	See women's sample above. 46% completed BA degrees, 20% MA. Data collected by A. René.
Occupational Therapist (f)	301	1978	37.2	17.0	10.5	Members, American Occupational Therapy Association and the Minnesota Occupational Therapy Association. 75% completed BA degrees, 22% MA. 37% were employed by clinics or hospitals (17% general, 13% psychiatric, 7% children's), 15% by educational institutions, and 11% by rehabilitation centers.
Occupational Therapist (m)	203	1979	36.9	17.8	10.3	See women's sample above. 62% completed BA degrees, 36% MA. 44% were employed by clinics or hospitals (18% general, 23% psychiatric, 3% children's), 14% by educational institutions, and 10% by rehabilitation centers.
Optometrist (f)	190	1979	37.8	18.9	12.0	Members, American Optometric Association. 60% were self-employed or in a partnership, 11% were employed by clinics or hospitals, 13% by a combination of employers; 75% reported private practice as their major activity.
Optometrist (m)	213	1979	39.8	18.8	14.3	Members, American Optometric Association. 83% were self-employed or in a partnership; 93% reported private practice as their major activity.
Personnel Director (f)	333	1978	38.3	15.1	9.1	Members, American Society for Personnel Administration. 29% had high school diplomas, 39% completed BA degrees, 11% MA. Major activities included administration (37%), recruiting and selection (18%), and a combination (32%).
Personnel Director (m)	206	1978	39.1	16.7	10.8	Members, American Society for Personnel Administration. 1% had high school diplomas, 61% completed BA degrees, 28% MA. Major activities included administration (38%), recruiting and selection (10%), and a combination (34%).
Pharmacist (f)	203	1979	33.7	17.4	10.2	Members, American Pharmaceutical Association, and pharmacists obtained with the assistance of the University of Minnesota College of Pharmacy; all were registered pharmacists. 83% completed BA degrees, 5% MA, and 9% PhD. 33% were employed by hospitals, 26% by independent pharmacies, and 21% by chain pharmacies. Major activities included dispensing (60%), management (12%), and a combination (18%).
Pharmacist (m)	222	1976	39.6	17.3	15.9	Obtained with the assistance of the University of Minnesota College of Pharmacy; all were registered pharmacists. 90% completed BA degrees, 4% MA, and 6% PhD.
Photographer (f)	249	1978	36.9	15.3	10.9	From *Professional Photographers of America, 1977; National Press Photographers Association, 1977;* and *Society of Photographers in Communication.* 21% had high school diplomas, 38% completed BA degrees, 13% MA; 35% received training on the job, 37% from photography courses (23% in courses not leading to a degree, 14% in courses leading to a degree), and 28% received training from a combination of sources. 51% were self-employed or in partnerships; the remainder were employed by studios, businesses, newspapers or magazines, or a combination of employers.
Photographer (m)	223	1978	38.9	15.1	15.1	See women's sample above. 24% had high school diplomas, 10% completed associate degrees, 31% BA; 44% received training on the job, 35% from photography courses (15% in courses not leading to a degree, 20% in courses leading to a degree), and 22% received training from a combination of sources. 56% were self-employed or in partnerships; 14% were employed by newspapers or magazines; the remainder were employed by studios, businesses, or a combination of employers.
Physical Education Teacher (f)	291	1979	36.6	18.0	13.1	Members, American Alliance for Health, Physical Education, and Recreation. 47% completed BA degrees, 52% MA. 84% were employed by secondary schools.
Physical Education Teacher (m)	210	1979	38.4	19.1	14.2	Members, American Alliance for Health, Physical Education, and Recreation. 18% completed BA degrees, 76% MA. 84% were employed by secondary schools.

Scale/sample	N	Year tested	Mean age	Mean years education	Mean years experience	Composition and comments
PHYSICAL THERAPIST (f)	332	1978	34.6	16.8	10.4	Members, American Physical Therapy Association, and a listing of Registered Physical Therapists in Minnesota. 82% completed BA degrees, 15% MA.
PHYSICAL THERAPIST (m)	226	1978	37.3	17.3	12.7	See women's sample above. 80% completed BA degrees, 17% MA.
PHYSICIAN (f)	321	1967	48.0	19.5	18	National sample from *American Medical Association Directory*, 1965.
PHYSICIAN (m)	240	1969	40.0	20.1	12.5	National sample from *American Medical Association Directory*, 1968.
PHYSICIST (f)	255	1973	38.8	Phd+	9.0	National sample of PhDs selected from *Women in Physics*, 1972, a roster compiled by the Committee on Women in Physics of the American Physical Society. 58% were employed by colleges and universities, 16% by government or national laboratories, and 12% by industry; major activities included research (52%), teaching (50%), and administration (11%).
PHYSICIST (m)	226	1977	40.4	21.1	12.2	Members, American Physical Society; all had PhD degrees. 40% were employed by educational institutions, 27% by government, and 27% by industry; major activities included research (47%), administration (13%), teaching (12%), and a combination (20%).
POLICE OFFICER (f)	206	1979	32.0	14.8	6.1	A national sample gathered with the assistance of the member police departments of the Police Executive Research Forum, also from participants in a 1978 International Association of Women Police training meeting held in Minnesota. 41% had high school diplomas, 18% completed associate degrees, 35% BA. Areas of work included patrol (46%), investigation (14%), and a combination of activities (21%); on the average they spent 39% of their time doing clerical work.
POLICE OFFICER (m)	294	1979	33.0	14.7	9.1	See women's sample above. 35% had high school diplomas, 28% completed associate degrees, 28% BA. Areas of work included patrol (55%), investigation (11%), and a combination of activities (14%); on the average, they spent 42% of their time doing clerical work.
PSYCHOLOGIST (f)	275	1966	43.0	Phd+	13.0	National sample from *American Psychological Association Directory*, 1966.
PSYCHOLOGIST (m)	245	1967	44.0	Phd+	14.3	National sample from *American Psychological Association Directory*, 1966.
PUBLIC ADMINISTRATOR (f)	195	1979	37.6	17.9	9.1	Members, American Society for Public Administration, 1978. 22% completed BA degrees, 65% MA. 69% were employed by government agencies, 11% by educational institutions.
PUBLIC ADMINISTRATOR (m)	210	1979	38.0	18.4	11.6	Members, American Society for Public Administration, 1978. 17% completed BA degrees, 73% MA. 82% were employed by government agencies, 5% by educational institutions.
PUBLIC RELATIONS DIRECTOR (f)	298	1978-1979	39.2	16.3	12.1	From the 1977 membership register issue of *Public Relations Journal*, a publication of the Public Relations Society of America. 63% completed BA degrees, 22% MA. 41% were employed by business or industrial counseling firms, 17% by health or welfare agencies, and 11% by educational institutions.
PUBLIC RELATIONS DIRECTOR (m)	302	1979	45.0	16.7	17.8	See women's sample above. 63% completed BA degrees, 29% MA. 71% were employed by business or industrial counseling firms.
PURCHASING AGENT (f)	158	1979	38.2	13.9	7.2	Members, National Institute of Governmental Purchasing, and write-in response to articles in purchasing publications. 19% had high school diplomas, 48% had some college education, and 20% completed BA degrees.
PURCHASING AGENT (m)	215	1979	41.1	15.8	11.2	See women's sample above. 27% had some college education, 44% completed BA degrees, and 18% MA.
RADIOLOGIC TECHNOLOGIST (f)	220	1978	31.6	14.5	9.4	From the 1977 American Registry of Radiologic Technologists; all were registered technologists. 29% had high school diplomas, 17% completed associate degrees, 6% completed BA degrees, and 36% received certificates or degrees in radiologic technology. 78% were employed by hospitals or clinics; 82% reported x-ray technology as their specialty; other specialties included nuclear medicine and radiation therapy.

Scale/sample	N	Year tested	Mean age	Mean years education	Mean years experience	Composition and comments
RADIOLOGIC TECHNOLOGIST (m)	239	1978	34.4	14.9	11.1	See women's sample above. 38% had high school diplomas, 24% completed associate degrees, 19% completed BA degrees, and 14% received certificates or degrees in radiologic technology. 72% were employed by hospitals or clinics; specialty areas included x-ray technology (65%) and nuclear medicine technology (13%).
REALTOR (f)	208	1977	44.3	13.7	8.3	Members, Women's Council of Realtors. 64% had high school diplomas, 26% completed BA degrees. 55% were employed by real estate firms, 36% were self-employed or in partnerships; sales specialty areas included residential (64%) and a combination (30%).
REALTOR (m)	175	1969	48.0	12.8	14.7	Brokers and salesmen listed in *State of Minnesota Roster of Licensed Real Estate-Business Opportunity Brokers and Salesmen, 1967*.
RECREATION LEADER (f)	264	1979	36.4	17.3	11.5	Members, National Recreation and Park Association. 49% completed BA degrees, 37% MA. 59% were employed by government; major activities included administration (41%), education (10%), program leadership (10%), supervision (10%), and a combination (24%).
RECREATION LEADER (m)	214	1979	38.6	15.9	13.9	Members, National Recreation and Park Association. 45% completed BA degrees, 40% MA, 11% PhD. 89% were employed by government; major activities included administration (66%), education (11%), and a combination (15%).
REPORTER (f)	200	1979	38.0	16.1	10.8	From *Alphabetized Directory of American Journalists*, 1978; all those selected for the sample indicated "reporter" or "writer" as their job title. Also, members of the National Federation of Press Women. 15% had high school diplomas, 69% BA degrees, 14% MA.
REPORTER (m)	201	1979	35.1	16.2	11.7	See women's sample above. 14% had high school diplomas, 72% completed BA degrees, 12% MA.
RESTAURANT MANAGER (f)	92	1979	41.2	15.0	12.9	Members, National Restaurant Association. 24% had high school diplomas, 23% had some college education, 5% completed associate degrees, 27% BA, 14% MA. 32% were restaurant owners and 55% held management positions; major activities included customer contact (24%), personnel management (20%), and a combination (37%).
RESTAURANT MANAGER (m)	159	1979	39.3	15.0	14.3	Members, National Restaurant Association. 15% had high school diplomas, 26% had some college education, 10% completed associate degrees, 40% BA, 6% MA. 61% were restaurant owners and 37% held management positions; major activities included personnel management (23%), customer contact (22%), and a combination (39%).
SCHOOL ADMINISTRATOR (f)	200	1979	43.8	19.9	7.8	Members, American Association of School Administrators. 61% completed MA degrees, 12% specialist certificates, 20% doctorate degrees (9% EdD, 11% PhD). 47% were employed by elementary schools, 27% by junior-senior high schools; major activities included administration (37%), student and faculty interaction (14%), and a combination (49%).
SCHOOL ADMINISTRATOR (m)	289	1979	43.3	20.1	12.1	Members, American Association of School Administrators. 55% completed MA degrees, 17% specialist certificates, 25% doctorate degrees (16% EdD, 9% PhD). 30% were employed by elementary schools, 9% by junior-senior high schools, 27% by school districts, and 15% by a combination; major activities included administration (50%), and administration combined with student and faculty interaction and school board responsibilities (38%).
SECRETARY (f)	366	1967	36.0	12.8	12.0	Composite sample: University of Minnesota; Pillsbury Company; Dow Chemical Company; Minnesota Mining and Manufacturing Company; and membership of National Secretaries Association.
SKILLED CRAFTS (m)	339	1969	42.0	11.6	18.0	National sample of carpenters, electricians, and tool- and diemakers from 14 major cities.
SOCIAL SCIENCE TEACHER (f)	183	1967	42.0	16.4	14.0	Members of women teachers' groups in Minnesota, Iowa, and Colorado; within each state, an attempt was made to balance samples between urban and rural areas.

Scale/sample	N	Year tested	Mean age	Mean years education	Mean years experience	Composition and comments
SOCIAL SCIENCE TEACHER (m)	239	1969	38.0	17.0	12.2	From roster of Minnesota high school teachers provided by the Minnesota State Department of Education.
SOCIAL WORKER (f)	201	1975	42.8	18.5	14.8	Members, American Association of Social Workers. 96% completed MA degrees. Major activities included casework (35%), administration (27%), and a combination (18%).
SOCIAL WORKER (m)	234	1975	41.8	18.7	15.1	Members, American Association of Social Workers. 95% completed MA degrees. Major activities included administration (46%), casework (27%), and a combination (12%).
SOCIOLOGIST (f)	203	1974	42.2	21.4	11.1	Members, American Sociological Association, all with PhD degrees. Major activities included teaching (48%), research (15%), administration (9%), and a combination (24%).
SOCIOLOGIST (m)	207	1974	40.3	21.0	11.4	See women's sample above. Major activities included teaching (45%), research (17%), administration (15%), and a combination (21%).
SPECIAL EDUCATION TEACHER (f)	200	1979	35.5	17.9	6.4	From a commercially compiled national listing. 46% completed BA degrees, 54% MA. 63% were employed in elementary schools, 20% in secondary schools; specialty areas included mental retardation (44%), learning disabilities (23%), and a combination (28%).
SPECIAL EDUCATION TEACHER (m)	250	1979	34.7	18.7	7.9	From a commercially compiled national listing. 40% completed BA degrees, 56% MA. 28% were employed in elementary schools, 48% in secondary schools; specialty areas included mental retardation (36%), learning disabilities (15%), and a combination (29%).
SPEECH PATHOLOGIST (f)	222	1978	36.2	18.2	10.0	From *Directory of the American Speech and Hearing Association, 1976.* 96% completed MA degrees or higher. 41% were employed by elementary or secondary schools, 14% by colleges or universities, 10% by hospitals, and 10% were self-employed or in partnerships. Major activities included therapy (67%), teaching (9%), administration (6%), and a combination (10%).
SPEECH PATHOLOGIST (m)	336	1973	40.3	18.8	13.0	See women's sample above. All held advanced clinical certification: 50% completed MA degrees, 36% completed the PhD. Major activities included therapy (27%), administration (16%), teaching (13%), and a combination (44%).
SYSTEMS ANALYST (f)	258	1975	32.9	15.9	7.9	Rosters provided by the Society for Data Processors, and from write-in response to articles in *Computerworld;* those selected for criterion sample spent at least 50% of their time in systems analysis. 16% had high school diplomas, 59% completed BA degrees, 16% MA. 67% worked in business-related areas, 14% in educational areas, and 9% in scientific areas.
SYSTEMS ANALYST (m)	361	1975	39.4	16.3	12.9	See women's sample above. 10% had high school diplomas, 49% completed BA degrees, 28% MA. 79% worked in business-related areas; the remainder worked in educational, scientific, and other areas.
VETERINARIAN (f)	308	1973	36.2	20+	11.0	Members, Women's Veterinary Medical Association, 1971; minimum D.V.M. degree. 79% of the sample were in private practice, the majority specializing in small animals; 13% were in research or teaching; 8% were in other areas.
VETERINARIAN (m)	204	1973	37.8	20+	11.0	National sample from the *American Veterinary Medical Association Directory,* 1972; minimum D.V.M. degree. 82% of the sample were in private practice; 13% were in research or teaching; 5% were in other areas.
VOCATIONAL AGRICULTURE TEACHER (m)	395	1969	40.0	16.6	14.5	From Minnesota, North Dakota, South Dakota, and Wisconsin; listed in *National Vocational Agriculture Teachers Directory,* 1967. Collected by C. D. Norenberg.
YWCA DIRECTOR (f)	206	1978	37.1	16.1	7.6	Obtained with the assistance of the Professional Directors of YWCAs in the United States. 12% had high school diplomas, 60% completed BA degrees, 18% MA.
YMCA DIRECTOR (m)	313	1978	38.4	17.0	13.6	Obtained with the assistance of the Association of Professional Directors of YMCAs in the United States. 68% completed BA degrees, 27% MA.

References Cited

Only those works cited in the text are listed here. The most complete bibliography of the Strong inventory is in O. K. Buros, *The Mental Measurements Yearbook*, Vols. 1–7, 1933–72 (Highland Park, N.J.: The Gryphon Press), where 1,267 entries are listed.

Barnette, W. L., Jr., and J. N. McCall. 1964. Validation of the Minnesota Vocational Interest Inventory for vocational high school boys. *Journal of Applied Psychology*, 48: 378–82.

Borgen, F. H., and G. T. Harper. 1973. Predictive validity of measured vocational interests with black and white college men. *Measurement and Evaluation in Guidance*, 6: 19–27.

Brandt, J. E., and A. B. Hood. 1968. Effect of personality adjustment on the predictive validity of the Strong Vocational Interest Blank. *Journal of Counseling Psychology*, 15: 547–51.

Cairo, P. C. 1979. The validity of the Holland and Basic Interest Scales of the Strong Vocational Interest Blank: Leisure activities versus occupational membership as criteria. *Journal of Vocational Behavior*, 15: 68–77.

Campbell, D. P. 1966a. Occupations ten years later of high school seniors with high scores on the SVIB life insurance salesman scale. *Journal of Applied Psychology*, 50: 369–72.

———. 1966b. The stability of vocational interests within occupations over long time spans. *Personnel and Guidance Journal*, 44: 1012–19.

———. 1968. Changing patterns of interests within the American society. *Measurement and Evaluation in Guidance*, 1: 36–49.

———. 1969. The vocational interests of Dartmouth College freshmen: 1947–67. *Personnel and Guidance Journal*, 47: 527–30.

———. 1971. *Handbook for the Strong Vocational Interest Blank*. Stanford, Calif.: Stanford University Press.

Campbell, D. P., F. H. Borgen, S. Eastes, C. B. Johansson, and R. A. Peterson. 1968. A set of Basic Interest Scales for the Strong Vocational Interest Blank for men. *Journal of Applied Psychology Monographs*, 52, no. 6, part 2.

Campbell, D. P., and J. L. Holland. 1972. A merger in vocational interest research: Applying Holland's theory to Strong's data. *Journal of Vocational Behavior*, 2: 353–76.

Clark, K. E. 1961. *Vocational Interests of Non-professional Men*. Minneapolis: University of Minnesota Press.

Clark, K. E., and D. P. Campbell. 1965. *Minnesota Vocational Interest Inventory*. New York: Psychological Corporation.

Darley, J. G. 1941. *Clinical Aspects and Interpretation of the Strong Vocational Interest Blank*. New York: Psychological Corporation.

Darley, J. G., and T. Hagenah. 1955. *Vocational Interest Measurement*. Minneapolis: University of Minnesota Press.

Diamond, Esther E., ed. 1975. *Issues of Sex Bias and Sex Fairness in Career Interest Measurement*. Washington, D.C.: Department of Health, Education, and Welfare, National Institute of Education, Career Education Program, Spring 1975.

Dolliver, R. H. 1969. "3.5 to 1" on the Strong Vocational Interest Blank as a pseudo-event. *Journal of Counseling Psychology*, 16: 172–74.

Dolliver, R. H., J. A. Irvin, and S. E. Bigley. 1972. Twelve-year follow-up of the Strong Vocational Interest Blank. *Journal of Counseling Psychology*, 19: 212–17.

Dolliver, R. H., and J. E. Kunce. 1973. Who drops out of an SVIB follow-up study? *Journal of Counseling Psychology*, 20: 188–89.

Douce, L. C. 1978. Career aspirations and career development of women in relation to Adventure Scale scores on the Strong-Campbell Interest Inventory. *Dis. Ab. Int.*, 38 (10-B): 5091.

Guilford, J. P., P. R. Christensen, N. A. Bond, Jr., and M. A. Sutton. 1954. A factor analysis study of human interests. *Psychological Monographs*, 68 (4, whole no. 375).

Hanlon, R. J. 1971. Validation of the Strong Vocational Interest Blank for Use in the Irish Republic. Unpublished Ph.D. dissertation, Social Science Research Centre, University College Galway, Galway, Ireland.

Hansen, J. C. 1976. Exploring new directions for SCII occupational scale construction. *Journal of Vocational Behavior*, 9: 147–60.

———. 1978. Age differences and empirical scale construction. *Measurement and Evaluation in Guidance*, 11: 78–87.

Hansen, J. C., and C. B. Johansson. 1972. The application of Holland's vocational model to the Strong Vocational Interest Blank for Women. *Journal of Vocational Behavior*, 2: 479–93.

Hansen, J. C., and J. Stocco. 1980. Stability of vocational interests of adolescents and young adults. *Measurement and Evaluation in Guidance*, 13, no. 3: 173–78.

Harmon, L. W. 1969. The predictive power over 10 years of measured social service and scientific interests among college women. *Journal of Applied Psychology*, 53: 193–98.

Holland, J. L. 1959. A theory of vocational choice. *Journal of Counseling Psychology*, 6: 35–45.

———— 1965. *Manual for the Vocational Preference Inventory*. Palo Alto, Calif.: Consulting Psychologists Press.

———— 1966. *The Psychology of Vocational Choice*. Waltham, Mass.: Blaisdell.

———— 1973. *Making Vocational Choices: A Theory of Careers*. Englewood Cliffs, N.J.: Prentice-Hall.

———— 1976. *The Occupations Finder*. Palo Alto, Calif.: Consulting Psychologists Press.

Hutchins, E. B. 1964. The AAMC longitudinal study: Implications for medical education. *Journal of Medical Education*, 39: 265–77.

Johansson, C. B., and D. P. Campbell. 1971. Stability of The Strong Vocational Interest Blank for Men. *Journal of Applied Psychology*, 55: 34–36.

Johansson, C. B., and L. W. Harmon. 1972. Strong Vocational Interest Blank: One form or two? *Journal of Counseling Psychology*, 19: 404–10.

Johnson, R. W. 1972. Contradictory scores on the Strong Vocational Interest Blank. *Journal of Counseling Psychology*, 19: 487–90.

Johnson, R. W., and C. B. Johansson. 1972. Moderating effect of basic interests on predictive validity of SVIB occupational scales. *Proceedings of the 80th Annual Convention, American Psychological Association*, pp. 589–90.

Kunce, J. T., R. H. Dolliver, and J. A. Irvin. 1972. Perspectives on interpreting the validity of the SVIB-M. *The Vocational Guidance Quarterly*, 21: 36–42.

Lonner, W. J. 1968. The SVIB visits German, Austrian, and Swiss psychologists. *American Psychologist*, 23: 164–79.

———— 1969. Bericht ueber Untersuchungen mit der deutschen Fassung des Strong Vocational Interest Blank for Men (SVIB), *Psychologische Rundschau*, 20: 151–56.

McArthur, C. 1954. Long term validity of the Strong Interest Test in two subcultures. *Journal of Applied Psychology*, 38: 346–54.

Rayman, J. R. 1976. Sex and the single interest inventory: The empirical validation of sex-balanced interest inventory items. *Journal of Counseling Psychology*, 23: 239-46.

Schlossberg, N. K., and J. Goodman. 1972. Imperative for change: Counselor use of the Strong Vocational Interest Blanks. *Impact*, 2: 25–29.

Shah, I. 1970. A Cross-cultural Comparative Study of Vocational Interests. Unpublished Ph.D. dissertation, University of Minnesota.

Spokane, A. R. 1979. Occupational preference and the validity of the Strong-Campbell Interest Inventory for college women and men. *Journal of Counseling Psychology*, 26: 312–18.

Stauffer, E., transl. and ed. 1973. [E. K. Strong, Jr., and D. P. Campbell.] Questionnaire d'intérets vocationnels: Manuel d'instructions. Issy-les-Moulineaux, France.

Strong, E. K., Jr. 1935. Predictive value of the Vocational Interest Test. *Journal of Educational Psychology*, 26: 332.

———— 1943. *Vocational Interests of Men and Women*. Stanford, Calif.: Stanford University Press.

———— 1955. *Vocational Interests 18 Years After College*. Minneapolis: University of Minnesota Press.

Tilton, J. W. 1937. The measurement of overlapping. *Journal of Educational Psychology*, 28: 656–62.

Trimble, J. T. 1965. Ten-Year Longitudinal Follow-up Study of Inventoried Interests of Selected High School Students. Unpublished Ph.D. dissertation, University of Missouri.

Webber, P. L., and L. W. Harmon. 1978. The reliability and concurrent validity of three types of occupational scales for two occupational groups: Some evidence bearing on handling sex differences in interest scale construction. Chapter in *Sex-Fair Interest Measurement: Research Implications*, Tittle, C. K., and Zytowski, D. G. (eds.), NIE Department of Health, Education and Welfare, Washington, D.C.

Whetstone, R. D., and V. R. Hayles. 1975. The SVIB and black college men. *Measurement and Evaluation in Guidance*, 8: 105–9.

Index